The Future of Real Estate Education

The Future of Real Estate Education: From Pedagogy to Technology brings together award-winning educators and researchers in the field to address the complexity and challenges of today's real estate degree programs.

Representing diverse disciplinary, geographic, and professional perspectives, the authors discuss innovative technology, inclusive pedagogy, curriculum development, and more in an updated global approach to real estate education. They share strategies and tools for teaching excellence and student achievement, offering guidance to fellow educators and administrators in creating dynamic learning environments, developing and leading successful programs, and mentoring the next generation of real estate professionals. The book highlights experiential and project-based learning, featuring engaging teaching methods to create impactful classroom experiences that build educational proficiency and foster the professional skills that employers seek.

This book will interest faculty and administrators in real estate degree programs, as well as instructors teaching undergraduate and postgraduate real estate courses. It is also relevant for professional educators and students pursuing professional education or a real estate degree.

Karen M. McGrath is an award-winning researcher specializing in real estate sustainability and pedagogy. She serves as Chair of the Accounting and Financial Management Department at Bucknell University, her alma mater, where she also oversees the real estate program. Dedicated to applied learning, Karen designs and teaches courses in real estate finance, investment, and ESG, bridging theory and practice to prepare students for leadership in an evolving field. She holds an MRE from NYU and a PhD from the University of Reading.

Elaine M. Worzala is an award-winning real estate educator and has written extensively on real estate education programs. Instrumental in the design of the Commercial Real Estate Finance major at the College of Charleston, the full-time master's program at Johns Hopkins University and the master's at the University of San Diego, she has over 30 years of experience in higher education. Dedicating her life to carrying on the Wisconsin tradition, she believes strongly in the multidisciplinary approach to understanding real estate and regularly employs the power of project-based/experiential learning to make the classroom come alive for her students.

Pernille H. Christensen is Course Director of the Bachelor of Property Economics (BPE) at the University of Technology Sydney, leading a program with 18 full- and part-time staff, and over 475 students enrolled across its three-year degree. She holds a Professional Bachelor of Architecture (1996), dual Master of Architecture and Master of City & Regional Planning degrees (2000), and an interdisciplinary PhD in planning, design, and the built environment (2012). Her teaching integrates academic and industry perspectives, preparing students to navigate and address contemporary complex challenges and shape the future of the built environment.

The American Real Estate Society (ARES) Real Estate Thought Leadership Collection Series

The American Real Estate Society promotes the global dissemination of research representing the forefront of critical thought in real estate, with findings applicable to all areas of industry, policy, education, and practice. ARES publishes a broad range of real estate topics within an international scope, including finance, economics, investment, business, development, housing, sustainability, and environmental and urban studies. ARES publications provide insider access to the latest high-level real estate research, case studies, reports, analyses, pedagogies, and reviews. These constitute an up-to-the-minute resource of interest and relevance to business decisionmakers, academic researchers and educators, industry professionals, and emerging real estate leaders.

ARES publishes six, peer-reviewed, academic journals in partnership with Routledge, Taylor & Francis that provide relevant and timely research of interest to real estate academics and practitioners worldwide: The *Journal of Real Estate Research* (JRER), *Journal of Housing Research* (JHR), *Journal of Real Estate Literature* (JREL), *Journal of Real Estate Portfolio Management* (JREPM), *Journal of Real Estate Practice and Education* (JREPE), and *Journal of Sustainable Real Estate* (JOSRE). For more information visit: https://www.aresnet.org/page/ARES-Journal-Info#rjer

Conference

ARES hosts an academic and professional conference each spring in a unique travel destination that attracts real estate researchers from around the globe. The event features formal paper presentations, panels and roundtables, exhibitions, and social and networking events.

Membership

Membership in ARES includes the subscription to the journals, discounted conference registration, and many other benefits. For more information visit: https://www.aresnet.org/page/Benefits.

ARES
American Real Estate Society

Transforming the Irvine Ranch
Joan Irvine, William Pereira, and the Big Plan
C. Michael Stockstill and H. Pike Oliver

Commercial Real Estate Analysis for Investment, Finance, and Development
David M. Geltner, Norman G. Miller, Alex Van De Minne, Piet Eichholtz, Thies Lindenthal, and Lily Shen

The Irvine Ranch
Fulfilling the Vision, 1977–2025
C. Michael Stockstill and H. Pike Oliver

The Future of Real Estate Education
From Pedagogy to Technology
Edited by Karen M. McGrath, Elaine M. Worzala, and Pernille H. Christensen

For more information: https://www.routledge.com/The-American-Real-Estate-Society-ARES-Real-Estate-Thought-Leadership/book-series/ARES

The Future of Real Estate Education

From Pedagogy to Technology

Edited by Karen M. McGrath,
Elaine M. Worzala, and
Pernille H. Christensen

Routledge
Taylor & Francis Group
NEW YORK AND LONDON

Designed cover image: Elaine M. Worzala

First published 2026
by Routledge
605 Third Avenue, New York, NY 10158

and by Routledge
4 Park Square, Milton Park, Abingdon, Oxon, OX14 4RN

Routledge is an imprint of the Taylor & Francis Group, an informa business

Library of Congress Cataloging-in-Publication Data
Names: McGrath, Karen M. editor | Worzala, Elaine M. editor | Christensen, Pernille H. editor
Title: The future of real estate education : from pedagogy to technology / edited by Karen M. McGrath, Elaine Worzala, and Pernille H. Christensen.
Description: New York, NY : Routledge, 2026. | Includes bibliographical references and index.
Identifiers: LCCN 2025051884 (print) | LCCN 2025051885 (ebook) | ISBN 9781032656465 hardback | ISBN 9781032625041 paperback | ISBN 9781032656458 ebook
Subjects: LCSH: Real estate business–Study and teaching | Real estate business–Study and teaching (Higher) | Real property
Classification: LCC HD1381 .F88 2026 (print) | LCC HD1381 (ebook)
LC record available at https://lccn.loc.gov/2025051884
LC ebook record available at https://lccn.loc.gov/2025051885

ISBN: 978-1-032-65646-5 (hbk)
ISBN: 978-1-032-62504-1 (pbk)
ISBN: 978-1-032-65645-8 (ebk)

DOI: 10.1201/9781032656458

Typeset in Sabon
by Newgen Publishing UK

Access the Support Material: www.routledge.com/9781032656465

Contents

Introduction

We are delighted to present this edited volume, inspired by the collaborative spirit and intellectual energy in the "Education Track" sessions at the annual American Real Estate Society (ARES) conferences.[1] What began as a panel discussion on the future of real estate education in 2016 evolved into a series of annual sessions over the following years that passionately explored the challenges, opportunities, and innovations shaping the field today with educators across a broad range and diversity of programs. This book is a testament to the diverse voices and perspectives that emerged from that initial session and the essay that captured that discussion (McGrath et al., 2020) as well as all the proceeding sessions that followed, and to the shared commitment among educators, practitioners, and researchers to reimagine real estate education for a rapidly changing world.

Why this volume?

Educational landscape

Real estate education has long struggled to define itself as a distinct academic discipline. Despite its central role in shaping economies, communities, and the built environment, it has often been marginalized within business schools and overlooked in broader academic discourse. As the original essay notes, real estate has been described as an "ill-defined mutation" (Dasso & Woodward, 1980), lacking a unified body of knowledge and suffering from limited recognition compared to fields like finance or accounting.

Yet the importance of real estate education has never been greater. The US Energy Information Administration projects significant growth in both residential and commercial real estate, with over 880,000 new housing starts annually and commercial floor space expected to expand by more than 34% by 2040 (US EIA, 2014). Despite this demand, university programs are not producing enough graduates with the skills and knowledge needed to meet industry needs.

This book explores how real estate education can evolve to better serve students, employers, and society to help meet this demand. It highlights the need for interdisciplinary approaches, active and experiential learning, and stronger connections between academia and industry. It also calls for a rebranding of real estate education – one that moves beyond transactional models to embrace its transformative potential.

Educational development

Real estate educators are increasingly called upon to be change-makers within their institutions. They must navigate complex pedagogical, technological, and societal shifts while preparing students for careers in a multifaceted and global industry. This volume showcases how educators are responding to these challenges by adopting innovative teaching methods, integrating real estate into broader curricula, and partnering with alumni and professional associations.

This book brings together educators, researchers, and practitioners in order to introduce a variety of pedagogical strategies that move beyond the traditional lecture. Chapters examine how game-based, experiential learning, and problem-centered instruction can transform abstract concepts into applied knowledge. Real-world cases demonstrate how authentic problems can be leveraged for authentic learning.

The book also emphasizes the importance of integrating broader perspectives into real estate education. Sustainability, interdisciplinarity, and global experiences are explored as essential elements for preparing students to address contemporary issues facing cities and markets. Alumni engagement and industry partnerships are shown to be vital not only for student learning but also for shaping and sustaining robust academic programs.

At the same time, the volume looks ahead to the technological and structural shifts reshaping the profession. Contributors explore how to teach responsibly about AI, and how generative AI can be thoughtfully integrated into real estate and urban planning curricula. Broader program-level strategies are also discussed, including lessons on curriculum design, building bridges across disciplines, and positioning real estate education to achieve world-class standards.

Origins of this volume

This book is rooted in the collaborative efforts of educators and researchers who participated in the 2016 ARES conference's "Education Track" panel and the discussions that have proceeded and expanded upon that initial panel session. Educators' shared experiences and insights formed the basis of the original essay, which has since become a foundational text in the field. The contributors in this book represent a wide range of institutions, disciplines, and geographic regions, reflecting the global nature of real estate education.

The volume builds on the essay's five key sections:

1. *The importance of real estate education* – Examining the strengths and weaknesses of current programs and the need for greater academic legitimacy.
2. *Real estate in the broader curriculum* – Advocating for integration across disciplines and highlighting the role of real estate in societal innovation.
3. *Changes to the education model* – Proposing new delivery methods, including experiential learning, cross-disciplinary learning within the university, university partnering with associations, impact partnerships, micro-credentials, and lifelong learning hubs.
4. *Working with stakeholders* – Emphasizing the role of alumni, industry mentors, and professional associations in shaping educational outcomes.
5. *Connecting with (prospective) students* – Rebranding real estate education to appeal to students seeking purpose, impact, and community engagement.

How did we get here?

Each of us has industry and academic experiences that inform our perspectives on how we teach in the classroom. We have decades of teaching experience among the editorial team, and what would be centuries of experience when we consider the contributions of the authors included here. Many of us also have industry experience, which informs us on what and how we teach in the classroom and our understanding of what an industry-ready graduate looks like. Each of us has unique approaches to teaching and student engagement, curriculum development, administration of programs, and how to integrate the use of new and innovative technologies, which inevitably continue to evolve as we progress through our careers. Below we share our journey into teaching and our teaching philosophy.

Karen

As an educator, I believe my role is to use my enthusiasm for real estate and my experience in both teaching and practice to inspire students to see just how deeply real estate affects their lives and communities. Real estate is everywhere; it shapes our cities, our economies, and our daily experiences, and yet many students arrive in the classroom with only a vague sense of its scope. I take seriously the responsibility of making the subject not only accessible but also engaging and relevant, so that students can connect the concepts to their own lives and professional ambitions.

My teaching philosophy rests on three principles: helping students understand real estate in ways that translate into professional application, providing multiple modes of learning to meet diverse needs, and cultivating critical thinking and problem-solving skills that extend well beyond the classroom. To accomplish this, I use a range of strategies. For example, I create opportunities for discussion and debate where students can grapple with real-world issues such as housing affordability or the behavioral aspects of investment. In larger classes, where discussion is more difficult, I ask students to keep reflective journals, linking real estate concepts to their own interests and experiences. These approaches encourage active engagement while also allowing students to discover which areas of real estate resonate with them most. Overall, my classes are designed to encourage students to apply theory to real-world problems. For example, in real estate finance, this means working with models, case studies, and projects that mirror professional practice. Across all courses, I emphasize written and presentation skills, preparing students to communicate effectively in both academic and professional settings.

I also bring a global perspective into the classroom. Real estate practices vary widely across borders, and I believe students should understand these differences. Whether comparing property ownership rules in Mexico, contrasting the home-buying processes in the US and the UK, or examining sustainability standards across countries, I encourage students to see real estate as a global discipline.

In the end, I view teaching as a dynamic process. Each class has its own personality, and it is my responsibility to adapt, learn, and improve alongside my students. What excites me most is that real estate offers endless opportunities for discovery. By helping students to connect with the subject, I hope to equip them not only with technical knowledge but also with the curiosity and critical perspective to become thoughtful, responsible leaders in the industry.

Elaine

As a conscientious educator, I feel my role is to use my enthusiasm and experience in the real estate marketplace to give the students the critical thinking skills that will enable them to become socially responsible leaders in the real estate industry. I enjoy encouraging the students to become aware of the role they can play in enhancing their communities given the political nature of the real estate industry. Since the rules often change, it is important to stay active in the industry and update lectures every semester to reflect the dynamic nature of the subject matter.

The nature of the courses I teach is rigorous and, in my opinion, designed to hold students to the highest standards of academic excellence. I do this with the thought that if students are encouraged and held to a high level of expectations, they will aspire to reach higher goals, learn more, and apply critical thinking skills to solve real estate problems that will help them in their professional and personal lives. I work hard to assist the students in learning to learn rather than learning a set of rigid concepts. At the same time, the students see my enthusiasm for my discipline and how I love what I do, and this rubs off on many of them. I am passionate about what I do and believe that I, through this process, can help students determine their passions while gaining valuable skills to help them succeed in their professional pursuits.

At its most basic level, I view my role while interacting with each student as that of a guide on their road of lifelong learning. My primary responsibility is to bring my knowledge, experiences, networks, and best efforts to the time and place where my students and I share common goals – to gain understanding and insight, reflect on the role of real estate investment, and apply this knowledge to explore and solve the many problems facing our world today. I also believe I have a responsibility to students stemming from my profession as an educator – to foster in students a thirst for exploring and learning about the world that lies beyond the classroom and any single discipline.

In summary, I take my role as a teacher seriously and want to help my students excel. If they excel, they will improve our profession. In the long run, that is why I have chosen to be an educator. Real estate is an integral part of any culture or society, and we need to have well-educated and knowledgeable professionals to ensure we take care of our finite resources and provide livable communities for everyone to enjoy.

Pernille

As a student interested in the systemic, interdependent relationships between the built environment disciplines, I was often frustrated by the disconnect of these disciplines in academia. As a practitioner with over twenty years of experience working in the built environment, I was able to transcend those siloed boundaries when given the opportunity to work on complex transdisciplinary projects, pulling from my experiences in architecture, planning, urban design, sustainability, and property finance. By working across disciplines and applying strategies from one discipline to another in innovative ways to solve complex issues, I created a niche role for myself.

As an educator, I continue to believe challenging disciplinary boundaries is necessary to help students bridge the "gap" between built environment disciplines – a necessity if we are to effectively address the complex nature of current social and environmental issues facing cities today. By integrating industry perspectives (my own and those of guest speakers) into the classroom, we can facilitate engaged discussions with students, and by using a variety of applied, real-world-focused strategies to bring those discussions to life, students are challenged to think critically about the wicked challenges we face today in the property industry. Students in my courses are exposed to case studies, tasked to apply their conceptual learning to real-world scenarios, and engage in active, experiential learning activities to help build deeper learning of key concepts. Through active, experiential learning, I believe students are more engaged, become better communicators, and learn deeper. Students are also exposed to current research to understand what the newest developments are in industry and to help develop their own research, analytical thinking, and reflective self-inquiry skills. They are challenged to expand their thinking beyond arbitrary disciplinary boundaries and think in a systems- and network-based manner, which is required when developing "out of the box" innovative solutions to the complex challenges faced in real-world practice environments. I am passionate about what I see as a pivotal moment of opportunity for change; if society is to transition toward a greener, more resilient future, we must educate our next generation of practitioners to think about the built environment in an integrated, transdisciplinary manner.

Scope of the book

We hope that by engaging with this book, readers will be able to:

- Discover innovative practices to help them enhance student engagement, career readiness, and social impact.
- Reflect on institutional strategies for curriculum development, faculty support, and industry collaboration.
- Learn new strategies to integrate and teach students about responsible use of AI in academic and industry settings.
- Recognize the interdisciplinary nature of real estate and its relevance across academic and professional domains.
- Envision a future where real estate education is inclusive, adaptive, and transformative.

We also hope that university leaders, program directors, and industry stakeholders will:

- Support faculty in delivering applied, experiential, and socially responsive education.
- Identify opportunities to strengthen partnerships between academia and practice.
- Champion initiatives that promote diversity, sustainability, and ethical leadership in real estate.

This book is organized into three thematic sections that explore both the theoretical foundations and practical applications of real estate education. It includes case studies, program models, and recommendations that can inform teaching approaches, curriculum design, faculty development, and institutional strategy. The book begins with "fun in the classroom" and offers ideas to engage students in active, experiential learning experiences. The subsequent section offers insights to help with the administration of real estate programs. Finally, we discuss the impact of technology on real estate education and offer some strategies to ensure students are prepared to use these new tools in an ethical and strategic manner.

We do want to note that because our authors are located around the world, we did need to standardize some of the terminology. We used the American versions of spelling as well as higher education terminology. For example, we used "major" rather than "course," "course" rather than "module," and "class" for an individual session. We tried to indicate both terms wherever possible with the American version first (major/course).

Looking ahead

As real estate education continues to evolve, we must ask: What kind of real estate education do we need for the future? How can we prepare students not just to succeed in the industry but also lead it toward more equitable, sustainable, and innovative outcomes?

This book does not offer a single answer. Instead, it presents a mosaic of ideas, experiences, and visions that together illuminate a path forward. It celebrates the work of educators who are redefining the boundaries of the discipline, and it invites readers to join in shaping the next chapter of real estate education.

We are grateful to the contributors whose insights and dedication made this volume possible. Their voices reflect the richness and complexity of the field, and the promise of what it can become.

Note

1 ChatGPT-3 (OpenAI) was used sporadically to reword original work by authors for a more cohesive, single voice. Chapter 18 contains screenshots from GPT-5 mini for demonstrative purposes.

References

Dasso, J., & Woodward, L. (1980). Real estate education: past, present and future—the search for a discipline. *Real Estate Economics*, *8*(4), 404–416.

McGrath, K., Wang, B., Jackson, B., Kämpf-Dern, A., Malone, K., Funk, D., & Geurts, T. G. (2020). The future of real estate education: A multi-faceted perspective. *Journal of Real Estate Practice and Education*, *22*(1), 40–55.

US Energy Information Administration (EIA). (2014). Annual energy outlook 2014. www.eia.gov/outlooks/aeo/pdf/0383(2014).pdf

Contributors

Adejimi Adebayo is a senior lecturer in real estate at Leeds Beckett University. Prior to joining Leeds Beckett, he was a lecturer in property management and development at Nottingham Trent University. At Leeds Beckett, he is responsible for delivering key real estate modules such as property valuation & investment, property development, and asset & portfolio management at both undergraduate and postgraduate levels. His teaching approach integrates practical scenarios and research.

Samuel Azasu (PhD) is a Counselor of Real Estate (CRE) and a professor at the University of Navarra (Spain). He was previously the academic director in charge of undergraduate, postgraduate, and executive courses at the University of the Witwatersrand in South Africa. Before that, he was Director of Teaching and Learning at the Department of Real and Construction Management at KTH, Sweden. His work in South Africa has been profiled as a case study in graduate employability by the International Finance Corporation of the World Bank Group.

Tanya Bansal joined the Real Estate Development Program at the University of Maryland in November 2014. She teaches both undergraduate and graduate courses, including real estate development principles and process, case studies, and the Capstone project. As faculty liaison, she has supported over 50 adjunct instructors, leading new faculty training and orientations each semester. A strong advocate for experiential learning, Bansal promotes the integration of site visits, industry guest speakers, and project-based assignments into the curriculum. Tanya's contributions extend to curriculum development, new program proposals, course scheduling, faculty and student recruitment, program outreach, and academic student advising. In 2018, she co-led a study-abroad program to St. Petersburg, Russia, and is currently developing a program in Chandigarh, India, for winter 2026. Originally from

India, Tanya holds an undergraduate degree in architecture, an MRED (2014), and an MBA (2023), both from the University of Maryland.

Sandy Bond is Professor of Practice at Bucknell University, with an international career spanning real estate appraisal, consulting, teaching and research. She was formerly Director of the Real Estate and Land Use Institute at California State University Fullerton. She integrates industry experience and academic insight into her teaching at both undergraduate and postgraduate levels. Sandy's research focuses on global real estate challenges, including the impact of detrimental conditions, such as earthquakes and climate change, on property values. She holds a PhD from Curtin University and a master and a bachelor degree from Massey University. Sandy serves on the editorial board of the *Journal of Sustainable Real Estate* and is a fellow of both the Property Institute of New Zealand and the NZ Institute of Valuers. Her contributions to property education and research have earned her the PRRES Achievement Award (2002) and the IRES Service Award (2016) for outstanding service to the international real estate societies.

Gavin Boyce is Head of Faculty and Research Partnership at the University of Sheffield Library. He holds a master degree in computing and a PhD in philosophy and is a senior fellow of the UK Higher Education Academy (SFHEA). He leads the library's development for supporting the digital scholarship needs of users with a focus on enabling computational access to library content for research purposes. Since the introduction of freely available Gen AI tools, he has been working with the library sector to understand the implications for how research libraries support the information literacy needs of their users when information discovery is mediated by such tools and the effect of their widespread use on independent learning.

Stephen T. Buckman is Fogelson Chair of Real Estate at Roosevelt University (USA). He previously taught in the MRED program at Clemson University and at the University of South Florida, following his postdoctoral work at the University of Michigan. Dr. Buckman has taught classes on resiliency planning and sustainable mixed-use real estate and has published extensively on the issues of resiliency and sustainability as related to climate impacts to the built form. He is a former Fulbright recipient, where he studied climate resiliency in the Favelas of Rio de Janeiro, Brazil. As a practitioner, he creates residential and horizontal developments and consults to developers. He also sits or has sat on sustainable real estate and resiliency boards such as the Coastal Risk Consulting group and the RISE network (Puerto Rico). He received his PhD in urban economic geography from Arizona State University, where his dissertation concentrated on the use of canalized rivers and canals to create more economically viable and sustainable areas in non-waterfront cities.

Pernille H. Christensen is Course Director of the Bachelor of Property Economics (BPE) at the University of Technology Sydney, leading a program with 18 full- and part-time staff, and over 475 students enrolled across its three-year degree. A passionate educator, she received the 2022 UTS Vice-Chancellor's Individual Teaching Award for her innovative, real-world-focused teaching that empowers students to become critical problem solvers and reflective thinkers. As a UTS Learning Futures Fellow, she championed pedagogical reform and mentored colleagues in active and experiential learning. Pernille teaches undergraduate and postgraduate courses, including introduction to property and the built environment, resilient urban development, property development process, and the Capstone project. Pernille's academic background reflects her transdisciplinary focus, including a Professional Bachelor of Architecture (1996), dual Master of Architecture and Master of City & Regional Planning degrees (2000), and an interdisciplinary PhD in planning, design, and the built environment (2012). Her teaching integrates academic and industry perspectives, preparing students to navigate and address contemporary complex challenges and shape the future of the built environment.

Éamonn D'Arcy is Professor of International Real Estate and Co-Head of the Department of Real Estate and Planning at the University of Reading. He has over 35 years of experience as a real estate educator and is Program Director of the full-time MSc Real Estate Program at Henley, which is one of the largest programs of its type globally. He is a past president of both the International Real Estate Society (IRES) and the European Real Estate Society (ERES). He has also served on the board of the European Public Real Estate Association (EPRA). His research and teaching interests focus on real estate economics, the operation of real estate markets in practice, and the internationalization of real estate involvements. In 2024, he was the recipient of the American Real Estate Society Education Award in recognition of his many significant contributions to the advancement of real estate education.

Ronald Dyer is Academic Lead for Digital Innovation and Senior University Teacher in Complex Project Management at Sheffield University Management School. With over 20 years of professional experience in project management, he has led major digital transformation initiatives across sectors, such as financial services, education, agriculture, and energy at institutions, including Goldman Sachs, Citi, and the Inter-American Development Bank. Ronald's academic interests include AI, VR, analytics, and game-based learning for enhanced decision-making in project delivery.

Nick French is a recognized expert and highly regarded property academic in the areas of property valuation and investment. He has worked as a professor at numerous universities in the UK, Europe, and the USA, teaching extensively in the areas of property valuation, real estate investment, and corporate real estate. He is a member of the Royal Institution of Chartered Surveyors (RICS) and serves as Chair of the RICS Global Valuation Standards Expert Working Group. Previously, he was also a member of the Professional Board of the International Valuation Standards Council (IVSC). Nick is the editor of the *Journal of Property Investment & Finance*, an award-winning, international academic journal. He has published over 350 articles in various professional and academic journals.

Tom G. Geurts, since graduating with a PhD in finance with a concentration in real estate from Pennsylvania State University in 1998, has taught as a professor at six universities, interspersed with three stints working as director of research at prominent real estate firms in New York City. He has given invited guest lectures at 11 universities all over the world, many of them multiple times. He has received two teaching awards at New York University in 2006 and at George Washington University in 2013. In 2022, he was awarded the Real Estate Education Award in recognition of his "many significant contributions to the advancement of real estate education" by the American Real Estate Society. Tom's teaching philosophy is that students should learn a theoretical foundation augmented by practical applications. For this purpose, he has created a number of educational games and has found that study-abroad trips are perfect for this teaching philosophy. Consequently, he has led study-abroad trips for five universities.

Rebecca Johnson is a GenAI ethicist and doctoral researcher exploring how human values, biases, and worldviews are embedded in GenAI systems. With a background in science, communications, and research ethics – including a year at Google's Ethical AI team – Rebecca integrates sociotechnical systems theory, post-phenomenology, and the MaSH framework (Machines, Society, and Humans) to explore values alignment and the societal impact of AI. Rebecca was named one of Lighthouse3's "100 Brilliant Women in AI Ethics" in 2020, is managing editor for the *AI Ethics Journal*, and serves on the editorial board of *AI and Ethics*. She convened Australia's largest GenAI ethics conference, *ChatLLM23*, its policy-focused follow-up, *ChatRegs23*. Since 2016, she as taught undergraduate and postgraduate students in the Faculty of Science and Arts and the Business School at the University of Sydney. Her work champions cross-disciplinary collaboration, integrating philosophical and social science insights to promote inclusive, value-sensitive, ethical AI development. More at https://ethicsgenai.com/.

Tobias Just has been Managing Director at the IRE|BS Immobilienakademie and Professor for Real Estate at the University of Regensburg since 2011. He is Course Director for the MBA Real Estate and all Executive Real Estate Programs of the University of Regensburg. Tobias teaches across undergraduate and postgraduate programs, including introduction to real estate markets, real estate economics, housing policies, and urban development. Tobias graduated in economics from Hamburg University in 1996 (equivalent to a master's degree); his PhD thesis on globalization's impact on fiscal and monetary policies was awarded the University's Science Prize in 2001. In 2009, Tobias concluded his professoral thesis on demographics and real estate at the Technical University of Berlin. Before joining the University of Regensburg, Tobias worked at Deutsche Bank Research on sector and real estate market topics in the strategic research division. This experience also shapes his teaching, in which he uses economic theory to solve practical real estate market problems.

Annette Kämpf-Dern is a recognized thought leader in holistic, sustainable management of the built environment, with academic credentials spanning economical civil engineering and business administration, an MBA, a doctorate, and further habilitation-equivalent achievements from universities in Berlin, Frankfurt, Chicago, Darmstadt, and Weimar. Annette's mission is to empower responsible change-makers by combining academic rigor with real-world impact through student-centered, problem-based learning, and industry collaboration in management, leadership, HR, entrepreneurship, and sustainability. A pioneer in integrating smart and digital technologies into teaching and practice, Annette empowers students to translate knowledge into responsible action. Annette has developed interdisciplinary curricula, organized international conferences and summer schools, and received the ARES Best Manuscript Education Award and the BMBF University Challenge. Annette cofounded the Real Estate and Leadership Foundation and the Transdisciplinary Workplace Research Network and leads the Real Estate Management competence group at gif E.V., Society of Property Researchers, Germany. As a crowd-fundraiser, she mobilizes resources to advance research, education, and knowledge transfer for a more sustainable built environment.

John A. Kilpatrick heads up Greenfield Advisors, Inc. in Seattle, WA. He's been involved in the real estate finance, investment, and development business for about 40 years, with an occasional foray into university administration and teaching. He's the author of six books (with number seven slowly underway), about 100-or-so refereed journal articles, chapters, one Congressional Testimony, and who-knows-how-many lectures, invited speeches, and ramblings at cocktail parties. He serves on the National Board of Advisors for the Carson College of Business at Washington State University. In 2017, Gov. Jay Inslee appointed Dr. Kilpatrick to serve as a director of the Washington State Economic Development Finance Authority, and in 2020, he was named to the Advisory Board of the US Global Leadership Coalition. He holds the MAI designation from the Appraisal Institute and has served for many years on the review board for their flagship publication, the *Appraisal Journal*.

Constantine Korologos (CRE, MAI, MRICS) is Clinical Assistant Professor at NYU's Schack Institute of Real Estate, where he teaches graduate courses in real estate capital markets, portfolio risk, valuation, and investment analysis. With over 30 years of teaching experience, he has played a key role in curriculum design, academic leadership, and mentoring future industry professionals. He previously served as director of the Hirsh Fellows honors program. Constantine brings over 38 years of real estate capital markets experience, having structured, underwritten, or advised on nearly $100 billion in global CRE transactions. His industry career includes senior roles at Equitable Real Estate, Moody's Investor Services, Bear Stearns, Wachovia Securities, and Deloitte Financial Advisory Services, focused on valuation, structured finance, CMBS, and advisory. He is a FINRA broker-dealer registered representative and regularly serves as an expert witness in real estate litigation matters. He is coauthor of *Real Estate Capital Markets: A Primer* (2024) and a contributing author to *The Counselors of Real Estate's Top Ten Issues Affecting Real Estate*. He is a frequent speaker and subject matter expert for CREFC, NAREIT, ULI, and The Counselors of Real Estate.

Moses Kusiluka (PhD) is currently serving as Chief Secretary of the Government of the United Republic of Tanzania. He formerly served as a faculty member and head of the Department of Real Estate and Finance and Investment at Ardhi University in Tanzania. Other positions he has held include Permanent Secretary in the President's Office (Tanzania), Commissioner for Lands for Tanzania, President of African Real Estate Society, Board Member of IREBS Foundation for African

Real Estate Research, and Visiting Professor at IREBS – University of Regensburg, Germany.

Dr. Luis Lozano-Paredes is a lecturer at the Transdisciplinary School, University of Technology Sydney, where he teaches across transdisciplinary subjects that bring together design, technology, and critical governance. His teaching practice is shaped by a commitment to complexity thinking, reflexive pedagogy, and participatory learning. Drawing on his background in architecture, urban economics, and science and technology studies, Luis designs learning experiences that are exploratory, systems-oriented, and grounded in real-world problem-solving. Luis places strong emphasis on teaching as a collaborative process of knowledge coproduction. He encourages students to engage deeply with ambiguity, navigate competing perspectives, and apply theory to practice, particularly in social and technological change contexts. He has developed a curriculum around digital ethnography, scenario thinking, the ethics of AI, and integrating GenAI tools to support critical inquiry and reflective practice.

Meagan McCollum is Associate Professor of Finance and Director of the Center for Real Estate Studies in the Collins College of Business at the University of Tulsa, a small private university in Oklahoma. In this role, she designed and initiated an interdisciplinary undergraduate real estate minor in 2021 that currently enrolls approximately 65 students from across the university's four undergraduate colleges. Through the Center for Real Estate Studies, which she launched in 2023, she engages with more than 300 undergraduate and graduate students annually in coursework, research, networking, and experiential learning opportunities in real estate. Meagan is a graduate of Samford University (BA, MBA), University of Alabama (MS), and Louisiana State University (PhD). Prior to her appointment at the University of Tulsa, she was a faculty member at Baruch College, City University of New York, where she helped redesign the undergraduate and graduate real estate curriculums. Her teaching focuses on helping students develop strong foundational knowledge in real estate principles as well as providing exposure to industry perspectives through experiential learning opportunities.

Margaret McFarland was Founding Director of the Graduate Programs in Real Estate Development at the University of Maryland starting in 2006 until she took emeritus status in 2018. She developed the curriculum and courses for the fast-growing program as well as mentoring over 50 industry professionals, many of whom were teaching for the first time. McFarland taught real property law and urban planning first as an adjunct professor and upon retiring from law practice as clinical faculty until 2022. McFarland has taught at both the undergraduate and graduate levels and is a strong advocate of using industry professionals as adjunct professors who can bring their knowledge to the classroom in an effective way. Her teaching reflects her multidisciplinary education and professional experience with an AM degree in Urban Studies from the University of Chicago and a JD degree from the University of Michigan. As a practicing attorney for over 25 years, McFarland advised clients primarily on corporate organization and commercial real estate matters with a focus on nonprofit governance and affordable housing finance, development, and management.

Karen M. McGrath is an award-winning researcher specializing in real estate sustainability and pedagogy. She serves as Chair of the Accounting and Financial Management Department at Bucknell University, her alma mater, where she also oversees the real estate program. Before returning to Bucknell, she taught undergraduate and graduate real estate courses at Texas A&M University and the University of Illinois Urbana-Champaign. Karen is the lead author of "The Future of Real Estate Education," the 2020 article that laid the foundation for this book. She chairs the American Real Estate Society (ARES) Education Committee and serves on the editorial boards of the *Journal of Real Estate Literature* and the *Journal of Property Investment & Finance.* Her research focuses on sustainability in the built environment, draws on nearly two decades of Wall Street experience, where she specialized in REITs and REOCs. She is a LEED Accredited Professional and holds the Fundamentals of Sustainability Accounting (FSA) credential. Dedicated to applied learning, Karen designs and teaches courses in real estate finance, investment, and ESG, bridging theory and practice to prepare students for leadership in an evolving field. She holds an MRE from NYU and a PhD from the University of Reading.

Sekhoho Ntene is a self-employed corporate trainer based in Johannesburg (South Africa). She has extensive experience in designing and implementing tracer studies for government training and education authorities in South Africa.

Olayiwola Oladiran is Lecturer (Assistant Professor) in Real Estate at the University of Sheffield and Co-Lead of the Shef.AI Pedagogy Interest Group. He is a senior fellow of the UK Higher Education Academy (SFHEA), an RICS Chartered Surveyor (MRICS), and a member of the RICS Yorkshire and the Humber Regional Board. Olayiwola is the coauthor of the textbook *PropTech and Real Estate Innovations: A Guide to Digital Technologies and Solutions in the Built Environment* and coauthor of the PropTech Education Integration Framework (PEIF). At the University of Sheffield, he leads and contributes to various modules, including real estate innovation and digital transformation, international real estate markets, real estate development, and applied valuation. Olayiwola is enthusiastic about advancing real estate education and scholarship through the integration of innovation and digital technology.

Tunbosun Oyedokun is Lecturer (Assistant Professor) in Real Estate within the Division of Urban Studies & Social Policy at the University of Glasgow. He holds a BTech and an MTech in Estate Management from the Federal University of Technology, Akure, Nigeria, and a PhD in urban studies from the Urban Institute at Heriot-Watt University, Edinburgh. He led the MSc Real Estate program at the university from 2018 to 2025 and teaches on various postgraduate courses in real estate and planning programs. He is passionate about excellence in learning and teaching, which led him to pursue an MEd in Academic Practice and earn recognition as a fellow of Recognizing Excellence in Teaching. He is also an associate fellow of the Higher Education Academy and a member of the European Real Estate Society. In addition to his work in real estate research, Tunbosun has a strong interest in pedagogic research, particularly in active learning, technology-enhanced learning, and teaching professional development.

Katherine A. Pancak is Professor In-Residence of Finance and Real Estate at the University of Connecticut and currently serves as Academic Director of Business Programs at the UConn Stamford Campus. She is a student-focused educator who consistently prioritizes pedagogical excellence and the enhancement of the student learning experience. Her teaching has been recognized through multiple prestigious honors, including the UConn School of Business Outstanding Undergraduate Teaching Award (received twice), the Innovation in Teaching Award, the UConn Stamford Campus Faculty Recognition Award (also received twice), and the national Educator of the Year Award from the Real Estate Educators Association. Katherine is the author of *Connecticut Real Estate: Law and Practice*, a widely adopted textbook for the state's real estate prelicensing curriculum, and has developed extensive instructional resources for use by real estate educators and professionals throughout the industry. She earned her undergraduate degree in economics from Mount Holyoke College and her Juris Doctorate from Boston College. Prior to entering academia, she was a practicing corporate real estate attorney.

Jeffrey G. Robert (PhD, MBA) is Lecturer in Real Estate at the University of Massachusetts. He has past appointments asa Collegiate Associate Professor in the Blackwood Department of Real Estate at Virginia Tech. He is a passionate professor who has been teaching market analysis for the past five years. His research interests are twofold. He focuses on applied real estate development research such as spatial and price externalities, and he dedicates research time to classroom pedagogy and curriculum design. He earned a PhD in housing (2019) from the University of Georgia and a Master of Business Administration (2011) from Bentley University. For additional information and any inquiries, he can be reached at jeffrobert@umass.edu.

Stephen E. Roulac is a distinguished educator and thought leader in real estate, known for his ability to distill complex theory and analytics into clear, compelling insights. With academic appointments and degrees from Harvard (MBA), UC Berkeley (JD), and Stanford (PhD), Dr. Stephen's work is defined by discovery, rigor, relevance, and impact. His teaching blends textbook mastery, creative innovation, and engaging storytelling, consistently earning high evaluations. He draws on a portfolio of globally ranked, award-winning research to inform his teaching and scholarship. He is one of only two academics – and the sole property strategist/analyst – honored with UC Berkeley's Millennium Award for transformative impact on real estate in the 20th century. His numerous awards include the American Real Estate Society Education Award. He has created distinct learning resources, pioneered educational research, advanced real estate pedagogy, and advanced the discipline's body of knowledge. Beyond academia, he is a professional speaker and expert witness, applying his teaching expertise in corporate training and professional education settings.

Andrew Stanton is Founder and Editor of PROPTECH-X, a leading source of insight and analysis in the PropTech and real estate sectors. Known as the "PropTech Real Estate Influencer," Andrew writes over 1.3 million words annually, having met 1,000+ founders, and critiqued 400 pitch decks. As CEO of PROPTECH-PR, "A consultancy for PropTech founders," he has advised over 130 PropTech companies with a combined market capitalization of £1.47Bn, focusing on operations, market positioning, scaling, revenue growth, and exit strategies. His advisory also supports global real estate firms. With 200,000+ followers, he has facilitated over 4,100 introductions and raised £2.1 million in funding. A former NED of nurtur.group, his expertise is trusted by senior executives across the industry globally. Known for deep market knowledge and an unparalleled network, he is a strategic partner for startups, scale-ups, and established firms looking to grow, derisk, and succeed in the ever-evolving PropTech landscape.

Elaine M. Worzala is an award-winning real estate educator and has written extensively on real estate education programs. Instrumental in the design of the Commercial Real Estate Finance major at the College of Charleston, the full-time master's program at Johns Hopkins University, and the master's at the University of San Diego, she has over 30 years of experience in higher education. She has three degrees from the University of Wisconsin-Madison, including one from the highly ranked master's program. She was a recipient of the prestigious James A. Graaskamp Award (2014) and the Real Estate Education Award (2018) from the American Real Estate Society. Dedicating her life to carrying on the Wisconsin tradition, she believes strongly in the multidisciplinary approach to understanding real estate and regularly employs the power of project-based/experiential learning to make the classroom come alive for her students. She focuses on building strong links to her classroom by engaging alumni and other professionals. To facilitate this, she is actively engaged in many professional and academic organizations around the globe.

Chapter 1

The complexity of simple teaching

The art of teaching students what they already knew but never realized

Nick French

Introduction

When I was asked to write a chapter on how to teach, I was hesitant as although I have won teaching awards during my 45 years of being an educator, I have never really thought about what I do and why it is that students and professionals find my lectures engaging and rewarding. I have been lucky, and I have been blessed with a natural aptitude to being able to communicate at the right level to the right audience. At university, my teaching loads have always been high with an average of 20 contact hours each week. In addition, I used to undertake 30 or 40 public lectures to practicing professionals each year. So, I have had a lot of time to hone my skills but never have I consciously dissected what it is that I do.

This chapter offers me a chance to think about it and hopefully identify what it is that makes my lectures successful. I hope that by reference to one case study topic, I can pass some of those insights on to the next generation.

What makes a good lecturer?

That is a difficult question to answer without appearing to be arrogant. I know, from student and public lecture feedback, that people consider me to be a good lecturer. I also know from my own experiences, both as a student and, latterly, as an observer of my colleagues, that many lecturers are not good at what they do; particularly in the university sector. In fairness, I was unusual when I became a lecturer, I chose lecturing as a career because I wanted to teach but most of my colleagues chose a university life because they enjoyed research. Something that I have done with some success but never as a main motivator. Below are some reasons why I believe I am successful at my trade as a lecturer.

DOI: 10.1201/9781032656458-1

Enthusiasm

I have always taught with relish and enthusiasm. I became a university lecturer to teach. It is what I do. Many of my colleagues were the opposite and saw lecturing and tutorials as a bane that distracted them from their research. Too many times, I have heard colleagues cursing the presence of students during term time. I relished their attendance and their curiosity and, for most of them, their dedication to learn.

What I am saying is that a principal requirement of being a good lecturer is aptitude; a desire to help the students to learn and achieve. I remember a time when I was visiting a fellow professor in Australia and I stumbled upon a mantra mug to give to him as a thank you gift, it simply said, "Those who can, do. Those who can't, teach. And those who can't teach become university lecturers." This may be a humorous statement, but there is more than a grain of truth in it and that is a sad indictment of our profession. But just as it is possible to teach people to act, it must also be possible to teach people to teach.

And, indeed, the analogy between the two professions may be useful to this exposition because the second trait that I think manifests itself in a good lecturer is that of being a frustrated thespian.

Performance

When I give my public lectures, I suffer terribly from nerves. Every lecture is like the first time and my adrenalin is pumping and I constantly question my choice of career. I once spoke about this with a friend who was in the Royal Shakespeare Company and we were amazed about how similar our experiences were in our respective roles. We both needed to be dressed correctly. In his case, it was as the wardrobe for the play dictated, in my case it was always a suit. We both needed to have time in the wings to gather our thoughts and go through rituals; checking the microphone, checking (in my case) the computer and projector, and making sure that there was a clock in my eye line to allow me to pace my delivery. It is a performance. Just as an actor learns their lines, it is all about preparation.

Prepare, prepare, prepare

There is another adage that says that "if you fail to prepare, you are preparing to fail." When I gave my first ever university lecture at the tender age of 22, I spent weeks preparing for a two-hour lecture. Not only did I need to have my slides (or in those days overhead projector acetates) written and in order, I also needed to understand my topic inside and out. I needed to understand what everything meant and to pre-empt every single possible question that the students might ask. That doesn't mean to say that I was never stumped by the inquisition of the audience, but it did mean that I had most angles covered.

Audience interaction: Questions and questioning

For most lectures that I have given, I have always encouraged questions and, more so, I have always asked questions of the audience. It is a two-way process. Their questions are there to seek clarity and my questions are there to steer the students towards their own understanding of the topic based on other life experiences. Analogies and metaphors are central to how I teach. So, I ask the students to answer certain questions to direct them towards a better understanding of what I am saying. One thing that is paramount to the process of asking the audience questions is to allow them to volunteer to answer. I never pick on people (albeit I often encourage others to speak when they feel more relaxed in the class and more confident). I also always listen intently and courteously to their answers and, if I feel what they are saying is right, I will give them affirmation but if they haven't yet cracked a real understanding of the point being made, I will never say that they are completely wrong. Most answers (when discussing concepts) are a curate's egg; they are good in parts. So, I concentrate on the elements that are helpful to the exposition and then ask for other opinions. This point is revisited in the case-study below.

And in reverse, when I am asked a question, I stop the lecture at that point and give my full consideration to the question being asked. Because we all know that in an audience of (say) 20, if one person asks a question then it is likely that another five or six are wondering about the same thing. Most times, I have the answer and most times, I give the answer time to be discussed. I will then weave that discussion back into the lecture's exposition to validate the importance of the question.

And that is important as it builds the respect of the attendees. The other thing that builds respect is when I didn't know the answer, I never tried to flannel the questioner with an inadequate response but always thank them for their question and promised that I would go away and then get back to them with a considered response. And I always did. With students, I would seek them out in a couple of days to address their question over a cup of coffee. With practitioners, I would phone them or write to them.

Respect

Treating your audience with respect is always important. They are there to learn, some learn at different speeds to others. Some will struggle to understand, others may understand and challenge your view. But it takes teamwork in the classroom. A good lecturer doesn't "talk at" the audience; they "work with" them. When I started, we didn't use the term "facilitator" but that is what teachers do; they facilitate the learning process. I always felt honored and blessed to play a small part in the education of my audience. And I think that students respected that in return.

Practical examples

When I started, I may have followed the old saying of "a teacher being one chapter ahead of the students" but as I grew older and wiser, my understanding of my subject became deeper and deeper. I devoured every article and every book on my subject (principally property valuation and investment), I ensured that I was constantly up to date with the real estate and finance markets and, most importantly, I spoke with colleagues in practice regularly, so all my lectures were anchored in the real world with topical examples.

I don't underestimate the importance of the academic "skeleton" of concepts and theory, but the complete lecture also needs the "skin" of practice. The students need to be able to relate to what you are saying and to apply the theory spoken to things that they see and understand. This is particularly true of the case study that I use below.

Simplicity and relatability

One of the comments that was made of my teaching was that I made complex issues understandable by using simple analogies and expositions. Again, I don't raise this issue to sing my own praises but, rather, to demonstrate a very important foundation of all good teachers. Keep things simple.

It is surprising how much everyone already knows. Life teaches life lessons, but it also provides a framework for exploring and applying academic concepts. If you can link everything that you talk about to things that the audience already understands then it can speed up the learning process. In the case study below, I will link lots of economic concepts to everyday things with which everyone already engages. But, in other lectures, I have introduced the stories of time travel with Dr Who to illustrate the concept of time value of money. It is easier for students to relate to a fictional character to understand present value than it is to introduce them cold to the mathematical formulas of finance. Math is a tool to get specific answers but without an understanding of what the math is doing it becomes a soul-destroying rote exercise. Many students have an innate fear of math, but this can be dispelled by helping them to understand the question and not concentrating solely upon getting the right answer.

Engagement and lack of distractions

In my introverted analysis of what makes a good lecture and a good lecturer, my final point is probably the most contentious. This is particularly true in the modern world of laptops and mobiles and the ubiquitous social media. I always ask my audiences (and with students, demand) that they turn off all their electronic devices. For the Millennials and Z-Generation, this request is akin to asking them to chop off an arm, but it is worth the perseverance. Obviously, to ask them this is part of a contract. In return, I will provide them with detailed notes of my lectures, and I promise to keep them engaged. The result is a much more focused learning environment for them and more enjoyable experience for me. And, by being engaged on only what is in front of them, me, they are better able to learn. Of course, to achieve this, you need the respect and trust of the audience but that returns to my comment above, teaching is a shared experience and not a monologue.

And in that regard, depending upon the size of the audience, always make eye contact with them. Not only does that make them feel part of the experience, but it also allows you to gauge, by the number of quizzical faces, how well you are doing in explaining the topic of the lecture.

Humor

The next requirement, in my opinion, is the most difficult as it relies upon your personality and how funny you can be. But the best lectures that I have seen in my life have one common theme and that is that the lecturer is genuinely funny. This is a quality that helps to keep the audience engaged, interested, and listening. As it is important to ensure that no offense is ever caused, it is best to find the humor in the topic and not to anyone's detriment. I often use myself as the brunt of the jokes as that is easy and safe but, however you do it, just be upbeat and amusing. It makes the audience so much more susceptible to the message that you are presenting.

Presentation

The final point is to me a much more mechanical requirement. Some of my best lectures are not based on PowerPoint (or equivalent) slides and fall into the category of "chalk and talk," albeit technology today means that it is more likely to be a whiteboard and pen. My first ever lecture, as noted, relied upon acetates to be my aide memoire and that is still true today when I am giving public lectures where the convention of a slide-based talk is rarely challenged. But, as I got older and more experienced, I was often able to develop my lectures as I went along, reacting to questions and comments.

But when I do use slides, there are certain very simple rules. Keep the font size large and readable from the back of the room, only have a couple of points or ideas on each slide and, most importantly, DON'T READ THE SLIDES. They are there as a prompt to free-flowing speech. The audience want the points noted in writing placed in context. They want examples of each to help them understand.

Be sure to spend time making the slides themselves engaging too. Use different layouts, use color, use clipart, or photos. You may be the main act of the lecture (to return to my thespian analogy), but your slides are the support act.

These are, to me, the most important elements of creating a good lecture and of being a good lecturer. Using that framework, I will present one of my best received lectures and how I direct the discussion and debate. I have probably given this lecture 200–300 times both at universities around the world and at professional conferences globally. Sometimes my audiences have been students, sometimes my audiences have been senior management of banks and real estate companies. In each case, with a little tailoring, the message has been well received and I hope that everyone learned and understood the concepts discussed better.

A case study lecture looking at the concepts of price, value, and worth

This is, in many ways, a 101 lecture but it is amazing how many senior managers have told me that they never understood the difference between price, value, and worth and that this lecture has helped them understand their valuations and their investment strategies for their property portfolios better.

Before I can describe the lecture, as I said above, I need to provide you with an understanding of what I am trying to get across in the lecture. This is a short explanation of the concepts that I am discussing.

Thee different concepts of value

There are three words in common parlance in the English language (and other languages) which are commonly used interchangeably. These are "price," "value," and "worth." Yet, in the context of property (and economics), the words have distinct meanings.

- Price is the actual observable figure at which a property asset is sold in the open market. It is an historic fact and can only be observed once the sale has been made.
- (Market) Value is an estimate of price where there is no actual sale. It is a proxy. An estimate of the figure that would be paid for the property asset in the open market were the property to be sold (after marketing) on the date of the valuation.
- Worth is a not a market-based figure. It is a subjective assessment of the financial benefit of that asset to a particular owner or potential purchaser at a particular moment in time.

In simple terms, an investor may look at the cash flow that a property investment generates and calculate that the property is worth "X" to them based on their forecasts of the future. The open market valuation for the same property, however, is "X-1" based on market evidence. Thus, the investor will be interested in purchasing the property; the difference reflecting the divergence between their forecasts and market expectations. Conversely, if an investor thinks that a property that they own is worth less than the market value, then they would consider selling that asset.

Worth is the driver of price. A successful bidder, at auction or sale/tender, will be the one who thinks that the item is worth the most and will outbid other bidders. That will determine the price, the observable exchange point. And value is just a professional estimate of price when there isn't an actual sale.

Worth is the driver that stimulates offers in the market; value is an estimate of the sale price in that market and price is the actual amount paid. These are three different concepts. But all of them are at a specific point in time. Just as prices fluctuate in the market according to economic conditions, so will value (as an estimate of price) and worth. Valuations do not have a shelf life. Values, as prices, go up and down.

This lecture is to emphasize the distinction between "price," "value," and "worth" and by the example of a pretend sale/tender, the lecture clearly helps the audience to understand this distinction.

The structure of the lecture

The strength of this lecture is audience participation. Asking them lots of questions and incorporating their own explanations into the exposition of the lecture. Effectively, this is a workshop (regardless of the size of the audience – I have done this lecture with as few as ten and as many as 400) and the lecturer is the facilitator (as discussed above).

As a result, this is a lecture with only a few slides and very few references to the same. They are there as a backdrop and not as a focal point.

The opening remarks

As with all lectures, it is important that the first slide says who you are (particularly for public lectures) but it also does something to capture the audience participation. In this case, I use a quote from Oscar Wilde with whom, for comic effect, I claim a tenuous affinity in terms of a shared nationality and spending a significant amount of time at an institution in Reading. In my case, it was the university, in his case it was the prison. As noted earlier, humor and self-deprecation can be very useful techniques in getting the audience to relate to you. This slide is shown in Exhibit 1.1.

But the quote is important as it provides me with a peg (outside the subject of property valuation) to hang my coat on. The misunderstanding of concepts.

The important questions

My first slide with content (not illustrated here) is the agenda slide where I talk about what I am going to talk about. Again, like the mantra for success of all papers and all lectures, "talk about what you are going to talk about, talk about it and then talk about what you have talked about." But it is also at this point that I ask everyone to put my handouts away and to

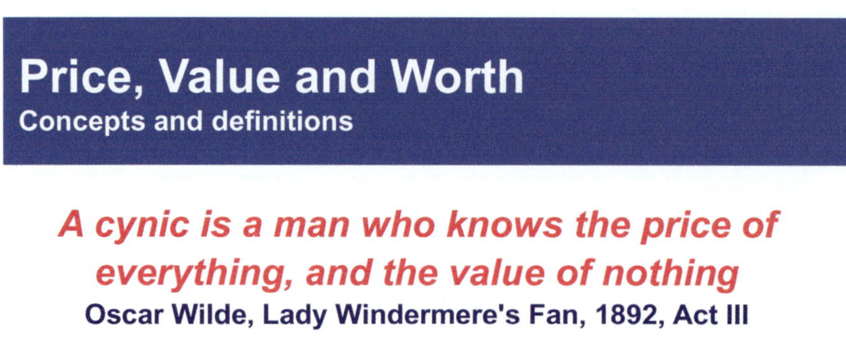

Exhibit 1.1 A PowerPoint slide with a thought-provoking quote and the instructor's personal information.

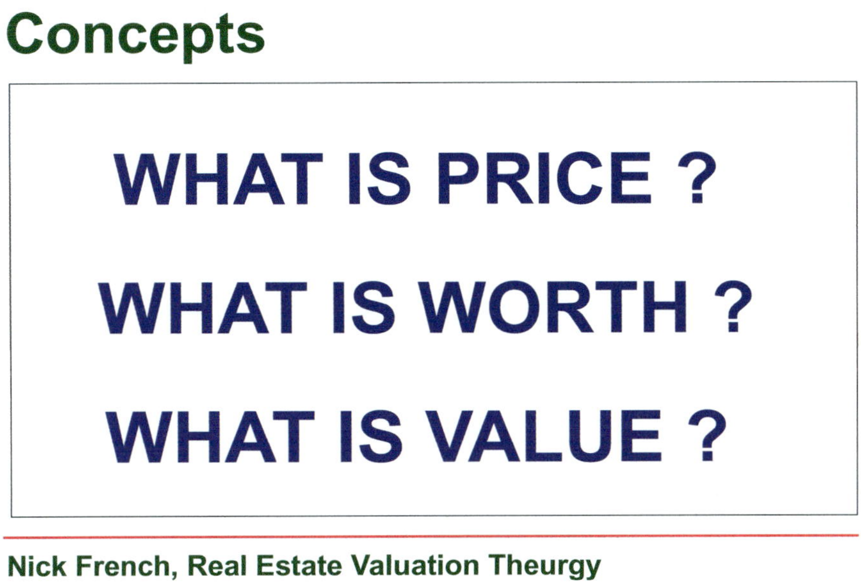

Exhibit 1.2 What is price? What is worth? What is value?

turn off (or put on silent and to one side) all electronic devices. You will get some pushback at that point but most of the audience will comply, and this creates peer pressure for others to comply. But I never made a big thing of it.

In Exhibit 1.2, I show what is pretty much the only slide that you need. It is just the three questions of what price, value, and worth mean. And the trick here is not to ask about the words in the context of real estate but, instead, in terms of everyday life.

What is price?

Start with the question. What is price? You will get some responses; some will say what something costs. Which is fine but the word "cost" has other implications in terms of economics. The cost of production rather than the colloquial use of what you pay for something. Talk about that. And then progress to whether price is the amount on the ticket. The ticket on a suit in a large department store, the ticket on the windscreen of a car for sale, the amount that an illegal street vendor asks for a "genuine" Louis Vuitton handbag when they were on vacation last year?

The majority of the audience will all say "yes" to each. Either by a show of hands or orally. So, you then throw the curve ball and ask whether the amount that someone pays for the item is always the number on the ticket. You will get a confused room at this point. Some will immediately recognize that isn't the case, others will start deliberating about what they understand and become more curious. Feed the curiosity by giving a real-life example. I talk about asking for a discount on the suit in a department store and how there is no flexibility. Then, I say that the same suit is next door in the boutique outfitters, and the ticket says more than the department store. The owner is serving you and they know their margins and know that they can get a sale by negotiating on price. The offer of less than the department store ticket is accepted and the deal is done. You are introducing the concept of haggling, of price only being determined when the deal is done. Everything before then is just marketing, it is an asking price. A starting point for negotiation. In theory, this is true of all retail stores, it is just that the large supermarkets and multiple chains prefer not to allow their staff the flexibility and responsibility of negotiating. Although that is not strictly true. In the UK, the managers in many big retailers are given the power to give a 10% discount if asked. Most people don't ask but they do have that discretion. Talk about things like this. The more examples of how the real-world works, the more they will buy (if you pardon the pun) into the concepts.

The same is true of the street trader, they will sell you that copy-handbag for much less than their opening offer. Show disinterest and the asking price starts dropping. Make a silly offer and the seller will totally engage with you. It is all the dance of negotiating. And eventually there will be a number that works for the seller and the buyer. That is when the deal is done. The price will be fixed at that point. But remember, the next deal with the next buyer, in this instance, where the buyer is a less skilled negotiator, could be at a higher number. The price is at a moment in time. It can change from moment to moment. This then allows you to introduce how stock markets work, how share prices change by the minute. The concept is that price is the number at point of exchange – but that a price can change over time and is influenced by how many players there are in the market or markets.

At all points, keep encouraging everyone to participate. Remember, it is their class, and you are just the facilitator. Once you feel that the discussion has run its course on "price," put up a summary slide, as illustrated in Exhibit 1.3, that defines what the class has agreed amongst them.

Price is an observable, historic (even by 1 minute), transactional figure and, by definition, you can only see price once it has happened. Anything prior to the transaction is "marketing," for example, asking price.

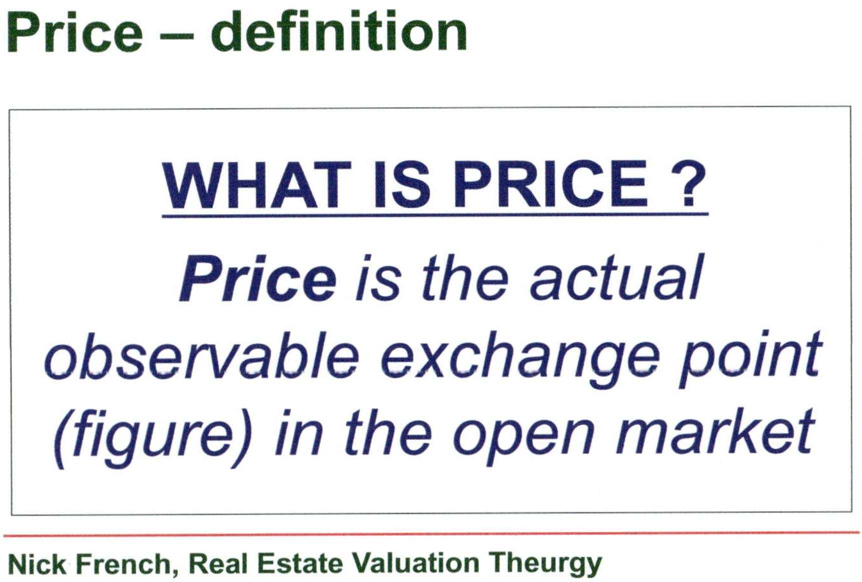

Exhibit 1.3 "What is price?" followed by a definition of price: "the actual observable exchange point in the open market."

What is worth?

This is a moment of reassessment. The room thinks that it has nailed its understanding of the word "price" but as soon as you ask them to define "worth," there is a new feeling of disquiet in the room as they try to differentiate their understanding of "price" from "worth." Remember that all their understanding and defining is coming from things that they already know. Most of the time we never question what we do when we shop or what we do when we decide we want something new. But a deep dive into the motivations of shopping will really help the audience to start appreciating the subtle differences in the three words of "price," "worth," and (latterly) "value."

The audience already knows all the answers, they just don't know that they know the answers. You need to keep pointing them in the right direction. So, the question to the audience is "what is worth?" A few will offer suggestions. Some will give you long economic definitions of utility, some will say it is the same as price and a few might say that it is individual to you. Which is it? Again, always respect the answers given. Say things like "that sounds like an economic definition to me, let's park it for the while and then return to it to see how it fits into our understanding at the end" or something of the sort. As I said, it is all about herding the group in the right direction, without losing any of the sheep along the way.

The next step is to go back to the suit example that you explored when discussing "price." Add in further information and say that the suit was actually pink and blue and then ask if anyone in the room would buy it at the ticket price of (say) £300? You will get a chorus of "nos." They do this because it isn't "worth" spending that much on a suit that they wouldn't wear. But now add in further information that they have just received an official invitation from the King of England to a garden party at Buckingham Palace. The invite says that the dress code is "pink and blue." You then ask how many of the audience would now be interested in buying the suit. The majority (they might not all be royalists, but everyone wants to go to a garden party at the palace) will now say that they will buy the suit for £300. In other words, circumstances have changed how much they consider the suit is worth to them.

Reinforce this concept that "worth" is all about someone's willingness to pay, an individual assessment of their bid, by referencing other real-life experiences. Maybe talk about how their attitude to buying things would change if they won a lot of money on the lottery. Or, how the importance of things changes as you get older. When you are young, you will pay a lot to go out, party, and drink. When you are older, maybe with kids, those things are not so important, and you choose to spend less (or nothing) on them so you can spend the money on your family. Worth changes with circumstance.

One example that always resonates with audiences is by asking them who goes skiing. A few will say "yes." Ask those few how much they will pay for a snickers bar at the bottom of the mountain. They will say about £2.00. Then ask the same people how much they would pay, at lunchtime, for the same bar at the restaurant at the top of the mountain. They all know and accept that it will be £4 to £5 but they never ask why? So, ask them. You will get answers that it costs more to get it to the top of the mountain. Point out that is not true as you just put it on the cable car that is going there anyway. There is no additional cost. Some will say it is because the restaurant has a monopoly which is partly true but as the owner of the shop at the bottom and the restaurant at the top is the same company, that doesn't ring true either. The answer is nothing to do with the supply side, it is all about demand. After skiing all morning, the consumer is sitting enjoying the views and is willing to pay more for the same chocolate bar. Circumstance in the guise of timing and altitude have made the Snickers bar worth more to them.

Thus, we have a working definition of "worth." It is the maximum bid that an individual will pay for an item. And it is at this point that you can return to the economic definitions that may have been mentioned by the respondents earlier. Because in terms of economics, "worth" can be considered as value in use, whereas "price" or market value can be considered as value in exchange.

Most of the delegates will nod an affirmation of understanding at this point. But I want to reinforce the points that I have made, and I introduce a class exercise to illustrate the same. I show them my "most favorite thing in the world" or that is what I say. It is a kid's book that turns into a pop-up train set. The reason that I chose this for my class exercise is that it is quirky and most of the audience won't have seen one. You can do the exercise with lots of other things. Maybe a toy car from your childhood (I've used the Corgi James Bond Aston Martin)? Maybe a nice watch? Maybe a particular flavored sandwich?

The important thing is to choose something that some people will covert and want and others will dislike and not want it at all. If you do this, you will find that there will be a whole range of views in-between.

My most favorite thing is the book: *Choo Choo, My Little Steam Train* which I affectionally call in the lecture, "My Little Choo Choo." Here it is illustrated in the slides, see Exhibits 1.4 and 1.5, from when I had to do the lecture remotely over Covid. In a face-to-face version of this lecture, I parade the book around so everyone can see it before making a grand

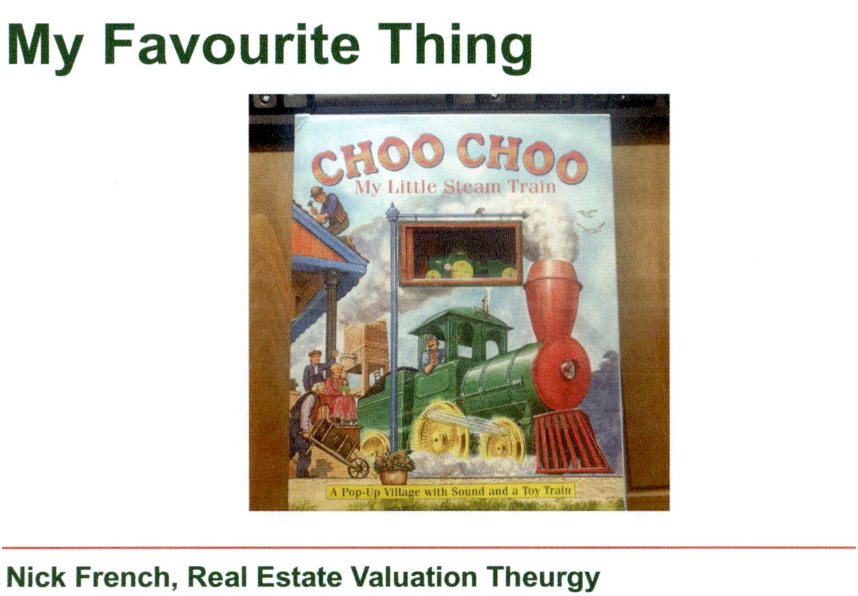

Exhibit 1.4 Cover page of *Choo Choo My Little Steam Train*. Photograph by the author.

Exhibit 1.5 Interior of the children's book illustrating the pop-up train.

reveal and opening it up to show the train set. I then set the train going on the track with great aplomb. Again, showmanship keeps the audience engaged and interested.

I then ask the audience to write down on a piece of paper how much they would bid for My Little Choo Choo. I explain that it isn't an auction and that it is more akin to a sealed bid where you decide your bid and then stick to it. I then go around the room (or a selection of the room) asking each member to shout out their bid. I then plot their bid, in real time, on the white board or flip chart; recording the amount of the bid and the frequency of each bid. And as we go around the room a chart appears before their very eyes. It is revealed to be a normal distribution (bell curve). Sometimes it is skewed to the left or the right but most times it is a standard curve with a central tendency with lower bids and higher bids on either side. Once this is fully plotted, as illustrated below in Exhibit 1.6, I ask the audience what each of the bids represent in terms of the concepts that we have been discussing and what the highest bid also represents. They will nearly all say that the individual bids that each of them made is "worth" and most will say that the final accepted bid represents "price."

Success. We have them understanding the concepts of "price" and "worth" which I then reiterate on a slide (see Exhibit 1.7 below) and point

Concepts – possibilities

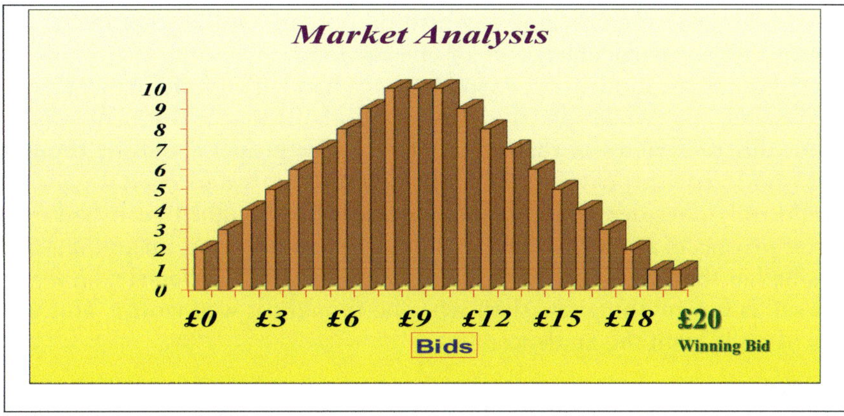

Nick French, Real Estate Valuation Theurgy

Exhibit 1.6 Illustration of a normal distribution curve of bids.

WORTH in context

- PRICE is an observable, historic transactional figure
- WORTH is a subjective judgement of the maximum bid for an item
- A rational bidder will bid up to their worth to buy an item. They will not buy if asking price is more than worth
- So what is VALUE?

Nick French, Real Estate Valuation Theurgy

Exhibit 1.7 Definitions of price and worth, finally asking "what is value?"

out that "worth" is the driver of all markets. If everyone thought that everything was worth the same, then there would be no markets apart from things of necessity (food or provisions, etc.). It is the fact that one person thinks that something is worth more than another that makes the market. This is particularly true of investments.

I tell the story about a conversation that I had with a fund manager who used to tell me (whilst playing 5-a-side football) that investment was all about different views of the future. If he had a property that he thought had good growth prospects in both income/rentals and capital gain, he would only consider selling it to someone who thought that it had even better prospects as they would pay him, as a capital value, an amount that was higher than he thought the property was worth. Conversely, he would not sell it for anything less than what he thought it was worth. This gets lots of nods from the audience.

What is value?

The last question of the day is "What is Value?" I tell the room that we know that "price" is the observable transactional figure and that we also know that "worth" is a subjective judgment for the maximum bid for an asset or item but that leaves the question, what is "value?" What is provided when an appraiser/valuer gives a valuation?

I point out that I am an appraiser/valuer and that when I provide an estimate of market value to my client that I am telling them a specific thing. I ask the audience what that is? Some will erroneously say "worth" but most of them will have got their ducks in a line and will say "price."

And that is what it is. VALUE is an estimate of PRICE. To reemphasize this, I return to referencing property and state that Value or Market Value is an estimation of the price that would be achieved if the property were to be sold in the open market.

This is almost the conclusion of the lecture but I now tell them that I am going to make them all into appraisers/valuers and I give them the scenario of going forward in time (in the Tardis with Doctor Who) by one week and that the successful purchaser of My Little Choo Choo is asking you for a valuation of the train set. Again, I ask them to write down what they think the value will be; not what they would bid personally but what the market would pay for My Little Choo Choo. Again, I will get a whole range of different figures. Some misunderstand the question and revert to what they think it is worth; many believe that value is the central tendency point but most will realize that value is at the top end of the graph as illustrated in Exhibit 1.8.

Market Value - comparables

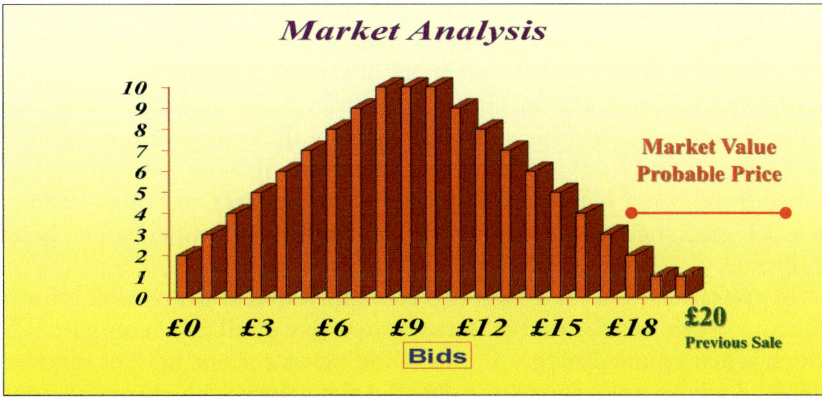

Nick French, Real Estate Valuation Theurgy

Exhibit 1.8 Normal distribution of bids indicating that the probable price skews to top end of prices.

And, at this point, you can start introducing the complexity of valuation. Last week the train sold at (in the example above) £20. It didn't sell at the point where most people thought it was worth of £10 which was the central tendency of worths. And you stress this; things sell at the highest bid, the top bid – and thus a valuation – will be at the top end of the graph. But that doesn't mean to say that its value is £20. This is a different point in time. Markets are ecosystems that feed on themselves. Any good agent of My Little Choo Choos will have shouted from the rooftops that it sold for £20 last week. It would be a headline in "Toy Train Sales Weekly." In other words, the market will be aware of that transaction and, more so, will be influenced by it. Some of the under bidders of last week may bid more this week, some new players in the market will anchor on the £20 figure as a starting point. Every bit of new information feeds on the previous and, as such, markets are constantly changing. Previous sales affect perceptions but, equally, other macroeconomic changes can change the market too. We call this market sentiment. Is the market bullish (they think that things are getting better) or bearish (they think outlooks are not good) or stagnant (they think the market is treading water)? All this will impact upon the hypothetical bids that underpin the valuation.

Value is the estimate of price at that moment of time. For the reasons noted above, it may be higher, or lower, or the same as last week's sales price. This is shown above by the range of "probable price" at the top end of the graph. The skill of the valuer is to read the market and give a figure within that range as Market Value. It will be anchored on the sale price of last week and, in reality, the sale prices of similar assets at a similar time in similar markets previously. This is called transactional data.

But the message for them to walk away with is that items transact for the highest figure (bid) in the market at that moment of time. A valuation is a snapshot on a particular day (the valuation date) and time – and just as stock exchange prices rise and fall, changing with time, value changes with time.

An appraiser/valuer is an applied economist that reads market information and previous sales (in real estate/property we call this "comparables") which when coupled with an understanding of current market sentiment will lead you to an estimate of price. But the valuer is answering the question of what will the market pay for the item at that moment. The valuer seeks to reflect the market's assessment and NOT to add value to something for which the market will NOT pay. VALUE is an estimate of PRICE when there is no sale.

Market Value

I have already started to introduce the term "market value" and explained that it is an estimate of price in the market. The final couple of slides links all that we have been discussing to the real-world definition of value. The International Valuation Standards Council (IVSC) has an internationally agreed definition of value that applies to all assets. This is shown in Exhibit 1.9, below, and I talk about the need for a consistent definition of value to be applied worldwide to ensure that all users, in theory, know what the figure means when they are provided with a formal valuation.

The audience generally shows a lot of appreciative and enlightened nods at this point. Property valuation is clicking into place in their minds. It should be noted that I have even given this talk to a room of professionals (investors/bankers/fund managers) all of whom work daily with property valuations. I have been surprised at how this appears to be a revelation in their understanding of market value. Even within a group of professionals, there is confusion between "price" and "worth." So, this isn't just a property valuation 101 issue.

A second slide on the same theme (Exhibit 1.10) reinforces the definition by some subtle changes to the wording to make it into a price definition on the assumption that the asset had been sold. That slide says:

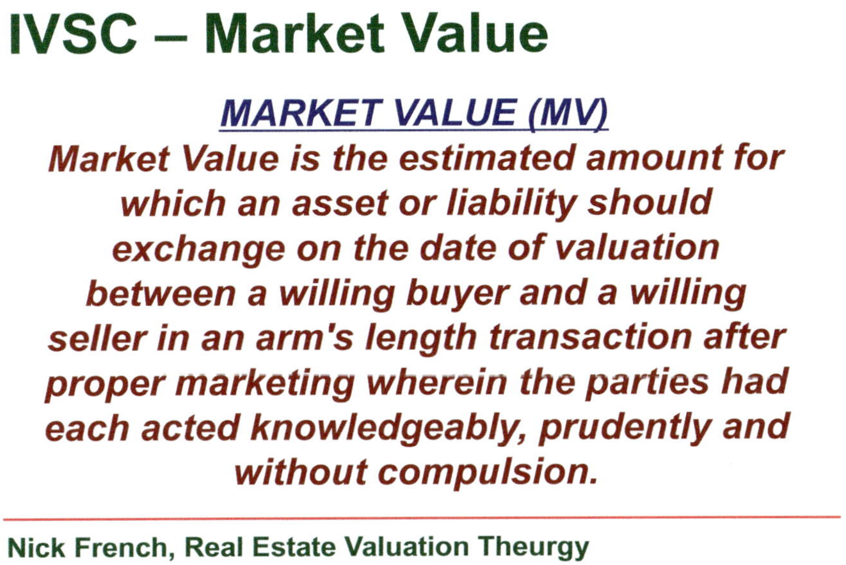

Exhibit 1.9 IVSC definition of market value.

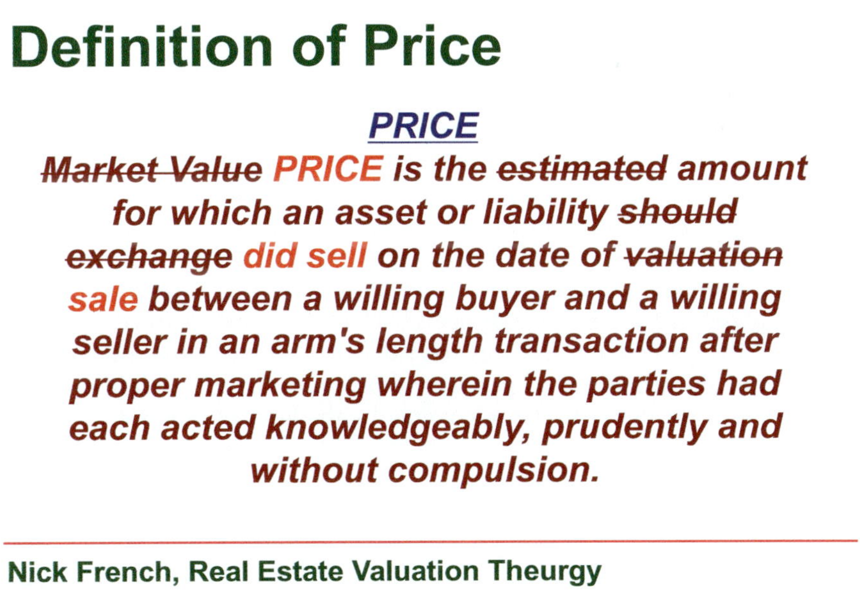

Exhibit 1.10 A definition of price.

And, there close the lesson. Spend a few minutes bringing together what the lecture has decided. Bearing in mind that the whole lecture has been developed based on what the audience already knew which is a point that I will discuss more in the conclusions. Thank the audience. Note that they created the lecture and they developed their own understanding. All you did was, hopefully, entertain and facilitate the learning process.

Conclusions

What I have tried to do with this chapter is to show you how you can teach a new subject, in this case real estate/property valuation, with reference to things that the students already know from their own life experiences. The case study is just one example of this technique and, of course, not all lectures lend themselves to this style. But in simple terms, you are (re) teaching students what they already knew but never realized!

But to do that you do need to think like they do and develop the lecture with them. The more that you can get them involved, the more they will learn and remember.

A few years back, I received a lovely email from an MBA student whom I have taught at Oxford University some 10 years earlier. He was very blunt in saying that, at the time, he wasn't sure about my lecture style as he initially thought it to be quite lightweight. But over the years he said the one lecture that stuck in his head was this one. He admitted that the understanding of price, value, and worth had been a bedrock of his endeavors as a property investor. All his investment decisions had been informed by that lecture and understanding the difference between price and worth had proved invaluable when identifying investment opportunities. The reason that he was writing was that he had just sold his company in a multi-million-dollar deal, and he wanted to thank me. That made me smile, albeit 5% of the profits would have been nicer.

But joking aside, that is what teaching is all about particularly with the younger students. You are privileged to be part of their learning. But that only really counts if they make use of what they have learned and that is why I always link my lectures to real world situations and examples. Property people are practical people and property lectures should be practical too. The academic skeleton covered by the flesh of practice.

Chapter 2

Game-based Learning and experiential learning in real estate education

Olayiwola Oladiran, Éamonn D'Arcy, Adejimi Adebayo, and Ronald Dyer

Introduction

The recent technological advancements and innovation in the real estate industry demand the integration of more effective and innovative pedagogical approaches to learning. Learners typically tend to attend teaching and learning support sessions with inner motivational resources that, when supported, can catalyze motivation, engagement, learning, and achievements (Patall & Zambrano, 2019). Some of the ways of supporting engagement and motivation in the classroom include fun and simulating learning environments through game-based learning (GBL), experiential learning (EL), and collaborative learning; these are vital for learners' academic well-being and achievement and have also been found to support learners' engagement (David & Weinstein, 2023; Nakata et al., 2022; Swacha, 2014). Educational institutions and administrators are therefore increasingly integrating positive psychology-based pedagogical approaches in learning (Chodkiewicz & Boyle, 2017).

Considering the increasing advancement in innovation and digitization in the real estate industry, students, educators, and industry professionals have advocated for more effective and innovative approaches to real estate education to facilitate student engagement and collaboration (Oladiran & Nanda, 2021). This chapter therefore aims to provide a review of GBL and EL, as conduits for facilitating collaborative learning, engagement, academic well-being, and achievement for real estate higher education students. It provides a case study analysis of GBL focused on the Blue Game at the University of Reading. This is followed by broader reflections on the merits and limitations of GBL and EL in real estate pedagogy. This chapter serves as a knowledge base and a reference for real estate educators to explore the opportunities that motivational, engaging, and EL environments provide.

DOI: 10.1201/9781032656458-2

Conceptualizing GBL and EL

Game theory

Game theory is a strategic framework used to understand and analyze the behaviors of rational individuals' decisions in competitive or cooperative situations (Osborne, 2004). Game theoretical reasoning is used widely in social and behavioral sciences and is also a standard feature in the curricula of a wide range of disciplines such as management (Breslau, 2003), studio art (Han, 2015), architecture (Rice, 2014), and sustainability (Sadowski et al., 2013). Exhibit 2.1 shows the classification of games based on the work of Osborne (2004). The Exhibit highlights that the information flow and availability have implications on the outcome of the games; thus, educators seeking to integrate games into their teaching and learning support should carefully consider the level of information (a)symmetry. Conceptualizing games in education through the lenses of information (a)symmetry is sensible; however, this concept implicitly assumes that parties in a game are always opponents seeking to outplay, outpace, or outbid the others. This may not be the case in all games because some games are set up without any direct interaction or interference from other players. In some cases, rather than focus on the other contestants, a player needs to focus on the accuracy and speed of his/her answers/solutions to win. Regardless, game theory provides valuable insights into various real-world scenarios, including business competition, negotiations, political strategy, and international relations. It helps decision-makers understand the incentives, strategies, and potential outcomes of complex situations,

Exhibit 2.1 The game theory classification

Information type	*Game type*	*Description*	*Examples*
Perfect information*	Strategic games	A model of interacting decision-makers which allows each player to be affected by the actions of all players, not only their actions.	Prisoner's Dilemma, Bach or Stravinsky, and matching pennies
Perfect information*	Extensive games	A sequential structure of decision-making explicitly allowing us to study situations in which each decision-maker is free to change his or her mind as events unfold.	Entry games, ultimate games, hold-up games, auction games and buying votes

Exhibit 2.1 (Continued)

Information type	*Game type*	*Description*	*Examples*
Perfect information*	Coalitional games	A model of interacting decision-makers that focuses on the behavior of a group of players. A set of actions are conceptualized more as being driven by every group of players rather than being only by individual players.	Resource allocation games, trade agreements, network formation games, environmental agreement games, and joint venture games
Imperfect information**	Bayesian games	Deals with games where players have incomplete information about the game and update their beliefs using Bayesian inference as they make decisions.	Information asymmetry in market transactions, adverse selection in the insurance market, and strategic entry into a new market

Source: Authors.

Notes: *All players have complete knowledge of the game's history including past moves and events.
**Players have information about the game that is unknown to other players and rationality extends to reasoning about uncertainty.

making it a valuable tool for making informed decisions and predictions. It is therefore a suitable base for students' skills development.

Gamification and GBL defined

Prior to any recommendations regarding the integration of such approaches, an understanding of what they are is required. Gamification is defined as the use of game design elements in a non-game context (Laine & Lindberg, 2020). For example, leveraging the mechanics, dynamics, and aesthetics of "for fun" games as a means of learner engagement improvement. The premise surrounding gamified approaches in learning supposedly allows students to acquire knowledge, hone skills, and foster positive traits through games built specifically for this purpose. Thus, its advantage rests in the provision of various forms of stimuli to involve and motivate students to stay active with their studies (Hishamuddin

Exhibit 2.2 Expectations from GBL in learning environments

Expectations	*Details*
Motivation	Games have been shown to motivate learners over a long period.
Engagement	Provides a wide range of engagement opportunities, thus informing multiple learning styles and learning goal alignment.
Adaptivity	Customizability and scenario-based approaches to learners, supporting learners in a way that reflects their learning style(s).
Failure	By building "safe" opportunities to fail in GBL environments, learners are encouraged to take risks, explore, and gain opportunities for self-regulated learning during the play process.

Source: Authors.

et al., 2018). Similarly, GBL emphasises a type of gameplay with defined learning outcomes. Its design process for learning involves balancing the need to cover the core knowledge and learning outcomes while integrating "game-play." The argument for the integration of GBL in learning environments rests on their perceived ability to provide motivation, engagement, adaptivity, and failure (Plass et al., 2015) as illustrated in Exhibit 2.2.

Gamification and GBL in pedagogy

There is much debate in learning about the ways through which engagement can improve learners' interests and performances. Part of the challenge with today's learners is their digital native (Prensky, 2005) origins vs. the cadre of people teaching them in higher education who are, for the most part, digital immigrants. Consequently, learning approaches need to not only be fit for the current digital demographic, but teaching staff need to be familiar with these approaches to ensure the best possible engagement.

Gamification and GBL both represent attempts to increase student engagement and bring innovative pedagogical approaches into the classroom. Integration of gamification and GBL approaches represents an opportunity for academics and learners to create a collaborative environment built on: effective, behavioral, cognitive, and socio-cultural engagement. To adopt such approaches, an understanding of the design process with a focus on the desired quality of the learning experience(s) needs careful consideration. Moreover, utilization of any GBL approach requires the suitability of the game as the preferable option to support the proposed learning vs. traditional approaches. To better understand the adoption approaches of GBL, academics need an understanding of serious play and how it informs strategies for learning improvement. Play is essentially a voluntary activity, with pleasurable engagement outcomes. Serious play approaches assume the premise of growth, intellectually, emotionally, or physically while experiencing a flow state (Kiili, 2005). For example, the state of complete absorption or engagement in activity and optimal experiences.

Gamification and gamified learning differ in some dimensions such as scope, primary focus, content integration, and gaming mechanism. In terms of scope, gamification does not entail transforming all aspects of education into a game; rather, it involves using game elements and principles to strategically enhance the learning process, particularly in a digital learning environment. Gamified learning, on the other hand, is the comprehensive approach to integrating games into learning. In this case, the entire learning and broader educational experience is gamified involving the use of educational games or simulations and the students' interaction with predominantly game-based educational content. Furthermore, gamification is not primarily about creating a complete game-like experience, rather, it enhances existing educational methods by adding some gaming elements. Gamified learning, on the other hand, primarily focuses on creating an entirely full-fledged educational game-based simulation to teach and support learning and skills development.

Gamification and gamified learning have their merits and demerits. Gamification in pedagogy is flexible and can be applied to a wide range of existing content or activities such as online courses, classroom exercises, and digital textbooks without the total development of a new game. Gamified learning, on the other hand, is more rigid. It involves the development of bespoke educational games or game-based content that are directly related to the learning objectives. In this case, the educational content cannot be delivered without the game. Gamified learning, however, has the advantage of an immersive game environment, characters, and storylines which have been shown to enhance student engagement in the learning process through active participation in game-like scenarios. In contrast, gamification pedagogy includes a learning environment that may remain largely traditional. It is therefore important that educators carefully consider both the pros and cons of both approaches to GBL to ensure that they synchronize harmoniously with the resources available, learning objectives, learners' composition, and the learning environment before deciding on their adoption approaches.

Exhibit 2.3 Core components of GBL

Components	*Description*
Game	Incorporates game elements such as rewards, badges, points, leader boards, challenges, levels, and progression.
Goals and objectives	Clear goals and objectives are set for students which enables the students to understand what they need to achieve and how that enables them to make progress.
Competition	Introduces healthy competition among students, motivating them to strive for better performance.
Problem solving	Involves solution-seeking or overcoming challenges.
Reflection and feedback	Requires that feedback is provided after the game. This may be in the form of a score to indicate the level of success or notes and tips to improve future performance.

Source: Authors.

GBL draws on the natural inclination of humans to play games, compete, and have fun. In theory, this makes learning more effective and enjoyable. Some of the core components of gamification are shown in Exhibit 2.3. The combination of the components situates GBL as a valuable teaching and learning support system. The use of techniques such as narrative and storytelling, problem-solving and several other styles can improve problem-solving, autonomy, mastery, and motivation to learn. These are core issues that educators constantly have to contend with. Problem-based or project-based learning, for instance, enables students to utilize their knowledge and skills to solve real-world problems. The competitive and reward-based elements can also boost students' motivation to participate in and "take charge" of their learning. The feedback they receive can support them in identifying their challenges and skill levels in a non-judgmental way. This will further enable them to identify their learning needs and areas for improvement. Real estate students engage with subjects such as property valuation, management, investment, and development which require qualitative and quantitative analytical skills and other soft skills. GBL is therefore a channel through which these skills can be developed simultaneously.

Lego Serious Play

Lego Serious Play (LSP) represents one such opportunity for gamified/GBL. LSP is a transdisciplinary process to create new methods of playing seriously with strategy (Gkogkidis & Dacre, 2021). The process involves posing a facilitated question, participants building a model in response to the question, participants sharing their model(s) to tell the story behind it, and participant reflection. The value of LSP approaches in real estate rests with:

- **Learning context:** Provide methodologies to support a better understanding of sustainability approaches in this domain by using LSP to build questions which engage students in defining sustainable business practices for new or existing builds.
- **Central questions**: Provide learners/students with a list of focused questions to assist in the analysis of real estate issues and connect them to the theoretical knowledge gained through the model-building process. Building questions to support the use of LSP for experiential purposes can include identifying main sources of income/financing to support urban planning projects, risks associated with the use of sustainable resources, and/or potential alternative solutions which balance economic realities with urban design challenges.

Utilizing gamified/GBL approaches with LSP, academics and learners build an understanding, influenced by theoretical interest in the subject domain that allows exploration of key questions that can be visually interpreted by students. It supports the establishment of connections between knowledge and experience that learners already have through learning materials while building new knowledge via interpretation of world views utilizing 3D modelling approaches. Finally, it allows for idea(s) sharing with peers and feedback solicitation through reflective processes bringing richer context to the subject matter.

Experiential learning

The model of EL was introduced by Kolb (1984) and it has since become a well-established pedagogical framework in the education literature. EL suggests that learning is accomplished through the integration of non-dominant models of dealing with the world and it primarily aims to translate experience into concepts that can be more easily assimilated by the learner. It is a student-centered approach that emphasizes the importance of direct, hands-on experiences in the learning process with a focus on active engagement and reflection. In EL, students learn by doing, reflecting on their experiences, and applying what they have learned to future situations. Within this framework, learning begins with a concrete experience which forms the basis for observation and reflection upon experiences; these are further assimilated into concepts and generalizations about

Exhibit 2.4 Stages of EL

Stages	*Details*
Concrete experience	Experience is gained through concrete activities or events.
Observation and reflection	The learner critically reflects on and records the lessons learnt.
Formation of abstract concepts	This involves deduction and analysis following reflection and observation.
Generalization	This final stage may lead to inferences being drawn and used to test hypotheses in future situations.

Source: Authors.

experiences that further guide interactions with the world (Oladiran & Nanda, 2021).

EL enables learners to understand abstract concepts that can be applied flexibly across a range of situations and allows them to develop their ideas from new experiences. This is a learner-driven process where knowledge and skills are developed through the transformation of experience. The four stages of EL are shown in Exhibit 2.4 based on the classification of Loo (2004).

Teaching methods should be tailored to various learning styles (Ronchetto et al., 1992), and the model of EL provides a platform for achieving this. These perspectives are essential for developing learning frameworks for real estate education where a wide variety of learning styles should be adopted to cater for the variation (Oladiran & Dickins, 2024).

GBL and EL in real estate education

The real estate subject intersects with various disciplines within higher education, including planning, construction, geography, law, and business studies. Consequently, learning outcomes may vary across higher education providers and courses. However, a common expectation in real estate education is that learners, including students and apprentices, are trained to become industry-ready professionals who are active collaborators. Due to the multidisciplinary nature of the real estate sector, real estate education should be designed to be collaborative, active, and engaging, enabling students to achieve core learning outcomes and develop relevant skill sets. The integration of GBL and EL will help achieve this in real estate pedagogy. The Blue Game illustrates the application of this in real estate pedagogy.

The Blue Game

The origins of the Blue Game at the Henley Business School, University of Reading date back to 2012 when the game was introduced as part of a "capstone" module for students undertaking the full-time MSc Real Estate program. Since 2012, over 1,800 students have played the game. The game was devised by Jürg Bernet at the EURO Institute of Real Estate Management (Bernet, 2021) in Switzerland and Jürg has acted as the "Gamemaster" for 12 editions of the game. The game fits the characteristics of GBL; its conceptualization is heavily influenced by classical "Game Theory" (von Neumann & Morgenstern, 1944, Nash, 1950) and its applications to the world of business and strategy (Brandenburger & Nalebuff, 1995). The objective of the Blue Game is to teach students "real estate strategy" within the safe confines of the classroom. The game takes place over four days with groups of up to six students taking on roles in the game such as investors, fund managers, and developers. One group is elected to take on the special role of "The Government" which acts primarily as a regulator, collector of taxes, and provider of subsidies. The business case used to support the game is the Australian office market, with the investors holding assets in Sydney, Melbourne, and Perth.

The game commences with the assignment of roles to the teams and the distribution of a "game box" containing further details on their roles, starting positions, funds, and game cards to record their interactions with the other teams in the game. The first morning is focused on introducing the teams to key game theory concepts, in particular "Nash Equilibrium." From this, they play a "mini-game" to reinforce the concepts they have learned. Following sessions on how to play and how to win, the teams are required to submit a value net of their relationships to other teams in the game and a financial statement of their initial position before the close of business that day.

Following feedback on the value nets and financial statements submitted, Round I commences on the second day of the game. This round is focused on using strategic moves to improve the teams' financial positions and in some cases to change their relationships in the game. As part of Round I, teams can bid for additional assets at an auction. Strategy coaching is provided by the game master throughout the game. Teams can submit drafts of their work at certain points in the game to obtain feedback. At the end of Round I, teams submit their reports on the round during the afternoon of day two. Following additional strategy inputs from the game master, Round II commences. In this round, teams are tasked with using strategic moves to improve the "green" performance of their assets and their overall "green" credentials. Reports from this round are submitted at midday on the third day of the game.

Following a further set of strategy inputs from the game master, teams commence the final round of the game. This requires them to use strategic moves to add "blue" or social value to their assets.

The final report on their activities over the game is submitted at midday on the fourth day of the game. This final report is the product of all the reports submitted through the week and has benefited from the feedback received from the various rounds. Teams are also required to submit a short presentation which outlines the strategic moves they made throughout the game to improve their position. On the afternoon of the fourth day, they deliver this presentation in person to a jury of industry experts. The game concludes with the awarding of prizes for the best presentations delivered that afternoon. The final report is assessed using Bernett's (2021) blue game assessment criteria covering four elements: Strategy, Execution, Analysis, and Performance. Each criterion has a number of elements on which the teams are scored.

The Blue Game is a serious simulation game for EL. Focused is placed on teams performing strategic moves to improve their positions relative to sets of broad strategic goals. It enhances a range of key skills, in particular teamwork and negotiations. Overall, the game provides a useful example of GBL designed to enhance the skillset of future real estate professionals.

Merits, limitations, and challenges of GBL and gamification in real estate education pedagogy

Merits

1. Enables real estate students to develop soft skills such as creativity, critical analysis, strategy, flexibility, and active listening.
2. Enables real estate students to develop an understanding of healthy competition with high ethical standards.
3. Provides a platform for better knowledge retention and understanding of complex concepts and ideas.
4. It supports the establishment of connections between knowledge and experience that learners already have through other learning media.
5. It facilitates peer-to-peer learning and team work.
6. It provides a platform for formative feedback and reflection, bringing richer context to the subject matter.

Limitations and challenges

Several factors can limit the integration of GBL and EL in real estate education. For real estate educators to integrate these concepts into their pedagogies, they need to develop a knowledge and understanding of the various GBL tools and approaches. Educators need to make a conscious effort to upskill through research and continued professional development (CPD). There is also insufficient documentation of the mechanism and issues associated with the integration of GBL specifically focusing on real estate education. This chapter is therefore a valuable contribution in this respect. Additionally, educators may be sceptical about the use of GBL for summative or formal assessment systems.

Conclusion

The labor market is getting increasingly competitive with jobs now requiring students to possess soft skills during the recruitment process. Data from the World Economic Forum (2023) shows that the top 10 skills that employers are seeking are:

1. Analytical thinking.
2. Creative thinking.
3. Resilience, flexibility, and agility.
4. Motivation and self-awareness.
5. Curiosity and lifelong learning.
6. Technological literacy.
7. Dependability and attention to detail.
8. Empathy and active listening.
9. Leadership and social influence.
10. Quality control.

Although knowledge is important for professional practice, the skills listed by the World Economic Forum suggest that students need a lot more than just knowledge to be valuable to potential employers. The real estate sector particularly continues to evolve in line with digital technological advancement and real estate students should be equipped with the skill-set required to lead the next wave of innovation. GBL and EL offer a viable and practical pathway to equipping real estate students with both the knowledge and skills that will position them for positive impact in the workforce. Real estate educators are encouraged to explore the game-based and EL techniques reviewed in this chapter to create impactful classroom experiences that build educational proficiency and foster professional skills that employers seek. Furthermore, informal settings such as games can provide opportunities for informal feedback, reinforce learning, and provide reassurance to students which can further enhance the education process.

References

Bernet, J. (2021). *The Blue Game: A Strategy Playbook for Responsible Investors and Managers in Real Estate*. EURO Institut für Immobilien Management.

Brandenburger, A. M., & Nalebuff, B. J. (1995). The right game: Use game theory to shape strategy, *Harvard Business Review*, July–August, 57–71.

Breslau, D. (2003). Rationalizing strategy: Game theory in management pedagogy and practice. *Social Analysis*, *47*(1), 53–64.

Chodkiewicz, A. R., & Boyle, C. (2017). Positive psychology school-based interventions: A reflection on current success and future directions. *Review of Education*, *5*(1), 60–86.

David, L., & Weinstein, N. (2023). A gamified experiential learning intervention for engaging students through satisfying needs. *Journal of Educational Technology Systems*, *52*(1), 52–72.

Gkogkidis, V., & Dacre, N. (2021). How to use lego serious play as a gamification teaching and learning framework? A responsible management approach. *SBS Working Paper Series on SSRN*. https://doi.org/10.2139/ssrn.3829949

Han, H. C. (2015). Gamified pedagogy: From gaming theory to creating a self-motivated learning environment in studio art. *Studies in Art Education*, *56*(3), 257–267.

Hishamuddin, M., Rahman, A., Ismail, I., Panessai, Y., Anida, N., Noor, Z. M., Syazwani, N., & Salleh, M. (2018). Gamification elements and their impacts on teaching and learning – A review. *The International Journal of Multimedia & Its Applications (IJMA)*, *10*(6), 37–46. https://doi.org/10.5121/ijma.2018.10604.

Kiili, K. (2005). Digital game-based learning: Towards an experiential gaming model. *Internet and Higher Education*, *8*(1), 13–24. https://doi.org/10.1016/j.iheduc.2004.12.001.

Kolb, D.A. (1984). *Experiential learning: Experience as the source of learning and development*, Prentice Hall, Englewood Cliffs, NJ.

Laine, T. H., & Lindberg, R. S. N. (2020). Designing engaging games for education: A systematic literature review on game motivators and design principles. *IEEE Transactions on Learning Technologies*, *13*(4), 804–821. https://doi.org/10.1109/TLT.2020.3018503.

Loo, R. (2004). Kolb's learning styles and learning preferences: Is there a linkage? *Educational Psychology*, *24*(1), 99–108.

Nakata, Y., Nitta, R., & Tsuda, A. (2022). Understanding motivation and classroom modes of regulation in collaborative learning: An exploratory study. *Innovation in Language Learning and Teaching*, *16*(1), 14–28.

Nash, J. F. (1950). Equilibrium points in n-person games. *PNAS*, *36*(1), 48–49. https://doi.org/10.1073/pnas.36.1.48

Oladiran, O., & Dickins, L. (2024). *PropTech and Real Estate Innovations: A guide to digital technologies and solutions in the built environment*. Taylor & Francis.

Oladiran, O., & Nanda, A. (2021). *PropTech Education Integration Framework (PEIF)*. www.researchgate.net/publication/356420161_PropTech_Education_Integration_Framework_PEIF_integrating_innovation_and_digital_technology_in_real_estate_higher_education

Osborne, M. J. (2004). *An Introduction to Game Theory* (Vol. 3, no. 3). Oxford University Press.

Patall, E. A., & Zambrano, J. (2019). Facilitating student outcomes by supporting autonomy: Implications for practice and policy. *Policy Insights from the Behavioural and Brain Sciences*, 6(2), 115–122.

Plass, J. L., Homer, B. D., & Kinzer, C. K. (2015). Foundations of game-based learning. *Educational Psychologist*, *50*(4), 258–283. https://doi.org/10.1080/00461520.2015.1122533

Prensky, M. (2005). Digital natives & digital immigrants. *Agency for European Integration*, 9(5), 23–26. https://doi.org/10.1108/10748120110424816.

Rice, H. E. (2014). *Exploring the Pedagogical Possibilities of Applying Gaming Theory and Technologies to Historic Architectural Visualisation*. University of York, Department of Archeology, MSc for Digital Heritage.

Ronchetto, J., Budkles, T., Barath, R., & Perry, J. (1992). Multimedia delivery systems: A bridge between teaching methods and learning styles. *Journal of Marketing Education*, *14*(1), 12–21.

Sadowski, J., Seager, T. P., Selinger, E., Spierre, S. G., & Whyte, K. P. (2013). An experiential, game-theoretic pedagogy for sustainability ethics. *Science and Engineering Ethics*, *19*(3), 1323–1339.

Swacha, J. (2014). An architecture of a gamified learning management system. In Cao, Y., Väljataga, T., Tang, J. K. T., Leung, H., & Laanpere, M. (Eds.), *New Horizons in Web Based Learning: ICWL 2014 International Workshops* (pp. 195–203). Springer International Publishing.

von Neumann, J., Morgenstern, O., & Rubinstein, A. (1944). *Theory of Games and Economic Behaviour* (60th Anniversary Commemorative Edition). Princeton University Press. www.jstor.org/stable/j.ctt1r2gkx.

World Economic Forum (2023). Future of jobs 2023: These are the most in-demand skills now- and beyond. www.weforum.org/agenda/2023/05/future-of-jobs-2023-skills/. Accessed 21 February 2024, 13:10 pm.

Chapter 3

Employing real problems for real learning in real estate market analysis

Jeffrey G. Robert

Introduction

For those unfamiliar with real estate market analysis, the course centers upon the evaluation of geographic areas for the development, expansion, or transaction of specific real estate products (such as apartment buildings, office towers, retail strip centers) within the context of demand and supply. To prepare professional skills, students are required to think beyond the memorization of definitions or the recitation of rote facts. Students must critically identify issues and make connections between topics. To quote a very common phrase in higher education, students must "think critically."

In market analysis, we differentiate geographic areas into markets and submarkets. Markets are larger in geographic size and provide macro-level trends about the economic health of the region. Submarkets are localized zones within the overall market that are more specific to the property type in question. With the identification of the market and submarket, students interpret large trends and compare macroeconomic conditions of the region to the localized economy of the submarket.

In addition to markets and submarkets, another geographic area of study within real estate market analysis is the market area, also known as the trade area for retail real estate analysis. Market areas are specific to real estate property and represent the spatial area where the majority of customers or space-users of the property originate. Once defined, the market area serves as the boundary for additional demand and supply analysis. Employers stress the cognitive skills required to delineate a market area and provide logical justification for an appropriate demand and supply analysis. Instructors who provide fun opportunities for students to learn and explore these core learning objectives will find that their students are more engaged in the classroom and are better prepared for real estate careers post-graduation.

DOI: 10.1201/9781032656458-3

Real problems for real learning

Market analysis is an excellent course to spark student interest and passion as it represents the proverbial "blank canvas" for developing real problems for real learning. As defined here, real problems must follow a basic set of principles to be effective and compelling. Real problems must depict the actual built environment or a humorous version of it (for a humorous example of this, see the Case of the Mountain Gas Station in Appendix A). Second, real problems must connect to industry applications and future careers. Students continually judge assignments on their own and decide if it is a credible representation of future work or merely classroom busy-work. Assignments that seem to replicate real-world problems are, by this perception, deemed more important than busy-work assignments. As a result, students will work harder on these real-world assignments and they will be more engaged when absorbing core content and skills.

At the beginning of the course, develop activities that are fun and relatable to students. Since many college students live in an apartment and, maybe for the first time, purchase and cook their own food, we discussed the site location of the local grocery stores. Working in teams, students consider where they shop for food. Trends emerge as students spatially plot their purchasing habits in relation to apartment locations. Using digital maps, we identify, describe, and provide a logical trade area for each major grocer in our local community. Next, we incorporate transportation information such as bus routes, highway systems, and parking constraints into the analysis and we evaluate the influence of grocery competition on consumer decision making. Afterwards, we layer into the activity higher cognition level hypothetical questions. For example, we might ask students what would happen if the closest grocery store closed. Where would they shop? How does the closure of a store influence the remaining grocery store trade areas? While most students recognize the basic answer that they need to drive further distances for shopping, the purpose of these hypothetical questions is for students to develop an analytical framework for prediction.

The prediction of a future outcome given basic information is an important skill desired in the real estate industry. Simulating real world problems for students to evaluate, analyze, and apply class concepts hones their prediction skills and makes these students more valuable upon graduation. In market analysis, we present two broad prediction-based questions to students: (1) predict the best parcel of land where a specific real estate project will be successful and (2) predict the best real estate project given a specific parcel of land.

Earlier, we described the need to create activities that are fun and relatable to students. Leverage student-centric real estate by using examples where students could have engaged with the content. If the company is not well known, provide articles about where the company has been successful or has been in the news. With this information, we can simulate a specific real estate project that is in search of land (market analysis scenario one from the previous paragraph). In the classroom, we discuss familiar companies like Topgolf, Amazon, Starbucks, or Home Depot. To provide an example of using a non-traditional company, few students have visited a beer spa (a beer spa is exactly as it sounds; soak in a tub of beer). While unfamiliar, the word beer engages some students, who find the concept fun and interesting. We use this experiential retail to find the best parcel of raw land or leasable space where a beer spa will be successful. Students assess the market areas where these retail businesses currently operate and make recommendations for an investor to successfully open a new beer spa. This activity provides students with an opportunity to explore and be flexible with their solution, which is a key aspect of real problems for real learning.

When developing real problems for real learning, allow students the greatest amount of creativity within the boundaries of the problem. Real problems should revolve around class concepts and align with the topics learned; however, there should never be one specific solution. In the beer spa example, students selected dozens of different locations where a beer spa could be successful. The location itself is mostly irrelevant. A student's subsequent justification and logical defense of that location is the graded portion of the activity. Assessing comprehension of the learning objectives follows a provided rubric, which is designed in the "yes; yes, but; no, but; no" format. Creating activities in this manner relieves student pressure to "get an answer he/she believes the professor wants." Moreover, developing activities with maximum creativity more closely resembles the future problems these students will encounter upon graduation (for the full activity, see Appendix B).

Providing student creativity within assignments requires more thought to develop, since students may pursue a direction different from the course learning objectives. However, we can make small modifications that promote creativity while providing assignment structure. In the last example, the instructor selected the real estate project to develop. To provide more student creativity in the activity but to remain on task, the instructor may modify the activity and let students select their own retail franchise to develop in a specific geographic region.

ICSC (formerly known as International Council of Shopping Centers) is a trade organization that "promotes marketplaces and spaces where people shop, dine, work, play, and gather." Retailers who are seeking to expand franchise locations provide "retailer fact sheets" to ICSC at trade shows and for digital dissemination. A retailer fact sheet includes site location criteria such as preferred square footage, frontage, real estate type (drive thru, end-cap, outparcel, etc.), and co-tenants. In addition, the fact sheet outlines the customer demographic and targeted growth regions. The last aspect of the fact sheet outlines the corporate contact information for the retailer. While not relevant for the actual graded assignment, it is important to keep these contact sections and make a connection for the students. These fact sheets are real. Companies, which many students will know and recognize, develop these fact sheets. These are actual people working in these companies who will engage with whoever finds property that suits their needs. Showing students that the work they are doing in the classroom reflects work they could be doing in their careers increases student effort and engagement. ICSC combines dozens of fact sheets into annual documents. In another activity, students scroll through many retailers and select the retailers that interests them the most. Equipped with the information specific to their retailer of interest, students begin the process of identifying the location, again either raw land or leasable property, where their retailer would be successful (for full activity with an example hypothetical ICSC factsheet, see Appendix C).

The ICSC retailer activity works best in small teams in the classroom. It is recommended to use a large "post it" type notepad paper for each team to adhere to a portion of the classroom wall. In too many classrooms today, student teams are trained to create a shared digital document where each student conquers one aspect of the assignment. Little discussion occurs in this format and the assignment is a box-checking exercise with minimal discussion or collaborative learning. Using large notepad paper interrupts the digital "divide and conquer" mentality and fosters conversation between students. The notepad paper becomes a gathering point to place ideas and to problem solve. As teams write on the large paper, the instructor can read the paper and engage with the students about their decision-making process. Generally, students gather information from university provided or free databases such as CoStar Group, ESRI, and the American Community Survey. (After teams finished writing on the notepad paper, a cell phone can text capture all the team's notes digitally. No time is lost rewriting large paper notes!)

In a situation where an instructor wishes to avoid the complexity of multiple retailer factsheets from ICSC, many companies post digital site selection criteria on their websites. Directing students to these digital locations remains impactful, since the instructor and students can have a brief discussion about the real-world application of the activity in the classroom. For example, one could use a local convenience store and gas station such as Sheetz, Buc-ee's, 7-Eleven, Wawa, or Casey's to name a few. This is a link to Wawa's site selection information posted on their website www.wawa.com/iframe/about-us/real-estate/site-submission-guidelines. These real-world scenarios can be another fun activity for students to determine an appropriate market area and location to develop for a specific retailer. Students clearly see the connection of the activity to practical knowledge and how it will help them succeed in a future role in the commercial real estate industry.

In addition to smaller problems and activities, using a larger course-wide team project presents another learning opportunity for students. A single major project incorporates many of the individual learning objectives of the smaller activities; however, students must combine skills and acquired knowledge to formulate overall decisions and recommendations. It is recommended that the instructor develop a story around the parcel of vacant land or the redevelopment project. A story provides simulated context and the chance to make a classroom assignment more real. Encourage the students to role-play the story and to become the professional team to answer the question for their "clients." In the story writeup, the use of industry language and its connection to the real-world increases student buy-in. Also, the final student report and presentation should represent a real-world deliverable or expectation. As an example, students might be required to produce an offering memorandum, which is more commonly associated with a real estate brokerage career, than a lengthy text-based report. Providing examples of offering memorandums from industry in class helps students visualize the deliverable they need to complete but does not reduce student creativity in the project outcome. Moreover, the examples from industry connect a student's potential career path to the in-class conversation, which tends to boost student engagement.

There are two main versions of the major course project. Yet, the goal remains the same: compel students to think like industry professionals and to produce quality content befitting an industry professional. The first version of the course project is to provide a parcel of land in search of a development project. Prepare a vacant green-field parcel of land for students and ask for an analysis regarding the highest and best use of the land given its location, characteristics, and constraints. Ensuring that the land can be used for multiple purposes through current zoning or that there is ample evidence that the local zoning board is willing to change the current zoning allows for students to explore various real estate product types as solutions. In addition to a flexible zone, a course project should include other complexities such as above average population growth, new employment entrants, or overlay zoning to force students into heightened analysis of the land. Use project sites where you have a connection to the owner or the developer. Without divulging trade secrets, provide the industry rationale for development after the course project has been submitted. Always reserve time in the last class to discuss the course project with the students. The instructor can provide insights into the actual development, if there is a site layout or architectural rendering; provide the image for students to discuss. Moreover, there may be a built-in hidden element of the project that some teams may have missed. An example of a hidden element may be a news article that discusses the relocation of a new employer into the area or an expansion of infrastructure, such as a highway or residential rail line. Discussing these hidden elements and providing opportunities for students to contribute as they integrate the semester's knowledge will help them succeed. Students really enjoy seeing project renderings and learning what will happen in an area that they have researched so thoroughly. In addition, the class can compare and contrast the actual development with their own recommendation for further insights and learning.

In the second version of the course project, students are provided with a building that requires redevelopment. While it would be ideal for student-learning to visit the property and tour the site, there are logistical limitations associated with visiting properties. If students cannot tour the property, pictures of interior and exterior spaces in addition to architectural drawings would help students better comprehend the redevelopment opportunity and any physical limitations therein. Again, the goals of this version of the course project are no different than the vacant parcel of land course project. Compel students to leverage class concepts to formulate solutions to real-world problems. To make the project more relatable, connect the redevelopment project to local news or national trends. For example, an instructor could use the redevelopment of antiquated commercial mall space or abandoned church complexes as redevelopment projects. Students remember content when they can relate to the project.

Embedded within every project, activity, and assignment is the need for students to analyze, evaluate, and formulate decisions or recommendations from data. While professors have the ability to package data and provide information to students, a better strategy is for students to search and find their own data points to analyze. Leveraging real estate technology in the classroom is paramount to cultivating a strong and career-ready student. For example, in the classroom, we utilize two main technologies: Esri and CoStar Group to evaluate actual market data. These global companies provide real time information on population demographics, migration trends, and help students identify the demand for various real estate product types in a specific geography. These technologies provide real-world data to students as they explore real locations to develop their own conclusions. This allows students to put classroom content and discussions into practice.

While the focus of this chapter has been on the development of real problems for real estate learning, there is a need to discuss a pivotal step after the completion of a real problem. Students need feedback and a follow-up discussion about the aspects of their work that were executed well and the areas that could have been improved. Students learn just as much from these conversations, where they look at examples where others may have gone wrong in their research, as they do from the actual evaluation and analysis. Furthermore, students gain valuable insights when they see the successful work products of their peers. It is important for educators to realize that some students may be more scared to make a wrong decision than they are confident to make a good decision. Being scared coupled with a lack of confidence induces paralysis and minimizes student effort and motivation to learn. However, when students learn from their peers and view examples of successfully completed work, they are more likely to succeed. In addition, students are excited to see their anonymous work praised in front of the class and they strive to produce even better work in the future.

Conclusion

This chapter outlined steps to create real world problems to enhance teaching and learning in a market analysis course. In summary, real problems for real learning must:

- Represent the built environment or some humorous version of it.
- Connect to the real estate industry or future career applications.
- Be relatable to students.
- Maximize flexibility and promote creativity.
- Require real world data and leverage real estate technology.
- Foster collaboration and teamwork.

At the conclusion of the real problem activity, engage with the students regarding the successes of the class and highlight specific areas for improvement. Provide ample feedback and encourage students to explore the next real-world problem, whether it comes in the classroom or from a real-world client.

Appendix A

The case of the Mountain Gas Station

In our humorous version of a real-world depiction, the instructor provides students with the Case of the Mountain Gas Station. At first, students laugh at the image, but afterwards the class becomes serious about the picture's connection to markets and trade areas. We discuss the need to analyze real estate demand and supply. Compared to discussions without humorous imagery, students are more likely to retain this class content conversation (see Exhibit 3.1).

Exhibit 3.1 A gas station and convenience store named "Santo's General Store" located at the top of a mountain surrounded by other rugged, snow-covered mountaintops. The store features a rustic design with large, red-framed windows, and a sign advertising "Local Gasoline." The landscape contrasts the store's function, which is to sell gasoline, since the high-altitude location makes vehicle travel impossible. Image created by Renzo Sanio.

Appendix B

Site selection for the development of a new beer spa

Activity prompt:
You work for a brokerage company. An investor just finished reading the CoStar article titled, "Want to Soak in a Tub Full of Beer?" The investor claims this is the perfect project for them. It is a classic case of a project in search of land (or in this case a building). Your job is to help them find the building to realize this opportunity. Your building does not need to be for sale or for lease. It can be currently occupied. For now, do not worry about the size of the building either.

When you are finished, upload your word or pdf document.

Be sure to answer the following questions and use the rubric:

- Identify the target end user for the new Beer Spa, provide a logical justification for your site location, and connect your location to the targeted end user.
- Using specific geographic distances, estimate the market/trade area of the project. Provide a map with drawn market/trade areas specific to your site and project.
- Estimate the number of potential end users in the market area.

Exhibit 3.2 Selection for the development of a new beer spa rubric

Criteria	*Ratings*			
Logical justification of the location	**4 pts** **Full Credit** Identified the target end user for the new Beer Spa and provided evidence substantiating their assumptions. Provided a logical justification for your location by aligning the end user demographics with the demographics of the market/trade area. There was discussion of consumer habits/behavior and key demographic indicators.	**3 pts** **Partial Credit** Identified the target end user for the new Beer Spa but provided little evidence substantiating their assumptions. Provided a logical justification for your location by aligning the end user demographics with the demographics of the market/trade area. Some attempt was made to connect the location to consumer habits/behavior and key demographic indicators, but the logic was either lacking some justification or was missing.	**2 pts** **Partial Credit** Identified the target end user for the new Beer Spa but did not provide any evidence substantiating their assumptions. Did not provide a logical justification for your location. Did not align the end user demographics with the demographics of the market/trade area. But there was an attempt to discuss consumer habits/behavior and key demographic indicators.	**0 pts** **No Credit** Failed to identify the target end user for the new Beer Spa and provided evidence substantiating their assumptions. Didn't provide a logical justification for your location. Didn't align the end user demographics with the demographics of the market/trade area. There was no discussion of consumer habits/behavior and key demographic indicators.

(*Continued*)

Exhibit 3.2 (Continued)

Criteria	*Ratings*			
Estimate the market/trade area of the project	**3 pts** **Full Credit** Provided a map with market/trade areas specific to the site, connected the geographic distance of the market/trade areas to end user's consumer behavior, and provided some proof for the end user's consumer behavior.	**2 pts** **Partial Credit** Provided a map with market/trade areas specific to the site but didn't connect the geographic distance of the market/trade areas to end user's consumer behavior or made an ungrounded assumption as to the end user's consumer behavior without proof.	**1 pts** **Partial Credit** Did not provide a map with market/trade areas specific to the site but attempted to connect the geographic distance of the market/ trade areas to end user's consumer behavior. Made one or more ungrounded assumptions regarding the end user's consumer behavior without proof.	**0 pts** **No Credit** Did not provide a map with market/trade areas specific to the site. Did not connect the geographic distance of the market/trade areas to end user's consumer behavior. Made many ungrounded assumptions regarding the end user's consumer behavior without proof.
Estimate the number of end users	**2 pts** **Full Credit** Estimated the number of potential end users in the market area and provided evidence.	**1 pts** **Partial Credit** Estimated the number of potential end users in the market area but did not provide evidence.	**0 pts** **No Credit** Did not estimate the number of potential end users in the market area and failed to provide any evidence.	

Professional writing	**1 pts** **Full Credit** Written professionally and formatted in a logical progression that improved ease of reading.	**0.5 pts** **Partial Credit** Written professionally and formatted in a logical progression that improved ease of reading, but there were a couple of minor grammatical errors/awkward sentence structures.	**0.25 pts** **Partial Credit** Written professionally and formatted in a logical progression that improved ease of reading, but there were many grammatical errors/ awkward sentence structures.	**0 pts** **No Marks** Not written professionally or formatted in a logical progression that improved ease of reading.
Total Points: 10				

Appendix C

Retail market analysis activity

Exhibit 3.3 Hypothetical ICSC factsheet

Retailer Name
Urban Cravings

Contact Information
Samantha Ryker – (555) 123-4567
samantha.ryker@urbancravings.com

Retail Category
Healthy Fast Casual

Total Number of Stores Currently Operating
215 (120 corporate & 95 franchise)

Geographical Area Preferred

- CA – San Diego, Los Angeles, San Jose, Sacramento
- TX – Austin, Dallas, Houston, San Antonio
- FL – Miami, Orlando, Tampa, Jacksonville
- NC – Charlotte, Raleigh, Durham
- TN – Nashville, Knoxville, Chattanooga

Typical GLA and Preferred Frontage
3000–4000 sf (3500 sf is preferred) – 55 feet of frontage

Type of Location Desired
In-Line, End Cap, End Cap with Drive Thru, Freestanding with Drive Thru (dependent on market analysis and projected sales)

Preferred Co-Tenants
Fitness centers, organic grocers, and lifestyle retailers targeting health-conscious customers

Typical Lease Term
7–10-year base term

Population Density Preferred
75k

Desired Income Range
$70k

Number of Stores to Open in 2024 in this Region
10

Number of Stores Projected to Open in 2025
15

New Developments/Concepts
6

Additional Comments
Takeout orders make up 40%–50% of our sales, so proximity to residential areas is crucial. While dine-in options are important, ensuring smooth drive-thru operations is a top priority for our concept. Due to our target demographic, we focus on locations with high foot traffic near fitness hubs or wellness communities. Cannibalization risk is low, but we aim to maintain a minimum 20-minute drive time buffer between locations to ensure market saturation is avoided.

Activity prompt:

Search for a retail building or unit for sale or lease in [desired state]. Select a business in the ICSC Factsheet posted in the course materials module.

1. Use one of the techniques from this class to estimate the trade area.
2. Once you have the trade area geographic boundaries, compare the demographics of your trade area to the demographics required by the business in the ICSC factsheet.
3. Would the business locate at your retail building location? Why or why not?

Exhibit 3.4 Retail market analysis activity rubric.

Criteria	*Ratings*			
Estimate trade area & demographic analysis	**5 pts** **Full Credit** Used one of the techniques to estimate the trade area for a retail business. Justified the trade area distance with the technique. Evaluated the demographics within the trade area and compared the demographics to the ICSC factsheet.	**3 pts** **Partial Credit** Used one of the techniques to estimate the trade area for a retail business. Didn't fully justify the trade area distance with the technique. Provided a basic analysis of the demographics within the trade area and compared the demographics to the ICSC factsheet.	**1 pt** **Partial Credit** Used the default drive-time distances without explanation to estimate the trade area for a retail business. Failed to justify the trade area distance with the technique. Did not connect the demographics within the trade area to the demographics to the ICSC factsheet.	**0 pts** **No Credit** Failed to provide a realistic estimate of the trade area for a retail business. Failed to justify the trade area distance with the technique. Did not connect the demographics within the trade area to the demographics to the ICSC factsheet.

(Continued)

Exhibit 3.4 (Continued)

Criteria	*Ratings*			
Business location	**4 pts Full Credit** Provided evidence and reasoning for the location of the business. Clearly stated why the business would or would not locate at the site.	**3 pts Partial Credit** Provided evidence and reasoning for the location of the business. Did not provide strong evidence why the business would or would not locate at the site.	**0 pts No Credit** Failed to provide evidence and reasoning for the location of the business. Failed to clearly state why the business would or would not locate at the site.	
Writing	**1 pt Full Credit** Written professionally and formatted in a logical progression that improved ease of reading. Provided endnote or footnote sourcing.	**0.5 pts Partial Credit** Written professionally and formatted in a logical progression that improved ease of reading, but there were a couple of minor grammatical errors/ awkward sentence structures.	**0.25 pts Partial Credit** Written professionally and formatted in a logical progression that improved ease of reading, but there were many grammatical errors/ awkward sentence structures.	**0 pts No Credit** Not written professionally or formatted in a logical progression that improved ease of reading.
Total points: 10				

Chapter 4

There are no real estate markets without the real estate capital markets

Constantine Korologos

Introduction

In order to learn about commercial real estate investments, valuation, finance, and development, students must understand where the capital comes from, and how it is priced. The goal of this chapter is to help develop a plan to teach capital markets to students who have some background in real estate finance, valuation, and investment analysis. For many undergraduate and graduate real estate programs, the study of the capital markets is limited to some discussion in finance and investment analysis courses, while other programs dedicate an entire semester to the topic.

We will begin with a look at how you might define what the real estate capital markets are, and then provide a brief history of the development of the markets. I have found that over my two decades of teaching the topic, "war stories" are a great way to connect the content to its application in a fun and realistic way.

Next, we look to help establish a connection between the broader capital markets and how trends drive capital in and out of real estate. We follow with a look at the components of the real estate capital markets; the four quadrants which reflect public debt and equity and private debt and equity. After establishing the components and their relevance in understanding why it is important to understand them, we finish with a brief look at analytical tools, a look into the future of the real estate capital markets and examples of sources that should assist you with creating a valuable applied foundation for the students to build on.

What are the capital markets and, in particular, the real estate capital markets?

Capital markets are financial markets where long-term debt or equity-backed securities are bought and sold. These markets facilitate the raising of capital by providing a platform for the issuance of stocks and bonds,

DOI: 10.1201/9781032656458-4

which are critical for both corporations and governments to fund their operations and projects. Capital markets are integral to the functioning of the global economy as they connect savers and investors with those who need capital to grow their businesses or finance government activities. The primary components of capital markets include:

- **Equity markets:** Where ownership in companies is bought and sold in the form of stocks or shares.
- **Debt markets:** Where bonds and other forms of long-term debt are traded.

These markets can be classified further into primary markets, where new securities are issued and sold for the first time, and secondary markets, where existing securities are traded among investors.

Real estate capital markets are a specialized subset of capital markets that focus on the trading of financial instruments related to real estate assets. These markets play a crucial role in providing the necessary capital for real estate development, investment, and operations. They encompass a variety of instruments, which will be discussed in more detail later in the chapter, including:

- **Mortgage-backed securities (MBS):** These are pools of real estate loans, usually residential, that are packaged together and sold as securities to investors.
- **Commercial mortgage-backed securities (CMBS):** Similar to MBS, but these are backed by commercial real estate loans such as those for office buildings, shopping centers, and hotels.
- **Real estate investment trusts (REITs):** Companies that own, operate, or finance income-producing real estate and allow investors to buy shares in portfolios of real estate assets.
- **Direct equity investments:** Investments made directly into real estate properties, often through private equity (PE) funds or joint ventures.
- **Mezzanine financing:** A hybrid of debt and equity financing that gives the lender the right to convert to an equity interest in the company in case of default, typically after senior lenders are paid.

Discussing these products and roles in the industry can provide students with insights into various career options.

The importance of real estate capital markets

Real estate capital markets are critical for the functioning of the broader real estate industry. They provide the liquidity needed for real estate investments and enable the flow of capital from investors to developers and operators. This is essential for the creation and maintenance of real estate assets, which are fundamental to economic activity, providing spaces for businesses, housing, and infrastructure.

For professors teaching this topic, it is important to convey that real estate capital markets are not just about real estate but also about the intersection of real estate with financial markets. The markets provide a platform for the valuation, risk management, and investment in real estate assets, thus playing a pivotal role in both the financial system and the real economy.

By understanding real estate capital markets, students will gain insights into how large-scale real estate projects are funded, how risk is managed, priced, and how real estate assets are valued and traded on a global scale. This knowledge is crucial for anyone looking to engage with the real estate industry, whether from a financial, operational, or regulatory perspective.

A brief historical context

Mid-20th century: Post-war expansion

Government involvement: The US government played a significant role in expanding real estate capital markets post-World War II. The creation of entities like the Federal Housing Administration (FHA) and the Veterans Administration (VA) in the US facilitated mortgage lending and homeownership.

Securitization beginnings: The concept of MBS began in the 1970s with the creation of government-sponsored enterprises (GSEs) like Fannie Mae and Freddie Mac in the United States. These entities pooled mortgages and sold them as securities, spreading the risk and creating a new market for real estate finance. A great book to assign the students is *Liars Poker* by Michael Lewis (2022), which looks at the early years of securitization.

Late 20th century: Growth and innovation

Commercial real estate finance: The 1990s saw significant growth in commercial real estate finance, with the introduction of CMBS. This allowed institutional investors to participate in the real estate market, providing more liquidity and capital for large-scale projects.

REITs: REITs, which were established in the United States in the 1960s, grew rapidly in the late 20th century, providing a way for individual investors to invest in diversified portfolios of income-producing real estate.

21st century: Maturity and complexity

Globalization of real estate markets: The globalization of financial markets has extended to real estate, with international investors increasingly participating in real estate markets across the world. This has led to the growth of cross-border real estate investment and the internationalization of REITs and real estate funds.

Financial crisis impact: The 2008 financial crisis had a profound impact on real estate capital markets. The collapse of the housing market and the subsequent credit crunch exposed the risks inherent in complex financial products like subprime mortgages and CMBS, leading to significant regulatory changes and a more cautious approach to real estate financing. Regulation evolved to address lessons learned from the crisis.

Technology and innovation: Recent years have seen the rise of technology in real estate capital markets, with the emergence of prop-tech, crowdfunding platforms, and blockchain-based real estate transactions, which are beginning to reshape how real estate is financed and traded.

Teaching foundation

Understanding the history of capital markets and real estate capital markets provides a crucial foundation for students, as it helps them appreciate the evolution, complexities, and interconnectedness of financial systems. This historical context will enable students to grasp the significance of modern practices, the importance of regulation, and the ongoing innovations that continue to shape these markets. Professors can use this historical perspective as a basis to explore more complex concepts and current trends in the capital markets.

The role of real estate capital markets in the economy

Facilitating capital formation for real estate

Real estate capital markets are crucial for raising the necessary capital to fund real estate projects, including commercial properties, residential developments, and infrastructure. By providing a platform for the issuance and trading of real estate-related financial instruments, such as MBS, CMBS, and REITs, these markets enable developers and investors to access capital. This capital formation is essential for the growth and expansion of urban areas, the creation of housing, and the development of commercial spaces, all of which are fundamental to economic development.

Providing liquidity to real estate assets

One of the primary functions of real estate capital markets is to provide liquidity to inherently illiquid real estate assets. Through securitization and the trading of real estate securities, these markets allow investors to buy and sell real estate exposure without having to directly purchase or sell physical properties. This liquidity facilitates the efficient allocation of capital, enabling investors to diversify their portfolios, manage risk, and respond to changing market conditions. This is a great place to introduce the concepts of diversification.

Risk management and pricing risk

Real estate capital markets play a critical role in risk management for both lenders and investors. By pooling and securitizing real estate loans, such as in the case of MBS and CMBS, the risk associated with individual properties or loans is spread across a broader base of investors. Additionally, the availability of real estate derivatives and other financial products allows investors to hedge against specific risks, such as interest rate fluctuations or changes in property values.

This is a great place to introduce derivative products used in risk management, including interest rate caps and swaps, demonstrating the sophistication of real estate finance and capital structures. Concepts surrounding the pricing of risk-based capital, helps solidify the foundations surrounding the relationships between the level of risk and the expected returns.

Enhancing market efficiency and transparency

The development of real estate capital markets has led to increased transparency and efficiency in the pricing and valuation of real estate assets. Publicly traded instruments, like REITs and MBS, provide continuous pricing information which helps in the assessment of market conditions and the valuation of underlying assets. This transparency is crucial for attracting investment, ensuring fair market practices, and maintaining confidence in the real estate sector.

Impacting monetary policy

Real estate capital markets are closely linked to the broader financial system and play a significant role in the transmission of monetary policy. Changes in interest rates, for example, directly affect mortgage rates, the cost of borrowing, and consequently, real estate investment. Central banks often monitor real estate markets as part of their policy decisions because of the sector's influence on economic activity, inflation, and financial stability. As these policies have an effect on the amount of leverage in the market, this is a good place to discuss the impacts of an active and aggressive lending market where borrowers have access to a lot of low-cost debt, and the downside effects when things go wrong as economic conditions change and borrowers may struggle to service or refinance that debt.

As monetary policy can have a material impact on capital markets pricing and liquidity, consider suggesting to the students to monitor Federal Reserve data (St. Louis Fed, for example), as well as reports by the chief economists of some of the larger money center banks. This gets them used to following the economy, while continuing to focus on specific real estate market supply and demand trends.

The relationship between real estate capital markets and the broader economy

Economic growth and development

Real estate capital markets are integral to economic growth. By facilitating investment in real estate, they contribute to the development of infrastructure, commercial spaces, and housing, which are critical components of economic development. The construction and real estate sectors generate significant employment and stimulate demand in related industries, such as manufacturing, materials, and services.

Wealth creation and distribution

Real estate is a key asset class in wealth creation and is often a significant component of both individual and institutional investment portfolios. The growth and performance of real estate capital markets can have a direct impact on wealth distribution, retirement savings, and overall financial security. Through mechanisms like REITs and real estate funds, a broader segment of the population can participate in real estate investment, contributing to wealth distribution and financial inclusion.

Financial stability and systemic risk

While real estate capital markets are essential for economic growth, they can also be a source of systemic risk, as seen during the 2008 financial crisis. The interconnectedness of real estate markets with the broader financial system means that disruptions in these markets can have widespread economic consequences.

The health of real estate capital markets is often a bellwether for broader economic conditions. For instance, a downturn in real estate can lead to reduced consumer spending, lower business investment, and financial institution stress, all of which can contribute to an economic recession.

Influence on consumer behavior

Real estate capital markets influence consumer behavior, particularly through their impact on housing affordability and mortgage availability. When real estate markets are strong and capital is readily available, consumers are more likely to purchase homes, which drives demand in other sectors of the economy. Conversely, when capital is tight and/or real estate prices are high, consumer spending can contract, affecting broader economic growth.

Globalization and cross-border investment

The globalization of real estate capital markets has led to increased cross-border investment in real estate. International investors play a significant role in some local real estate markets, particularly major cities, influencing prices, development patterns, and economic activity.

This cross-border investment also means that economic conditions in one region can have ripple effects across global markets. For example, a slowdown in a major economy like the United States or China can affect real estate markets globally, impacting investment flows and economic stability.

Teaching considerations

When teaching these concepts, professors should emphasize the dual role of real estate capital markets as both a driver of economic growth and a potential source of risk. Students should understand how these markets facilitate investment and capital allocation, while also recognizing the broader economic implications of market fluctuations and crises.

Incorporating case studies, such as the 2008 financial crisis, can provide valuable lessons on the importance of regulation, transparency, and risk management in maintaining the stability of real estate capital markets and their relationship with the broader economy. Additionally, discussing current trends, such as the impact of globalization and technological innovation, will help students appreciate the evolving nature of these markets and their continued significance in the global economy.

Key components of real estate capital markets: The four quadrants

Real estate capital markets consist of various financial instruments and platforms that facilitate the flow of capital into real estate investments. These components can be broadly categorized into public and private debt and equity markets. A few things that may be valuable to discuss with the students, include how the various public and private sources of debt and equity capital expand the options of capital sources, and through unique structures, increase liquidity.

Public debt

Mortgage-backed securities

MBS are securities that are backed by a pool of mortgages. Investors receive periodic payments derived from the interest and principal payments made by homeowners or commercial property owners. They include RMBS backed by residential mortgages and CMBS backed by commercial real estate loans, such as those for office buildings, shopping centers, and hotels. Market participants include GSEs like Fannie Mae and Freddie Mac, private financial institutions, and institutional investors.

REIT bonds and mortgage REITs

REITs may issue bonds to raise capital for acquiring or developing properties. These bonds are a form of unsecured debt that must be repaid with interest, taking priority over the equity shareholders. They provide a fixed-income investment opportunity backed by the revenue-generating properties owned by the REIT.

Mortgage REITs are similar to their equity counterparts in terms of their tax structure (discussed in more detail below) and invest in income-producing mortgages.

Private debt

Commercial real estate loans

Loans provided by banks or private lenders to finance the acquisition, development, or refinancing of commercial properties. They are typically senior secured debt, backed by a first lien on the property, taking a priority position over other claims on the property's cash flow and assets.

Mezzanine debt, on the other hand, is a hybrid of debt and equity that gives the mezzanine lender the right to convert the loan to an ownership or equity interest in the event of default. As it is collateralized by the equity in the ownership entity of the property (the borrowing entity), they only get to replace the borrower and take on the obligations of that entity, including the mortgage that is senior to them. This is an area that I constantly find myself having to explain several times, so it is worth using examples to clarify the priority of claims.

Private mortgage/debt funds

These are funds that pool capital from private investors to provide mortgage loans, typically to commercial real estate borrowers that may need more leverage, flexibility, or possibly the borrowers do not qualify for traditional bank financing. They offer higher yields to investors in exchange for taking on higher risks associated with real estate lending. Of course, higher yields mean higher costs for the borrowers as well. They also use repurchase agreements, or REPOs, to leverage the capital available to make loans, providing higher yields and a larger pool of capital.

Public equity

Real estate investment trusts

Equity REITs are companies that own and operate income-producing real estate. They are registered with the Securities and Exchange Commission (SEC) and traded on major stock exchanges. The REIT tax-structure provides some unique benefits as compared to most listed companies in that in exchange for not having to pay corporation tax, they are required to distribute 90% of their taxable income to shareholders.

In addition to exchange-traded REITs, there are also non-exchange-traded REITs (NTRs) which facilitates equity share ownership. Unlike private REITs, which do not have to be registered with an exchange or with the SEC, or like an equity REIT which are listed on major exchanges, NTRs are SEC registered and compliant, but may only be acquired through FINRA-registered investment advisors (RIAs). It is useful to demonstrate the differences between listed equity REITs and NTRs using data from REIT websites, highlighting the similarities, available public documentation, and transparency of data and financial reporting vs. the differences including limited liquidity and investor suitability. Blackstone's BREIT (www.breit.com/) is a great NTR to study. Both traded and non-traded REITs provide investors with exposure to real estate without the need to buy and manage properties directly, offering liquidity, and diversification.

Real estate exchange-traded funds

An exchange-traded fund (ETF) is a basket of stocks and fixed-income securities which are traded on an exchange. ETFs that focus on real estate securities, including REITs and real estate-related companies, trade like stocks on exchanges, allowing investors to gain diversified exposure to the real estate sector with the ease of trading through a single security.

Private equity

Direct investment: Institutional and high net-worth investors

These investments involve the direct ownership of real estate properties, typically by individuals, general partner (GP)/limited partner (LP) structures, institutional investors such as pension funds and insurance companies, or PE firms. Investors have control over the property and its cash flow, bearing all the equity ownership risks and rewards associated with the asset.

Sovereign wealth funds and other international sources

Significant amounts of institutional capital come from international sovereign wealth funds, pension funds, and insurance companies, who want to diversify their investment holdings into the United States. Canadian, Asian, European, South American, and Middle Eastern capital regularly looks to the United States as a target for safe, stable real estate investment opportunities.

Real estate PE funds

These PE funds represent pooled investment vehicles that raise capital from investors to acquire, develop, and manage real estate properties. These funds can target core investments, which are more stable lower-risk assets, as well as targeting higher returns through value-add or opportunistic investments. Data services, such as Preqin, provide good transparency into what is a very private investment structure (for a list of Sources, Tools, and Resources for Studying Real Estate Capital Markets, see Appendix A).

Fun and engaging ways to teach the content

Because the capital markets are complex, and students rarely have any kind of experience with them in which to easily build their knowledge, it is critical to actively engage the students during their learning. Below are some fun and engaging ways for professors to bring the capital markets to life in order to facilitate deeper learning.

Case study simulations

Professors can create case studies based on real-world scenarios involving public and private debt and equity deals. Students can be divided into groups to analyze and propose investment strategies, considering the risks and returns of different components of the real estate capital markets. You can add a competitive element by turning it into a mock investment pitch, where each group presents their analysis to a panel of "investors" (which could include the professor or invited industry professionals).

Real estate investment game

Develop a classroom game where students manage a portfolio of properties using a combination of public and private capital. The game could simulate market fluctuations, changes in interest rates, and other real-world factors that impact real estate investments. Introduce unexpected events (like a sudden market crash or regulatory change) to see how students adapt their strategies in real-time.

Field trips or virtual tours

These can be some of the best opportunities to bring the field into the classroom. With the learning outcome in mind, arrange visits to real estate projects, REIT-managed properties, or financial institutions involved in real estate finance. If physical visits aren't possible, virtual tours can also be highly effective. After the tour, have students identify the types of capital (public/private debt or equity) likely used to finance the project and discuss the pros and cons of these choices.

Portfolio management simulation

Real actual deal data is always difficult to secure, but extremely valuable when you can. Use financial software, such as excel or ARGUS to create examples that allow students to manage a portfolio of real estate assets. They can adjust the mix of public and private debt and equity and see how these changes impact the portfolio's performance over time. The good thing about public equity and debt structures (CMBS) is the transparency that you can access. Data sources like Trepp for CMBS, and Freddie Mac and Fannie Mae, can provide great granular data that you can use to create portfolios of investments. Incorporate challenges like economic downturns or new regulatory requirements that force students to reassess and rebalance their portfolios. The Fed posts its stress testing economic scenarios every year (see www.federalreserve.gov/publications/2025-str

ess-test-scenarios.htm) along with the top bank results. These scenarios can provide a real look at the way the Fed is assessing capital markets risk.

Debates and role-playing

A few ways of generating participation in the classroom is through debates and role playing. Organize debates where students take on roles as different market participants (e.g., a REIT manager vs. a PE investor) and argue the merits and risks of their respective positions.

Have students switch roles mid-debate to help them understand multiple perspectives within the real estate capital markets. Mock credit committee's and mock loan workout negotiations can provide practical experience and facilitate learning to think and speak on your feet.

Real estate "Shark Tank"

Invite industry professionals (such as real estate investment managers, REIT executives, or capital market analysts) to participate in a "Shark Tank" style event where students pitch real estate investment ideas. Students work in teams to develop their investment pitch, focusing on how their understanding of real estate capital markets underpins their strategy. The guest speakers act as "sharks" and provide feedback, ask tough questions, and decide whether they would "invest" in the idea. This activity underscores the practical value of understanding real estate capital markets in convincing investors and making informed investment decisions.

These methods can make the content more engaging and help students apply theoretical knowledge to practical situations, thereby deepening their understanding of real estate capital markets. By incorporating these fun and interactive teaching methods, professors can make the study of real estate capital markets engaging and memorable. These activities not only convey the importance of the subject matter but also equip students with practical skills and a deeper understanding of how real estate capital markets operate in the real world.

Taking it to the next level: Integrating tools like AI and property technology (proptech) into your real estate capital markets teaching toolbox

Teaching the future of real estate capital markets, particularly the impact of technology and AI, can be an engaging and forward-looking topic for college students. To make the learning process effective and enjoyable, professors can utilize a variety of teaching strategies that combine theoretical knowledge with practical applications. Here's a guide on how professors can approach this subject.

Start with a historical context and evolution

The purpose is to help students understand how far the real estate capital markets have come and set the stage for discussing future developments. Begin with a brief review of the history of real estate capital markets, focusing on key technological advancements (like the introduction of securitization and digital trading platforms). Highlight how these innovations have shaped the markets we see today.

Introduce key emerging technologies and AI applications

- **Blockchain:** Discuss how blockchain technology can be used for property transactions, title recording, smart contracts, enhancing transparency, and reducing fraud.
- **AI and machine learning:** Explore how AI is being used for property valuation, predictive analytics, automated underwriting, and risk assessment. Discuss whether AI can improve decision-making by analyzing vast amounts of data more accurately than traditional methods.
- **Proptech:** Explain how technology is transforming property management, leasing, and real estate services through Internet of Things (IoT), virtual reality (VR), and augmented reality (AR).
- **Fintech (financial technology) integration:** Examine how financial technologies are being integrated with real estate markets, particularly through crowdfunding platforms, digital payments, and online investment platforms.

Use multimedia presentations, such as videos and infographics, to visually illustrate these technologies. Incorporate guest speakers who are experts in these fields to provide real-world insights.

Engage students with hands-on technology demonstrations

Give students practical exposure to the technologies impacting real estate capital markets. Examples can include:

- **Blockchain simulation:** Conduct a mock property transaction using a blockchain platform. Students can play roles such as buyers, sellers, and regulators to see how blockchain ensures transparency and security.

- **AI tool demonstration:** Use AI-based software to analyze real estate market data. Show students how AI can predict market trends, assess property values, or identify investment opportunities.
- **Proptech app exploration:** Assign students to explore various proptech apps (like property management platforms or virtual tour apps) and present their findings on how these tools are transforming the real estate industry.

Organize discussions on technology's impact

This will encourage critical thinking about the benefits and challenges of integrating technology and AI into real estate capital markets. Organize debates on topics such as "Will AI replace human jobs in real estate?" or "Is blockchain the future of property transactions?". Divide the class into teams to argue for or against these propositions. Alternatively, host a panel discussion where students can share their views on the ethical implications of AI in real estate, such as privacy concerns and the potential for algorithmic bias.

Use case studies on technological disruption

Create opportunities to show real-world examples of how technology is changing the landscape of real estate capital markets. Present case studies of companies or projects that have successfully integrated technology into their real estate operations. Examples might include the use of AI for property management, blockchain for real estate transactions, or crowdfunding platforms for real estate investments. Assign groups to research and present on a recent technological innovation in the real estate market. Each group could focus on a different technology, analyzing its impact on the market, the challenges faced, and future potential.

Host a real estate tech innovation workshop

Use this to foster creativity and innovation among students by organizing a workshop where students brainstorm and design their own technological solutions for challenges in real estate capital markets. They could develop ideas for new proptech tools, AI applications, or blockchain innovations. After the workshop, host a pitch competition where students present their ideas to a panel of judges (which could include the professor and guest experts). Offer feedback and discuss the feasibility of their ideas in the real world.

Leverage online platforms and simulations

Use this to provide a dynamic and interactive learning environment. Use platforms that simulate real estate investment and trading, allowing students to experiment with digital assets, REITs, and other market instruments. This helps students understand how technology influences investment strategies.

VR tours

Incorporate VR technology to give students virtual tours of properties or developments, showing how these tools are being used in marketing, sales, and investment decisions in the real estate industry.

Discuss regulatory and ethical considerations

Assign students to research and present on how governments and regulatory bodies are responding to new technologies in real estate, such as blockchain or AI. Facilitate discussions on ethical issues related to AI and technology in real estate, such as data privacy, algorithmic bias, and the digital divide. Encourage students to consider how these issues might shape the future of the industry.

Encourage continuous learning and industry engagement

We need to prepare students for the ongoing evolution of real estate capital markets. Encourage students to attend (virtually or in-person) industry conferences, webinars, and events focused on real estate technology and AI. This keeps them updated on the latest trends and innovations. Assign readings from leading publications, blogs, or white papers on real estate technology and AI. Follow up with class discussions or written reflections on how these readings apply to their understanding of real estate capital markets.

Conclusion

By leveraging a range of sources, tools, and innovative teaching methods, professors can provide students with a comprehensive and engaging understanding of real estate capital markets. This multidisciplinary approach, blending theoretical knowledge, practical application, and creative thinking, prepares students to navigate and shape the rapidly evolving landscape of real estate finance. Emphasizing the transformative role of technology and AI, this framework equips future professionals with the critical skills and insights needed to succeed in and contribute to the dynamic future of real estate capital markets.

Appendix A

Sources, tools, and resources for studying real estate capital markets

Books and textbooks

Real Estate Finance and Investment, William B. Brueggeman, Jeffrey D. Fisher & Stephanie Yates. (2024). A comprehensive textbook covering fundamental and advanced topics in real estate finance and investment, including valuation, market analysis, and risk management. McGraw Hill. Seventeenth edition.

The Real Estate Capital Markets: Evolution, Structure, Participants, Merrie Frankel, Hugh Kelly, and Constantine Korologos. (2025). Provides a deep dive into the structure and evolution of real estate capital markets, covering both theoretical frameworks and practical applications. Cognella. First edition.

Commercial Real Estate Analysis and Investments, David M. Geltner, Norman G. Miller, Jim Clayton, and Piet Eichholtz. (2014). Focuses on commercial real estate with detailed discussions on market dynamics, valuation techniques, and investment strategies. Authors are working on revisions expected to be available in 2026. Cengage published the third edition and Routledge will be publishing the fourth edition.

Real Estate Principles: A Value Approach, David C. Ling, and Wayne R. Archer. (2024). Focuses on how value is central to virtually all real estate decision-making, by providing valuation and decision-making tools that can be applied in a variety of real-world situations. McGraw Hill. Seventh edition.

Real Estate Investments Module, Blended Teaching. (2025). Provides a classbook with curated videos and other classroom contents including class assignments, quizzes, and exams for real estate investments that professors can customize for their classes. They also have real estate principles and finance .

Data providers

Bloomberg Terminal. A powerful tool for accessing real-time financial data, market news, and analysis on global real estate markets. They have a university program for students. University must have a lab to house the terminals. They also have some certification programs for students. www. bloomberg

CoStar. They offer a student certification package through university programs. www.costar.com

Green Street Advisors. Access private and public market insights validated by industry-leading commercial real estate news, research, and data models that have led the market for decades. www.greenstreet.com

Moody's Analytics/REIS. Offers commercial real estate market data, including property-level trends, rents, vacancies, and investment performance. www.moodys.com

MSCI Real Estate. Provides global real estate performance indices, analytics, and research, widely used by institutional investors. Subscription service for data and reports. www.msci.com

National Association of Real Estate Investment Trusts/European Public Real Estate Association (FTSE – NAREIT/EPRA). A key resource for information on REITs, including market data, performance analysis, and policy updates. www.reit.com

National Council of Real Estate Investment Fiduciaries (NCREIF). This organization serves the institutional real estate investment community, representing the largest, most robust and diverse database of country-specific real estate assets in the world. NCREIF produced the first property level return index, the NCREIF Property Index (NPI), dating back to 1978 to capture investment performance records that meet the rigorous scrutiny and review of major investors and academia. Regularly publish data as well as white papers on commercial real estate trends. Ncreif.org

National Investment Center (NIC). This association tracks the seniors housing sector of the real estate industry. They regularly publish performance data, statistics as well as white papers on the senior housing sector. They have a subscription service for the data although in the past they have worked with university programs. www.nic.org

Preqin. Preqin data covers a wide range of topics, including PE, venture capital, hedge funds, real estate, infrastructure, and natural resources. It covers the entire investment process, including investors, fund managers, funds and performance, transactions, portfolio companies, service providers, and market trends. www.prequin.com

RealPage (Axiometrics). A data source for monthly performance of the apartment sector. The company tracks individual properties or portfolios owned by both private and publicly traded apartment REITs, as well as properties owned and managed by private investors, developers, and management companies in more than 300 markets, totaling over 16,500 properties and 4.4 million units. Axiometrics delivers its data and analysis through a set of affordable, sophisticated tools that enable clients to improve property and investment performance at a fraction of the cost of the additional revenue generated. www.realpage.com

SNL Financial (Part of S&P Global). Provides comprehensive data and analysis on real estate companies, REITs, and real estate capital markets. www.marketplace.spglobal.com

Trepp, LLC. A leading data provider for commercial real estate debt securitization transactions, offering insights into market trends, property values, and capital flows. Trepp does work with universities by providing training and academic access. www.trepp.com/treppeducation

Investment analysis tools and software

ARGUS Enterprise. Industry-standard software for real estate valuation, cash flow analysis, and portfolio management, used by professionals and academics alike. They offer free access for 50 licenses on computers at universities. They also have student pricing for student certification. www.altusgroup.com/education/argus-university-program/

CoStar Portfolio Strategy. Provides tools for analyzing real estate investment strategies, including portfolio optimization, risk assessment, and market forecasting.

Excel with Real Estate Add-ins (e.g., @RISK, RealData). Excel-based tools and add-ins for modeling, forecasting, and analyzing real estate investments, incorporating features like Monte Carlo simulations and scenario analysis.

Python and R (with Real Estate Libraries). Programming languages that can be used for advanced data analysis, financial modeling, and simulations in real estate finance.

Rockport VAL. Rockport VAL is the (present) and future of commercial real estate cash flow modeling and valuation. They have a program to work with faculty to learn the product and then teach it to their students. www.therockportgroup.com/resources/val-training

Professional associations and certifications (including links for student memberships where available)

Appraisal Institute. Offers courses, publications, and certifications related to real estate appraisal, with a focus on valuation techniques and market analysis. Student affiliate membership is free. www.appraisalinstitute.org

CCIM. A certification for commercial real estate professionals. Begin building your professional network in college by joining CCIM Student

Membership at $50 open to full-time undergraduate and graduate students. www.ccim.com

Commercial Real Estate Finance Council (CREFC). Offers educational resources, certification programs, and networking opportunities for professionals in real estate finance and capital markets. www.crefc.org

NAREIT. A key resource for information on REITs, including market data, performance analysis, and policy updates. www.reit.com/nareit

The Counselors of Real Estate (CRE). A global consortium of credentialed real estate problem solvers, who provide expert advice on complex real property and land-related matters. Its 1,000 members from 22 countries and the US territories bring professionals from all specialties of the real estate industry together. Membership, which is extended by invitation only, although qualified members can self-apply, www.cre.org. Students and professionals can subscribe to their free publication *Real Estate Issues.* https://cre.org/real-estate-issues/

Urban Land Institute. A global network of real estate and land-use professionals in a variety of disciplines. Student memberships are 75% off the Associate membership price per year. www.uli.org

Industry reports and white papers

CBRE global research reports. In-depth reports on market trends, economic outlooks, and capital market developments across various real estate sectors. www.cbre.com/insights

JLL real estate trends and insights. Offers quarterly insights into national and global real estate investment trends, capital flows, and market performance. www.jll.com/en-us/insights

Cushman & Wakefield Market Beat Reports. Regular reports that provide analysis and forecasts for commercial real estate markets worldwide. www.cushmanwakefield.com

PwC and Urban Land Institute's "Emerging Trends in Real Estate". An annual report that provides insights into the latest trends, opportunities, and challenges in the global real estate markets. Free with some association memberships like ULI. https://knowledge.uli.org/en/

The counselors of real estate's top ten issues affecting real estate. An annual report that provides the current and emerging issues expected to have the most significant impact on all of the real estate sectors during the coming year. https://cre.org/top-ten-issues/

Chapter 5

Experiential learning in the classroom

Using scavenger hunts as a means of actualizing learning

Pernille H. Christensen

The pedagogical foundation

Experiential learning is a process in which "knowledge is created through the transformation of experience" (Kolb, 1984, p. 48). Teaching staff can support this process by giving students opportunities to demonstrate their understanding of learned concepts to real-world projects and scenarios (Frontczak, 1998). One type of experiential learning is place-based learning, also called field-based learning, which takes place outside the classroom. Place-based learning activities allow students to directly engage with and critique their environment, thereby deepening their understanding of abstract concepts (Krakowka, 2012; Wurdinger & Allison, 2017; Shahanaz, 2018).

Place-based learning can be implemented as either long- or short-term experiences. Long-term place-based learning experiences, such as internships and study abroad programs, are not uncommon in real estate education, and several papers describe how these are developed and implemented. These are highly beneficial experiences but also entail substantial time and financial commitments, limiting accessibility for some students. In contrast, short-term place-based learning activities, which incur minimal cost, are less commonly reviewed in real estate education literature. Apart from property development and real estate site visits, which are generally like traditional field trips, short-term place-based learning remains underutilized in property/real estate education.

Place-based learning activities can help make complex concepts more easily understood. Course materials must be clearly and creatively linked to real-world scenarios, guiding students through the observation process for this approach to be effective (Thyroff, 2019). One effective method is the scavenger hunt technique, which has been employed in various disciplines to link course content with real-world learning, such as in

DOI: 10.1201/9781032656458-5

management (Barclay & York, 1996), geography (Krakowka, 2012), and nursing (Tinnon, 2014).

Many of the scavenger hunt activities described in the literature use "seek-and-find" type activities for non-learning purposes (e.g. increasing awareness of campus resources or building student camaraderie). If utilized in this way, and students cannot see the connection to subject objectives, they may perceive the activity as a waste of time (Rugan & Nero, 2013). To address this concern, the Central Park scavenger hunt activity was developed based on Kolb's experiential learning theory (Kolb, 1984). It offers students a structured learning experience in which they identify implementations that they have learned about in class, make observations related to their implementation, critique and reflect on the implementation success and challenges, and synthesize their learning experiences through the creation of the deliverable.

Frontczak highlighted the importance of guiding students through the four phases of the experiential learning cycle after any field experience to ensure "complete and valuable learning" (1998, p. 31). The Central Park scavenger hunt activity therefore takes students through the steps of connecting theoretical concepts to real-world scenarios through observation and reflection, thereby distinguishing it from other simple "seek-and-find" activities. The aim of this experiential learning activity is to bridge conceptual and theoretical learning to real-world implementation of concepts and, in the case of this subject, sustainability interventions, to promote deep, active learning, increased engagement with the content, improved understanding of how concepts are implemented in real-world scenarios, and a critical assessment of the benefits, challenges, and risk associated with implementation (Lumpkin et al., 2015).

The setting

Developing experiential, place-based learning activities that offer hands-on, active learning while linking learned theory with applied concepts in real-world scenarios can be challenging. Potential obstacles to implementing experiential learning activities include transportation requirements, time commitment, logistical challenges, and organizational requirements (Wurdinger & Allison, 2017). Additionally, instructors may have student safety, time limitation, class size, and expense concerns associated with incorporating experiential learning into their courses (Krakowka, 2012). However, this scavenger hunt activity is comparatively straight-forward and easily actualized, even with large class sizes and time constraints, and incurs minimal to no costs.

Our activity was conducted on campus and through the adjacent urban precinct; however, the activity could be conducted entirely on campus, for example if transportation is a concern, or entirely off-campus if appropriate for the class. To manage student numbers, the scavenger hunt activity is combined with a University of Technology Sydney (UTS) green roofs tour. this helps us to manage larger student numbers (we split the class in half starting with the tour, and half starting with the scavenger hunt). Each activity takes 45–55 minutes, depending on the group sizes and how many elevators we need to use on the tour.

We start by meeting the full group at the meeting point on the Alumni Green (itself a green roof) in the center of campus. Students are given instructions on how to complete the scavenger hunt, and the learning goal is explained. We also remind students that they represent UTS and our program, and what we expect of their behavior. Students self-select into groups of two to three (to add a collaborative component to the activity), and (just for fun) can earn bonus points for finding unique implementation examples and/or taking photos from different perspectives than other teams. Half the teams are selected to start the tour, while the other half are walked to the starting point of the scavenger hunt. At the designated time, we reconvene at the meeting point, and students change to the other activity. At the end of the second activity, students return to the classroom to complete the deliverable.

The combined activities are conducted in a standard 3-hour block class with class sizes ranging from 40 to 65 students each year. The scavenger hunt activity has also been run as a standalone activity in 60- and 75-minute class sessions previously, with questions related to the green roof tour removed from the brief/assignment. Student participation may also be a concern for some instructors; however, experience shows that students are enthusiastic about engaging in student-led learning activities outside the classroom and value the novelty of the experience. Students note that they "found [the scavenger hunt] tasks to be a great incentive to promote engagement and participation." Specifically, students "liked that this class was more interactive than other subjects" and that "the self-guided tour [scavenger hunt] was practical and fun and I learnt cool things." One student further explained that the "stand out activity was ... the [scavenger hunt] tour of Central Park. Being able to identify and critique what we had learnt in class was extremely helpful."

Undergraduate students in the Introduction to Resilient Development elective spend the first half of the semester learning about urban resilience, urban systems, and triple bottom line theory, as well as applying that theory to real-world case examples in active learning activities in class. The second half of the semester focuses on built environment solutions and the opportunities, challenges, and risks these can bring to a project (e.g.

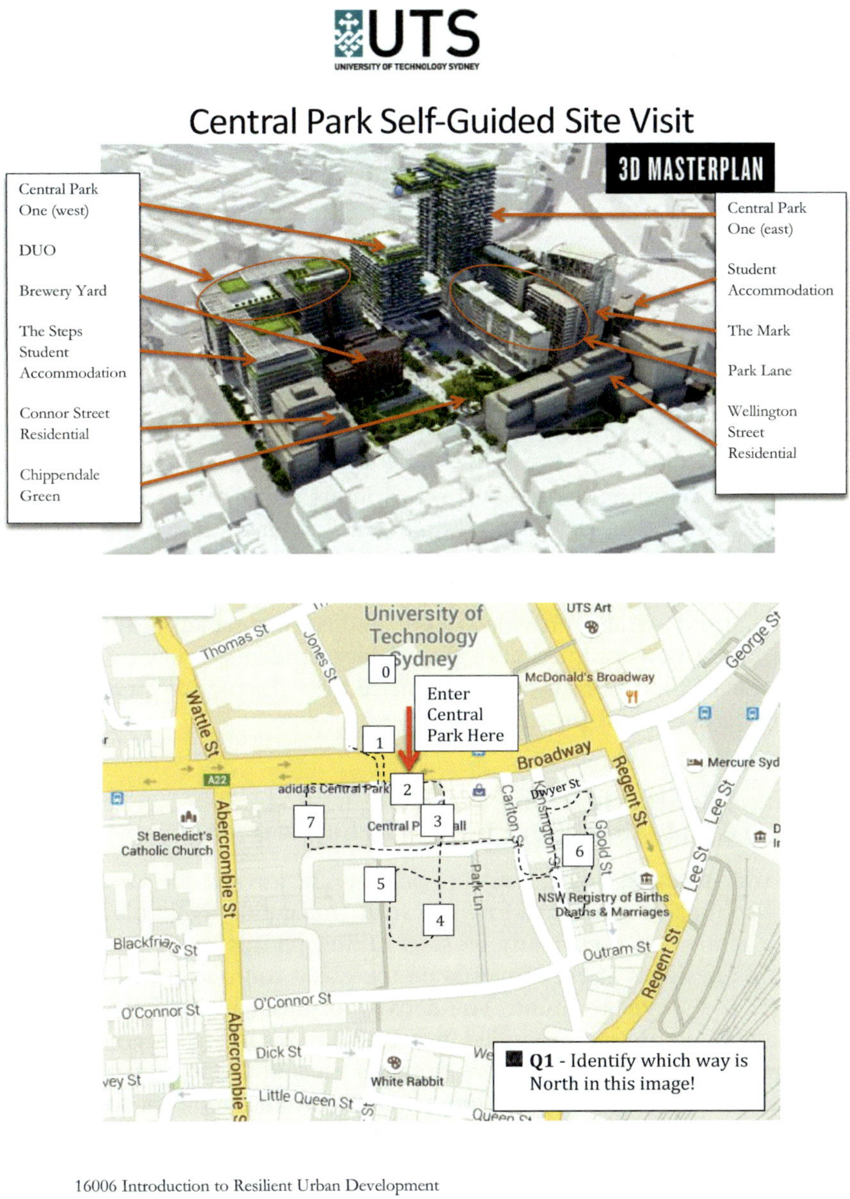

Exhibit 5.1 Overview image and map of scavenger hunt.

covering strategies for water sensitive urban design, regenerative design and development, transit-oriented development, security and placemaking, green infrastructure and precincts, etc.). The UTS Green Roof Tour/ Central Park scavenger hunt is the final in-class activity before their final research presentations and offers students the opportunity to consolidate their learning by investigating built environment solutions implemented in place.

Students are given an annotated precinct map (see Exhibit 5.1) with key points identified where they must locate the real-world applications of theoretical concepts and/or applied implementation examples which they have learned about in class. For example, at Stop #2 they must locate the southern hemisphere's largest green wall, investigate the installation type and irrigation system up close, take a photograph, and highlight key discussion themes prompted in the guide. They are also provided a guide (see Exhibit 5.2). In total, twelve photo-ops are identified on the map, and eleven discussion/reflection prompts are included in the guide. Student teams are expected to complete and submit photos and written responses by the end of class. Three supplemental YouTube videos (e.g. about the heliostat) and a few readings (e.g. a news article about the Halo art installation) are also provided in the guide to further support the learning exercise. Upon completion of the activity, students return to the classroom, upload their photos and summarize their discussions in a Word or PowerPoint document for submission.

The experiential learning activity: What are they doing and how are they learning?

At the tour meeting point, students pair up and review the Central Park scavenger hunt document before we start (full guide available from the author); teams are then ready to start taking photos and responding to reflection questions as they investigate the green roofs and green walls or complete the scavenger hunt. The activity begins with half the students starting with an instructor-guided group tour of four UTS green roofs and three green walls (Stop #0) where students learn about the different types of green roofs and green walls implemented on and adjacent to campus, the contribution these make to biodiversity in the precinct, the maintenance challenges different installation types create (and the adaptations our facilities team have made as they learned), and how these interventions are part of the larger green infrastructure network plan for Sydney. The tour also offers the opportunity to see and investigate the adjacent Central Park green wall from multiple angles.

Stop No 0

We will kick things off with a walking tour of UTS Green roofs – consider what this contributes to the UTS/Central Park/Ultimo precinct. What commitment does this represent for UTS towards sustainability goals?

Q2 – All semester, your weekly modules have linked to the UN SDGs to help communicate how what you are learning contributes to these larger goals we have set as a society. Review the UN SDGs (first presented in Module 1) and answer: To what UN SDGs are the green roofs, green walls and the associated initiatives you've heard about today contributing? Explain your answer.

P1 -Photograph each green roof we visit today and have each team member included in at least one photo.

Stop No 1

As you approach Central Park One from UTS, note which way is north on the diagram above, and have a look up at the green walls. Green walls of this size were a first for Sydney and were the tallest in the world when they were built. Have a look at the plant types included here. Is there anything particularly thriving or dying off? What type of installation Plants have to be replaced by hand - look up towards the top of the building and you can see "window cleaning platforms" used by the vertical garden maintenance crew. Look around at the people in the street. Is anyone else looking up/taking photos of the walls?

P2 -Photograph the green wall from in front of UTS Tower (include at least one team member in photo)

Green Wall Quick Facts

- Designer Patrick Blanc
- Height 116m
- Size of garden: 21 panels covering 1,120m2
- Number of Plants Approx. 35,000
- Number of species: about 383
- Maintenance Team of 6 people x 4 days/wk.

Stop No 2

As you cross the road, take a closer look at the green walls. The garden is essentially a hanging hydroponic system. The use of hessian means that no soil is required and that the green walls are a very lightweight. A team of 6 gardeners spend 4 days/week maintaining the façade and planter boxes. Tasks include planting, pruning, weeding, maintaining the irrigation system, pest management and training the planter boxes. Think about what factors may have contributed to this level of maintenance being viable at this site.

The hessian needs to be kept at a constant moisture level and would not tolerate outdoor water restrictions common during a Sydney drought. It is irrigated with recycled water, which will never be restricted in a drought, unlike potable water from the mains supply. The water that drips off the walls is also collected and recycled. The water is not suitable for drinking, but residents can wash their clothes in it!

P3 -Photograph the green wall up close. Can you see how the green wall works? (include at least a hand or foot of a team member) – be creative and use the photo to demonstrate how the system works.

16006 Introduction to Resilient Urban Development

Exhibit 5.2 Sample of scavenger hunt document demonstrating what information is included at Stops and how the questions and photo guidance is offered.

Upon completion of the UTS green roofs & walls tour, students reconvene at the meeting point and groups switch to the other activity. The students who started with the tour will then begin the student-led team learning activity where they (at Stop #1) build on the new learning from the tour by investigating the southern hemisphere's largest green wall from across the street and then crossing the street to investigate up-close the green wall typology, and the apparent issues with the installation (Stop #2). For students who started with the scavenger hunt activity, they will build on and supplement their initial team observations about the green walls throughout the tour and can ask questions and clarify their understanding.

The guide includes key facts about the precinct, the building and the interventions they will investigate. Students are prompted to identify and photograph implemented solutions and to reflect on how the implementation aligns with their in-class learning through discussion topic prompts, which direct them to consider specific things related to what they are seeing.

Stop #3 has students enter the building to investigate the largest digital wall in Australia and to read the information about the installation to consider whether and how this contributes to the social sustainability goals of the development. At this stop, they must also investigate (at least) one of the internal green walls. They are asked to pay attention to the impact of the heliostat, which is cantilevered above the glass-topped atrium, on internal daylighting. Links to a news article and a video are provided as additional learning resources for students to watch/read during the activity. This helps students investigate the installation more thoroughly so that they can assess its impact on the space and the users of the building.

Stop #4 has them moving through the building, down an escalator lined with an internal garden, and out into the park, which was created by the developers and deeded back to the city as part of the Voluntary Planning Agreement for the development. In the park, they view another video about the Halo art installation and consider its contribution to the community, before walking the site to assess potential security risks of this public space and to identify whether any protective security interventions have been implemented. Students are also referred back to the video they watched at the previous stop and asked to investigate the heliostat mirrors from their new angle and to assess whether there is any lighting impact for the lower-level apartments.

Students then walk over to the Go-Get SuperPod (Stop #5) to read about the resident and community discount program and consider how this type of amenity can enhance future transit-oriented development (TOD) projects, and whether this kind amenity may be able to contribute to reducing cars and traffic in the city. From here, students also get a great view of the historic brewery chimney and its reuse as an exhaust chimney for the central thermal plant, as well as the three cooling towers that protrude from the top of the old brewery building. Students are provided additional learning support discussing the central thermal plant to help them understand what they are seeing as they circle the old Brewery; this information links back to and builds upon the pre-class online learning module students completed in preparation for the class session, and demonstrates how historic buildings can be repurposed as well as it enables students to see the concepts implemented in place.

Stop #6 has students walking back across the park and through to the other side of the precinct. Here, they investigate the historic preservation and conservation of historic worker terraces as part of the Spice Alley food market. Students consider how conservation can add value and help amenitize a project as well as how the creation of ethnic food markets, such as Spice Alley, can contribute to addressing the diversity and inclusion agenda of Resilient Sydney (a policy initiative that was previously discussed in class).

The final stop on the tour walks students back towards campus with a stop (#7) at DUO 84, a newer green wall and garden designed to be protected from the tunneled winds coming down Broadway. This installation demonstrates how lessons learned from earlier installations across the precinct have improved the installation method and efficiency, demonstrating current best practices in urban greening.

Activity deliverable

When teams have completed both activities, they return to the classroom to create a PowerPoint or Word presentation that incorporates the photographs they have taken and the responses to the discussion/reflection questions in the guide. It is common to hear teams talking in animated voices about what they have seen and learned and enthusiastically working out what highlights/key points they want to include from their discussions.

The activity is focused on enabling the students to actualize their learning, rather than being a formal assessment, per se. As such, the assignment has a low point value towards their overall grade for the class. Teams earn one point for each question answered and each photo taken (max. 12 points each). Up to three bonus points can be earned from the photos. Despite the low point value for the bonus, many student teams actively try to earn the bonus points by finding and taking unique photos/perspectives/insights at each stop to capture interesting insights about the installations and/or their learning experience. Informal feedback indicates that this extra effort further helps them to understand the concepts/understand the technical implementation which they are investigating.

For smaller classes where we can complete both the green roof tour and scavenger hunt activities more quickly, I will ask student groups to volunteer to share their photos and insights. This is always a great opportunity for peer learning.

Student and industry feedback

The Central Park scavenger hunt is a highlight of the Resilient Urban Development course and one that students rave about on student feedback surveys. Not only is the scavenger hunt a fun, engaging activity that gets students out and learning onsite, but both the deliverable for the activity and the student feedback indicate that the scavenger hunt facilitates a deeper learning experience for students to ensure they understand how they can apply what they have learned in practice. Students note that the activity helps them to link together concepts learned throughout the term, to reinforce the concepts to ensure they are properly learned, and to link the theoretical discussion with the practical application of associated sustainability interventions. Feedback from students also indicates that the activity effectively promotes a deeper learning of concepts learned in class. For example, the activity prompted one student to undertake additional learning on their own time "When I did the site tour of Blackwattle Bay in my own time, the work we had done in groups at Central Park helped massively," while another student notes that "the knowledge [they] have obtained [from identifying and reflecting on learned concepts in the scavenger hunt] has quite literally transformed my view on the importance of considering sustainability when engaging in a development."

Furthermore, when we did student focus groups as part of a recent curriculum redevelopment, students from the course indicated that they now feel empowered to have conversations with their employers about what they have learned and to make suggestions on projects where interventions may be appropriate but are not currently being considered. It is important to note that student feedback themes align with the subject learning objectives focusing on "understanding the relationships among urban structure, resource consumption, and sustainability at the urban, precinct and/or building level" as well as "understanding the challenges and practical application of principles of environmental, economic, and social sustainability to urban development at the urban and precinct scales" and "understand the environmental risks posed by patterns of development, the strategies available to manage risk, and adapt urban development patterns to mitigate risk."

Similarly, industry partners and industry advisory board members highlighted that this activity is one their student workers talk about with them at work, noting this activity as a "best practice example" of an applied, experiential learning activity that effectively assists students to actualize their in-class knowledge in a manner that helps prepare them for work in industry. Employers have told us that students from this class are confident when talking about sustainability interventions for buildings as well as larger urban resilience challenges to which their projects can contribute solutions.

Conclusion

While this subject focuses on resilient urban development, the experiential learning activity described is extremely adaptable to other real estate/property development classes focused on valuation, property management, construction, market analysis, and so forth. For example, in a valuation subject, one might have students investigating a particular building to assess its value, and incorporate a scavenger hunt to help them fully understand key valuation concepts (e.g. location importance, surrounding uses, site characteristics, building characteristics, etc.). Or, in a property management subject, student teams might be split up to visit different grade-A buildings to identify amenities (e.g. elevator [type], dashboards for communication, sustainability measures, tenant engagement activities, or whatever other factors are relevant in the local market). Students in a construction or development subject might be asked to visit a building and identify LEED (Greenstar, BREEAM, WELL rating system) attributes and use these to assess the building's "green" rating.

The scavenger hunt activity described above is an award-winning (was recognized as part of a received learning and teaching award in 2022), 7-year-tested experiential learning strategy that can be used to teach any subject where students can investigate concepts in an applied, real-world setting. The activity has not significantly changed since its inception, although it has been refined through the years. Originally, it was offered in week 2 to "set the stage" for what students would learn in the subject. However, this placement ultimately ended up being more of an icebreaker activity than facilitating a deeper learning of concepts, as it *preceded* the learning modules. The placement of the activity was quickly identified as a missed opportunity and it was moved, along with the sustainable precincts learning module, to the penultimate week. This change has been supported when students were asked to consider the activity's placement in the subject curriculum on the end-of-term student feedback survey. The initial delivery of the activity also did not include the green roofs tour;

this was added post-Covid to bolster student learning of green roofs presented in the sustainable precinct's module. Combining the activities serves the additional benefit of helping to manage the larger class sizes and size restrictions for groups and enables us to have flexibility in its deliverable. During Covid, the scavenger hunt was re-envisioned as an online activity where students worked in teams (offer some social connection during a challenging time for many students) and "walked the site" using video materials created to simulate walking through the activity, Google maps and Google images. Despite being online, this was still a popular activity, demonstrating the power of participatory, experiential learning.

Although this chapter focuses on how the scavenger hunt activity was applied in an undergraduate elective, it should be noted that it has been utilized successfully in a similar postgraduate subject. Student feedback surveys and comments (from both undergraduate and postgraduate cohorts) indicate that students at both levels value the learning experience and feel it has helped them to consolidate their learning, while our industry partners have offered feedback that this activity builds confidence in students to talk about the application/integration of sustainability and urban resilience concepts and interventions on projects they are undertaking in the workplace.

Although some students may initially start off the activity less enthusiastically, experience has shown that by the completion of the activity, students are typically engaged and enthusiastic about their learning. Working through the activity prompts, students focus on key concepts, identify implemented interventions, and have in-depth discussions amongst their teams about the success of the interventions and how they might use this information in their future careers. Taking photos at each stop helps them to capture their learning and keeps the activity fun as team members must be included in photos (this also ensures all students participate). Because the scavenger hunt is a student-led, team-based learning activity, students feel empowered in their learning, with peer-learning opportunities presenting themselves naturally. Students note that the activity assists with learning and applying the class material in an authentic practice-focused manner, and our experience after running this activity for seven years (and from the quality of the student deliverables) has shown it produces incredibly positive student learning outcomes. Ultimately, the hands-on learning offered in the activity cannot be achieved by reading about concepts in a textbook or replicated in a traditional classroom-based lecture setting.

References

Barclay, L. A., & York, K. M. (1996). The scavenger hunt exercise: Symbols of organizational culture. *Journal of Management Education*, *20*(1), 125–128. https://doi.org/10.1177/105256299602000113

Frontczak, N. T. (1998). A paradigm for the selection, use and development of experiential learning activities in marketing education. *Marketing Education Review*, *8*(3), 25–33. https://doi.org/10.1080/10528008.1998.11488641

Kolb, D. A. (1984). *Experiential learning: Experience as the source of learning and development*. Englewood Cliffs, NJ: Prentice-Hall.

Krakowka, A. R. (2012). Field trips as valuable learning experiences in geography courses. *Journal of Geography*, *111*(6), 236–244. https://doi.org/10.1080/00221341.2012.707674

Lumpkin, A., Achen, R. M., & Dodd, R. K. (2015). Student perceptions of active learning. *College Student Journal*, *49*(1), 121–133.

Rugan, E. G., & Nero, M. D. (2013). Library scavenger hunts: The good, the bad, and the ugly. *The Southeastern Librarian*, *61*(3), 7–10.

Shahanaz, D. (2018). Meta-analysis on experiential learning in management education. *Management Today*, *8*(1), 95–102.

Thyroff, A. (2019). Teaching qualitative marketing research: An experiential approach. *Marketing Education Review*, *29*(1), 75–87. https://doi.org/10.1080/10528008.2018.1514979

Tinnon, E. A. (2014). Scavenger hunt: A creative teaching strategy to introduce pharmacological concepts and ethical concerns. *Teaching and Learning in Nursing*, *9*(3), 104–107. https://doi.org/10.1016/j.teln.2014.03.004

Wurdinger, S., & Allison, P. (2017). Faculty perceptions and use of experiential learning in higher education. *Journal of e-Learning and Knowledge Society*, *13*(1), 27–38.

Chapter 6

Negotiating a real estate strategy in a shrinking city

A case study

Tobias Just

Introduction: Shrinking cities

Demographic developments are among the key determinants of real estate demand (Mankiw & Weil, 1989). The number of households is decisive for housing market dynamics, while the number of people of working age is one of the factors determining demand for office space. Real estate investors and project developers are primarily interested in investing in growing cities when it comes to urban development, and indeed, the global trend towards urbanization has remained intact for centuries (Glaeser, 2011). However, urbanization is not a linear process. Economic and societal structural change has repeatedly led to phases of urban decline. The rise and fall of great powers have always been accompanied by the rise and fall of great cities (Kennedy, 1987). In most cases, the phenomenon of shrinking cities is a gradual process that also requires specific real estate expertise, and this too is a global phenomenon (Pallagst et al., 2013).

For example, the population of the US cities Buffalo, Pittsburgh, Cleveland and Detroit fell by almost 50% between 1970 and 2006 (Hartley, 2013), and in a recent study, Sutradhar et al. (2024) conclude in their simulations for the development of the United States that by 2100, around half of the approximately 30,000 US-cities will be affected by population decline. And even in China, which has experienced strong urban growth in recent decades, numerous cities are simultaneously shrinking (Wang et al., 2022).

Such population declines can lead to sharp decreases in property values, and this also implies that urban infrastructure is underutilized. Consequently, it is more difficult for new businesses to settle in the area, as infrastructure costs rise. This can set in motion a downward spiral that can be slowed or even halted if measures are taken early to limit the shrinkage process. Thus, it is important for real estate professionals with assets in shrinking locations and for city representatives to look at the dynamics in these regions.

DOI: 10.1201/9781032656458-6

This chapter analyzes an idealized situation of a shrinking German city in the form of a case study. Students are assigned in teams with different roles and asked to develop a negotiation strategy for this case study, and then to present it in a real negotiation session with the other stakeholder groups, in order to achieve a good result for their specific role and the city, respectively.

Case studies are particularly suitable for deepening teaching content and highlighting specific aspects that have been discussed in class. These lessons become clearer because actual cities, projects, and actors can be linked. Students learn critical thinking skills and increase their problem-solving skills. Hypotheses for a solution must be developed and are then tested for their realism in the discussion (Lundeberg et al., 1999). Overall, case studies make it easier for students to relate theory to practical problems. This better prepares them for challenges in their future work (Herreid, 2011). In this specific example, students also learn three other aspects. First, strategy is the result of a team effort. Second, students learn to defend their strategy before other groups. Third, during the negotiation, students learn that urban projects can give rise to unplanned dynamics that must either be prepared for or responded to quickly. Preparing for and following up on such negotiation cases is therefore an important experience for students.

The case of a shrinking Eastern German city

Preliminary remarks

The case study is used within a lecture of a real estate MBA program. Students hold at least an undergraduate degree, have a basic knowledge of real estate economics, and on average, five years of professional experience in the real estate industry. The fact that this group is very heterogeneous may be an advantage, but it is not necessary for the purposes of using the case. The case is part of a lecture on the implications of demographic developments for real estate markets. Students have learnt beforehand which factors are decisive for demand and supply and, consequently, price developments, and how structural changes lead to demographic processes, which in turn impact on the real estate industry.

In the preparatory lecture, current population projections are discussed and price estimates based on positive or negative population dynamics are addressed. The varying time lags on the supply side compared to the demand side are an important aspect, because excess supply persists for a long time in cities with declining populations.

The effects of an ageing population on structural changes in demand on the housing market are also discussed in the lecture, namely that there will be more demand for senior-friendly apartments and fewer single-family homes in an ageing population.

Students also heard introductions to behavioral economics and game theory. Though negotiation strategy is only taught later during this program, it is reasonable that students get some basic concepts in preparing a negotiation beforehand. In our case, the students are experienced real estate professionals with average work experience of five years, who have usually previously led negotiations during their careers.

The teaching case presented here describes an ideal-typical (not real) situation in an East German municipality from which many young people moved away following reunification in the early 1990s. Within a few years, the population in Eastern German cities shrank rapidly and the remaining population continues to age (Burdett, 2006; Just, 2013). The resilience of local households can be fostered by a sense of ownership or belonging to the region, the convenience of being located near favorite shops or other amenities, appealing views, proximity to family and friends, as well as a positive relationship with neighbors (Wiles et al., 2009). Moreover, housing supply responds more slowly to a decrease in demand by comparison with its reaction to an increase in demand. In many cities, the building stock has not yet been adapted to the new requirements, as there are very different interests among stakeholders. Vacancy then remains elevated for a long time, leading to disamenities for the population (Accordino & Johnson, 2000).

The case: A small city in Eastern Germany

The demographic and economic development in this case does not describe a specific situation, but a development that was seen in many cities in Eastern Germany: for example Rostock or Chemnitz, the number of inhabitants fell by 20% in the years after 1990, and in the cities of Suhl or Gera by as much as one third. Even though all these cities have since bottomed out (see Exhibit 6.1), none of them have reached the population levels of the years prior to reunification, and smaller peripheral cities have seen a permanent decline in population. Above all, development in these Eastern German cities has also been worse in recent years than in many Western German cities. The average development of all independent cities in Germany has been significantly more positive than in the above-mentioned Eastern German cities.

As Germany experienced significant positive net immigration from southern and Eastern Europe, particularly during the years 2009–2022,

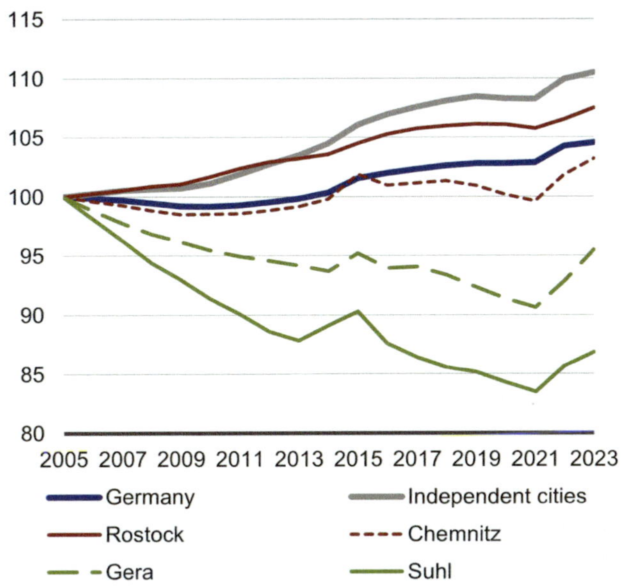

Exhibit 6.1 A graph showing the population in different German regions.

the population in many German municipalities is likely to shrink again in the next few decades when net immigration might diminish.

Four teams (City, Public housing, Private landlords, Tenants) of approximately four to six students are formed for this case study. The mayor represents the city and has two advisors who help him or her in terms of argumentation. From the lecture notes, students can learn about expected price declines in demographically challenged cities as well as typical price and rent burdens in such regions experiencing population decline. It is important to note that prices and rents in these cities are significantly lower than in attractive regions with high levels of migration. This is important because it means that tenant households are not necessarily suffering from significant financial strain and investors can only expect low returns.

Students are asked to develop a negotiation strategy for a discussion the next morning in class. This preparation can be done within 90 minutes, but it is recommended that students develop their negotiation strategy as homework the day before negotiations. Students may use the internet and the lecture material on demographics.

The case study enables students to apply lessons learned from course materials to test their understanding of:

- **Demographic trends:** Students will learn in an applied manner that trends must be addressed at an early stage, as the challenges increase every year, and a downward spiral can develop.
- **Establishing partners:** The strongest negotiating partners in shrinking regions are sometimes different from those in growth regions. This must be taken into account in negotiation situations.
- **Public–private sector collaboration:** Good solutions in shrinking regions require cooperation between the private and public sectors and sometimes the reconfiguration of familiar structures.

The case study relates to the housing market of the ideal-typical (not real) town of Gonelitz in Eastern Germany. The number of inhabitants has fallen by around 20,000 to 50,000 since 1990 and, according to current projections by the State Statistical Office, the number of inhabitants could fall by a further 10,000 over the next 20 years. The unemployment rate is 10% and there are no metropolitan regions in the immediate vicinity.

There are currently 30,000 residential units in Gonelitz, 5,000 of which are vacant. Most of the vacant residential units are in typical prefabricated housing estates that were erected during the time of the GDR. Many of these buildings suffer from a refurbishment backlog. Most of them are held by a municipal housing association. This municipal housing association holds approximately 25% of the total housing stock in Gonelitz, a figure matched in many Eastern German cities 20 years ago (even if only a few municipalities still have such a high proportion today). Another quarter of the apartments are owned by large private companies, a quarter by small private landlords, and a quarter by homeowners. These figures are based on typical ownership structures in eastern German cities. In fact, the home ownership rate in many cities is even lower than 25%.

In addition to the typical East German prefabricated housing estates, there is also a historic city center characterized by half-timbered houses. Some of these are listed historic buildings, have poor energy efficiency, and are mostly not barrier-free/handicap accessible. This is an important aspect, as the population in Gonelitz will age rapidly in the coming years, with the number of over-80-year-olds, for example, set to triple in the next few decades. This ageing is worsening because the younger residents are moving away, and this has led to the population decline. It is therefore important to adapt the housing stock to the shrinking number of inhabitants on the one hand, and to the growing number of old people with limited mobility on the other hand.

Different discussion groups

The class is divided into four groups. In the "City" group, one student is designated as the mayor and takes on the role of moderator of the negotiation. The mayor is assisted by two advisors. The mayor and his team are given the task of designing a housing strategy for Gonelitz. This strategy should take demographic trends and fiscal limits into account and must be capable of gaining majority support.

The remaining students are distributed randomly and evenly among the other three groups (teams) representing: (1) the municipal housing association, (2) private landlords and homeowners, and (3) tenants. To make the discussion more complex, the group of private landlords can be subdivided into large and small owners or into homeowners and investors. However, this distinction is not necessary to obtain the main findings. Each group acts as a team. This means that they need to arrive at a single strategy that represents their team, that is, the tenants team. If there is more time, it is possible (and interesting) to subdivide the groups into smaller, diverse sub-teams (e.g. one group could be young tenants and another group could be older tenants).

Each of the four groups receives a worksheet (see Exhibit 6.2) with preparatory questions. Each team is then given the task of preparing for

Exhibit 6.2 Preparatory worksheet for the negotiation round

	City	*Public housing*	*Private landlords*	*Tenants*
What are your targets for this meeting? Prioritize				
With whom do you want to cooperate?				
What can you offer to other negotiation partners? Why should they cooperate with you?				
What information do you have?				
What information do you need? (Make assumptions)				
What is your greatest challenge/risk?				
What is your greatest opportunity?				

negotiation the following day. The teams should fill out this table and are asked to anticipate the perspectives of their negotiating partners.

Typical negotiation dynamics

The mayor is asked to open the meeting. She/he can explain her/his strategy, but this is not mandatory. In most cases, the mayor decides to outline a rough plan. This plan usually consists of three elements: moderate demolition of existing properties (prefabricated buildings), incentives to move to the old town, and investment in low-barrier/handicap accessible housing. Financing is usually open.

Negotiations then unfold across three dynamics: (1) the municipal housing company tries to justify its raison d'être by offering affordable rents; (2) the private housing companies defend themselves against possible demolition and try to acquire shares of the municipal housing company; and (3) tenants fight for affordable rents and resist change.

The municipal housing association recognizes two strategic partners: the tenants, as protection against the possibility of sale, and the mayor, as the person with authority to issue directives. Landlords usually act as if they are financially strong problem-solvers who want to acquire assets. They try to push down the price of the public housing association's units (in the event of these being offered for sale). It is important to note that students can perceive from the lecture material that landlords and private investors are not necessarily rich, as house prices have likely come down in this city. What is more, tenants often act cautiously, rarely with a problem-solving mindset. Here, it is important to note that students can perceive from the lecture material that tenants are not necessarily poor, as their rents have not been rising. So, at least the group of employed tenants spends a comparatively lower proportion of their income on housing, which is significantly less than households in attractive metropolises.

Small and large landlords often have different perspectives. This leads to tensions and can weaken the negotiating position of the landlords. If two different landlord groups are involved, the mayor and the tenants will try to polarize the interests of the two groups. In both scenarios, the position of the landlords is diluted and thus weakened during negotiations.

Most negotiations end with the mayor drafting a strategy that includes partial sale of the municipal housing company to private housing companies (usually the larger ones) with a redevelopment requirement. Partial demolition is also considered in order to make the city center relatively more attractive. Business relocation, tourism, and national funding opportunities are often discussed as *deus ex machina*, or as unexpected solutions to a seemingly unsolvable problem.

Lessons learned

This case study is taught at the end of a lecture on demographics and real estate within the economics course of an executive MBA class. Students learn that demographic developments have significant impact on real estate market dynamics: unexpected outward migration leads to falling rents and prices, and ageing leads to structural shifts within the demand for housing.

As part of this case study, students are expected to apply this knowledge to the case of a shrinking city. During the discussion, students will deepen their understanding of theories and recognize the asymmetry of price reactions in growing and shrinking cities. Students will also learn to develop their own small-scale negotiation strategies in an urban context, to present these to others (within their respective team and between teams), and to understand that in such negotiations, not all parties can win when a shrinking pie has to be divided.

The case is not so much about applying specific negotiation tactics, these will be taught later in the following management module, but after the case study ends, it is reasonable to give feedback on students' negotiation styles and tactics. Students can apply what they have learned in lectures on behavioral economics and game theory, as the case study also involves searching for potential negotiating partners.

At the end of the case study, students are directed to key questions: first, who are the most powerful people in the negotiation process (follow the power). Often, reference is then made either to the mayor or to the landlords. The representatives of the municipal housing association are very quickly recognized as powerless. Their vacancy rate is high, so the need for a state-owned housing company is questionable. The decision to sell is logical. It is therefore understandable that the representatives of the municipal housing association are often the most vocal group, as they have a lot to lose.

Tenants could have the greatest influence during the negotiation process, as they are the largest group in terms of numbers, have at least one common denominator (affordable rents), and can use this to put pressure on the mayor. Regardless of whether they rent out many or few properties, private landlords are likely to have their hands tied to some degree when setting rents, in view of the relatively high vacancy rate in the city and the existence of a municipal housing association with rental problems. Residential rents in Gonelitz are low. In fact, real residential rents fell significantly in many Eastern German cities during the years of population decline.

It is therefore also unlikely that private landlords would want to take over the local authority's existing properties at a price that would satisfy the local authority. There would have to be considerable financial incentives. At the same time, because tenants would then possibly expect a medium-term housing supply shortage and therefore rising rents, resistance to such sales is to be expected. Given the low homeownership rate, tenants have significant political power, as they are a relatively homogenous and numerically strong group.

The second question during debriefing is who in Gonelitz is most likely to have the financial means to renovate/restructure existing buildings (follow the money). In most conversations, students respond that this is the private landlords. This reflects the everyday experience of many students, characterized by the fact that landlords are wealthier than tenants. However, this is not likely true in this case because the population is ageing and the unemployment rate of 10%, though still elevated, is significantly lower than 20 years ago. At the same time, rents in Gonelitz are likely to be low. At around EUR 6 per square meter in Suhl or Gera, housing rents are about one third square meter of those in Munich or Frankfurt and less than half those in Berlin. However, disposable incomes in Suhl or Gera are like those in Berlin and merely one third lower than those in Munich. In a city like Gonelitz, people in employment – 90% of the working population – are therefore likely to have a comparatively high residual income (net income minus monthly recurring expenses for housing, insurance, or mobility). On the other hand, it will be difficult for many landlords to build up sufficient reserves from current rental income to carry out renovation and maintenance investments. In this case, tenants are therefore both politically influential and financially strong. What is more, private landlords would require and negotiate financial assistance for renovation. Tenants might do so less, as they internalize the benefits of renovation in case of ownership (no tenant–landlord dilemma).

A solution must therefore always place great emphasis on the interests of tenants. It is therefore essential that the mayor form a close alliance with tenants. In this respect, it is remarkable that in most negotiations, the mayor first gives the floor to either landlords or the municipal housing company. This makes no sense either politically or in terms of negotiating tactics. Students learn how to structure negotiations strategically.

Most groups try to solve the case by increasing immigration. However, this will ultimately require a solution outside of the case: recruiting a company, additional support measures, or infrastructure expansion. If the mayor were to succeed in stopping outward migration, the net result for the city would be similar. This could be achieved by increasing the home ownership rate, as willingness to move decreases with home ownership, especially in countries with high transaction costs (Germany). In this respect, the sale of the municipal company's housing stock to create private residential property could be in the interests of the city and its residents, that is, the mayor and tenants. As the proceeds from vacant residential units are negative, even giving away individual units would be part of the solution.

With this case, students learn that the recommendations "follow the money" and "follow the power" do not always lead to the actors who are the usual suspects, and that negotiators must be prepared to understand the interests of all negotiation partners. In addition, it is learned that loud negotiating partners (in this case the municipal housing associations) can sometimes be ignored if they have neither money nor influence. A strong mayor could prevent vocal representatives of the housing association from taking the floor or even exclude them from negotiations. The significance of municipal housing associations can also be discussed in this case. In regions with a growing vacancy rate and low rents, public housing stock can be put to the test more quickly than in tight housing markets, where economic and political perspectives always clash.

The limitations of this case lie in the fact that it involves the restructuring of a structurally weak area and that initially, it is primarily about reducing a growing problem. This cannot provide a sustainable solution to the urban structural problem. Ultimately, there is no clearly calculable solution here, as neither rents, vacancies, costs, nor income are explicitly mentioned. The solution to the case, however, lies partly in the lecture notes (low relative housing costs and high transaction costs) and partly in structuring the negotiation and analyzing the different interests.

For the mayor, it is important to communicate clear goals at the outset and to recognize that the tenants are his or her most important partners because they represent most of the city. The mayor should try to use the public housing association as a bargaining chip. It should not play a major role in the discussion. It will be important for investors to recognize that tenants can bear part of the necessary investment costs; they are not necessarily poor. It is equally important to recognize that investors have only limited resources of their own.

In addition, students receive feedback on whether they were able to communicate their strategy clearly and whether they arrived at a jointly supported strategy as a team. This is not always the case and can result in the team being divided by others. For example, if there are differing views between private homeowners and institutional investors, a skillful mayor can exploit a disagreement to formulate an offer to just one subgroup.

A good result is achieved when, at the end of the discussion, the mayor proposes a strategy that the tenants and some of the investors can agree to, that is, because the investment burden is shared between these groups. To this end, part of the Public Housing Association's housing stock could be sold to tenants in order to increase homeownership. Because rents are low, there is no great need for a separate municipal company. The city can channel any proceeds from the sale into maintaining the city center.

There is no formal evaluation (grades) for this case study, as it is an exercise within the context of a lecture. The case can be supplemented by a sustainability aspect, as many vacant buildings from the GDR era are energy inefficient. Privatization allowing former tenants to become owners of their property would also make sense from this perspective, because here too the typical tenant–landlord dilemma would be resolved more easily by internalizing the energy costs saved after refurbishment than in a rental situation.

Finally, the discussion can be livened up by the moderator taking on the role of the media and sending messages, for example, in form of giving additional information, to individual groups. For example, news could circulate that a foreign private equity investor is interested in the public housing company and is proposing a price significantly above the net asset value. A new party that radically represents tenant interests could also be announced, or a radical citizens' movement could be formed. This sometimes helps to revitalize discussions but is not decisive for solving the case.

Conclusion

The case study relates to Germany, but many of the lessons can also be applied to shrinking cities in other countries. The main lesson is that these issues are not insignificant and that many cities have experienced periods of declining budgets and that this has led to considerable challenges for the real estate sector. Students should learn from this case study that there is often no simple market solution but that a joint urban strategy is needed. This can, but does not have to, be moderated by city representatives. Students also learn that there may still be investment opportunities in such cities, but that these are more likely to be found in submarkets than in the real estate market. Therefore, distribution problems arise.

Teaching with such a stylized case study gives students the opportunity to take on roles, combine their theoretical considerations with practical suggestions and, above all, present these to a group. Discussion also deepens their understanding of the concepts, as students are forced to justify their positions.

The case study is part of a lecture on demographics within an executive MBA program. Students have an undergraduate degree and about five years of professional experience. If you want to use a similar case study in an undergraduate lecture, this should take place towards the end of the course, and students will need more preparatory material, for example, statistics on rent levels, prices, incomes, and a short textbook text on the implications of shrinking cities (e.g. Pallagst et al., 2013).

References

Accordino, J., & Johnson, G. T. (2000). Addressing the vacant and abandoned property problem. *Journal of Urban Affairs*, *22*(3), 301–315. https://doi.org/10.1111/0735-2166.00058

Burdett, R. (2006). *German Cities: Success Beyond Growth? Urban Age*. London School of Economics. Retrieved from http://eprints.lse.ac.uk/33352/1/Burdett_German_cities_2006.pdf

Glaeser, E. (2011). *Triumph of the City. How Our Greatest Invention Makes Us Richer, Smarter, Ggreener, and Happier*. Penguin Books.

Hartley, D. (2013). Urban decline in rust-belt cities. *Economic Commentary*, *2013*(06). Federal Reserve of Cleveland. https://doi.org/10.26509/frbc-ec-201306

Herreid, C. F. (2011). Case study teaching. *New Directions for Teaching and Learning*, *2011*(128), 31–40. https://doi.org/10.1002/tl.466

Just, T. (2013). *Demografie und Immobilien* [Demographics and real estate] (2nd ed.). Oldenbourg.

Kennedy, P. (1987). *The Rise and Fall of the Great Powers*. Random House.

Lundeberg, M. A., Levin, B. B., & Harrington, H. L., (Eds.). (1999). *Who Learns What From Cases and How? The Research Base for Teaching and Learning with Cases*. Routledge.

Mankiw, G. N., & Weil, D. N. (1989). The baby boom, the baby bust, and the housing market. *Regional Science and Urban Economics*, *19*(2), 235–258. https://doi.org/10.1016/0166-0462(89)90005-7

Pallagst, K., Wiechmann, T., & Martinez-Fernandez, C. (Eds.). (2013). *Shrinking Cities: International Perspectives and Policy Implications*. Routledge. https://doi.org/10.4324/9780203597255

Sutradhar, U., Spearing, L., & Derrible, S. (2024). Depopulation and associated challenges for US cities by 2100. *Nature Cities*, *1*, 51–61. https://doi.org/10.1038/s44284-023-00011-7

Wang, Q, Xin., Z., & Niu, F. (2022). Analysis of the spatio-temporal patterns of shrinking cities: Evidence from nighttime light. *Land*, *11*(6), 871. https://doi.org/10.3390/land11060871

Wiles, J. L., Allen, R. E. S., Palmer, A. J., Hayman, K. J., Keeling, S., & Kerse, N. (2009). Older people and their social spaces: A study of well-being and attachment to place in Aotearoa New Zealand. *Social Science & Medicine*, *68*(4), 664–671. https://doi.org/10.1016/j.socscimed.2008.11.030

Chapter 7

Appraisal in the classroom

John A. Kilpatrick

Introduction

Real estate valuation is a critical part of a real estate program. Both undergraduate and graduate students should at least be introduced to aspects of valuation, preferably as an exciting capstone before they go on to their real estate careers. In a business curriculum, the course goes together with investments, perhaps even integrated with it, and should methodologically coordinate. In a non-business curriculum, such as urban planning, the valuation coursework is necessary as there are so many cost-benefit analysis decisions regarding the built environment. Appraisals are vital to public policy decision making, in eminent domain decisions, property taxation, and urban redesign.

Many of the teaching tools available for appraisal courses were designed for training professional appraisers, and thus treat the discipline as entirely self-contained, rather than part of a larger academic exploration. While this chapter cannot cure this, perhaps it can outline ways to adapt existing tools to make the valuation part of the curriculum more enjoyable for the students and teachers, with an eye to how valuation fits within the bigger picture of the real estate industry and an academic major.

This chapter does *not* anticipate teaching or training students to become practicing appraisers. That would be a very different curriculum taught in a very different way. Instead, the target audience here is faculty who recognize that real estate students will deal with appraisals regularly and will need to understand some of the fundamentals to better use those tools in the bigger real estate equation.

Market efficiency and the need for valuation

Business students will learn the efficient markets hypothesis as part of their finance training, but students from other disciplines may need a brief

DOI: 10.1201/9781032656458-7

introduction. This holds that in an informationally efficient market, prices should already reflect available information. If a market for a particular asset is efficient, then market prices should already reflect market value and so in theory an appraisal is unnecessary. Of course, even highly efficient securities markets have some inefficiency, which gives rise to a huge industry of stock market analysts.

Real estate markets are famously inefficient, both informationally and transactionally. Buyers and sellers may have very different preferences, information, and motivations. Transactions require a significant and costly amount of intermediation.

Most appraisals in the United States are conducted for one of five reasons:

1. To assure a lender that the underlying collateral (a fee simple interest in the real estate) is sufficient to support a mortgage.
2. To aid the tax assessor in property taxation.
3. To determine market value in eminent domain actions.
4. To aid investors in investment and disposition decisions, including property renovation or redevelopment.
5. Estate management, probate, or matrimonial dissolution.

Usually, the appraisal will be based on contemporaneous sales of like-kind properties (Sales Comparison Approach), by an analysis of future cash flows using net present value techniques (Income Approach), and/or by some kind of replacement cost analysis (Cost Approach). In most circumstances, though, no contemporaneous sale of identical property is available. Even if the contemporaneous sale of the property itself existed (as in the case of an appraisal for a mortgage loan on a newly acquired property), that sale is only one data point in an analysis and may or may not reflect market value at a given point in time.

Broad outline of the academic appraisal course

Understanding that no two curricula will be identical, initial questions should be asked concerning how the appraisal body-of-knowledge will fit into the overall program. Things to be considered include:

- Is this an undergraduate or graduate curriculum?
- In which academic discipline will this be located (business, urban planning, architecture, or other)?

- Will this be a stand-alone valuation course or integrated into another real estate course?
- If integrated, will it be a lower-level review course in real estate or an upper-level real estate investments or real estate market analysis course?

Depending on the answers to these questions, the overarching outline will be similar but likely with different emphases.

- **In a stand-alone valuation course developed for a business curriculum:** Additional emphasis may be placed on investment criteria, with a more direct tie into finance topics. Usually, this course will come after introductory courses in finance and real estate. Depending on how many courses the program has (typically more courses will be a major whereas less will be a concentration or minor) and the valuation course may be contemporaneous with real estate market research or investments.
- **In a stand-alone valuation course for a non-business curriculum (say, urban planning):** The emphasis may be on market research and highest-and-best use analyses.
- **In an undergraduate real estate program:** This course may be best taught as a lecture series with homework and exams focused on individual topics.
- **In a graduate program:** This course may surround a case study, broken into modules, with the final product being a rudimentary appraisal of a commercial property, with an emphasis on either investment (business) or redevelopment (urban planning) decision making.

This material can also be incorporated directly into a foundations course in many disciplines. As such, it would best fit later in the class after a full development of the real estate basics. Additionally, the valuation course may actually be the capstone after a series of courses on financial analysis, appraisal standards, and market research.

Specific contents of the academic appraisal course

A practitioner-oriented appraisal curriculum often begins with an extensive review of the history of valuation, the history of appraisal standards and regulation, and theoretical underpinnings of real estate economics. Much of this can be truncated for academic students, and the theoretical underpinnings will generally be referenced from prerequisite economics courses. The academic curriculum will dive directly into the fundamentals of appraisal methods.

What are you valuing

It may seem perfunctory, but appraisal standards set forth a series of steps to define this. Most appraisal assignments begin with some simple request from a client to "value the property at 123 Elm Street." Appraisers need to develop the scope of work in order to hone in on important questions which need to be asked at the onset. Common examples include:

- The valuation of an easement (in which case, the nature and extent of the easement needs to be fully understood).
- Valuation of a leasehold or leased fee estate.
- Valuation of a remainder estate.
- Valuation of a partial interest, such as a tenancy in common or a condominium subject to certain conditions and restrictions.

Often, the client doesn't realize that there are limitations on the bundles of rights which have implications for valuation, and the appraiser is in a teaching role to help the client understand.

- **Market value or some other kind of value:** Most appraisals in the United States are for federally regulated mortgages, tax assessments, or eminent domain acquisitions, and the focus is on the market value. Note that in some circumstances, such as an appraisal for portfolio value or in litigation, the term fair market value may be used with certain specific definitions applying. Alternative values may include, but are not limited to, value in use, liquidation value, or investment value.
- **Date of the valuation:** Most often, the effective date of the appraisal is contemporaneous with the date of the report itself. However, a valuation may be requested as of a date in the past, often to settle a dispute or an estate, or a date in the future, to value a property after completion of development. Note that appraisals are dependent on the market as it existed in the time leading up to the date of value. If a retrospective value is requested, then data from today cannot be used to value the property, other than to confirm market trends.
- **Conditions of the assignment:** Clients will often impose certain conditions, or in the case of Federally funded acquisitions, legal instructions. Appraisers are obligated by law not to accept instructions from a client, even legal instructions, which would impair the credibility of the analysis.

- **Extraordinary assumptions and hypothetical conditions:** The former are assumptions which are believed to be true, but if found to be false could have a material impact on the appraisal. For example, the appraiser believes that the zoning will be changed and has substantial support backing this up. The latter is a condition which is known to be false but is invoked for specific purposes. For example, a contaminated site may be valued as if it was clean to settle a legal dispute. In both circumstances, the appraisal must clearly delineate the assumption or condition and note that it has an impact on the value determination.

All of these scope-of-work determinations serve as important predicates to the analysis itself and must be determined even before data is gathered. Answers to these questions indicate what data will be informative or not.

Market research and the highest and best use analysis

An appraisal is typically focused on either a site in search of a use or a use in search of a site. The former is typically the appraisal problem, while the latter is generally the purview of economic geographers. However, there is an immense overlap between these two disciplines.

The statistically minded should begin to see that, appraisal practice is Bayesian. This is particularly apparent in market analysis, where a skilled and experienced appraiser will base the analysis on surrounding land uses, prior knowledge of the market, and experience with particular property types.

Valuation is mostly focused on a specific existing or proposed property in a specific location. The current or proposed use will drive the market research which will feed the highest and best use (HBU) analysis. Valuation is interested in market demand for a particular use versus the market supply of competing properties. This implies delineation of a market area, which will differ depending on the nature of the property. A single-family residence may only compete with similar residences in the same neighborhood, while a super-regional shopping mall may draw customers from many miles around. If the existing use of the property is also the HBU, then market area delineation and market research are greatly simplified. However, if this is a property with a potentially higher and better use, or if the appraiser has been asked to explore alternative uses for a development site, then the market research is probably more complex than the ultimate valuation exercise which it drives.

Market research often does not get the attention it deserves, since there is a presumption that the current use is also the HBU. All too many appraisals simply present a raft of economic and demographic data in the place of real market area delineation and market research, and reach a predetermined conclusion about the property use. In an academic setting, the market research discussion really provides students with an opportunity to bring to the table other tools and techniques from other courses and life experiences. Teachers using case studies in the classroom find this as one of the more enjoyable and useful portions of the course. Market research can be broken down as follows:

- What is the market segmentation for the property?
- What drives demand for the given property?
- What constitutes competing supply?
- How can we discern if the market is changing over time?

This drives the HBU analysis in the following steps:

1. What are the legally permissible uses for the site? Most often, this is dictated by current zoning, but it may hinge on probable zoning changes. This requires extraordinary assumptions about probable zoning changes, which must be based on a valid rationale. Other factors may include building codes, covenants, and restrictions on the site, pre-existing easements and permitted encroachments, or other regulatory restrictions.
2. Of the legally permissible uses, which ones are physically possible? Size, shape, ingress and egress, topography, and even geology of the site may impact the physical adaptability. Often the issue is a simple one. For example, a site may be zoned for retail, but an optimum retail establishment in this market will require off-street parking and the site is not sufficiently sized for both a building and off-street parking.
3. Of the uses which are legally permissible and physically possible, which ones are financially feasible? For a development site or a property which is in transition, this can be the most complex component of the entire appraisal. The question really is, will the economic benefit (i.e., the value) exceed the cost of putting a particular use in place? Naturally, the economic benefit is driven by market supply and demand factors and ultimately requires at least a cursory estimate of the final value. Hence, if there are alternative uses for the site, the appraiser will virtually need to value the property with each use in place, and then compare each of those uses to the cost of putting that use in place. By the time the appraiser has completed the financial feasibility step, the value of the site in alternative uses is actually known. Not every alternative

use may be financially feasible, and in some situations, there are no financially feasible uses for a given site. This may result from a high cost of construction, lack of market demand, or excessive supply of alternative properties in the market.

4. Of the uses which are financially feasible, which one and only one specific use results in the highest value.

This ties back to the definition of value determined in the scope of work decision. For example, market value usually refers to the most probable price resulting from an arms-length transaction. What if an appraiser finds that the most probable annual market rent for a retail establishment ranges from $20 to $25 per square foot. However, there is one outlier in the market, which is renting at $30, with no discernable explanation. Naturally, the client may want to value the property based on the $30 outlier, but since this is found not to be probable, a market value determination based on the higher rent would not be credible and the report would be misleading.

Any asset valuation, not just real estate, depends on market comparables, or "comps," which have recently sold in the same or similar market as the subject property. Valuing art, gems, businesses, collectables, and even automobiles, boats, and airplanes, all depend on comparable analyses. The outcome of the HBU analysis informs comparable selection. For example, if the HBU is determined to be a single-family residence, then other single-family residences in the same market which have recently sold would be used as comparables.

The HBU analysis should be conducted at least twice – once on the "as is" condition and once "as if vacant." If the value determination "as if vacant" is higher than the "as is" valuc, after accounting for the cost of demolishing the existing structure, then the HBU is a vacant development site irrespective of the current use of the property. For example, an older, dilapidated residence on the edge of a neighborhood in transition to commercial use may still have a few good years left in it as a dwelling, but the value of the vacant site, after accounting for demolishing the house, may be more than the existing use as a house.

Data gathering and preliminary analysis

Having determined an HBU for a property, what resources are available for gathering useful data? Broad market research often just uses secondary sources, but actual valuation will need specific data on recent sales, rental rates, construction costs, and land values. Sometimes this data was already gathered in the HBU portion of the assignment.

Complicating matters is the fact that there are some "non-disclosure" states, where transactional data is not recorded along with deed data at the courthouse. Data availability varies widely from state to state, and even from county to county within states.

Common sources of data will include:

- **Multiple listing services (MLS):** There are, at last count, about 440 MLS in the United States. In most cases, these are only useful for residential sales data, and while the data is usually quite complete, it should be verified carefully with an eye to property-specific hyperbole.
- **Local tax assessors:** The quality of data from this source varies from excellent to poor. Further, because the data is gathered and used for property tax purposes, it is not always up to date. In fact, in many jurisdictions, properties are only reassessed every few years. This data should be verified carefully.
- **Data aggregators:** There are presently several firms providing commercial and residential data by subscription. These serve as nationwide commercial MLSs and are dependent on volunteer contributions from real estate brokers and appraisers. The services are usually dependable and can provide good data in non-disclosure locations.
- **Local appraisers and brokers:** In non-disclosure states, appraisers and brokers can be very protective of data sources and will often charge other appraisers for data. However, for students and researchers doing local projects, they can often be very helpful.

What kind of data do your students need for a valuation?

- **Recent comparable sales data:** Recent arms-length transactions of comparable properties reflecting the same basis of value (market, investment, etc.) and the same bundle of rights (e.g., fee simple interest) are most important. What constitutes comparability? There is an overarching four-step process that most professionals use for this, usually taken in this order:
  - **Transactional comparability:** Property rights, financing terms, and sale conditions.
  - **Recency:** This may be one year for residences or commercial property, but several years for rural land.
  - **Location:** Typically. the same market, such as a neighborhood for residences but a broader market as determined in the market analysis for commercial property.
  - **Physical characteristics:** This last category can often be the most challenging. Most real estate in the United States is valued in some

fashion on a square foot basis (or acre for land or by room for a hotel). The physical size of the comparables should bracket the subject. Other physical characteristics to be considered include age, degree of depreciation, style (to the extent it is a material factor in valuation), construction quality, and important amenities. For example, valuing a high-rise Class "B" office building in the suburbs of a major city will usually require sales of other high-rise Class "B" offices similarly situated. Use of a Class "A" building in the CBD may not be useful without significant adjustments.

- **Recent comparable rental data:** This is of obvious importance for commercial properties that may be valued by investors based on capitalized income. However, residential rental data should be analyzed if there is significant investor interest in the neighborhood.
- **Construction cost data:** This may come from one of the national construction cost aggregation services or from local contractors, engineers, architects, or construction cost estimators.
- **Local comparable land data:** Local land value for sites comparable to the subject's location is important but may be unobtainable in built-up neighborhoods or areas where comparable development sites simply don't sell. Alternatively, one can use a land extraction technique to estimate the contributory value of the site to the sales of comparably situated properties. Note that the sales selected for such an analysis don't necessarily need to be comparable for the subject, just that the sites themselves need to be comparable. For example, if an appraiser valuing a downtown office building notes that a department store across the street on an identical lot just sold, then a land extraction applied to the department store sale could provide a good indicator of land values downtown.

Approaches to value

The data will be applied across alternative valuation methods which are bundled into three overarching categories, called the approaches to value.

The sales comparison approach directly compares the sales prices of comparable properties to the characteristics of the subject. Academics with a mathematical bent will recognize that as a regression model (also called the hedonic pricing model), which applied to a valuation problem, is a form of the sales comparison approach. In practice, appraisers use much smaller data sets and apply adjustments in a non-parametric, somewhat heuristic manner, to arrive at a reconciled indication of value. The adjustments are preferably quantitative, with mathematical adjustments made for property transactional, market conditions, locational, and physical characteristics (in that order). Specifically, which characteristics are used can be a function of property type, local practice, appraiser experience, and market forces. For example, the paint color of a house may influence buyers, but may not have any material impact on its value. The quantity and quality of elevators will have a material impact on the value of a high-rise office building, but not so on a two-story industrial building. Agricultural land will usually be valued as a function of its productivity for farming (there are actual metrics available for this) while residential development land will have very different metrics which are material to value.

Often, calculating specific mathematical adjustments is difficult and adjustments may not be linear. Alternatively, appraisers frequently rely on qualitative adjustments, such as rank-ordering the comparable properties based on various characteristics. For example, rank-ordering the sales of several office buildings, including the subject, based on square footage of available rental space may give a reasonable indication of the range of values. In the end, the valuer is trying to emulate the thought processes of market participants, keeping in mind the needs and expectations of the client as well as the methodology usually followed by other appraisers.

The income approach generally includes two different methods: income capitalization (similar to perpetuity valuation in finance) and discounted cash flow (net present value). The former is based on the typical way an investor will pay for an income-producing property. The appraiser computes a modified annual operating cash flow, called net operating income (NOI), which is all cash inflows and outflows before computing debt service, plus factors for likely vacancy and collection issues and reserves for replacement (which can be estimated with physical depreciation). The NOI is then divided by a capitalization rate ("cap rate"), which is usually determined by examining sales of comparable properties, as detailed below.

$$\text{Value} = \frac{\text{NOI}}{r}$$

In the absence of good comparables to estimate the cap rate, appraisers can use the band of investments method, which recognizes that the cap rate is the weighted average of the bank debt service rates on loans for property of this caliber and the required rate-of-return on investor equity for this type of property. Finance students will recognize the similarity to the weighted average cost of capital (WACC). The implicit assumptions are that NOI and cap rate are either stable or will change in a predictable manner over time.

$$r = (1 - \text{LTV})R_e + (\text{LTV})M$$

The discounted cash flow method is useful for projects with a finite duration and dissimilar annual cash flows. The periodic cash flows, negative or positive, are discounted back to the present using the expected or required investor rate of return. Debt service or interim interest on a development project, as well as capital infusions from debt or equity, are part of the cash flow determination. In a commercial development, which may have "lumpy" cash flows for a few years then turn into a steady positive cash flow at a predictable point in time, a capitalization method can be employed when the cash flows stabilize to determine the value as of that time in the future (e.g., the end of a development period when occupancy and cash flow level out) and then that value is discounted along with all of the other cash flows back to the present.

The cost approach recognizes that the value of a property is related to the cost of acquiring the land and constructing a replacement building, after accounting for depreciation, any functional or economic disutility, and adding the entrepreneurial incentives to undertake the project. Site values can be determined by gathering local sales data or conducting a land extraction from a recent sale, and construction costs can come from an estimating firm or a national data aggregator. The cost approach is the least reliable, but it is an important support for the other approaches and may be the only approach useful when there is limited sales data or when valuing specialized properties.

Reconciliation

The appraiser should now have three estimates of value: one from each of the three approaches. In a perfect world, these would all be close to one another. Indeed, the experienced appraiser will look for any differences among these three approaches to inform corrections during the analyses. The appraiser has to make a judgment as to whether one of the approaches is better supported by data, analytical accuracy, and emulating the thought processes of market participants. In some cases, the appraiser may weigh the indicated values from each of the approaches. The result of this process is the reconciled opinion of value. It is important to note that this is a professional opinion, informed by good data and recognized methods, but nonetheless an opinion.

A valuation case study

While this case study appears simple, it presents several basic concepts for students to understand the fundamentals of valuation. It could be used as a classroom discussion or it could be modified for students to complete some of the calculations. It is based on an actual appraisal with publicly available data, though all personally identifiable information has been redacted.

You have been asked to appraise a 2,064 square foot dwelling on a 0.70-acre site in a residential neighborhood in a typical small American city. The property was purchased in two interrelated transactions: the lot containing the dwelling was purchased first and the adjacent vacant lot was purchased the next year.

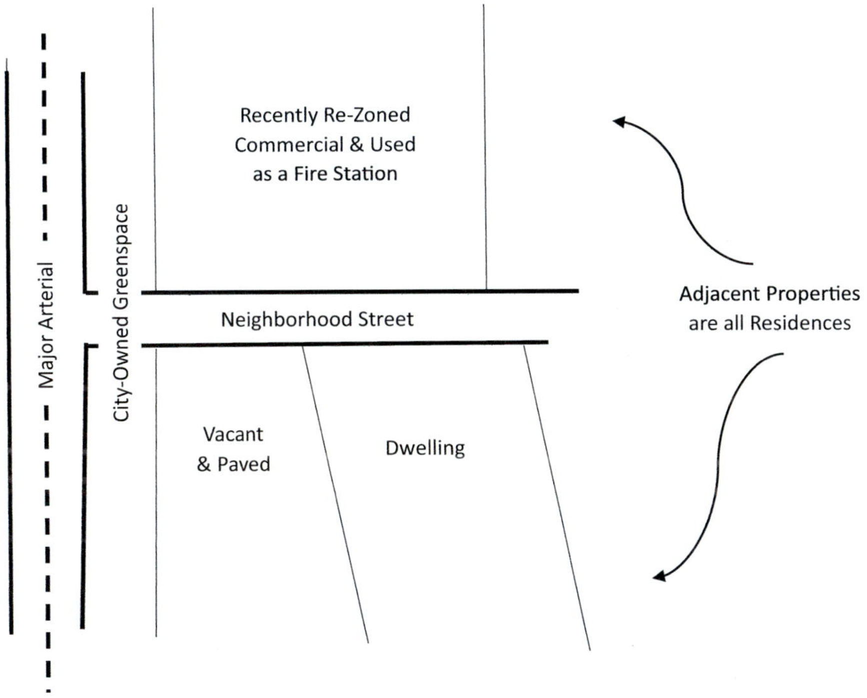

Exhibit 7.1 Sketch of appraisal case property to be valued.

The site is on a corner. The site and the properties across the street have been rezoned for commercial use, as shown in Exhibit 7.1. The owner has converted the dwelling office use and paved the adjacent vacant lot for desirable off-street parking. Even though the city zoning ordinance does not require off-street parking for this zoning category, the available on-street parking is inadequate for employees and customers.

After the preliminary information is gathered, it is time to begin the task of determining the HBU. Legally, the property could continue to be re-used as an office, in which case the two lots together, totaling 0.70 acres, provide more than sufficient footprint to operate a business. Conversely, the owner could revert the property to residential use. As it turns out, comparable commercial properties do not have similar lot configurations, research indicates that the adjacent lot, while useful, is actually excess land and could be sold off as a separate building lot.

The related concepts of excess land and surplus land often confuse even experienced professionals. Consider two residences, both of which sit on a typical residential lot. The first has a lot size of about a quarter of an acre, which is reasonably sufficient for that neighborhood. The second has a lot size of about a third of an acre. Is the larger lot worth more than the smaller one? Perhaps, but not proportionally. While the larger lot may indeed contribute to the overall utility – and hence value – the extra land could not be sold off as a separate lot. The extra land is generally considered to be surplus. The property in this case study (often called the "subject property") has sufficient land to both operate the business or support a residence and the owner can then sell off the extra land as a separate building lot.

All of this is intertwined with the HBU determination. There are at least two different legally permissible uses, and the physical adaptability of the site is different under different scenarios. Fortunately, the financial feasibility portion of the equation settles the matter – after more research you find that continued use as a business/office is more valuable in this part of town than reversion to a residence and a vacant residential lot.

You need to consider all three approaches to value: cost, income, and sales comparison. In fact, the sales comparison approach will be used twice. First, it is needed to value the site, and secondly to value the excess land. In that exercise, not presented here, the excess land is valued at $19.69 per square foot. In the income approach, suitable rent comparables are found and the value is determined through direct capitalization of the estimated NOI resulting from renting the property "at the market" rates.

Small, privately held owner-occupied office space is most commonly valued using the sales comparison approach, as shown in Exhibit 7.2. Of course, finding comparables for somewhat unique properties can be a challenge. Particularly in small markets, you may have to look back over a period of several years prior to the date of value, and in rapidly moving markets, this can lead to erratic and large market conditions adjustments. This exhibit is one example of a sales adjustment grid with six recent sales comps. Pricing trends over time were determined with a matched pairs model and showed that small commercial properties in this market were increasing in value by 19.78% per year during the salient period.

The depreciation factors for each comp, as well as the subject, are determined from local tax assessment records. The most recent data available was 2022, but this gave a benchmark of comparison. Sales comparables that had less depreciation than the subject property are adjusted downward. Two of the comps have sites with slopes, limiting utility for parking and potential redevelopment. One comparable has superior utility (better ingress/egress). Two of the sites have superior locations while two have inferior locations. One comparable also sold with a cell tower lease on the property, and the comp had to be adjusted for the present value of this additional income that creates value. Qualitative adjustments tend to be somewhat heuristic, but appraisers often rely on judgment, experience, and some ad-hoc sensitivity analysis to develop a reconciled "opinion of value."

Note that in this example, the comps are weighted. Comp 6 was less "like" the subject than the other five comps and was weighted half as much as the others. The final determination of value via the sales comparison approach was $636,151, which includes $274,951 for the excess land. A keen observer will recognize that the apparent precision of this number, to the nearest dollar, would most likely not be supported by the precision of the data or the methodology. There is a fair amount of debate in appraisal circles as to how, when, and by how much to "round" these results. As this number would subsequently be reconciled with value determinations from the income approach and the cost approach, at this point it is not rounded.

This example may work well for an undergraduate introductory course in real estate but may be too basic for a more advanced course for graduate students or in a course integral to a Finance major. In most situations, courses in real estate will want to incorporate some aspects of income analysis, such as a DCF model, and show how that impacts investment or development decision making.

Exhibit 7.2 Sales comp adjustment grid for appraisal case study.

Comp # -->	*Subject*	*1*	*2*	*3*	*4*	*5*	*6*
Transaction		1.5 yrs ago	2.2 yrs ago	1.5 yrs ago	2.3 yrs ago	0.7 yrs ago	0.8 yrs ago
Price		265,000	535,000	762,000	500,000	189,000	1,200,000
Cell Tower		0	0	0	0	0	-112,500
Net Value		265,000	535,000	762,000	500,000	189,000	1,087,500
Acres	0.70	0.17	0.25	0.23	0.29	0.36	0.39
GLA Sq Ft	2,064	1,860	3,344	7,316	4,634	2,688	5,164
$/SF		142.47	159.99	104.16	107.90	70.31	210.59
Transaction		Equal	Equal	Equal	Equal	Equal	Equal
	Adjustment	*0*	*0*	*0*	*0*	*0*	*0*
Mkt. Cond. Adj.	*Comp Age (Years)*	1.5	2.2	1.5	2.3	0.7	0.8
	Adjustment	30%	44%	30%	45%	14%	16%
Location	Good	Superior	Inferior	Inferior	Inferior	Equal	Superior
	Adjustment	-10%	10%	10%	10%		-10%
Depreciation	26%	15%	16%	13%	80%	47%	28%
	Adjustment	-4%	-4%	-6%	25%	10%	1%
Zoning	O (Office)	Central Business	Multi-Fam 12	Central Business	Light Industrial	Commercial-Med	Commercial-Med
	Ajustment	*0*	*0*	*0*	*0*	*0*	*0*
Topo	Flat/Moderate	Flat/Moderate	Sloping	Flat	Flat	Slight Slope	Flat
	Adjustment	0	5%	0	0	5%	0
Utility	Very Good	Superior	Roughly Equal	Equal	Equal	Equal	Equal

	Adjustment	*-10%*	*0%*	*0*	*0*	*0*	*0*
Adjusted Prices		143.66	254.59	139.65	215.86	92.46	221.72
Weighting		2.00	2.00	2.00	2.00	2.00	1.00
Indicated	$175/SF						
Indicated Total	361,200						
Excess Land	274,951	13,944 SF	$19.69 per SF				
Net Value	***$636,151***						

Conclusion

There is a lot that's not in this chapter! One could craft great sections in an appraisal survey course on the history of the profession, on appraisal regulations, appraisal standards, or special topics in the industry. One could, and perhaps should, discuss the future of the profession and how to develop a career as an appraiser.

But this chapter really isn't about training practicing appraisers. Likely students for this coursework will be engaged in areas such as investment, lending, or urban development. They will need to regularly deal with appraisal reports but not write them. Hopefully, this chapter will aid the teacher in understanding and incorporating this important body of knowledge into the real estate curriculum. As such, it is important to tie this back into the other disciplines which make up the real estate curriculum, and show how valuation impacts all of them, and all of them in turn impact the valuation analysis.

Chapter 8

Integrating sustainability into real estate programs

Lessons learnt from three case studies

Sandy Bond, Stephen T. Buckman, and Pernille H. Christensen

Introduction

Climate change, and the need to address it, has become a global issue high on political agendas around the world. The significant and costly damage caused by climate-change-related extreme weather events only heightens this need. Estimates indicate that the built environment is responsible for approximately 42% of greenhouse gas emissions globally, with building operations responsible for ~27% and an additional ~15% contributed by the embodied carbon of just four of the core building and infrastructure materials (cement, iron, steel, and aluminum), although it should be noted that these percentages vary substantially from country to country (Architecture 2030, 2023).

Despite these factors, the real estate industry has been slow to make significant strides to improve environmental sustainability, leaning on profit before environmental benefits (Christensen, 2012, 2017; Buckman & Sobhaninia, 2022). Yet, the impacts of climate change have begun to erode the profit margins for property developers and investors, particularly as many sought-after sites for development lie directly in the path of climate change. This is happening around the world from coastal communities at risk of sea-level rise and hurricanes to mountain regions dealing with fires, drought, flooding, and landslides. The negative financial impact of climate change has increased the focus on sustainable buildings for property owners, investors, and developers who are becoming more and more financially incentivized to include climate change assessments and relevant mitigation measures in their projects.

Moreover, the introduction of ESG and the increasing requirements for reporting on these aspects to institutional investors and shareholders has increased the focus of property and asset managers, corporate real estate holders, and large corporate lessees on how well buildings meet not only environmental sustainability requirements, but also the social and governance goals of their organizations (Christensen et al., 2022).

DOI: 10.1201/9781032656458-8

Given the importance of these factors, it has become clear that real estate students would greatly benefit from understanding the impact of climate change and appropriate mitigation and adaptation actions which can be taken to strengthen the resilience of our built environment. Broader social and governance aspects of sustainability are also impacting value, leasing decisions, and worker productivity and satisfaction.

But how do you integrate sustainability into an already existing (full) real estate program? Academics who have introduced new subjects in existing programs know the frustrating and lengthy processes required to do so. To help programs interested in expanding their sustainability offering(s), this chapter first discusses why it is important to include sustainability in the real estate curriculum, the barriers preventing the inclusion of sustainability considerations, and offers three examples of how this can be done:

- By integrating sustainability thinking in a holistic manner throughout the program.
- As a standalone sustainability-focused course.
- By including sustainability in an existing course.

To accomplish this task, we introduce three case studies. The first is a case that demonstrates a best practice approach for how programs can take a holistic approach to sustainability integration, reflecting the new "business-as-usual" expectations that sustainability is no longer simply a niche, value-add proposition, but a requirement for all quality new development. By integrating sustainability courses throughout an undergraduate program with exposure in every sub-disciplinary "stream," with at least one course delivered in every semester of the program, students graduate with a deeper understanding of sustainability and how requirements for responsible, sustainable development can directly impact all areas of real estate including finance, investment, valuation, management, planning, construction, and development decision-making. The second is a is a stand-alone undergraduate course focusing on teaching the students about the important altruistic aspects of sustainability in the built environment. The final case is a course in a Master of Real Estate Development (MRED) program that focuses on how sustainability can improve profits for (often financially conservative) postgraduate students.

In presenting the approaches taken in developing and implementing sustainability into these three types of cases, we hope to demonstrate how educators can craft a sustainability-focused course or a program where sustainability is integrated throughout all aspects of property, at the appropriate level and with consideration of their student base. Thus, these three case studies should be looked at not as a rigid blueprint, but as a foundation on which you can develop new subjects or a more integrated program curriculum.

Why do we need to teach sustainability in real estate programs

Before introducing the case studies, we briefly discuss what exactly we mean by "sustainability", why the topic of sustainability should be included in a real estate program, and the barriers to doing so. "Sustainable development" is broadly defined as "development that meets the needs of the present without compromising the ability of future generations to meet their own needs" (World Commission on Environment & Development, 1987). While the Commission focused its attention in the areas of population, food security, the loss of species and genetic resources, energy, industry, and human settlements, the focus of this chapter is solely on the role that the built environment can play in ensuring a sustainable planet.

With this said, we believe the present socioeconomic climate demands the teaching of sustainability in the real estate classroom. Four areas influence this need:

- **Industry demand:** In a rapidly changing climatic world where the best sites for real estate development are located in climate-impact-intensive areas, there is a demand by industry that students have some level of knowledge about sustainability, sustainable development, and responsible investment practices. It is no secret that the best sites for development are also the most likely to be climate-impacted by issues such as drought, forest fires, flooding, and sea level rise, to name a few. Take Charleston, South Carolina, where many of the Clemson MRED students find employment. Charleston is consistently named one of the best places to live and visit in the United States; however, the city is built at sea level, experiences continuous flooding, and is prone to being hit by hurricanes. Thus, for students to work in an area such as Charleston, they must understand the impact of climate change and how to approach development from a sustainability perspective. Furthermore, industry is demanding that students understand how climate might impact development and be able to propose strategies to mitigate climate risks sustainably.
- **Developers and real estate professionals have a fiduciary responsibility:** Developers have a fiduciary responsibility to both investors and end users. They must supply the best product not only in terms of financial returns for their investors, but also structural integrity for their end-users. Thus, students must be knowledgeable about both the fiscal

impacts of climate events and be able to propose appropriate sustainable design solutions to mitigate those impacts.

- **Asset and facility management:** Asset and facility management must consider the impact of the climate more than ever before. Firstly, they must manage assets in such a manner as to maintain a competitive advantage; this includes considerations such as green rating certificates (e.g. LEED, GreenStar, BREEAM) as well as other sustainability-driven interventions to a building (e.g. low-energy lighting, sustainable materials), as these can increase property value. Secondly, the actual management of the facility to ensure that it is maintained and fortified for the changing climatic landscape. Finally, from a social sustainability perspective, managing social governance initiatives for the buildings they manage.
- **Developer profits:** Understanding that some of the most valued and in-demand development locations are in areas prone to climatic conditions, it becomes necessary for students to understand what the pros and cons of a development site are and how a development can best utilize a site to protect the long-term profitability of the development. This not only involves site analysis but also requires an understanding of beneficial development strategies, from the bricks and sticks of vertical development to ESG initiatives.

An integrated, holistic approach to integrating sustainability in a program

The first case presented in this chapter is focused on taking an integrated, holistic approach to bringing sustainability in to the whole program (course at UTS), When the opportunity presents itself to reconsider your program, it provides an opportunity to evaluate all aspects of your program in the context of emerging industry trends, to assess how well your program develops graduates to be competitive in the job market with skills that fill industry needs, to evaluate what opportunities exist for your program to better meet industry challenges and trends, and identify changes to your program to better meet industry demands and thereby make your program more competitive against other similar programs. This was the situation when the Bachelor of Property Economics (BPE) program at the University of Technology Sydney (UTS) prepared for UTS course (program) accreditation, as well as their external Royal Institution of Chartered Surveyors (RICS) and Australian Property Institute (API) accreditations in 2023–24. When staff talked with their industry partners and the Industry Advisory Committee members in preparation for the first workshop, among the key trends that emerged were sustainability and property technology (proptech). Industry partners consistently identified sustainability thinking and understanding of how to address climate change impacts on assets as a critical graduate skill, while noting that the ability to use current and emerging proptech effectively to improve processes and decision-making was an essential technical skill. The focus on this case study will be on integration of sustainability in the program. However, a similar approach was taken to integrate proptech and industry-standard software skills into the program as well.

To address this feedback, the staff first assessed how and in which subjects sustainability was being taught in the BPE program. There was extensive discussion about how the program could better prepare graduates to be industry-ready with a deeper understanding of how to implement sustainability at the asset and portfolio level, as well as the potential impacts and costs of implementing sustainability strategies. The option of creating a stand-alone sustainability subject in the curriculum was discussed, but with consideration of industry partner feedback about the scope of sustainability thinking in practice, it was decided to instead integrate sustainability thinking holistically across all aspects of the program. The belief is that in so doing, students understand that sustainable development is no longer a niche offering but instead students understand that sustainability considerations impact decisions across the sector relating to property management, valuation, financing, investment, and development, as well as impacting opportunities when dealing with planning and regulatory bodies.

To accomplish this, at least one course is offered each semester (most semesters will include two or three), and sustainability will be integrated into at least one subject in each sub-disciplinary stream. It was identified that this holistic strategy to integrating sustainability thinking would best ensure that learning is appropriately scaffolded to provide regular learning exposure and development throughout the program (see Exhibit 8.1). In addition, as part of reworking the program intended learning outcomes, a new learning objective: "Technology and Sustainability: Employ creative and innovative use of technology and sustainability approaches to addressing built environment challenges." was developed to demonstrate to students and industry partners that these skills are being actively developed throughout the program.

As can be seen in Exhibit 8.1, the color-coding of each subject identifies the sub-disciplinary stream(s) it contributes to, as well as which subjects integrate sustainability and/or proptech and software development skills, contributing to the new Technology and Sustainability Attribute, as well as which subjects contribute to the new Indigenous Attribute. Sustainability

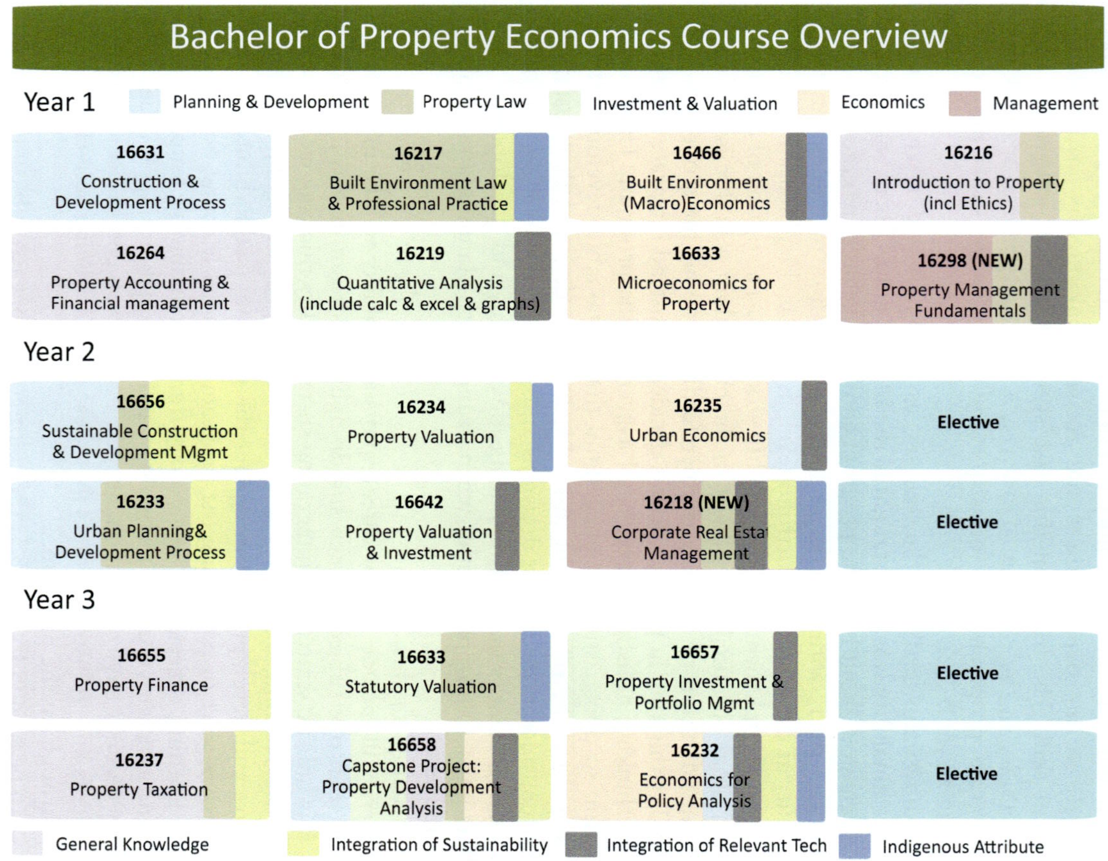

Exhibit 8.1 Map of BPE program identifying sub-disciplinary streams, and integration of sustainability and proptech throughout the program.

becomes integrated through 13 courses across each of the sub-disciplinary streams as follows (see Exhibit 8.2).

Graduates of the BPE program pursue jobs in each of the sub-disciplinary streams identified in Exhibit 8.2. When graduating from the BPE program, they will have a deep understanding of how to apply sustainability thinking in their property sector and employment role, will understand how to mitigate the environmental, economic, and social impacts of climate change in assets and portfolio valuations, investment, management and development, as well as understanding potential planning and legal implications of pursuing (or not) sustainability integration in a development project, an asset that they manage, or a valuation that they are completing for financing purposes.

Courses include theoretical and conceptual learning as well as application through applied exercises and real-world problem-solving scenarios. These may include modeling the impacts on a property valuation, developing and/or assessing a portfolio investment strategy, reviewing local planning regulations to identify opportunities to improve the development potential for a site, assessing an existing building and developing a strategy to improve its sustainability by creating a sustainability implementation plan, understanding the potential ethical implications of the use of AI (artificial intelligence) in sustainability monitoring and reporting, or participating in field visits and on-site activities to see and assess real-world sustainability implementations.

This approach to holistic integration of sustainability was developed with staff through a series of four workshops: (1) Trends & opportunities, "Who will our future graduate be?", and vision setting; (2) Identifying opportunities we want to pursue, general course redevelopment strategy; (3) Reconsidering the sub-disciplinary streams, rethinking content scaffolding and analyzing where to best integrate sustainability, software and technology; 4) Assessment of stream proposals and finalizing the curriculum.

Exhibit 8.2 Identification of sustainability integration for each sub-disciplinary area

Sub-disciplinary stream	*Semester*
General knowledge	Year 1 Autumn, Year 3 Autumn + Capstone Project
Planning & development	Year 2 Autumn, Spring + Capstone Project
Property law	Year 1 Autumn + Capstone Project
Investment & valuation	Year 2 Autumn, Spring, Year 3 Autumn, Spring + Capstone Project
Economics	Year 3 Spring + Capstone Project
Property management	Year 1 Spring, Year 2 Spring

This process was based in action learning and utilized action research strategies to facilitate each workshop. While the process was developed for an undergraduate program, the process could also be replicated to successfully develop an approach for a postgraduate program.

While we believe that integration of sustainability across the program represents best practice, we recognize that this is only possible for most programs at initial program development or at times of significant review and redevelopment. In the following two sections we offer two additional case examples of how an existing subject may be reframed to include sustainability and resilience thinking and how taking a multi-disciplinary approach can help facilitate the development of a new subject focused on sustainability and climate change across a range of disciplines.

Designing a new, stand-alone, multidisciplinary sustainability course

If you are unable to fully integrate sustainability thinking across your existing program, one option is to design a course from scratch. Such a course might introduce the concept of sustainable development and explore the business concepts of the triple bottom line (environmental, economic, and social sustainability) and ESG (environment, social, and governance), with particular focus on how these are applied in sustainable urban planning, property development and valuation/investment. Urban resilience and sustainability challenges faced by global cities might also be explored along with the causes and urban effects of global warming. These factors and effects include but are not limited to issues relating to population growth, greenhouse gas emissions (and reduction), carbon footprint and decarbonization strategies, energy consumption (and alternative energy development strategies), air quality and waste challenges, urban systems, and their impact on sustainable development. Finally, sustainable solutions and practices at the building level might be discussed and demonstrated. Use of national and international case studies, guest lectures, in-class/online group discussions and exercises, and, where possible, field trips are excellent strategies to actively engage undergraduate students in learning about these concepts and challenges.

One example of this approach is Flagler University's offering for undergraduate students studying in either business or natural sciences programs (it was open to either, and available as an elective), which asked students to consider "Why" the topic is important. Why are real estate investors and developers (and other business sectors) going green? Noting the growing demand for sustainable, energy-efficient buildings, students learn about climate change, the concept of sustainability, and sustainable design features. Understanding that property appraisers/valuers are now also required to consider sustainability when valuing property and how these factors impact the value of commercial property is increasingly important, as is understanding that sustainability plans are increasingly required by property investors and property managers. The subject is designed to encourage participants to consider their own environmental footprint and also that of the wider property sector, including emissions related to transportation to/from a property. Whilst the subject has a commercial property focus, it facilitates the evaluation of both residential and commercial property in a sustainability context.

Learning objectives

This course has six learning objectives:

- Identify, describe and evaluate the concepts of sustainability and how these apply to the built environment.
- Evaluate and discuss how buildings contribute to climate change.
- Identify the main drivers and barriers to "green" property development and propose methods to address the barriers.
- Identify and discuss the various renewable energy systems available (solar, wind, photovoltaic, etc.) in terms of how they aid in the reduction of a building's energy use and greenhouse gas emissions.
- Assess the components of the US Green Building Council's LEED rating system in comparison to other rating systems in use throughout the world and determine which building features contribute to a cost-effective higher rating and better environmental performance.
- Identify and assess the main features within a building that support the business case for "going green" by impacting positively on the building's rental and investment value, compared to a similar conventional building without these features.

Assignments and activities

Student learning was assessed through a variety of strategies: homework assignments, a major assignment, a class presentation, and a final examination. Homework assignments were designed either to ask students to reflect on assigned readings and videos or to conduct short research-based explorations. For example, one homework assignment required students to discover their own energy use and carbon footprint using three identified online calculators. Students were also asked to discuss the pros and cons of each online calculator and identify the ten most carbon-saving actions they can take, and the pros and cons of each. The purpose of this task was to make the students more aware of the environmental outcomes of their choices in terms of appliance selection, energy and water usage, waste disposal, transportation and from a non-building perspective, food choices, etc. and to help them identify ways that they could modify their behaviors to conserve energy and reduce their carbon emissions.

The major assignment required students to complete an in-depth analysis of a green-rated building and compare it to a similar conventional building in terms of its sustainable design features and environmental performance. The report emphasizes empirical work (from a site visit to the building) and research. Based on the findings from the major assignment, each student also made a short (15-minute maximum) PowerPoint presentation to the class. This helped students to think critically about sustainability features and their impact on building performance, and also to understand how sustainable commercial development performed differently from non-"green" commercial buildings.

To achieve close alignment between theory and practice, the class content was linked to real-world industry scenarios through three guest speakers from industry and a series of field trips. These activities helped students understand how what they are learning is relevant in the real world.

Guest speakers

- The first guest speaker demonstrated how to assess a home's suitability for solar panels and the financial projections involved.
- As the Tag! Children's Museum operation and facilities manager, the second speaker discussed the unique environmental features of the museum that helped improve operational sustainably while also educating the community on how to live in an environmentally sensitive way. The Tag! campus is master-planned and designed by PLACE Alliance, and employs low-impact, high-performance development strategies and building materials to reduce environmental impact.[1]
- The final speaker was the executive director at The St. Johns Housing Partnership (SJHP). He explained what housing affordability is and outlined the services that SJHP provides to the community, including the Weatherization Assistance Program (provides energy-efficiency improvements to homeowners), the Emergency Repair Program (provides emergency home repair services to low-income and elderly single-family homeowners in need of assistance), and the State Housing Initiatives Partnership Program (SHIP) (assists residents who need major repairs or accessibility installations in order to remain safely in their homes).

In addition, a unique and broad range of field trips was provided to help students understand how sustainability can be applied in different contexts. Tours were held at an off-the-grid container home, a Jewish temple, a middle school and three University buildings. Site visits enabled students to learn at a conceptual level about implementing sustainability features. In addition, students could see first-hand the variety of sustainability strategies available and to note that the aesthetics of these features when implemented are often different from their pre-conceived ideas. They also learned about the broader implications of sustainability features (e.g. how a silver/highly reflective roof-system can reduce the heat island effect around the building), and tenant behavior implications (e.g. one social sustainability initiative in which the local café now donates leftovers to local community members in need).

Reframing an existing course to include sustainability and resiliency thinking

The final case study looks at presenting and introducing a course on sustainability and resiliency to graduate-level, fiscally conservative students that are enrolled to "get a job". It requires a very different approach than a course offered to undergraduate students. The title of the course is "Mixed-Use Development: Sustainable Mixed-Use Development." It is taught as a standard semester-long 16-week lecture/seminar-focused class. The course is part of the MRED program at Clemson University where the students are getting a professional degree and courses are focused less on gaining new knowledge for knowledge's sake, and more on gaining knowledge that expands their marketable skills that will get them a well-paying job. Understanding this, it is important to tailor one's subject to the student cohort. Thus, sustainability thinking in this subject was geared towards developing skills that enable students to be more marketable in the private sector.

In this postgraduate MRED approach, while the merits and needs of sustainability are discussed, the emphasis is on how sustainability development strategies can be used to increase return on investment (ROI). This is of particular interest for this graduate program, as most of the students want to work in the Carolinas or Florida, ground zero for sea level rise and hurricanes.

Emphasizing the financial return aspects of sustainability and resiliency is always important to demonstrate that you can do good and make money in the process. The course highlights that the days of simply throwing up a building, getting a nice ROI and moving on are gone. With the world becoming increasingly fragile due to climate change impacting our cities and coastal areas, this fragility is now impacting developers, who are being forced by lending underwriters, the community, and governments to create more ecologically and socially sustainable developments. Coastal communities, which have been go-to for developers for their visual recreational amenities, are becoming increasingly untenable, and banks are beginning to stop their traditional funding of 30-year fixed-rate mortgages in coastal communities because they feel it's a "bad investment" since many of these communities are predicted to be underwater in 30 years. While all this may seem to be a hindrance for developers, it also creates a new avenue for development and marketing – a new frontier of profit potential. This is the driving force behind the structure of the course. Upon completing this course, students are geared to highlight that developers will be at the vanguard creating sustainable communities, and in turn the future of our urban world.

Learning outcomes

This course has four learning objectives:

- Introductory understanding of sustainability and resiliency.
- What makes a sustainable/resilient city.
- How mixed-use development helps to foster sustainability.
- How the real estate sector uses these concepts.

In addition to lectures and readings and a comprehensive final exam, students were asked to complete a series of applied-learning assignments, engage with guest speakers, and participate in field trips. It was necessary first to shepherd the students into a sustainability and resilience mindset. To accomplish this, six assignments helped students to develop this mindset.

Assignments and activities

The first assignment is the "Envision Assignment". Students are asked to envision their community when they were eight and draw it on paper. This activity helps students see the possibility of a more contained and focused community in which their needs are still met (learning objectives 1 and 3). The second assignment is centered on "Sustainable Indicators.. Students are asked to apply what they have learned about sustainability indicators to examine a city that has been ranked on the "Achieving a Sustainable Urban America" list by writing a short essay (learning objectives 1, 2, and 3). The third assignment is the "Plan Content" assignment. In this exercise, students either select a community sustainability plan or are given one. Student teams are each given an Excel spreadsheet to rate the plan using a score sheet given to them by the instructor (learning objectives 1, 2, and 3). The fourth assignment is entitled "Resilient Cities." Students choose a city that they are familiar with, or one they would like to learn about, and are asked to write an essay describing the city, the city's climate vulnerability, what's the risk if the city does nothing, what can be done in the urban form to combat vulnerabilities, and to propose an effective way to implement a resiliency plan for this city or improve upon an existing plan (learning objectives 1, 2, and 3). The fifth assignment deals with "ESG." Students write a short essay diving deeper into one of the three aspects (E, S, or G) as it pertains to real estate by examining a real estate company that employs ESG and what they do to profit from their ESG initiatives (learning objective 4). Lastly, there is a "Final Development Analysis." For the final project, students are split into three-person groups (depending on the size of the class) and asked to further analyze how real estate deals with the issues of climate change, and how these issues can be dealt with to create increased value. Each team is given a different development and provided with a brief case study write-up from *Returns on Resilience: The Business Case* (ULI, 2015). Students must expand on each section of the case study by seeking outside sources to delve more deeply into the case. Deliverables include a 15-page paper and a 15-minute presentation followed by 5 minutes of question and answer (learning objectives 1–4).

In addition to the above, students were exposed to four guest speakers (in person or via zoom) and two field trips. The speakers and field trips helped to solidify and personalize the broader that were discussed in class. Furthermore, they provided a holistic, real-world perspective on the learning objectives of the class. In course evaluations, students often indicate that these are the most rewarding learning experiences in the course.

- The first guest speaker, as a native of Frieberg and a sustainability expert, spoke on Frieberg. Frieberg is a unique sustainable town as it was destroyed during WWII and the city had the foresight to rebuild the town in a more walkable, sustainable way. This speaker took the broad ideas of the sustainable city and humanized it (learning objectives 2 and 3).
- The second speaker was the president of a consulting firm specializing in helping the real estate community through the use of geospatial modeling, data analytics, and risk assessment technology. His firm specializes in site location for real estate developments, and spoke to the students about taking into account the impact that climate change will have on their site (learning objective 4).

- The third speaker was the Land Development Manager for a major developer that is also a large landholder in the upstate of South Carolina and throughout the Southeast United States. The company has become famous for being a sustainable land steward. The speaker spoke about the need to use land wisely and how to pick the right developer to develop the land in a sustainable way (learning objectives 3 and 4).
- The final speaker was the CEO and co-founder of a green residential investment company that offers UK residential property expertise and software to help institutions to future-proof and grow their portfolios in a sustainable way. She spoke on how to be a green investor and make money doing it (learning objectives 3 and 4).

What should be noted about the guest speakers is that they all centered on how money can be made through sustainable real estate practice, whether that be through land banking, creating a built form that that saves community resources and money, investing wisely in sustainable developments that create value for the investors, or picking the correct site to ensure your development is not negatively impacted by climate change.

The last component of the class included two field trips in order to provide students with a hands-on experience of getting out onto a site and seeing development in action.

- For the first field trip, we toured the Clemson Experimental Forest, managed by Clemson University, and met with the head of the university's department responsible for the land holding. He explained that, as a public land grant university, Clemson has a responsibility to sustainably and equitably manage their land holdings to ensure they are available for present and future generations to enjoy and to help maintain the university's fiscal solvency.
- For the second field trip, students learned about modular housing as a sustainable, affordable built form. We toured an affordable housing development that alumni of the MRED program were developing in Spartanburg, SC. The development was unique in that it was being built entirely by modular construction techniques. The developers spoke to us about how the modular construction techniques were used and how they saved time, energy, and in many ways are more sustainable. A key takeaway for students was how the townhomes looked like traditional "bricks and sticks" ground-up homes and didn't look like what many of the students thought of as affordable housing. In addition, they were shown how this type of construction could save money and create more profit potential for both the developers but also the owners and tenants of the houses.

Conclusion

With growing demand for knowledge of green buildings, improvements in environmental and economic outcomes, and the need to consider ESG and sustainability when valuing and investing in real estate, the chapter highlights an opportunity to educate real estate students on evolving sustainability and resiliency topics so that they are better equipped and more "job-ready" when they enter the workforce. We have outlined three different strategies to incorporate sustainability into real estate programs for different types and levels of students. Lessons learned along the way include the need to ground teaching in real-life scenarios as well as be sure the students are exposed to current research on why to "go green." Finally, and most importantly, there is an urgent need to address climate change through both the built environment and our own actions and choices and exposing students to these issues will make them much better real estate professionals. Finding excellent guest speakers and including site visits to a diverse range of buildings makes subjects "come to life," as students can see what they have learned applied in practice. Additionally, it is important to include the economics of "going green" to address the myth that green buildings and energy/water efficient buildings and landscaping add significant costs. By investigating the payback period of green features, comparing sales for green/sustainable buildings are conventional buildings, and reviewing international research, students learn the benefits of creating sustainable development. Smart design is essential to achieving outcomes, and it is commonly cheaper to build an efficient new building than to retrofit an existing building. Given that only 1–2% of the building stock are created new each year, students need to understand the importance of also developing effective and cost-efficient strategies for existing buildings as future professionals to have maximum positive impact as real estate developers, investors, and managers.

Note

1 For information on the museum, see https://tagmuseum.org/our-plans/

References

Architecture 2030. (2023). Why the built environment? www.architecture2030.org/

Buckman, S., & Sobhaninia, S. (2022). The impact and perceptions of sea-level flooding and climate change on the real estate development community in Charleston, SC: Results of a ULI member survey. *Journal of Sustainable Real Estate*, 14(1), 4–20.

Christensen, P. H. (2012). *Key strategies of sustainable real estate decision-making in the United States: A Delphi study of the stakeholders*. UMI 3550422, Clemson University ProQuest Dissertations & Theses.
Christensen, P. H. (2017). A post-global financial crisis (GFC) framework for strategic planning, assessment and management decision making for US sustainable commercial real estate. *Journal of Property Investment & Finance*, 35(6), 589–618. https://doi.org/10.1108/JPIF-11-2016-0085
Christensen, P. H., Robinson, S., & Simons, R. (2022). Institutional investor motivation, process, and expectations for sustainable building investment. *Building Research & Information*, 50(3), 276–290. https://doi.org/10.1080/09613218.2021.1908878
ULI. (2015). *Returns on Resilience: The Business Case. ULI Center for Sustainability*. The Urban Land Institute.
World Commission on Environment & Development. (1987, October). *Our Common Future*. Oxford University Press.

Chapter 9

Using price-to-rent ratios to evaluate housing markets

Katherine A. Pancak

Overview

The median home sales price in the United States was $420,400 at the end of the third quarter of 2024, up from $327,900 four years earlier, an increase of 28% (FRED, Federal Reserve Bank of St. Louis, 2024). There were geographical differences during this time, with a four-year increase of 21% in the Northeast and 35% in the West. House price increases have been attributed to numerous factors including inflation and demand outpacing supply.

Those statistics alone, however, don't tell us enough about house prices. Prices are driven by both market conditions and speculative factors (expected capital gains) (Bram, 2012).[1] Therefore, an increase in house prices is driven by either strengthening market conditions or speculation. The ratio of prices compared to rents for a given area should stay consistent if changing market conditions cause an increase (or decrease) in both prices and rents. It follows then that increases in prices compared to rents could be due to speculative factors.

For potential homebuyers and real estate investors, evaluating house prices compared to rent (price-to-rent or P/R ratios) provides an additional metric for understanding housing price dynamics to be used in conjunction with traditional real estate appraisal methods. P/R ratios can shed light on whether it is better to buy or rent in a particular market, whether prices in a market vary from fundamentals, and whether a specific property purchase price is in keeping with market conditions.

With this learning exercise, students can explore the creation and use of P/R ratios by (1) tracking historical P/R data for a geographic market, (2) examining differences in P/R ratios between markets, and (3) comparing the P/R ratio for a specific property with benchmark data. The exercise lends itself to a Real Estate Principles course. While it is developed for a US audience, it could be adopted for international users. Note that the ability to conduct this exercise assumes that the data remains available

DOI: 10.1201/9781032656458-9

on given data websites. If not, alternative data sources would need to be explored.

Introduction to P/R ratios

For students that are already familiar with basic finance and financial statement analysis, one way to introduce the concept of P/R ratios is to liken it to the price/earnings (P/E) ratio used in stock price analysis. The P/E ratio is one way to judge stock prices, indicating how much equity investors are willing to pay for a share of a company's stock (the current "P" price of the stock) per dollar of the company earnings (the "E," which can be calculated as either actual, trailing or expected potential earnings per share over a specified time period). For example, if the stock of a company was selling for $120 and its earnings per share was currently $6, the stock P/E ratio would be 20. P/E ratios are relatively straightforward to calculate with information that is widely reported for publicly traded companies. Interpretation is the more complex part of the analysis and requires comparison to benchmark P/E ratios, whether it be current or historical statistics for the company, industry or business group, comparable companies, or overall market. In general, a high P/E ratio indicates either that investors are expecting higher future earnings growth (which would then bring down the P/E ratio to comparable levels in the future) or the stock may be overvalued.[2]

Working off the foundation of P/E ratios, students can then move on to a better understanding of P/R ratios. What a house could be rented for, even for an owner-occupied house not intended to be rented, can be viewed as the house's "earnings" for an investor. A P/R ratio can be constructed by looking at the current house price compared to potential current rental earnings. It is calculated by dividing a house's value by what the house could be rented for per year.

A simple hypothetical exercise can serve as a starting point for understanding this calculation. Assume a house just sold for $600,000 and after closing the house is rented for $2,500 a month ($30,000 a year). The house's P/R ratio can be calculated by dividing price by annual rent: $600,000/$30,000 = 20.

Invite students to think about this metric. If house prices were too high compared to rents, a housing consumer would rent instead of buy. This would lead to a reduction in demand for buying and an increase in demand for renting houses. Theoretically, house prices would decrease, and rents would increase until equilibrium was reached. The opposite would happen if house prices were too low compared to rents, a housing consumer would choose to buy rather than rent. This would lead to an increase in demand for buying and a decrease in demand for renting, with prices increasing and rents decreasing until equilibrium is reached.

Another way to encourage students to think about this is to look at the P/R ratio as a multiple – how much buyers are willing to pay for a house in terms of years of rent. In the above example, students can find that the buyer was willing to pay the equivalent of 20 years of rent to buy the house. Be sure to remind the students that this ratio is simplistic since it does not consider total costs of buying versus renting nor the time value of money. And, of course, they are not actually buying the house!!

So, what does a P/R ratio tell students about a housing market, and how can they decide whether prices are high, low, or normal? They need to compare a calculated P/R ratio to a benchmark by looking at what is historically consistent for the geographic area where the house is located as well as the property characteristics.

What is a good P/R ratio

The above title is not the way to approach the P/R ratio (although it is catchy!), as there is not a good or bad level per se. As with P/E ratios, a P/R ratio provides a benchmark, and therefore useful information as to whether it is cheaper to own or rent in an area, as well as whether housing is fairly valued or in a bubble. It should be noted that P/R ratios don't tell us whether a house is affordable since it does not consider area income and cost of living.

P/R ratios construction can take different forms. Ideally, P/R ratios would start by comparing same house price and rent values, and then aggregating these property-specific P/R ratios to create a regional P/R ratio. However, price and rent data for the same house has been difficult to obtain. Therefore, most P/R ratio studies construct regional P/R ratios using regional data for owner-occupied house prices compared to regional data for tenant-occupied rents.[3] These regionally constructed P/R ratios provide region-specific benchmarks that can provide insights into current and historical market conditions. However, comparing regionally constructed P/R ratios across markets can be problematic since different regions may have a different quality and income-range of owner-occupied versus tenant-occupied housing.

When looking at regional P/R ratios, a higher P/R ratio compared to an area's long-term average P/R ratio may indicate that house prices in the area are veering from economic fundamentals and overpriced. Also, a high P/R ratio compared to the long-term average suggests that it may be better to rent than to buy in the area at that point in time. This can be good news for rental property investors and landlords since demand for rental housing will increase. A low ratio compared to the long-term average for an area suggests that it may be better to buy than rent. This is good for potential homeowners but not so favorable for landlords, as there is lower demand for rentals and rents could fall negatively impacting the landlord's ability to pay their mortgage and impact their overall return on their investment. However, regional ratios diverging from long-term averages may also be indicating a change in economic activity for the area, such as gain or loss of jobs.

Various online sites report on P/R ratios for different areas.[4] For example, *SmartAsset* calculated the P/R ratios for the 50 largest US cities using US Census Bureau 2019 1-year Community Survey data (Wallace, 2022). The reported range was San Francisco, California with a P/R ratio of 51.79 (and a median home value of $1,217,500) to Detroit, Michigan with a P/R ratio of 5.67 (and median home value of $58,900). The article also discusses P/R ratio variation over time by looking at historical national P/R ratios (data source not provided). The article explains that the national ratio rose from 22.73 in 2005 and to 24.50 in 2007. After the 2008 housing bubble burst, home prices fell, and rentals grew more expensive. This led to a reported fall in the national ratio below 20 in 2011 and then to 18.27 in 2021.

The Motley Fool published an online article providing general guidelines for understanding P/R ratios (Waterworth, 2024). The article suggests that a ratio of less than 15 means that it is cheaper and more affordable to buy versus rent, a ratio of 16–20 leans towards renting as a better option over buying, and a ratio of over 21 makes renting a better choice. While appealing as benchmarks, these ratio numbers are not market specific and depend on data used for ratio construction which in the above cases are time dependent as well. So, discuss with students that there is room for interpretation.

Florida Atlantic University publishes regional information on P/R ratios at the BH&J National Price-to-Rent Ratios Monthly Report (Florida Atlantic University, 2025). The site provides monthly P/R ratio data for 100 metropolitan areas using Zillow data (Granzer, 2023). A metro area can be chosen from a drop-down menu to view actual monthly P/R ratios for the metro as well as the historic average (expected) P/R ratio (dating to 2015). The site calculates the premium or discount of the actual ratio to the expected ratio, noting that what is important is the change in the P/R ratio through time relative to the historic average. An actual ratio above the historic average is presented as a premium and indicates renting is preferred, while ratios below the historic average imply buying is supported by the market conditions. It is assumed that the greater the premium (or discount), the stronger the stronger the signal is for renting (or buying).

Calculating P/R ratios

As part of a real estate course, students can access online real estate databases to calculate both regional index-based and property-specific P/R ratios. Zillow is one such online source of US housing data (www.zillow.com). There are other online housing data sources, but none that appear to currently provide the extent of property-specific information needed to create P/R ratios with easy and free access.[5] An international audience looking to analyze a local market would need to either find a different data provider or engage students in looking at a US market.

Regional P/R ratios can be created using Zillow regional indexes. The bottom of the Zillow homepage provides a Research link. From that page, at the top toolbar, there is a link to Data, then Housing Data. This data page can also be found directly at www.zillow.com/research/data. Under Home Values, a Zillow Home Value Index (ZHVI) can be generated at the United States, Metropolitan Statistical Areas (metro), state, county, city, zip code, and neighborhood levels. The ZHVI index shows the typical home value (for homes in the 35th to 65th percentile range) and market changes across a given region and housing type. It is available as a smoothed, seasonally adjusted measure and as a raw measure. This housing data is provided by month starting in 2000 and can be downloaded as an Excel spreadsheet.

Likewise, see Zillow Observed Rent Index (ZORI), a smoothed measure of the typical observed market rate rent across a region by month based on the rental housing stock, starting in 2015.[6] Rental data is available at the metro, county, city, and zip code levels. Looking at both indexes for either metro or zip code, monthly data for price and rent can be downloaded to an Excel spreadsheet, and monthly P/R ratios can be calculated. Current and historical monthly P/R data can be generated for use in benchmarking and trend analysis.[7]

These Zillow indexes have housing quality comparison constraints when creating metro-level and even zip code-level P/R ratios. As discussed previously and in academic research on P/R ratios, different housing stock indexes are being looked at – an estimated home value index compared to an index reflecting changes in rental housing stock rents. Also, Zillow data only offers a relatively brief time series of rent estimates which does not allow for analysis of P/R ratios before the beginning of the Great Recession.

Zillow data also allows for the creation of property-specific P/R ratios, by looking at Zillow's property-specific estimates for price (referred to as "Zestimates") and rent (referred to as "Rent Zestimates"). These estimates are created by Zillow using a proprietary neural network that considers square footage and location, past transaction history, tax assessment records, public and user-submitted data, and sales and rentals of comparable homes (Zillow Home Value Index Methodology, 2023 Revision). It should be noted that these estimates are just that – an estimate and not perfect. Typically, the models will do a better job on properties that are more heterogeneous as the data is more prevalent.

A property-specific P/R ratio can be created by entering the address of a house at the Zillow website. If it is not currently on the market, the page will show the Zestimate and monthly Rent Zestimate (if it is on the market, scroll down for those estimates). The property P/R ratio can simply be calculated by using the Zestimate/(Rent Zestimate × 12).

For example, a specific property in Stamford, Connecticut was researched in November 2023. Zillow reports that it is 1,865 square foot single family home on a 7,405 square foot lot, with four bedrooms and three bathrooms. It last sold in 2001 for $297,000 (past transaction data can be found on the property Zillow page under Price History). The house Zestimate is $754,100 and Rent Zestimate is $4,411. Based on this, a P/R ratio can be calculated as $754,100/ ($4,811 × 12) = 13.06.

Student exercise

This exercise is envisioned as a student research project; the language below is written as it would be presented to students. It is suggested that students work in groups of two. It can also be used for an individual or larger group project and as a written assignment instead of a presentation. Prior to beginning the exercise, faculty should give students baseline knowledge on P/R ratios as detailed above. Every group should pick a different one of the top 100 metros. All research will be conducted related to this metro.

Metro overview

A list of US metros, with data from the US Census Bureau, can be found at en.wikipedia.org/wiki/Metropolitan_statistical_area. Clicking the metro name will lead to detailed information. An internet search can provide further information.

- Choose one of the top 100 US metros (by population).
- Explain the metro's geographic region and cities included in the metro.

- Provide a brief overview of the metro population, economy, and climate.

Metro P/R ratio

The BH&J National Price-to-Rent Ratios Monthly Report provides monthly P/R data for 100 metros, using Zillow.com data. Go to https://business.olemiss.edu/news/2024/11/beracha-and-johnson-price-to-rent-ratios-11-24/index.html. Choose your metro.

- Report on the current P/R ratio (actual) and historical average ratio (expected) for your metro.
- Is your metro's current ratio above or below average?
- Give three reasons why you think that is.
- Does this tell a home consumer that it is better to buy or rent in this metro and why?
- Briefly look at the current reported ratios for three other metros and compare them to the P/R ratio for your metro. Why do you think there are differences between metros?

Property-specific P/R ratio

While regional analysis can serve as a generic benchmark, drilling down to property-specific information is important given the heterogenous nature of real estate. Go to Zillow.com. Enter the address of a house for sale (or search and find a house for sale in a town within your metro). On the property page, scroll down to find the Zestimate and Rent Zestimate. The property P/R ratio can simply be calculated by Zestimate/(Rent Zestimate × 12).

Describe the property

- Report on the calculated property P/R ratio.
- Compare the property-specific P/R ratio to the metro actual and historic ratios reported by BJ&H (as found in the section above).
- Briefly compare and comment on differences between the property-specific P/R ratio and the benchmark metro P/R ratios.

The above research can serve as a standalone exercise. If time permits, students can develop their own P/R ratio benchmarks, looking at P/R ratios at a more local level. While the best analysis would be done at the neighborhood level, Zillow rental data is only available at the zip code level.

Zip-code P/R ratio

Explore the P/R ratio for the zip code where the specific property you looked at above is located.

- What is the zip code for the specific property you researched above? Zillow provides estimates of housing values at the metro, state, city, zip code, and neighbor levels. Go to Zillow.com, scroll down to the bottom toolbar and proceed as follows:
  - Click Research.
  - From that page, at the top toolbar, click Data.
  - Then click Housing Data.
  - To view data on housing value, under Home Values, choose ZHVI All Homes (SFR, Condo/Co-op) Time Series, Smoothed, Seasonally Adjusted.
  - Choose zip code then download the associated Excel spreadsheet; note that you will have to search the large Excel database for your zip code area (it helps to sort by the zip code or state column).
- Report on home value for your zip code for the most recent month. Zillow also provides estimates of rents at the metro, county, city, and zip code levels. Again, go to Zillow.com and proceed as follows.
  - Scroll down to the bottom toolbar and click Research.
  - From that page, at the top toolbar, click Data, then Rentals.
  - To view data on rent, under Rentals, choose ZORI (Smoothed Seasonally Adjusted): All Homes Plus Multifamily Time Series.
  - Choose zip code and then download the Excel spreadsheet.
- Report on monthly rent for your zip code for the most recent month.
- Based on the zip code home value and rent, create a P/R ratio for your zip code for this month.
- Briefly compare the calculated zip code P/R ratio with the previously determined metro and property-specific P/R ratios.
- Discuss the advantages of looking at benchmark P/R ratios on a more local level.

Exercise assessment for this exercise as a project can consider all three steps. A simple rubric may give 20% for part 1, 30% for part 2, and 50% for part 3. If the exercise consists of a presentation, a suggested presentation length would be ten to fifteen minutes, and a percentage of the overall grade can be given to presentation skills.

Conclusion

The amount of information that is now freely available online to help assess housing markets has grown rapidly in the past decade. This chapter provides instructors with an engaging project to give students an opportunity to develop knowledge and skills related to housing P/R ratios. Faculty should note the limitations of using P/R ratios. In particular, it doesn't account for future area job growth or other economic activity (positive or negative). For example, an increase or decrease in expected area jobs would likely affect the ratio, and ratio analysis would need to take that into account, Additionally, regional P/R ratios constructed with different quality data sets are not necessarily comparable across different markets as houses in different income bracket areas may sell in different ratio ranges. Just as when looking at P/E ratios for valuing stock, students should view the P/R ratio as a useful starting point in evaluating house prices, but it should not be viewed as the only factor to consider.

Notes

1 There are numerous other academic and practitioner articles written on P/R ratios, including Beracha and Johnson (2012), Gallin (2008), Leamer (2002), and Pancak (2017).
2 Time permitting, students can explore and discuss P/E ratios with information found online. While many schools have paid financial data services, stock quotes including P/E ratios can also be found for free at various online sites, including Yahoo! Finance (https://finance.yahoo.com). Benchmark P/E data can also be free found online, including published online by NYU (New York University, 2025).
3 For example, Gallin (2008) used a Freddie Mac house price index that measured changes in single-family home values as a proxy for house prices and rent data from an index for tenants' rent from the Consumer Price Index.
4 Time permitting, students can research and discuss current P/R ratios reported online and take note of how those ratios were constructed and what data was used.
5 Sources of housing data are continually evolving and could also provide needed data for learning purposes. For example, CoStar Group provides access to data to professors and students for academic research and use in the classroom (https://elearning.costar.com/about), and its Homes.com site has residential listing, sales, and rent data (www.homes.com).
6 Zillow (2024, Housing Data section) reports that ZORI is a repeat-rent index that is weighted to the rental housing stock to ensure representativeness across the entire market, not just those homes currently listed for rent. The index is dollar-denominated by computing the mean of listed rents that fall into the 40th to 60th percentile range for all homes and apartments in each region, which is once again weighted to reflect the rental housing stock.
7 Zillow allows personal and non-personal use of its data if the use states that "Data provided by Zillow Group" (2024, Zillow Terms of Use). Therefore, when referring to Zillow information in this chapter, data is provided by Zillow Group.

References

Beracha, E., & Johnson, K. (2012). Lessons from over 30 years of buy versus rent decisions: Is the American dream always wise? *Real Estate Economics*, *40*(2), 217–247. https://doi.org/10.1111/j.1540-6229.2011.00321.x

Bram, J. (2012). To buy or not to buy? The changing relationship between Manhattan rents and home prices. *Current Issues in Economics and Finance*, *18*(9), 1–6. https://ssrn.com/abstract=2190587

Florida Atlantic University College of Business. (2025, April 28). *BH&J National Price-to-Rent Ratios Monthly Report*. https://business.olemiss.edu/news/2024/11/beracha-and-johnson-price-to-rent-ratios-11-24/index.html

Gallin, J. (2008). The long-run relationship between house prices and rents. *Real Estate Economics*, *36*(4), 635–658. https://doi.org/10.1111/j.1540-6229.2008.00225.x

Glanzer, J. (2023). *Renting Beats Buying in Vast Majority of U.S., Florida Atlantic University News Desk*. Florida Atlantic University. www.fau.edu/newsdesk/articles/jan2023-rent-vs-buy.php

Leamer, E. (2002). Bubble trouble? Your home has a P/E ratio too. *UCLA Anderson Forecast Report*, 1.1–1.11. www.anderson.ucla.edu/documents/areas/ctr/forecast/PE_ratio.pdf

New York University. (2025, April 28). *PE Ratio by Sector (US)*. https://pages.stern.nyu.edu/~adamodar/New_Home_Page/datafile/pedata.html

Pancak, K. (2017). Variation in local house price–rent ratios. *Journal of Housing Research*, *26*(1), 79–94. https://doi.org/10.1080/10835547.2017.12092129

US Census Bureau & US Department of Housing and Urban Development. (2024, October 27). *Median Sales Price of Houses Sold for the United States* [MSPUS]. Federal Reserve Bank of St. Louis. https://fred.stlouisfed.org/series/MSPUS

Wallace, N. (2022, February 28). Where to buy: Price-to-rent ratio in U.S. cities. *SmartAsset*. https://smartasset.com/mortgage/price-to-rent-ratio-in-us-cities

Waterworth, K. (2024, September 28). *Price to Rent Ratios*. The Motley Fool. www.fool.com/investing/stock-market/market-sectors/real-estate-investing/basics/price-to-rent-ratio

Zillow. (2023). *Zillow Home Value Index Methodology, 2023 Revision: What's Changed?* Zillow Market Trends. www.zillow.com/research/methodology-neural-zhvi-32128/

Zillow. (2024, August 29). Zillow terms of use. www.zillow.com/z/corp/terms

Zillow. (2024, October 27). Housing data. www.zillow.com/research/data

Chapter 10

A blueprint for successful real estate study-abroad trips

Tom G. Geurts

Introduction

Real estate is local; however, its investors are increasingly global and they create global well-diversified portfolios to reduce their risk. Universities should include this aspect in their curriculum by offering a global real estate course. It is one thing to learn about global real estate investment in theory; however, it is more powerful to receive hands-on experience through a study-abroad trip. Indeed, one of the barriers to creating a global portfolio is the institutional framework of the country that the institutional investor wants to invest in, including a country's culture and its treatment of foreign investors (Geurts & Jaffe, 1996). What better way to learn about this than actually going to other countries, meeting real estate professionals in their own environment, and touring local real estate projects, with a secondary benefit for participating students: making new and useful connections that can help their career.

Suggested course outline

The course outline for a study-abroad trip should resemble a regular course outline as much as possible, so both the students taking the course and colleagues realize that this is an academic course just like any other which, if applicable, is particularly important for the tenure review process. Faculty members who are not involved in study-abroad trips can be dismissive of the value of these experiences, especially if "everyone" can lead one (e.g., administrators without a formal academic background). Students might also sign up with the expectation that this will be a "fun trip" with lower academic importance. This attitude should be discouraged from the start, since it can be a recipe for undisciplined behavior during the trip; this tends to be less of an issue with graduate students, since they are typically more mature and understand the learning experience being offered.

DOI: 10.1201/9781032656458-10

There are three unique components for this type of course: (1) Pre-Country Visit, (2) In-Country Visit, and (3) Post-Country Visit (see Appendix A for more details). Each of these components will be discussed in detail in subsequent sections, however, first I will explain the (learning) goals of the three components.

Pre-country visit

The first component is to educate students about the country, companies, and projects that are going to be visited, as well as to familiarize them with each other and the business culture they will be exposed to. Ideally, at the end of this component the students will be knowledgeable about the country that they are going to visit, understand the itinerary that the professor has planned, and feel comfortable traveling to the country as a group. When in-country they should be able to rely on the knowledge that they have gained during the preparation to enhance their learning experience, to make the most of the social–cultural experiences, both as part of the program and during their free time, and know what to do and where to go if they get separated from the group.

As will be discussed later, it is very important that there should be enough free time during the in-country visit, so that the students can explore beyond what has been planned. This means that they should already learn where they can (safely) go and how to get there. This is not without risks, especially when it comes to undergraduate students. There are faculty who have strict curfews and monitor the hotel floors where students are staying. I have never subscribed to this philosophy, instead giving my students freedom to explore, as long as they are on time to participate in the scheduled program. It is my experience that if you treat the students as mature adults, they will live up to that standard. Furthermore, this is also the reason why I stress group-work during this initial pre-trip component, because students will typically do activities together while in-country. To further facilitate this group dynamic, each group must divide the following roles amongst themselves (see Appendix B for more details):

- **Project leader:** Sets the direction and guides the group to a successful conclusion.
- **Transportation officer:** Organizes and leads the group when traveling in-country.
- **Communications officer:** Serves as the main contact for the professor and chronicles the trip on social media.
- **Culture officer:** Ensures that the group behaves appropriately when in-country, guided by the countries' local culture.

In-country visit

During the second component the emphasis switches to learning about real estate topics in the country that is being visited, comparing them to the home country. Consequently, at the end of the in-country visit each group will need to do a presentation on a topic that they chose during the pre-country visit lectures. Examples of topics that I have used are:

- If you are an American investor looking to buy a commercial property in [City], what and where would you buy?
- Discuss the investment climate for real estate investors in [City/ Country].
- What are the lessons that American investors can learn about [Real Estate Topic] from [Country] best practices (e.g., social housing, sustainable buildings)?

Post-country visit

I never had student meetings after the country visit, just two deliverables: a group paper and an individual reflection paper. Lack of additional meetings allows the in-country component to end on a high note for the students with their group presentation and closing dinner. Another meeting post-country would feel anticlimactic. Instead, the students wrap up their two deliverables remotely. These deliverables function as a culminating experience and provide reinforcement that this is a serious educational trip.

Building on the in-country deliverable (the presentation), the group writes an extensive paper, due two weeks after the conclusion of the trip. Part of this paper was already researched before the trip took place and clearly more information was gathered during the visit, which was already presented in-country. The students now must merge these components into one deliverable.

Students have more freedom when it comes to the individual reflection paper, which should be related to aspects of in-country visits:

- Organizational aspects of a firm/organization that was visited.
- Analysis of a management function of a firm/organization that was visited.
- Any social and cultural aspects of the country that was visited.

Clearly, the learning goal of the first deliverable is similar to the one of the in-country visit, while the learning goal of the second deliverable is more holistic and can result in impactful testimonials supporting the importance of study-abroad programs. I have read some fascinating experiences, many unrelated to the materials taught.[1] These deliverables give students something to concentrate on during the trip, as they will see all aspects in light of their deliverables. It is essential for the professor to point out how the various lectures and visits are connected throughout.

Pre-country visit suggested content

Going to another country requires understanding the history, economics, politics, and (business) culture of the country. I have found it useful to have a contemporary book about the country as required reading. Two examples: *Reimagining India: Unlocking the Potential of Asia's Next Superpower* (2013) and *A Brief History of Argentina* (2011). An ideal book contains a chapter about the aforementioned topics, so that students become familiar with those different aspects of the country. However, trusting that the students read the book is not sufficient, I also assign each group a chapter to present. Specifically, there should be a minimum of four presentations:

- History.
- Socio-cultural environment.
- Economic-financial environment.
- Political–legal environment.

More details about the length of this component and exact content of each lecture can be found in Appendix C.

These assignments also allow students to get to know each other better in preparation for the trip. Working together to create these presentations hopefully creates camaraderie and trust, because when they are in-country, they will need to work together and rely on each other as they navigate unfamiliar areas.

The second part of this section is designed to teach students about the specific industries and firms to be visited, in preparation for the group projects. This requires that the instructor already has some sense of the visits that will take place. I always have fixed visits planned, which makes this process easier (e.g., the Central Bank). Consequently, during the pre-country visit component, I give a presentation about the history and monetary policies of the country's Central Bank. A logistical note: provide students with a map of locations to be visited with the address and contact information to ensure that anyone who get separated has the resources to meet back up with the group. Although this has never happened to me, dispersing this knowledge creates a sense of comfort for the professor and for the student. Of course, with every student having a cell phone, this aspect has become less important.

During the discussion of the (finalized) itinerary, the professor should give a short presentation about the firms, organizations, and projects that will be visited as well as business culture. For example, if CBRE or a similar global real estate service provider is visited, I talk about the history of the firm and give the students a sense of what the firm does. Alternatively, this can be allocated to the student groups, where they do the research and present it to the rest of the class. This does not have to go into too much detail, but it should give the students a sense of what to expect for each visit. These short presentations thus serve as a tool to prepare and excite students for the trip.

Finally, I always stress that being punctual, attentive, and asking questions is essential to meaningful firm visits. First, students should visit websites and publications created by the firms and organizations that are to be visited students and think about questions that they could ask each firm. For this purpose, a "Visit Preparation Form" is useful (see Appendix A). This can also be used as a deliverable for grading purposes. Encouraging student engagement provides the organizations and presenters with a sense of reward and respect, while enhancing students' experience and understanding. Students should understand pre-country that these companies are hosting them at no cost and realize that engagement provides mutual benefit. Example prompts that can be used to encourage student engagement include: "What cultural differences do you observe?" or "Study the levels of security at the American Embassy".

In summary, the lectures before the trip should be a mixture of short presentations by the professor about the companies, organizations, and projects being visited, as well as the general business, culture, and behavior during the trip. This should be combined with presentations by the student groups on big picture topics of the country being visited, using the chapters of the book that has been assigned.

In-country visit suggested content

The ideal program is a mixture of guest lecturers, company and project visits, and social-cultural events. This is also the optimal sequence for a day during the trip. The lecture should be done in the morning when the students are still relatively fresh, depending on the activities of the evening before. After lunch, a visit to a company or project and in the evening a social-cultural event (see Appendix D for a sample itinerary).

The lecture can be done by the professor, but a guest lecture by a local expert is preferred. In my experience it is very easy to find good speakers who are willing and able to present. Sources for speakers and visits include:

- **Local university:** There will be experts on a range of subjects who are well-versed in lecturing, with the right facilities to host a group. However, a university speaker may be less flexible in their presentations. They tend to want to give a presentation that they do in one of their own classes, which might not be perfectly tailored for your specific student audience.
- **Government agency:** In particular the Central Bank, which has a wealth of expertise and relevant information about interest rates and economic activity, including building activity. However, although experts in their field, they are not always the most exciting speakers.
- **The US embassy or consulate:** While my personal high-ranking contact at the Office of Real Estate Acquisitions and Disposals of the US Department of State has helped me facilitate these visits, I expect that even without such a relationship it should be easy to set up a meeting. I like to juxtaposition the Central Bank speaker in the morning with a speaker from the US embassy or consulate after lunch, as views sometimes conflict. Larger embassies are also willing to show the students around the building and discuss resources. Although of lesser educational value, students like that aspect a lot, since embassy operations tend to be a black box for most people.
- **Consulting companies:** These organizations like to make long-term connections and relationships. Furthermore, they typically are also good speakers and know their topic very well. Finally, they are more flexible in creating custom presentations, as long as the topic that the professor matches the area of their expertise.
- **Real estate advisory companies:** CBRE, JLL, and Knight-Frank have representatives everywhere. Typically, they are willing and able to give a presentation on the characteristics of the local real estate markets, which is always very interesting and insightful. I sometimes take students to a small local real estate advisory firm in addition to more globally oriented "big names," afterwards encouraging a discussion about the differences between the two firms with respect to the information that they provided and their views on the market.
- **Commercial local real estate developers:** I have actually stopped approaching these types of firms, as they are less interested in providing speakers. The latter tends towards building tours, which may be reasonable for the afternoon program.

For the afternoon program, consider architects who are willing to provide a guided tour of the city. Government or semi-government agencies, such as social housing organizations, are typically proud to show off the buildings that they manage, and it can be interesting to see how projects differ by country. Many students are unaware of how social or affordable housing is supplied in other countries, hence a visit like this can be eye-opening.

For the evening program, I typically schedule three events during the course of the trip and let the students be free for the other evenings. On the first night of the trip, an opening dinner at a restaurant with local specialties is used to help set the tone for the whole trip. Keep the dinner a bit formal to remind the students that this is an educational experience and there may be consequences for unprofessional behavior, while still encouraging the social aspect as students mingle. They are excited to be in the foreign country and it is good to talk about their expectations on that first evening. This can be a returning topic during the closing dinner, which is the third social event typically held on the last evening of the visit. One warning, this goodbye dinner can be raucous, since the trip is almost over, most of the work is done, there is no threat of punishment anymore, and the students feel liberated and relaxed. I am also more relaxed, partaking in multiple toasts memorializing the invariable high points of the trip.[2] Typically, alumni and professionals who have helped with the trip are also invited and that can have a sobering effect.

Somewhere in the middle, but preferably earlier to the start, I organize a local culture event. For example, tango dancing instruction in Buenos Aires or a visit to a Biergarten in Germany. Another such event would be to mingle with local university students, which unfortunately has often proven difficult if the university is not in session. The logical starting point for such an event is discussing it with the colleague of a local university who will present to the group. When the professor is interested and able to get students to attend, the event is typically a big success. This event should happen early during the visit because inevitably friendships are created and the local students will show the visiting students around. Sometimes one or two local students even attend the closing dinner.

Although the other evenings are free of events, a consequence of too much freedom can be that the students are not completely fresh the next morning. While I advise against too early of a start, even a 9:00am start provides the possibility to attend a two-hour lecture in the morning. It is best to have lunch close to the location where the morning lecture took place. Ensure that there is plenty of time scheduled for lunch, since this always takes longer than expected. Restaurants are not always well-equipped to serve large groups in a speedy manner.

Transportation

Ensure that there is enough travel time, because traffic in a big city can be slow when taking a bus or delayed when taking public transportation. It is my experience that universities want to hire a bus to go everywhere. Nevertheless, I always manage to insert at least one trip using public transportation, because it is my belief that this is an important experience for students to have. In Europe especially, metros and trams typically move faster than a bus. However, this requires that the professor knows how to get tickets and where to enter and exit.[3] When taking the bus, make sure that there is enough slack in the schedule, parking is available, and loading/unloading is safe.

Debriefing

The time between the morning lecture and the arrival of the food can be filled with a debriefing session. Students are sometimes left wondering what was exactly meant by certain statements or fail to see connections between the different presenters. These debriefing sessions are as important as the lectures themselves and this is where the professor adds value, inserting the socio-cultural, economic-financial, and political–legal context of the country. Try to draw in the students who presented on these topics during the pre-country visit component as "experts." For example: A question regarding the speaker's view on capital flows into real estate can be posed both to a representative of the central bank and, separately, to a speaker of the US embassy or consulate. Typically, their views do not match driving an interesting discussion about why, what the consequences are, etc. This is when students start to realize how important market transparency is and how a lack thereof constitutes a risk for global real estate investors.

Finally, debriefing individual students can be less planned and can happen during lunch or over a drink. Asking them specific questions such as "So, what is the most interesting thing you have observed thus-far" or "Did you like the (country-specific) food we ate on the first night" forces them to think about their experiences and gives the professor an opportunity to remind the student that they need to write an individual reflection paper. On the other hand, asking such a question in a group-setting during lunch or while having a drink in the hotel bar, often leads to spirited discussions about what the students found interesting.[4]

Deliverable preparation

Free time during the country visit is also important for students as, for many, this will be their first time in a country or even abroad. Giving them time to relax and process what is going on, is not wasted time. The students can gather their thoughts, write down notes about what they have learned for their deliverables, but also use the time to explore aspects of the city that they are interested in, which are not on the pre-planned itinerary.

Since the students must present at the end of the trip, they must also have time to work on this deliverable while they are there. Consequently, I meet with all groups at least once to discuss how things are going and to hear the progress they are making. This can lead to spontaneously organized trips to look at another area, museum, or project, to gather more information for their group project. Administrators and presumably peer-reviewers, tend to frown upon the label "free time" since it sounds like no learning takes place. Hence, always label it "group work", but explain to the students that they could use that time as they see best. However, the students do need to report back.

It is also advisable to schedule time for students to rehearse their presentations. This is especially important if outside observers (e.g., from visited firms and/or alumni) are invited to the final presentations. Students want (and need) to rehearse as they want their presentations to be taken seriously.

Suggestions for success

Making a preparatory visit to the country is essential. Meeting with some, if not all, of the speakers helps them to give more targeted presentations. It also gives the opportunity to change or add speakers if the quality of the speaker is below par and/or if there is a gap in the program.

Navigating the city where the trip will take place gives a sense of the travel times, enabling an efficient schedule of visits. Having dinner and taking photos at the restaurants where the welcome dinner and closing dinner will take place, are details that students always appreciate. It provides them with an idea of what to expect. The same applies to the hotel where everybody will be staying. It is important to inspect the amenities that are available. For example, it should have at least one conference room for meetings with the students and for them to work including space for rehearsing their presentation. The hotel should be centrally located, but not too close to the main "party-area" of the city. And, of course, the hotel needs to have reliable Wi-Fi. Twice, I decided to switch hotels after making the preparatory visit.

Overall, this preparatory visit will give students confidence when the professor can say that all aspects of the visit have been finalized, since it means that the students know that they can rely on you.

Additionally, set clear rules and expectations and enforce them; I personally subscribe to a "two strikes and you're out" rule. Others may include: When using public transit, all the students need to be in the same train or metro car with you. Or when walking, while the professor leads the group, the teaching assistant (TA) brings up the rear and students should always stay in front of the TA. Depending on the group size, these clear rules make it much easier to keep oversight. This is more about safety than anything else.

Finally, and this is probably the most important factor for success: A TA who is organized, independent, and reliable. The TA's main role is to make sure that the program runs as it is supposed to be, and they therefore should check all components of the next day, by making a quick phone call or email the day before. The professor needs to ensure the quality of the educational component during the trip, however there are many aspects that facilitate the educational component, which ideally the TA takes care of. For example, checking that the bus will be at the hotel on-time, making sure that a museum that is scheduled to be visited, is actually open. If going by public transportation, making sure that everybody knows which metro to take and where to get out, etc. The TA must be somebody who is organized themselves but also can operate independently. Ideally, the person speaks the local language however, that is not required, since many people in other countries speak English. Another reason to have an independent person is that inevitably a mishap occurs. I have had students end up in the hospital and the big question then becomes: Do you stay in the hospital with the student or can you rely on your TA? Clearly, the professor needs to be in the hospital to make sure that everything goes well, however, once the sick student has been settled in, staying with the sick student becomes the responsibility of the TA, so the professor can continue to educate the other students. Being able to rely on the TA for this important task is paramount.

Budget

It is important to remember that budgets will vary a lot, since costs vary greatly from country to country and change over time. Also, at some schools, some of the costs were included in students' tuition. Here are the main budget items:

- A copy of the aforementioned contemporary book about the country for every student.

- Cost of preparatory visit.
- Opening and closing dinner.
    - A note on this item: A separate source for funding can be the Office for Alumni Relations at your own university. When going to a larger city, there might be alumni interested in meeting with current students, and I have found that in those cases the Office for Alumni Relations was willing to pay for the event.
- Cost of the socio-cultural event.
- Honoraria: Typically, only speakers from a local university request an honorarium.
- Travel in the city, either by renting a bus or by using public transportation.

Conclusion

The best practices discussed are the result of continuous feedback by the students. To highlight this, I have included some quotes from recent student evaluations.[5]

- **Preparedness:** "Cultural preparations were great, especially as we needed it for the interaction with our client and it played a big role in our interactions there."
- **Varied topics and format:** "Germany has such an international presence, is a big player within the EU and US relations, etc. so it provided a lot of variation in the type of site visits we participated in. There is also just so much history here that it was a great addition to the work/cultural pieces."
- **Holistic programming:** "We learnt a lot about the culture and got international experience."
- **Encouraging independence:** "Students are allowed to direct the project as needed and the professor only interjects or provides guidance when necessary."
- **Practical nature of coursework:** "I liked the hands-off approach of Professor Geurts. He was extremely smart on helping us only when we really needed help. The rest of the challenges we tackled on our own which gave us more confidence."

Reading these comments reminds me how much of an impact these study-abroad trips have, but also how much fun they can be. It is a lot of work, but also extremely rewarding for the student and me.

Notes

1 One female student went with her group to the red-light district in Amsterdam, which is actually a safe area. The student paid a prostitute for her time and

proceeded to ask her questions about her life, experiences, dreams, disappointments, etc. The student labeled this as a life-changing experience, since she came from a sheltered environment, and now she finally started to understand how less-fortunate people lived.

2 Students also let their hair down (too far), like the one time when I wanted to interrupt the speech of a student and the student said "shut the f**k up, Geurts." It was a very hilarious moment and she apologized the next day.

3 It happened once that a student fell asleep in the subway, however we managed to get them out in the last second.

4 Especially the local food and drinks can lead to heated, yet friendly and amusing, discussions. Once during such a discussion, a student on a trip to Germany in the early 2000s, loudly proclaimed that bottled sparkling water, which was a standard offering with food in Germany, would never be a success in the United States. Pellegrino would beg to differ!

5 For more quotes, see Wellner et al. (2015).

References

Brown, J. C. (2011). *A Brief History of Argentina*. Checkmark Books.

Chandler, C., & Zainulbhai, A. (Eds.). (2013). *Reimagining India: Unlocking the potential of Asia's next superpower*. Simon and Schuster.

Geurts, T. G., & Jaffe, A. J. (1996). Risk and real estate investment: An international perspective. *Journal of Real Estate Research*, *11*(2), 117–130. https://doi.org/10.1080/10835547.1996.12090817

Wellner, K., van Gool, P., & Geurts, T. G. (2015). Lessons learned from thirteen years of international real estate study abroad programs hosted by universities in the United States, The Netherlands, and Germany. *Journal of Real Estate Practice and Education*, *18*(2), 117–140. https://doi.org/10.1080/10835547.2015.12091748

Appendix A

Visit preparation form

Pre-visit	Your name
	Company/Organization name
	Company/Organization website
	Other relevant sources of info
	Name(s) of the speaker(s) and their title/role in the Company/Organization

Pre-visit	Your name
	What do you think s/he is/are going to talk about?
	Description of the main activities of the Company/ Organization
	Questions (write a minimum of 3)
	What would you like to know? Formulate this in a series of at least three questions, which you can ask the speaker(s) during the visit. The questions you write below should help you better understand (a) how the visited company works, (b) major processes in the company, and/or (c) help improve your recommendations to your client.
	1.
	2.
	3.
	4.
	5.
Post-visit	**Summary of the main points of the presentation**
	Reflection
	What was the most interesting thing you learned on this visit and why?

Pre-visit	Your name
	What specific information did you learn that can help you improve your recommendations to your client?
	Other Notes

Appendix B

Team roles

Introduction

Each team consists of three or four members, and each member will have a specific role with its own responsibilities. This document describes the responsibilities of each member and their typical characteristics.

It is important that you study your own responsibilities and the responsibilities of the other team members. A good team member fulfills their responsibilities to the best of their ability while respecting the roles of others. Conflicts often arise when:

1. A person does not fulfill their assigned tasks, or
2. A person performs tasks that are not their responsibility.

Besides the typical responsibilities, tasks associated with the actual consulting project, such as secondary research, primary research, and data analysis, need to be distributed among the members, balancing workload and skill set.

Note: In three-person groups, #3 and #4 are combined.

Team roles table

Member	*Characteristics*	*Typical responsibilities*
1. Project Leader	– Leadership experience – Good communicator – Good listener – Able to delegate – Good writer	– Sets the direction and guides the project to a successful conclusion. – Creates a good work environment. – Serves as liaison with professor/client (if applicable).

Member	*Characteristics*	*Typical responsibilities*
2. Technology Officer	– Tech savvy – Strong organizational skills	– Creates and coordinates document share and database. – Maintains the PowerPoint deck(s). – Schedules and manages virtual meetings.
3. Communications Officer	– Knowledge of social media – Strong communicator – Skilled writer	– Chronicles team experience. – If applicable: contacts client to develop stories. – Finds out what can be publicly communicated. – Promotes trip via social media.
4. Culture Officer	– Expert on local culture – Experienced traveler – Good writer	– Leads team in-country. – Ensures surveys/interviews are culturally sound. – Ensures deliverables reflect understanding of local culture.

Appendix C
Sample syllabus

[Course Number]
[Course Name]
[Location]

Semester Year

PROFESSOR: *Dr. Tom G. Geurts, FRICS*
OFFICE HOURS:
OFFICE LOCATION:
EMAIL:

GRADUATE TEACHING ASSISTANT:
EMAIL:

CLASS MEETINGS: 01:30PM–04:00PM on Monday 1/28, 2/4, 2/25, 3/4, 4/1, 4/15, and 4/22.

LOCATION:

Course description

This course will go to Berlin in Germany. Berlin's role in Europe has gotten stronger and stronger after the fall of the Berlin Wall and reunification of Germany in 1989. With the expansion of the European Union to the former Eastern Bloc countries, the "schwerpunkt" of the European Union has also shifted eastwards, since countries such as Poland and the Czech Republic are quickly developing countries that export and import goods, services, and people to the original western core countries of the European Union. Indeed, growth in the more recently admitted countries of the European Union is larger, for example Poland's GDP will grow by 4.3% in 2018 versus Germany's growth of 2.3% in the same year. Germany's economy benefits from the faster growth in eastern European countries due to its proximity and transportation route to these countries. For example, France, where the growth of GDP will only be 2% in 2018. With these economic benefits comes growing political influence in the eastern European countries, which has grown even more due to Great Britain leaving the European Union ("Brexit").

This growing economic and political power can be clearly seen in Berlin, where the Government District around the completely refurbished Reichstag has grown rapidly with many new modern buildings and the former Berlin Wall area that was formerly a "no-go zone" has been rebuilt, for example as high-end retail, like the Potsdamer Platz. Indeed, Berlin is still full of exciting construction sites and the city is a vibrant place to visit.

In preparation of the trip the students will be provided with the information necessary so they can obtain a working knowledge of the industry in which their client operates, as well as the institutional and cultural framework of Berlin and its role within the European Union. Essential in this stage is that the students develop a meeting schedule of whom they want to meet and why, when in Berlin. Based on this I will arrange such visits. Clearly, if I see omission(s) in the program I will discuss this with the students.

Final analysis of the consulting project will be accomplished through onsite meetings and faculty-facilitated discussions, which will give the students an "on-the-ground" perspective of the economic, social, political, and legal realities of Berlin (Germany) in a larger global context. Work with the local host client will consist of a number of visits to the firm and meeting with key personnel. At the end of the trip there will be a formal presentation of the deliverable and feedback from the client.

Course objectives

By the end of the course students should be able to:

1. Utilize a formal consulting framework to design and execute a custom-tailored process to answer the key business questions identified by a client organization. This process should include:
    a. Developing working hypotheses.
    b. Designing and implementing a data collection plan.
    c. Synthesizing data to answer key questions identified by client organizations.
    d. Developing creative, well supported, impactful and actionable recommendations and implementation suggestions.
    e. Communicating, effectively and professionally, in written and oral form while executing a project plan as a team to respond to the challenges identified by the client.
2. Demonstrate a deep knowledge of the structure and dynamics of their client's industry, and of the central topic/theme of their project.
3. Demonstrate a broad knowledge of the economic, social, political, and cultural aspects of the country where their clients are located, as well as demonstrate an appreciation for the implications that cultural and institutional distance have on global business practice.

Structure of the course

This course is comprised of a formal classroom-based Consulting Abroad Program (CAP) and its associated overseas engagement, two components of one highly intertwined experiential learning experience. Co-curricular offerings, such as consulting skills trainings and formal assessments like the Global Mindset Inventory and Cultural Orientations Indicator, reinforce the course by allowing students to acquire skills and develop increased awareness of their individual strengths and improvement areas. Students are expected to take advantage of the portfolio of tools provided by Global & Experiential Education (G&EE) that are intended to assist them in optimal learning and performance.

This course is unique in that it is a three-credit experience with three faculty teaching the same core GMBA requirement. Although the faculty all use a similar syllabus with similar evaluation tools, please keep in mind that every class is unique. Each instructor may have a unique approach, each client has varying needs, and each program travels to a different location with its own unique culture and customs. Consequently, it is inevitable that students in each course will have differentiated experiences, although extensive coordination between the faculty minimizes this difference as much as possible.

As one academic experience both the Washington, DC and onsite program are regarded as one in terms of preparation, deliverables and grading. Expectations of academic engagement and professionalism are thus equivalent while students are engaged in the United States as well as overseas; one grade will be provided for the entirety of the experience.

This course is eminently creative, practice oriented, and team-focused. Students will be expected to take a leadership role in managing their own learning process. Students are expected to be highly entrepreneurial in finding the necessary sources of information to properly assess the current business landscape and in developing a sound proposal for their client. These sources include, but are not limited to, physical and online archives, industry experts, other professors, and potential consumers of the client's products and services. The professor will facilitate access to some of these sources, but they should be viewed as a starting point rather than the only sources of information needed to address the client's needs.

The campus-based and onsite experiences are closely aligned with the core curriculum of the Global MBA program. Students should expect to use knowledge gained in these courses as a foundation in performing, developing hypotheses and ultimately constructing a final deliverable for their clients.

Pre-requisites

Mastery of the management tools covered in the courses taken during the fall semester of the MBA program as well as progress toward the mastery of concepts in required spring core coursework of year one will also be assumed.

Technical requirements

All students enrolled in this course are required to have a personal Skype account; in years past this has been the most reliable and affordable means of holding conference calls with clients. Any expenses incurred for Skype communication are the sole responsibility of the student. Students may also utilize their WebEx account, provided free by the University.

Students are expected to be participating in an active learning experience while overseas; such an engagement requires access to the tools of global business including: a laptop computer or tablet, and preferably a smart phone.

Brief client project descriptions

There are three projects for three clients:

1) **GETEC:**

- *Company Info:*
  GETEC considers itself to be an enabler of the transition toward renewable energies and their vision is to be the leading energy efficiency company, offering smart solutions and optimal business models.
- *Project Information:*
  Conceptual design of an innovative contracting Business Model for the market entry in United Kingdom, considering the (expected) regulatory framework post-Brexit.
- *Core Subject Areas:*
  Energy, Finance, Strategy, Decision Analytics, and Operations Management.

2) **Peccato:**

- *Company Information:*
  Peccato was founded in 2006. They currently have three high-quality fashion stores but need a better way to "stand out" among the competition. Thus, they want to know how to better market their brand.
- *Project Information:*
  Develop a marketing and branding campaign for their stores.
- *Core Subject Areas:*
  Marketing.

3) **BEOS:**

- *Company information:*
  BEOS is an innovative real estate firm that converts and/or refurbishes existing industrial real estate into new and updated usage. Founded in 1997 and now operating with an interdisciplinary team of more than 140 employees, the company currently manages an inventory of 80 commercial properties with over 1,150 tenants, rental space of more than 2.6 million square meters and a total investment volume of more than EUR2.6 billion.
- *Project information:*
  BEOS with its six German offices is a fast-growing organization along its concept of "radical decentralized." The original founders have sold their BEOS-shares to the international group of SwissLife Asset Managers and have transitioned from leading the firm as co-CEO's to becoming Supervisory Board members. The management of BEOS

wants to take a fresh look at the organization and leadership structure of the firm within the new European context of SwissLife and make sure that the current management team is working optimally.

- *Core Subject Areas:*
  Real Estate, Strategy, and Human Capital Management.

Assignments and evaluation

Grading

Group work (60%)			*Deadline*
Project game plan report	10%	Organize	February 4
Input report	10%	Frame	March 4
Progress briefs	10%	FOCUS	Biweekly
Client written report – draft	Ungraded	Understand	April 15
Team presentations – draft	Ungraded	Understand	April 15
Team presentations – external panel	5%	Understand	April 22
Final client written report	15%	Synthesize	May 17
Final client presentation and slide deck	10%	Synthesize	May 17
Individual work (40%)			
Class participation	35%		
Midpoint peer evaluation			April 22
Onsite participation			
Visit preparation forms and Site visit leadership			
Final reflection	5%		June 7
	100%		

While most of the work will be conducted in teams, we expect that differences in the effort invested, level of engagement with the whole program (remote and in-country), and the value delivered towards the team's output as observed by the client, your peers, and the faculty member and the graduate assistant may result in differentiated grades for each individual student.

Explanation of course requirements

1. Project game plan report (10%)

Students should start working on the Project Game Plan as fast as possible, based on the Understanding phase of the Friga model. Each team will submit a first draft, which will be a "living document" as the students learn more about the Client and Project. This report will include:

1. A statement summarizing the client engagement issue/topic/challenge.
2. A descriptive outline of the client written report. The outline should include fully drafted text for every aspect of the report that is already known/researched. Where "blanks" remain, a list of remaining research questions the team is still pursuing should be embedded into the report.
3. A full bibliography in APA style.
4. Appendix A – (if applicable) Drafts of any primary research instruments (survey, interview protocol, focus group protocol, etc.).
5. Appendix B – A list of defined milestones/due dates for team project, inclusive of expected interviews and "touch base" meetings with clients and other individuals.
6. Appendix C – A detailed description of the roles and responsibilities for each team member.

All game plan reports should be posted on Blackboard by **February 4**. Teams should also create a brief PowerPoint summarizing the game plan report. You will be required to present this information informally in class on **February 4** and again on **April 1**.

2. Input report (10%)

A stated learning objective of this course is the development of broad knowledge of the economic, social, political, and cultural aspects of the country where your clients are located, as well as the demonstration of deep knowledge of the structure and dynamics of the client industry, and of the central topic/theme of your project.

To make immediate progress toward these central objectives of the course, all teams will be expected to define research topics that are critical to the specific industry of their respective client project beginning in the first phase of the consulting process. These topics should be based on the initial hypothesis formulation for the client's presenting problem. In addition to outlining tentative recommendation hypotheses, the team's initial research findings should be synthesized to present the landscape as you see it from your preliminary research. A bibliography must be included to support this assignment.

This assignment (exclusive of bibliography) should not exceed five double-spaced pages. Wherever possible, teams should make use of bullets, summary tables, figures, and charts in their reports to make the report visually appealing and quickly digested. All in-text citations should be parenthetical endnotes; a full reference list should be attached at the end of the assignment. Use the APA style guide to cite the sources.

In the appendix, please include the following:

1. Scope of Work Agreement (at least a tentative version that you have discussed with your client in the first meeting).
2. Memo summarizing major takeaways from the first client meetings.
3. The TEAM FOCUS process map template filled out to the best of your ability based on the limited information you have obtained at this point in time. You will keep tweaking this document as the project progresses.
4. Your Team Charter.

3. Progress briefs (10%)
Routine measures of student progress, challenges, and successes are critical in order for the faculty mentor to successfully provide assistance to teams as they develop their client deliverable(s). To formalize the communication of progress **biweekly** progress briefs must be provided to the instructor. These may take the format of a single-page memorandum addressed to the instructor and sent by the team leaders by the established deadline.

4. Draft client written report, draft and external panel presentation, final report, and final presentation (30%)
The main deliverable in this class will be a professional, client-responsive, and actionable client report. Each report will differ depending on the task assigned and client needs. The draft written report will be graded exclusively by the professor but may be informed by feedback from the client. Reports will be graded on the following criteria:

1. Responsiveness to client needs/requests.
2. Comprehensiveness of research (primary and secondary).
3. Specificity and "actionability" of recommendations made to client.
4. Creativity.
5. Professionalism of the report, presentation materials, and actual delivery of the proposals.

A draft written report and copy of the presentation will be due on **April 15**. There will be a presentation in front of a panel of external experts on

Monday **April 22**. Students will receive feedback from the professor on the draft written report and from the panel of experts on the presentation. Students are expected to revise and update the report and presentation in accordance with this feedback.

The final presentations to the clients will be scheduled for the last day in Berlin, thus **May 17**. The clients will be asked to provide explicit feedback on the quality of the work of the team, both in terms of content and delivery. The final report and presentation grade will be based on assessment by the professor with feedback from the client.

Final presentations will be delivered to the client on your assigned day in country. You should email the client an electronic version of the report and the PowerPoint **one full day** before the presentation and bring a hard copy of the revised report to the presentation for each client present. You should also bring copies of the PowerPoint handout for the client. Adhering to this timeline will require forward planning and should be discussed with your project team.

Final presentations will be graded on the following criteria:

1. Ability to keep to the established time limit.
2. Clear, easy-to-read, professional text and graphics.
3. Persuasiveness, on-stage confidence, and energy of presentation.
4. Full-room eye-contact, speech clarity, body posture/gestures.
5. Ability to respond to questions from client.

5. Class participation (35%)

As an active learning experience your continued and rigorous engagement is critical to the progress of your project work as well as your academic success in the course.

Class Attendance and Participation

Class attendance and participation is mandatory and will be evaluated strictly and on an individual basis. Your grade will depend on quantity of your participation and, most of all, the quality of your participation. Your participation grade may be negatively affected by unprofessional behavior in the Washington, DC (e.g., inappropriate comments, classroom distractions, chatting with classmates) as well as onsite (e.g., tardiness, lack of preparation for business visits and client meetings, attentiveness at required events).

It will be particularly important to prepare for the required sessions and activities where we have external guests. These people are experts in their domains and are willing to share their knowledge with us just for our benefit. Let's honor this by ensuring all are particularly professionally engaged during these sessions.

Midpoint Peer Evaluation

In an effort to assist in the development of each student as a learner and consultant a midpoint peer evaluation will be provided by and to each team member. This evaluation, an operationalization of the TEAM (Talk, Evaluate, Assist, and Motivate) model, will serve as an opportunity to provide sound and constructive feedback to team members with the aim of encouraging team productivity and efficiency. Consistent feedback from past participants illustrate that this is a critical opportunity for teams to share constructive feedback to all team members to improve project performance and professional development.

Consulting Abroad Program Seminars

Feedback from students consistently points to the need for skills building to compliment the structure and requirements of the formal CAP classes. In response, G&EE hosts a series of mandatory co-curricular trainings that emphasize the skills building critical to performance in CAP. These sessions are intended to supplement your classroom instruction and attendance is counted toward your course participation grade.

To capitalize on the framework the Global Mindset Inventory provides, CAP seminars are designed to give all students opportunities to intentionally reflect on areas of improvement discovered through their GMI results.

Below is tentative schedule of CAP Seminar topics:

CAP event topics

Month	*Topic*
January	TEAM FOCUS Framework / Client Relationship / Goal Setting
February	Cultural Orientations Indicator Debrief
March	Consulting Reports
April	Effective Presentations (Goal-Setting)

Onsite Participation, Visit Preparation Forms and Site Visit Leadership

Engagement while onsite in client meetings, business visits, and required cultural activities is critical to the success of each student. To facilitate this, students will be expected to be active participants in onsite activities and prepare for meetings through the production of formal site visit forms. Leadership roles will be assigned for each site visit and responsibilities provided by the instructor.

6. Final reflection (5%)
Students are required to submit a written reflection paper on their experience in the CAP including: the client organization, the destination city, or other site visits and business meetings in the project destination.

The paper can cover, but is not limited to, any of the following aspects of the business meetings/visits: (1) Organizational information of the host, (2) Any particular aspect of the host organization's management functions that interests you, (3) What aspect of the business meeting discussions that strikes you the most, (4) What are the take-aways you have from this visit, or (5) any social and cultural aspects of the destination cities. The length of reflection should be three double-spaced pages due no later than **June** 7.

Required reading materials

The McKinsey Engagement: A Powerful Toolkit for More Efficient and Effective Team Problem Solving (2008) by Paul N. Friga.
Other readings will be provided on Blackboard.

Course policies

Academic Progress and Travel Clearance
All students participating in the Consulting Abroad Program are required to maintain good academic standing. The university reserves the right to remove students not making successful academic progress – with assessment on an ongoing basis – and such students will not be authorized to travel for the overseas engagement of the program. Such students will be required to complete this requirement in a subsequent year.

Group work

This course intends to replicate the conditions under which a team of consultants work jointly to address their client's problems. As a result, group-work will be the norm rather than the exception. It is critical that team expectations are set from the beginning of the engagement. Given the amount of time that you will have to spend working together every week it is advisable that, from the beginning, all the members of the team agree on reserving specific blocks of time to plan and distribute the work, discuss and integrate it, and produce the reports and presentations as required.

All members of the team are expected to be prepared to discuss any aspect of the group's work at any time.

Portable electronic devices in the classroom

Many use laptops to help them take notes or reference the Internet as it relates to in-class discussion. However, no student is expected to be surfing the web, checking email, sending text messages, or working on other class assignments. Out of respect for the instructor and fellow classmates, it is expected that you will use your laptops and other electronics judiciously. Bear in mind that cold-calling is fair game at any point during class. Participation grades will be impacted for any student who is unable to respond or who provides a far less than satisfactory response.

Professional conduct

All students enrolled in the CAP are representing the George Washington University during their project work and expected to conduct themselves in a professional manner. Students who fail to do so will receive a written warning and be subject to removal from class sessions and/or the project team. Egregious behavior may result in immediate suspension from the project teams, with return to the United States at student expense, and/or receipt of a failing grade in the course. Students should refer to the complete participation agreement which must be signed electronically prior to travel and is provided in the appendix of this syllabus.

Academic integrity

Academic dishonesty is defined as cheating of any kind, including misrepresenting one's own work, taking credit for the work of others without crediting them and without appropriate authorization, and the fabrication of information. **ANY ASSIGNMENT INCLUDING PLAGERIZED MATERIAL (see Academic Integrity Code for definition) WILL RECEIVE AN F**. NO EXCEPTIONS WILL BE MADE.

Late assignments

No late assignments will be accepted. Note that 5 minutes late constitutes a late assignment. Students are expected to make arrangements to hand in assignments prior to the deadline. If you anticipate a course absence the day an assignment is due, you should plan to complete the work ahead of time, turning in the assignment early via email. Alternative methods of assignment submission should be sought prior to the class period. Failure to turn in assignments before class will result in a zero for the assignment.

Final grades

Final grades will reflect the student's total points earned in the course. Students will be able to track progress in the Blackboard gradebook. All grades are final. There will be no extra credit offered in this course.

Grading disputes

If a mistake occurs in grading, students are requested to submit a written request for a grade change outlining what is believed to be the error in grading. I will respond back to you as soon as possible in writing.

Attendance

Attendance and participation in both formal class meetings and required co-curricular programming in Washington, DC and all official activity in Berlin are mandatory and will be evaluated strictly on an individual basis. To receive a high grade in participation, you must come to class prepared and must contribute frequently and with high-quality, substantive comments.

Student support

Disability support services

Any student who may need an accommodation based on the potential impact of a disability should contact the Disability Support Services office.

For accommodation, overseas students are directed to contact Global & Experiential Education (G&EE) early on in the planning process. G&EE will liaise with Disability Support Services and in-country travel providers to establish eligibility and coordinate reasonable accommodations.

Overseas preparedness and emergency response information

Successful preparation for your CAP engagement will require careful attention to meetings prior to travel and after arrival at your destination. **On-campus orientation:** As a part of your preparation for international travel Global & Experiential Education will hold a pre-departure travel

briefing during one CAP class session. During this meeting students will review health and safety resources, University travel policies, and situational protocol. This is one of many opportunities to seek out the expertise of this office to best prepare for a healthy and safe overseas experience.
In-country orientation: Students should expect to participate in an in-country orientation during the first day of the overseas program. In this session faculty will share information about location-specific emergency and non-emergency procedures related to health and safety for the duration of your program.

Class outline

Each lecture will have a specific theme in order to ensure that we cover all relevant topics before we go in-country. *Each class, except the first two, will start with brief 7–10-minute presentations from each team on that lecture's designated theme.* Please see class descriptions:

Date	*Topic*	*Preparation*	*Assignments*
January 28: Introduction	1) Discussion of berlin and doing business in Germany. 2) Discussion of the clients and their projects. 3) Discussion of global mindset. 4) Creating a team, managing a team, and expected deliverables. 5) In-country scheduling.	Read: "Team Roles" by Tom G. Geurts. This document is posted on Blackboard.	None

Date	*Topic*	*Preparation*	*Assignments*
February 4: Focus on the Clients	1) Student presentations of the first draft of the project game plan reports. 2) Discussion of project game plan reports. 3) Identification of auxiliary visits in Berlin.	Each group should have spoken with their client at least once.	Submission and presentation of project game plan report
February 25:	Time to work on the input report.		None
March 4: Focus on Secondary Research	1) Student presentations of the input reports. 2) Discussion of input reports.	By this date teams should have done significant amount of data gathering in regards to the industry and work environment relative to their respective projects.	Submission and presentation of input report
April 1: Focus on Primary Research	1) Presentation of findings of orientation trip by the professor. 2) Presentation of updated project game plan reports. 3) Discussion of updated project game plan reports.	By this date teams should have done significant amount of information gathering in regards to hypothesis testing.	Presentation of updated project game plan report

(Continued)

Date	*Topic*	*Preparation*	*Assignments*
April 15:	1) Final preparation for trip. 2) Guest speaker from G&EE about in-country trip and its requirements. 3) Round table discussion about final client presentation. All teams are expected to share constructive feedback for each team.	By this date teams should have begun to synthesize their secondary and primary research, and have their first set of actionable recommendations for their respective projects.	Submission of draft client written report
April 22:	External panel: Three previousstudents and/or field experts will be invited to judge the presentations.		Presentation of draft client written report
June 7:			Submission of final reflection report

Modifications to the syllabus

This syllabus represents the best possible plan at this time. The instructor reserves the right to make revisions to any item on this syllabus, including, but not limited to, any class policy, the course outline and schedule, examination schedule, grading policy, required assessments, etc. Changes will be announced on Blackboard.

Appendix D
Sample itinerary

Itinerary Consulting Abroad Program Germany

Sunday *Berlin* *Casual*	*Monday* *Berlin* *Casual*	*Tuesday* *Berlin* *Business Professional*	*Wednesday* *Berlin* *Business Smart*	*Thursday* *Berlin* *Business Smart*	*Friday* *Berlin/Dresden* *Business Smart*	*Saturday* *Dresden* *Casual*
	Breakfast Daily brief	Breakfast Daily brief	Breakfast Daily brief	Breakfast Daily brief	Breakfast Daily brief	Breakfast Daily brief
Independent airport transfer to hotel	Orientation Business visit: Real estate developer	9–10:30am Client Meeting 1 11:00–12:30pm Client Meeting 2 Debrief	Business visit: US Embassy Debrief	Business visit: Consulting firm Debrief	Academic visit: University of Berlin (lecture on German legal and financial framework)	Cultural activity: City Tour

(Continued)

Itinerary Consulting Abroad Program Germany

Sunday Berlin Casual	*Monday Berlin Casual*	*Tuesday Berlin Business Professional*	*Wednesday Berlin Business Smart*	*Thursday Berlin Business Smart*	*Friday Berlin/Dresden Business Smart*	*Saturday Dresden Casual*
Lunch on own	Group lunch	Lunch on own	Lunch on own	Networking lunch	Lunch w/ University of Berlin Students	Lunch on own
Hotel check-in	Cultural activity: Holocaust Memorial	2:00–3:30pm Client Meeting 3	Business visit: Real Estate Law Firm	Client meetings Facilitated	Train to Dresden	Cultural activity: Winery
Government district walking Tour with Dr. Geurts		4:00–5:30 Client Meeting 4	Debrief	Team Work		
		Debrief				
Welcome dinner	Dinner on own	Dinner on own	Dinner with local alumni	Dinner on own	Dinner on own	Group dinner (winery)

Chapter 11

Top twenty tips for (adjunct) professors

Tanya Bansal and Margaret McFarland

Introduction

Most real estate programs, both undergraduate and graduate level, use adjunct professors to supplement a limited number of full-time faculty. There are a few exceptions, but generally, real estate still struggles to be recognized as a discipline at many institutions, whether based in a business school, an architecture, or a planning school, such as the program at the University of Maryland, where these authors are based. The real estate program at Maryland is based in a multidisciplinary school of architecture, planning, historic preservation, and real estate development. There are about 20 similar multi-disciplinary programs around the United States. But more commonly, real estate degree programs are based in the business school or department, often with a more limited focus on finance or investment. In fact, real estate programs are not standardized at all in the United States and literally are "all over the map" (McFarland & Nguyen, 2010)!

As an adjunct, you can make a difference in any of these academic settings, as there are very few real estate programs that have sufficient full-time faculty to cover the range of courses for a full-fledged real estate degree. The good news is that this creates an opportunity for you. Most real estate programs need you and your fellow industry professionals to take the plunge and try teaching, particularly once you are advanced in your career and your experience becomes more valuable. The challenge, of course, is to take your experience and figure out the skills for delivering your knowledge in a formal academic setting. Maybe you have mentored some students for a few hours or hosted a site visit or even done a guest lecture. If you found you enjoyed engaging with bright minds that need not only knowledge, but professional skills, you should consider taking on the challenge of teaching a full course. Your new aspirational title: adjunct professor.

In this chapter, the terms "adjunct" or "adjunct professor" refer to real estate industry professionals who contract to teach one or more courses in

DOI: 10.1201/9781032656458-11

a real estate program. Most adjuncts teach less than a full load of courses and typically are not required to provide service or research output to the university. For this chapter, we focus on tips for adjuncts who are teaching a full course as a solo professor.

The 20 tips set out below are based on having identified, engaged, nurtured, and mentored more than 50 industry professionals over 25+ years working with the University of Maryland's graduate and undergraduate real estate programs. We work with industry professionals to engage with our students from orientation to final capstone competition. Industry professionals provide site visits, internships, guest lectures, mentoring, and most crucially, teaching.

If you are reading this as a current or prospective adjunct professor, we hope you will find our tips helpful to a successful start, or continuing journey, in academia. And notwithstanding the focus on part-time adjuncts, we believe those of you who are already teaching full-time may find some useful teaching tips here.

Top 20 tips

1. ***Do* have experience** in your field. Our rule of thumb is to look for industry professionals with at least ten years of experience to come in as adjunct professors. Even better if you have been in the field for 20+ or even 40+ years. If you have this experience, you have the applied knowledge and experience to be outstanding adjuncts. And if you are retiring and looking for a way to "give back" to the industry, teaching is ideal.

Of course, there are exceptions when an outstanding program alum just cannot wait to come back and teach for their program. But in most instances, teaching is so much more rewarding, less stressful, and more effective for the students, when you have experience to back up the concepts you are covering.

2. ***Do* take a trial run.** Before you sign a course contract, we highly recommend that you try out at least one or two guest lectures to be sure you "like" teaching before you sign on for a full or even partial class. Pro Hint: It is actually less work, and easier to teach a class solo, than to coordinate with another professor, although we have worked with adjunct professors who have taught jointly with us and found it worked for them.

3. ***Don't* teach for the money.** Most institutions do not pay much for adjunct professional faculty. The amount paid per course could range as low as $2,500 or at the high end, but rarely, $10,000. So, it is best not to think about how much time you are putting in (particularly the first

time you teach a course) or to compare it to the money you are making in industry. As they say, you are doing it for the love of it – and the students – and as a gift to the industry by preparing the next generation of real estate professionals. It is definitely not about compensation!

4. ***Do* teach a course more than once.** This assumes you are asked. We are humans; we need to practice to get better. Teaching is no different. The first time through a course is the hardest and takes the most time. You will likely find you want to tweak your lectures, add more in-class exercises, even change-up who to use as a guest lecturer, or all of the above and more. Many of us keep a duplicate syllabus throughout the term, making changes or noting modifications we want to make the next time around.

The real ease and maximum joy in teaching typically comes in the 3rd, 4th, and 5th time teaching a course. You are on a roll and you will be putting in less time to boot. About the seventh time teaching a course you might want to take a sabbatical (academic speak for a semester off) or switch to a different course if your program is willing to let you. Also, you should consider what course structure that you want to teach. Not all programs will have flexibility for when the course is offered that they are asking you to teach, particularly when you first come in the door, but if you have the option to request the semester, day(s) of the week, and time the course is offered, do make it as convenient as possible for your schedule.

And, a word of caution, the real estate program needs you, your program director for sure needs you, but don't plan on making a career as a part-time adjunct professor. Not only is the compensation not life-sustaining, but the curriculum can change abruptly, or full-time faculty can be hired that have your expertise, or your desired class is no longer offered.

5. ***Do* figure out your best teaching style.** Yes, most courses will involve some, or more than some, lecturing as part of the content delivery. So, figuring out your best teaching style is another reason to teach a course more than once. Is your best style Socratic? Raising a topic and asking students to answer a pointed question and reacting/affirming/revising their answer? Personally, we have found this method difficult when many students, particularly at the undergraduate level, have not delved into the material deeply, or sometimes at all.

At a minimum, do not drone on without eliciting feedback or input from students throughout your presentation (see Tip #8). And, do not read from the textbook – or even your slides. Sadly, we had one very young adjunct lecturer who filled the lecture hour by reading the textbook word for word. Definitely not acceptable.

You likely have heard of, and experienced yourselves, teaching by the case study method. The textbook required by your institution may or may not provide case studies and questions for discussion. But using your experience, or that of a guest lecturer, to extract the broader conceptual understanding from a real-life case, is usually a very effective way to have student engagement, and hence, learning.

While you can refer to or use case studies from your own real estate experience, do be careful that the class, or any one lecture, does not turn into a series of "war stories." Reports from the field, site visits, and guest lectures which might be actual war stories can be useful and engaging but remember as an instructor you need to connect the "war story" to the concepts and skills the students need to master. Active learning, sometimes called applied or experiential learning, is very effective, and hopefully supported by your institution. And you, as an industry professional, are in the best position to teach from site visits and real-world problem solving.

6. ***Don't* be late.** Unlike parts of the business and government worlds where being 5, 10, or even 15 minutes late in some settings is considered acceptable, this is not the case in academia. Classes start on time. Get to campus 10–15 minutes, at least, in advance. If you are running late or cannot make it to your class for an unforeseen reason, inform your students as soon as possible as well as your program liaison so they can officially inform the students. Most accrediting standards require that the time missed in class be made up. Check with your program on how they manage that circumstance.

7. ***Do* be prepared.** Being prepared means you have an outline, if not a script, for what you will cover in each class, and the mechanisms you plan to use to engage students (see Tip #8). Your syllabus is a contract with the students. Some institutions allow changes after the beginning of the course, but often only a limited amount and only with significant advance notice to the students – typically at least two weeks. Changing course content or assignments frequently, or in the middle of the course, is a source of frustration for the students and will likely result in low student evaluations. Plus, it is truly unfair to diligent students and laggards alike if they are confused about what the topic or assignment is and when it is due.

If you are disorganized or unprepared, students will likely note that in the student evaluations. If this happens, you may not get invited to teach again. But, if you do, definitely work on improving that score. Believe us, it is harder than you think to stay on track and get the students all the information they need and the support they would like.

8. ***Do* engage students during class.** We are not fans of the "Sage on the Stage," where the professor lectures without interruption for the entire class period. While we do not forego all lecturing and content delivery from the lectern, we often use an icebreaker for 10–15 minutes at the beginning of a class or to break up 90+ minute class session. It could be in the form of a short three-question snap quiz that you then use to generate discussion at the beginning of class. Or, you can ask one or two students (in advance or on the spot, depending on your student's shyness quotient) to discuss something they read on the topic of the day.

We often give short assignments for everyone to bring to class. A favorite for eliciting engagement during class is to assign each student to bring in a one-page news report on real estate happenings within the last two weeks. The news could be from anywhere in the world. We give students a template to use that requires them to not just summarize but explain how the news item relates to the topic of the week. See Appendix A for a sample example of a news report template.

These short assignments also are turned in and graded and can be returned to students with comments. We have found that any assignment that is not part of their grade gets short thrift, while multiple small assignments keep students engaged in and out of class.

Another way to mix it up is to prearrange with one or two students to present or discuss a subtopic for the day. This is particularly useful in mixed graduate and undergraduate classes, where the graduate students can become experts on a topic and present a partial lecture or lead a discussion. Post-COVID, where it has been more difficult to engage students, you might try an in-class exercise with groups of three or four students to read together a short case study or news item and write a short summary to share with the class. Get them thinking; get them talking!

9. ***Do* follow the syllabus but you can also add your own creativity and experience.** Many universities have a policy that you can modify up to 20% of a program-approved syllabus. In virtually any course you teach you will find you are not able to cover everything in the topic area, let alone the textbook, *if* the course uses a textbook. In our experience, most undergraduate courses have a prescribed syllabus and textbook selected by the program. However, you typically are able to change the order of the syllabus, adjust the amount of time spent on particular topics, and/or add guest lectures and unique assignments.

In some cases, programs are open to hearing about alternative textbooks that you would prefer to teach or would recommend they consider. Courses with multiple sections, such as introductory courses, are harder to modify, but it never hurts to make suggestions to your program director. In some cases, you may be asked to propose a new course, say in a trending area such as proptech (property technology) or greentech (green technology). In that case, you would work with a faculty member to draft a new syllabus or modifications to an existing course.

10. ***Do* make assignments weekly**. You will find plenty of faculty who disagree with us but we believe strongly that assignments every week, or even every class period, are the most useful of all the alternative assessments as they become integral to the learning process. Some people use an opening class pop quiz, but we prefer the more engaged, fewer surprises approach to assignments, though a mix of both can also work.

The weekly assignments don't have to be long. They just have to be enough to be sure they have read the assigned material, listened to a guest lecture, or paid attention during a site visit. Smaller, multiple assignments keep students engaged. One technique is to have a major project as the learning/assessment tool and break that project into smaller weekly assignments as the students produce their project over time. The reality is that without a weekly assignment many students will not engage with the assigned material that week at all, and other classes where assignments have been made will get priority and you will find your students unprepared for your class.

And besides, as we like to remind our students, all humans learn by practicing. Requiring them to practice every week is the way to knowledge and mastery. We often ask at the beginning of a class when they see the syllabus with weekly assignments: How many of you are dancers? musicians? athletes? How often do you practice? Of course, the answer is "every day." To get good at something you have to practice!!

11. ***Do* make assignments that advance knowledge and skills.** Use assignments as a means for students to learn. Assignments that require the student to use and apply knowledge, rather than repeating information back to you as the instructor, will show the students understood the material but also that they can apply it.

Unlike full time professors, who are research focused and not likely to have industry experience, you can take students on site tours and introduce them to your friends and peers in the industry thereby greatly enhancing their learning. Site visits provide valuable experiential learning opportunities, allowing students to engage in real-world environments. Frankly, they will remember the site visit and the short 10–20-minute presentation from a developer, investor, or property manager long after they have forgotten much, if not all, of the rest of your course.

If site visits are not allowed or difficult to arrange, then do bring the real estate world to the students by bringing in guest speakers to present the latest trends to the class, like mass timber construction, dead malls, office conversions, the housing shortage, self-driving cars, and so on.

We often assign a "Key Points Memo" to confirm learning from assigned readings, site visits, and guest lectures. These memos are kept to a one to two-page limit, making grading straightforward. In these memos, students are required to highlight up to three "key" important takeaways, as opposed to providing a summary. An alternative to key points memos for introductory undergraduate students is to provide them with a form to fill in with a block for each point that they can use during the site visit or guest lecture. See Appendix B for a sample key points memo.

Presentations are another way to assess student learning while improving their oral communication skills. We recommend using a presentation grading rubric so that they are incentivized to focus not only on the content of their work but how well they can communicate it. See Appendix C for a sample of the rubric that we use which assesses the content and organization of the material and their presentation skills.

Some faculty are very successful in generating online discussions among class members through the class management online system. This promotes learning through interaction virtually as well. And, there is the tried-and-true method of assigning grading points for participation which can encourage preparation and engagement both online or in-class.

Need we say, we are not fans of multiple-choice quizzes or exams (see Tip #12). They are not learning mechanisms, and are not very effective in assessing actual knowledge gained, let alone knowledge retained.

Cautionary note: As we move ever faster into the AI-generated future, short memo assignments as well as critical book reviews and research reports are going to be a bigger challenge as an AI-generated paper can cover virtually any topic. Your institution may have rolled out seminars or workshops or tips on how to use AI effectively in your teaching and assignments. Academia is all abuzz on how to do this. Take advantage of every coaching or mentoring opportunity you can in this regard.

12. ***Do* require a final in-class assessment.** For this, we encourage you to have a final exam or a major project report and/or presentation. Some courses, such as real property law, might be assessed well with a written essay and short answer exam. However, we are big fans of assigning a major project from day one. Project-based learning is the current nomenclature for such assessment tools.

You can create fictional or actual scenarios of a real estate issue (e.g., property management, appraisal, market analysis, entitlements), all of which are assessed well through project learning. If you break the project up into pieces (weekly or biweekly) with draft submissions returned with comments, you will get engagement and better outcomes (learning).

For example, you could assign each student a "real" site to analyze, require them to conduct basic site context, market and financial analyses at an introductory level. This engages students outside the classroom when they visit the site and gives them a taste of what it would be like to work on acquisitions, finance, or market analysis, for instance. At the end of the term, each student (or group if class size requires) presents the analysis of their site to the class. If each student or group has a different site, it engages the students in the analytical tools applied to more than one place or type of real estate.

Pro Tip: A major project assignment with specific formats required and short clear instructions will enhance the student's learning and the quality of the reports and presentations you get back. The clearer and more detailed your instructions, the better the students will learn and produce a quality product.

However, in large undergraduate courses of 50+ students, project presentations may not be feasible. So, in that case, what is a good final exam? Assuming your program does not have a standard exam for the course, you will be designing an exam yourself. So, yes, the easy way is to have 100 multiple choice questions with a few True/False questions thrown in. While perhaps necessary if you have 100 students and no teaching assistant, this is the least desirable type of exam. An exam where the student must apply their knowledge based on a "real" scenario, in short answers or several paragraphs, will give you a much better sense of how much the student learned and understood the material. More work for you to grade, but so much more valuable for the students.

Do give the students a review sheet that has all the topics that will be on the exam. In our view, an exam should not be a guessing game as to what the instructor considers the most important concepts and skills to test. In other words, "don't hide the ball." Let them know what to study so they can perform well on the exam, and coincidentally, as they study, they will be reviewing the parts of the course that you consider most important for their success in the real estate industry.

And, above all, avoid giving take home exams. While convenient for students and professors alike, take-home exams are deadly in the era of AI or even other outside assistance to the students. In short, you do not really know who took that exam at home, and giving one puts students in an ethically challenging situation. Hence, our best advice is to never give a take home exam.

13. ***Do* return grades promptly and return them with comments.** You should grade all assignments and return them promptly for them to be useful to you and the students. Even those short weekly memos or quizzes. The feedback helps you know what students are learning (or not). The returned assignments, particularly in the first few weeks, help them adjust their study habits so that they find out early on if they are not doing well, and, in enough time, for those adjustments to make a difference to their course grade.

A graded assignment that is given back more than a week later has lost most of its pedagogical value. You want students to improve and acquire knowledge and skills in your field. Prompt feedback in the form of written comments (which now can be done online at most institutions), along with grades, is the best way to help your students improve over time. And, seeing that improvement is so gratifying. Without frequent feedback students won't know how well they are learning or where they can improve.

Even if your program does not require prompt return of grades or written comments, believe us, you will enjoy the process much more if you do and your students will be learning so much more.

14. ***Don't* inflate grades but be aware of your institution's guidelines.** Figuring out how to grade fairly and not too hard and not too easy is one of the biggest challenges for instructors – adjunct or full time. It is one of the most daunting tasks for an instructor. Different institutions have different grading protocols and guidelines. So yes, follow those if provided. However, a good rule of thumb is: if everyone in an introductory course is getting an A, you are not making challenging enough assignments. Conversely, if most of your students are getting Bs and Cs or below, and there are few to no As, the assignment is probably too challenging or is beyond the background students bring to the class. Another good reason to make assignments early and often in the course. You can adjust accordingly.

When it comes to graduate classes, some programs allow Cs, but you may be strongly encouraged to look at grading only with As and Bs. The theory being that if a student simply shows up and does the work, they deserve a passing grade. We are not fans of this approach, as peers and supervisors in the future will not overlook a poorly presented or researched project. Getting "real world" feedback on their performance is one of the benefits an adjunct professional instructor can bring to students. Think of it as giving them a tough, but fair, workplace review.

Of course, it is possible, particularly in a small advanced graduate class, you might have all A or B students. In that case, where you have a limited number of students, say under 12, you will just have to use your best judgment!!!

15. ***Do* respond to students in a timely manner.** At our institution, being responsive to students does not require you to hold in-person office hours. Typically, students rarely show up at those set aside hours, although if you are on campus anyway, you can always put a couple of open-door office hours on the syllabus. More realistically, you should have your syllabus inform students how they may reach you (email, text, phone) to set up an individual appointment. Be sure you check those channels daily. Our rule of thumb is to try to respond to a student within 24 hours or less.

For most adjunct professors and most issues, you can resolve a student issue with a Zoom session or phone call but it is also a good idea to give time for students to informally meet you either before or after class. If possible, come to campus early or commit some time for scheduled or unscheduled meetings after class.

There are student issues that adjunct professors are not well equipped to handle, particularly mental health or harassment issues, reasonable accommodations, and cheating suspicions. Be sure you know who on campus handles these issues and refer students as soon as you become aware of any of these problems (see Tip #17). Hopefully, your program will hold a faculty orientation before the semester starts and if not, you should be sure to ask for information on how to handle difficult students and issues.

16. ***Do* be a mentor, but not a friend, to your students.** It is an ethics thing! In our experience both as instructors ourselves and as mentors to adjunct faculty, wanting students to "like" you is not good for anyone. You want their respect, not their friendship. You also need to give them respect but not be a pushover for every complaint or request.

A class is not a popularity contest nor should you take a poll, or show of hands, for what kind of homework, or assignments, or exams they would like. You are kind, friendly, accessible, and open-minded to hear their concerns, but firmly in charge. You are a mentor, a source of knowledge; but you are not there to be a friend. You are not there to be liked. Some full-time faculty, or adjuncts, manage to engage with students outside of class, but in our view having seen this go awry, it is best avoided. Questions of favoritism, or inappropriate behavior, true or false, are just too easily raised. And, do not meet with a student alone in a closed-door room or office! Need we say more?

We note also that getting high marks on student evaluations because you asked them to do "not much" is not satisfying to you or your program. Your students have paid, often out of their own pocket, or with costly loans, for the course you are teaching. Give them their money's worth – even if they complain about too much work. Better to have complaints they had to work too hard than the class was an easy A.

Two great come backs when overwork complaints arise: "Are you concerned you will learn too much?" "When you tell me you're not getting your money's worth, then I'll listen". All said with a smile and using an empathetic voice. Often the complainers will tell you at the end how grateful they are that you made them work so hard and how much they learned. If you are lucky, you may even be told "it's the best class I've ever had."

Finally, connecting with students after they graduate and are out in the industry as full professionals can be rewarding for sure. They now are no longer your student and it is an excellent way to expand very fruitful professional associations for them – and you! Hello Linked-In.

17. ***Do* reach out to your program faculty liaison.** This is especially important if you have serious questions or concerns. You don't have to wing it. Examples of problems you may want to bring to the liaison's attention include: students who don't make it to class at all more than once, or ever on time; students missing exams or multiple project due dates; and students asking for "reasonable accommodations." There are federal requirements for these accommodations and an office on virtually any campus to support faculty who receive and approve these requests, typically with your input. Be sure to check with your liaison to find out how the federal policy on reasonable accommodation requests works at your institution.

18. ***Do* take advantage of resources that the university has to offer.** Often, there is a teaching and resource center that will have tips, resources, and free workshops for effective teaching on topics like enhancing student engagement, creating a positive classroom climate, and hybrid teaching. University libraries are a great resource for preparing syllabi. Do not buy the book, always check the university's library first to see if there is a copy available. Plus, many textbook publishers will provide a review copy gratis to a professor. Libraries also have case studies, newspapers, trade publications, and databases that you can access to prepare your teaching materials. Consider meeting with your school librarian to learn about different resources. In our library system, we can post articles and book chapters electronically for students at the online interactive teaching site for our course.

Do make sure you get a good orientation to the online course management and other online systems the students use for posting syllabi, assignments, and returning comments and grades to students. These online tools are much easier (once you get the hang of them), than the old gather up papers, scribble comments, enter grades in a separate spreadsheet, and return to the student!

19. ***Do* participate in as much of campus life as possible.** First off, be sure to go to every meeting of adjunct faculty called by your program. Not only will this endear you to your program, but you will find the connection to the program faculty rewarding, both adjunct and full-time. You will often gain helpful teaching tips and important information on resources at your institution. Parking permits anyone??

Many programs are in schools where you may be invited to attend (optionally) school-wide retreats or orientation sessions or to attend special awards dinners or scholarship events. Attending these kinds of events will enrich your experience and the students love seeing you there, so do partake if you can fit them into your schedule.

Participating in your program's student orientation, recruitment events, or a search or admissions committee also can be very rewarding. You might even be asked to participate in a research project by full-time faculty or to make a presentation at an academic conference such as the American Real Estate Society (ARES). We would highly recommend participating in as many of these activities as you can.

The more places and people you know on campus, the more you will enjoy the experience and likely find valuable connections back to your professional world. In other words, say "yes" to as much as you can.

20. ***Don't* panic.** It is both easier (and harder) than you think to be an adjunct professor. And remember – you know more on your subject than the students do! On the plus side, you get to share your knowledge and realize how much you really know after all those years of experience. It is rewarding to be asked for your advice and realize you can help a young person advance their life and career. Don't miss out. Call your local real estate program and ask to come and give a guest lecture. Get your feet wet and see if teaching is for you!!!

So, there you have it! Our top twenty tips for being an effective and engaging adjunct professor. Plus, one final admonition: Enjoy!! Teaching is the most rewarding thing we have done in our careers. Between us we have done everything from land use planner, practicing attorney, practicing architect, project manager, project analyst and property manager and we can both say that teaching is one of the most satisfying things we have ever done. Don't miss out!!!

Reference

McFarland, M., & Nguyen, D. (2010). Graduate real estate education in the U.S.: the diverse options for prospective students. *Journal of Real Estate Practice and Education*, 13(1), 33–54. www.jstor.org/stable/24863107

Appendix A
Sample News Synopsis (1–2 Pages Max)

Student Name:
Due Date: (the date submitted – no late entries accepted)

Title:
Author:
Source:
Date of Article: (must be within 3 weeks of due date)

SUMMARY OF ISSUE PRESENTED: (very short; typically, one short sentence, putting in the form of a question usually enhances your analysis below; if it is on the topic of the week, you receive 5 extra points)

SUMMARY OF FACTS: (bullets, no sentences, 1/2 page or less)

ELABORATION of ISSUE AND FACTS: (elaborate on sections above in short sentences, no more than 2–3 paragraphs)

Appendix B
Sample Key Points Memorandum

FROM: Student Name
SUBJECT: (Textbook or other Reading; Guest Lecture; Site Visit)
DATE:

I. INTRODUCTION

II. SHORT HEADER OF THE FIRST KEY POINT
Make sure the header is a good short description of your POINT. Follow the header with a brief 1–2 paragraph explication of the point in your own words. Explain why you find it to be "key" or "important" as opposed to other points made.

III. SHORT HEADER OF A SECOND KEY POINT
Same directions as First Key Point.

IV. SHORT DESCRIPTION OF A THIRD KEY POINT
Same directions as above, for as many points as you are going to make.

V. ANALYSIS OF THE KEY POINTS
What do the points you identified above have in common; are they related at all? Compare and contrast them.

VI. CONCLUSION
In your conclusion, tie together if there is a tie, the key points you have selected, any compare and contrast points between them, and relate to your own experience or professional aspirations.

Appendix C
Oral presentation assessment rubric

Name of presentation	*Grading scale*				
	Poor	*Fair*	*Passing*	*Above average*	*Excellent*
Structured content Storyboard – (beginning,middle, and end) Summarize what I will present Present information Summarizc what I presented	1	2	3	4	5
Simplicity The Rule of 3's and 5's 3 key points with 5 supporting points each, OR 5 key points with 3 supporting points each	1	2	3	4	5

Name of presentation	*Grading scale*				
	Poor	*Fair*	*Passing*	*Above average*	*Excellent*
Professional presentation of self Effective body language (posture, gestures, movement, etc.) No verbal litter (e.g. um, ah, like, so, etc.) Articulate clearly (slow, slow, slow)	1	2	3	4	5
Audience engagement Dynamic/Energetic presentation Do not turn back to the audience Do not read from notes	1	2	3	4	5
Visual presentation PowerPoint 10/20/30 Rule 10 slides (maximum) 20 words (maximum per slide) 30-point font (minimum) No sentences Interesting images (not distracting)	1	2	3	4	5

Chapter 12

Engaging alumni and industry professionals

Building connections, not transactions

Karen M. McGrath and Elaine M. Worzala

Introduction

In the world of real estate education, the classroom is just the beginning. The real magic happens when instructors, alumni, industry professionals, and students all come together; not just for lectures, but for mentorship, collaboration, networking, and long-term investment in everyone's success.

However, engaging alumni and professionals is easier said than done. It's not about a one-time event or a mass email with vague requests. It's about crafting intentional, mutually beneficial relationships that make people want to stay involved. The good news? There's a proven playbook, and it starts with shifting the mindset from "asks" to "opportunities." This chapter will help provide readers with some practical advice from experienced instructors who have been on both sides of the equation.

So, let's walk through what it looks like to create a thriving, people-powered real estate program, one connection at a time.

Be specific with the ask

When it comes to engagement, the more specific that you can be the better! Open-ended asks such as "would you like to be involved in our program?" or "we'd love your support" are vague and just not explicit enough. It leaves room for potential participants to say "sure" and then never actually get engaged or involved. Alumni and professionals are more inclined to say yes when they know exactly what they're being asked to do, as well as the kind of impact that they will have.

So instead of the vague language used above, use language that is clear, actionable and tied to outcomes such as:

- "The students are going to be learning about {insert relevant topic here}, and given your expertise in this area they would really benefit

DOI: 10.1201/9781032656458-12

from hearing about your experience. Would you like to do a guest lecture for us?"
- "We're looking for industry judges for our spring case competition, would you be interested?"
- "Your new development project is really exciting; can you arrange a site visit for our students?"
- "We'd love to name next week's real estate club tailgate after your firm. Would you consider sponsoring the event?"
- "Would you be willing to sponsor student access to Argus training this semester?"

People respond better when they know what they're being asked to support and how. Specific asks are easier to consider, easier to say yes to, and easier to feel good about. Alumni at many schools are particularly interested in giving back, and when they take on some of the above initiatives it is a win–win–win for them since they are helping the students, their company, and they're also reconnecting with their college experience and other alumni.

Start small and let relationships grow organically

Don't feel like you need to open with an ask for a six-figure donation. Every relationship starts somewhere; in fact, many of the most committed alumni and industry partners began with something as simple as being a guest speaker for a class, joining a panel discussion, reviewing a few resumes, or buying pizza for the real estate club or for the students on a site tour. These "entry-level" engagement opportunities are low-stakes, and low-cost, but high-impact. They give alumni and professionals a taste of the program's energy, they allow them to connect with students, and they often can lead to bigger involvement over time. Just like in a real estate project, small investments, when nurtured, can lead to big returns.

Always say "thank you" (and mean it!)

Gratitude should never be an afterthought. Whether someone gives money, time, access, or advice, it's crucial to acknowledge their contribution in a personal and thoughtful way.

While people love to help, they also like to be thanked for their efforts. For guest lectures, it's always nice to give a small token such as a pen, coffee cup, T-shirt, or water bottle that is branded with your department, center or university logo and colors. These gifts often become topics of conversation, and will continue to market your program or university for years to come. Even if you don't have the resources for physical gifts, you can, and should, always say thank you in a multitude of ways. Highlighting experiences or gifts by tagging people, companies, or organizations on platforms such as LinkedIn brings both your program, and donors, additional visibility while demonstrating how much their support was appreciated. Ask students to email the contributor individually; this not only allows the students to express what they got out of the experience, but it also helps students see the importance and value of networking. But, don't forget to embrace old school traditions. Handwritten thank you notes are especially powerful in an age of digital everything. It really does stand out so not only should you embrace this practice, but encouraging your students to do it as well can also work to your (and their) advantage. That extra effort tells the person that their contribution was noticed and appreciated, and the individual often remembers the personal touch. For example, one student created a handmade thank you card for a guest speaker, and that individual remembered their involvement in the class four years later!!

Beyond being good manners, saying thank you also acts as a form of subtle public relations for your program. When people feel seen and appreciated, they talk about it. They share it with colleagues. They post about it. And that builds the kind of organic visibility that money can't buy.

Make engagement a two-way street

One of the most effective ways to keep alumni and professionals coming back is to ensure that they benefit from the relationship, too. Companies are always looking for new talent, and industry organizations are looking for new members. Engaging professionals and organizations benefits the students, but when you invite alumni and professionals to engage in activities such as speaking in the classroom, being mentors, offering interview coaching or resume feedback. or participating in site visits where they can showcase their work and their firm, they get value in return. They get brand exposure, access to student talent, opportunities to recruit, and a chance to remain connected to the cutting edge of real estate education. When engagement feels reciprocal and rewarding, it becomes sustainable and effortless.

Real estate clubs: Where the magic starts

If centers, discussed below, are the engine room, real estate clubs are the fun "lido deck" of the ship: available to everyone with an interest in real estate, active, and alive with energy. These student-led organizations are often the most accommodating, engaging way to connect with alumni and professionals. In addition, they provide the students with leadership and management skills that will help them in their careers. We would encourage you to make the real estate club open to anyone on campus as real estate is multidisciplinary and students from economics, political science, or engineering might be interested in being part of the group.

Active real estate clubs will typically host:

- Evening speaker panels and networking events.
- Social events like mixers, tailgates, or site tours.
- Skill-building workshops or software tutorials.
- Case competitions and group challenges.
- Professional networking opportunities.
- Career fairs and other company recruitment efforts.

Because they're student-driven and flexible, clubs are ideal places to involve young alumni and early-career professionals. With the proper guidance from their faculty sponsor, they best reflect what students want to engage in. For alumni, they offer a low-pressure way to reconnect and give back, and they often serve as the proving ground for future advisory board members or donors. One event that is extremely effective is the speed networking events that are run like speed dating events. Students spend 5–10 minutes with each professional, and they get to talk to 8–10 professionals during the event. This can be done as one-on-ones, but if you have younger students, it can be better to team them up as they may feel more comfortable with a fellow student. Clubs are also one of the best ways to demonstrate student enthusiasm and energy to external stakeholders. When professionals see a vibrant, motivated group of future industry leaders, they want to be part of it.

Create a career pipeline that works both ways

Your students want jobs. Your alumni want talent. Faculty (and/or the real estate program) are the intermediary. Engaged faculty can make the introduction. Whether it's through internship placements, resume workshops, interview coaching, or employer meet-and-greets, career engagement is a key reason why professionals stay involved. It keeps them close to the talent pipeline, and helps students feel like the program is a launchpad, not just a lecture hall. See Appendix A for a list of career-based websites that might be useful for helping to advise students and source positions.

The best career engagement efforts also help students develop real-world confidence. Resume reviews and mock interviews, especially when delivered by alumni, can be incredibly impactful, and foster lasting relationships.

Partner with local or national industry associations

Another often overlooked partnership are the professional organizations that are established to facilitate networking and career development. Whether you're located in a major metropolitan area with significant real estate or a smaller college town market, chances are there are local real estate professional organizations ready to partner with you. For more information on some of the various associations related to real estate, see Appendix B.

A few things that most industry associations offer to universities include:

- Student memberships that often include access to their websites with both resources as well as career pages curated by their members.
- Scholarships for both tuition but also to attend their annual meetings or other events. For example, Commercial Real Estate Women (CREW) have an annual scholarship program where the winners get money, membership, a travel stipend to attend their annual meeting, a summer internship and a mentor.
- Internships and mentorship programs.
- Access to members that can be guest speakers or provide field trips. For example, The Counselors of Real Estate offer a "Counselors in the Classroom" program.
- Additional resources including research grants and opportunities for both faculty and students. For example, the National Association of Office and Industrial Properties (NAIOP) has a Distinguished Fellows Program for faculty to engage with the association.

Most of the active real estate associations today know that they are not very diversified, and they have set up programs to engage with university programs in order to benefit from early access to talent and visibility on campus. By engaging in with these associations, your program gains credibility, connections, and potential funding. Never assume that just because you're not in a major metropolitan area, industry groups won't want to engage with your program or students. In reality they are often eager to get involved and participate; you just need to make the effort and open the door.

Build a dream team: Real estate advisory boards and alumni associations

To formalize your relationships with industry leaders and alumni, you may want to consider establishing a Real Estate Advisory Board composed of committed professionals. Often this group is made up of devoted alumni who are eager to give back to their alma mater. The university alumni association can, and should, be used to attract graduates. However, industry professionals that are not graduates can also be asked to help out. Typically, they are engaging because they are interested in recruiting your students. This board can help guide the program's strategic direction, serve as ambassadors to their networks, and lead the charge when it comes to fundraising, especially for larger gifts and endowments.

Alongside your board, you should consider a Real Estate Alumni Association. In fact, that might be easier to set up than the Advisory Board. Alumni are vested in not only the real estate program but also the reputation of the university and, as mentioned earlier, there is a feel good, nostalgic air to their engagement and involvement as they replay their college experience. It is recommended from our experience that you do not limit your group to just those from your small real estate program, but that the association is inclusive of anyone currently working in the real estate profession. They may have a political science degree, but they are a "dirt lawyer." The older alums (who typically have more money) did not have an established real estate program to go to when they were in school, but they want to give back and use their university network for business development and engagement just as much as the younger professionals. This group can help plan networking events and/or conferences, engage in mentoring the students, and/or promote the program across regions and sectors.

Just be mindful of your university's advancement office as well as their alumni association. Be sure to coordinate with them so you are not duplicating fundraising efforts or bombarding the same people repeatedly with multiple asks. You may want to consider focusing your alumni association on smaller, engagement-rich gifts that can fly under the radar while making a big impact for the real estate students in your program.

Consider establishing a real estate center

A well-structured real estate center can be the backbone of everything from career placement to public programming. With dedicated staff and strong leadership, a center can:

- Plan and manage site visits, field trips, speaker panels, and conferences.
- Coordinate with industry partners and alumni on outreach and engagement.
- Maintain directories, career databases, and internship pipelines.

- Run advisory boards, student support efforts, and employer relations.

Some centers are research-focused, funded by organizations like the National Association of Realtors (NAR), and tasked with producing market insights and thought leadership. Other centers are programmatic, focusing on teaching, networking, and student experience. The strongest centers find ways to integrate both research and programming: supporting curriculum, coordinating career services, and building strong external ties with the industry.

Centers can also provide a way for a larger donor or donors to get recognized. When a center is named, this is usually the result of a large gift being given to the university, and it is often structured as an endowment. This gift signals both the donor's and the university's commitment to real estate, which adds an element of prestige to the program. But even more importantly, it also provides long-term operational support as the endowment is kept in perpetuity with funding coming from earned interest. This ensures a level of financial stability from which the program can operate, benefitting students and faculty alike. Indeed, a named center creates visibility, anchors fundraising, and helps build a legacy for donors who want to make a lasting impact.

Most centers will have a Center Director as well as some support staff. These individuals could be responsible for teaching, research, developing curriculum, or simply serving as a bridge between students and industry. However, their presence helps unify the program's academic and engagement strategies and gives the real estate a platform or seat at the table within the hierarchy of the university. They can also provide another naming gift opportunity as recently programs have been able to attract endowments for the Center Directors to ensure funds are available to keep these positions open.

Don't underestimate the power of in-kind giving

Big checks are great, and sure, everyone loves a donor wall. But you know what else people appreciate? The person who buys pizza at a club meeting or the drinks at a happy hour; that person becomes a legend to the students that benefit from that gift. In addition, many companies have programs that provide student access to data (CoStar Group) or software programs (ARGUS). In-kind gifts are one of the most underused, high-impact tools in the engagement toolbox. They make events possible, show generosity in action, and often open the door to deeper involvement. So, don't just ask for money. Ask for support. Ask for time. Ask for snacks.

Conclusion

The takeaway: real engagement is built on real relationships. Engaging real estate alumni and industry professionals is not about one big ask, it is about building long-term relationships with a lot of smaller asks that can grow into some big gifts. Start with real conversations because people do not just want to give, they want to belong. They want to mentor, advise, connect, and contribute in meaningful ways. And when they do, everyone wins.

To build that kind of engagement you need to be clear, be intentional, be generous with your gratitude and your time, and always look for ways to create mutual connections and/or value. The best real estate programs don't just teach, they build a community between the students, the faculty, the industry, and the alumni. When you turn your real estate program into a true community, the possibilities extend far beyond any classroom or conference room. They build a foundation for the future for your program but also our professional real estate industry.

Appendix A

Career resources

- **BL Next:** A non-profit seeks to educate and empower student-athletes to lead successful careers in commercial real estate after their college sports journeys end. https://bluelightre.com/
- **IHire:** This job board has industry communities and one of them is real estate. You can put your information in and they will send you alerts on openings in your chosen career path and/or location.
- **LinkedIn:** This job board has the ability to search by career path and full or part-time positions as well as internships.
- **Professional associations:** Most of the associations above have career pages as well that have listings for internships and permanent careers.
- **Project destined:** A nonprofit that provides students with training, networking, mentorship, job and internships in real estate, entrepreneurship, and finance. https://projectdestined.com/
- **Select leaders:** A job board supported by most of the commercial real estate associations and organizations. Students can find jobs and internships throughout the United States. www.selectleaders.com/
- **SEO careers:** A nonprofit that prepares Black, Latino, and Native American undergraduate students for summer internships across Wall Street and real estate. https://career.seo-usa.org/

Appendix B

Additional resources to help build a real estate program network: Professional associations and certifications (including links for student memberships where available)

- **Appraisal Institute:** Offers courses, publications, and certifications related to real estate appraisal, with a focus on valuation techniques and market analysis. Student affiliate membership is free. And, they have a scholarship for a graduate and undergraduate students each year. www.appraisalinstitute.org
- **CCIM Institute:** This organization provides a certification for commercial real estate professionals. CCIM stands for Certified Commercial Investment Member and focused on commercial real estate. It is a multi-course process with exams and a final project. CCIM Student Membership is $50 and is open to full-time undergraduate and graduate students. www.ccim.com
- **Commercial Real Estate Finance Council** (CREFC): Offers educational resources, certification programs, and networking opportunities for professionals in real estate finance and capital markets. www.crefc.org
- **CORENET Global:** For corporate real estate professionals. Student memberships are $25 per year. www.corenetglobal.org
- **CREW Network:** Members join individual chapters, located throughout the US. Student memberships prices vary by chapter, so see the local chapter website for pricing. Best to join in January if interested. www.crewnetwork.org. The CREW Network Foundation also awards 50 student scholarships each year to both graduate and undergraduate students.
- **ICSC (formally known as the International Council of Shopping Centers):** For those interested in retail real estate. Student memberships are $50 per year. www.icsc.com/
- **NAIOP:** Commercial Real Estate Development Association. NAIOP members are primarily professionals in the commercial real estate development industry. The organization provides advocacy, education, research, and connections to foster business opportunities for professionals engaged in development and redevelopment. In partnership with local chapters, they connect and serve a diverse network of leading CRE professionals. They have six scholarships (two $2500 scholarships for undergraduates and six $5000 scholarships for graduate students as well as $1000 in travel funds to attend the national conference. www.naiop.org/

- **National Multifamily Housing Council (NMHC):** NMHC is the primary resource for industry research, insight, analysis, and expertise on apartment industry issues. Access everything NMHC researches, advocates, and publishes here. www.nmhc.org/research-insight/
- **National Association of Multifamily Housing (NAMH):** the NMHC is where rental housers and suppliers come together to help meet America's housing needs by creating inclusive and resilient communities where people build their lives. NMHC provides a forum for leadership and advocacy that promotes thriving rental housing communities for all. www.nmhc.org
- **National Association of Real Estate Investment Trusts (NAREIT):** A key resource for information on REITs, including market data, performance analysis, and policy updates. www.reit.com/nareit
- **Royal Institution of Chartered Surveyors:** A global organization for real estate professionals. Student membership is free. www.rics.org
- **Society of Industrial and Office Realtors (SIOR):** This organization includes primarily commercial real estate brokers that work in the industrial and office sectors. They have over 4,000 members in over 50 countries. They also have a foundation that provides the 2024 Mildred C. Hanson, SIOR Memorial Scholarships for one outstanding graduate and undergraduate student demonstrating significant promise and commitment to the real estate profession. The scholarship is for $8000. Some of the local chapters also award scholarships to students at their local universities. www.sior.org
- **The Counselors of Real Estate (CRE):** A global consortium of credentialed real estate problem solvers, who provide expert advice on complex real property and land-related matters. Its 1,000 members from 22 countries and the US territories, brings professionals from all specialties of the real estate industry together. Membership, which is extended by invitation only, although qualified members can self-apply, www.cre.org. Students and professionals can subscribe to their free publication *Real Estate Issues*.
- **Urban Land Institute:** A global network of real estate and land-use professionals in a variety of disciplines. Student memberships are 75% off the Associate membership price per year. www.uli.org

Chapter 13

Building real estate bridges across the university curriculum

Meagan McCollum

Introduction

Real estate is at its core an interdisciplinary field of study. In practical terms, real estate encompasses a diverse set of knowledge and skills, including law, architecture, economic development, banking, interior design, urban and city planning, finance and investment, sales and negotiations, accounting, construction, engineering, and management, among others. For example, CREW Network, a major international professional association for real estate, lists 37 distinct qualified fields of commercial real estate – areas of specialty – that potential members may work in to qualify for membership in the organization (CREW, 2025). Given the broad nature of the field, it is counterintuitive that real estate programs are often siloed in academic departments that restrict access to the curriculum to the broader student body. This is especially pertinent for undergraduate students, who are the focus of this chapter.

University administrators at my small private university strongly encourage faculty to think creatively and collaboratively when proposing any program additions or changes. When I joined the University of Tulsa as a finance faculty member, there was only a single introductory course offered in real estate. At the behest of students and alumni stakeholders, I propose expanding the course offerings in real estate at the university. My college dean was enthusiastic about the idea but was equally adamant that I think critically about how to effectively utilize existing courses, faculty, and resources as much as possible when designing a real estate program. This mandate forced me to be both creative and strategic from the beginning in my journey of launching a program.

Program design and implementation

Restrictions on course enrollment can often range from practically necessary to unduly burdensome.[1] Sometimes the required prerequisites make

DOI: 10.1201/9781032656458-13

sense, for example, requiring students to successfully complete an introductory finance course and introductory real estate course before taking a more advanced real estate finance course. Such a set of prerequisites will ensure students are prepared to engage with the material contained within the course with only limited review of fundamental concepts. However, a course like real estate finance in some institutions carries a series of prerequisites such that enrollment by students other than those with a major or concentration in real estate or finance becomes incredibly impractical.

Removing unnecessary barriers to enrollment in real estate classes was important to me when I started on real estate course development at the University of Tulsa. At the time when I joined the university, there was only a single introductory real estate course offered – Principles of Real Estate. Even though it was advertised as an introductory course, in practice over 90% of the students enrolled in the course were finance students within a year of graduation. The University of Tulsa, like many other universities that offer real estate within a business school environment, required that a student complete a suite of core business courses, including classes in economics, finance, accounting, management, marketing, and statistics, prior to enrollment in an entry level real estate course.

Having such a deep stack of prerequisites for an introductory course was a barrier to growing the number of students enrolled in real estate coursework. Indeed, requiring an introductory finance course prior to enrollment in real estate principles was the primary bottleneck for student enrollment. In developing a program where one of the key goals was accessibility across our undergraduate student body, I needed to eliminate unnecessary barriers to enrollment while still ensuring that students who engaged with the curriculum would be prepared for the content.

Therefore, the first step I took in working on curricular development in real estate was the reformulation of our existing Real Estate Principles course. With the goal of enrolling students in the real estate minor across multiple colleges, not just the College of Business, I reviewed the existing course content and prerequisites. A practical first step to increasing student access, I proposed changes to the course prerequisites that eliminated many of these requirements, keeping only successful completion (a grade of "C" or higher) of one semester of economics and one semester of College Algebra or higher-level math. This change would allow for enrollment of non-business majors as well as increase access to business students by enabling many to take this course earlier in their program of study. Some of my departmental colleagues were initially skeptical of this proposal and expressed concerns about a change that would allow finance majors to take a course that could be counted towards their major without having previously completed the business core finance course. Ultimately,

I won the support of my department and college curriculum committee to make these changes with the promise to monitor the progress of students who enrolled without prior finance coursework and revisit this change if there were widespread disparities in student learning outcomes as compared to students who enrolled with prior finance coursework.

As a result of this change, instructors of the real estate principles course could no longer assume that students enrolled in the course had a working knowledge of time value of money, net present values, or other basic finance concepts before enrollment. To the extent that these skills were still important for parts of the course material, they were introduced alongside the corresponding real estate concepts. For example, time value of money concepts were introduced alongside mortgage calculations. However, the overall content of the class was reimagined alongside the revision of the prerequisites to include material on real estate economics, law, environmental issues, urban planning, public policy, valuation, market analysis, in addition to topics that used TVM concepts such as mortgages, buy vs. rent comparisons, and basic DCF analysis of real estate investments.

In the first cohort of students enrolled in the newly reformulated introductory real estate course, approximately half had not taken the previously required Business Finance course prior to enrollment in Real Estate Principles, while the other half had successfully completed this introductory finance course before enrollment. Retrospectively, there was no statistically significant difference in the grades earned by students with prior finance coursework and those students who had no prior finance coursework in the first four semesters of offering the newly formulated class. Anecdotally, students who had taken several finance courses prior to enrollment found the quantitative material easier than their peers, however, several students who were introduced to TVM concepts for the first time through real estate commented that they found the concepts intuitive and appreciated learning them alongside a concrete application (e.g., mortgages or real estate investment returns). Other observations through conversations with students included that many students appreciated the opportunity to "try out" real estate early in their college career and they enjoyed class discussions with classmates from diverse academic specialties.

A few years after implementing these changes, an opportunity arose to place the Real Estate Principles course in the general education curriculum during an overhaul of the general education requirements of the university. However, in order to apply to place a course on the menu of options for students to choose from to fulfill their general education requirements, a course could have at most one prerequisite. Real Estate Principles had two prerequisites – one semester each of economics and math. This prompted a second look at whether completing coursework in both subjects was necessary to drive desired student learning outcomes.

I worked with colleagues from across campus to gain insights about the population of students that completed an introductory economics class with a grade of "C" or higher and found that over 95% of students who fit this criterion had also completed math course work equivalent to or exceeding the College Algebra prerequisite. This insight enabled me to go back to my department and college curriculum committee to ask that the formal math prerequisite be removed. After this permission was secured, Real Estate Principles was accepted as one of the courses that could go toward fulfillment of the social science general education requirements for the university. I anticipate that this change will result in more students from diverse majors across the university having the ability and incentive to enroll in a real estate course early in their program of study. This should drive increased enrollment in both this specific class and also in the real estate program as a whole.

While creating an accessible introductory real estate course was an important first step in designing a real estate program, my next step was to do a deep dive into the existing undergraduate curriculum to identify any existing coursework that aligned with a real estate program. The first class I identified as meeting this goal was an undergraduate course already actively in the course rotation for the business college, Real Property Law. At the time, this course was primarily taken by students majoring in energy management. I reached out to the professor teaching this class and explained my vision for creating an undergraduate real estate minor and had a conversation about course content, enrollment, and cross-listing. Later, when selecting courses from other colleges that I wanted to include as electives for the minor, conversations with the existing faculty teaching those classes were instrumental in getting the minor approved by the university level curriculum committee. Ensuring that I had personal buy-in at the faculty level was key in gaining support for launching a new program that drew curriculum from multiple colleges. Forging connections with faculty across campus also allowed me to gain insight into the profile of majors outside of the business school that made sense to target for enrollment in the real estate minor.

Finally, to complete the minor I designed a new course, Real Estate Finance. For this course, the prerequisite of introductory finance was retained,[2] and therefore made this course a de-facto "capstone" for our minor. In this course, students explore more advanced topics such as REITs and securitizations. They also complete case studies that involve more complex pro forma and DCF analysis than in the principles course. Although the only other formal prerequisite for this class is Real Estate

Principles, students typically enroll in this course during their final year of study.

With three required classes secured – Real Estate Principles, Real Property Law, and Real Estate Finance, I rounded out the formulation of the minor with the requirement to complete one elective course (see Exhibit 13.1). The list of available courses is intentionally broad including courses found in other colleges, such as urban sociology or introduction to GIS mapping. Or students can complete a real estate internship for course credit. Periodically, special topic courses are available as elective courses as well, allowing specialty topics within real estate to be offered as demanded by student enrollment. For example, an elective course in professional certifications and credentials where students could complete educational requirements for a real estate salesperson license. This has proved to be a fruitful testing ground for new courses. Recently, a special topics course in Real Estate Market Analysis was approved as a permanent course in the university bulletin after being offered three times as a special topic elective. The class will be offered at least once an academic year in the Spring semester. Concurrently it was approved as an option for one of the three required courses for the minor (see Exhibit 13.1), solving an enrollment bottleneck created by Real Property Law only being offered in the Fall Semester. By including courses outside of the finance core or even the business school offerings as elective options in real estate as well as ensuring that the courses within the business school do not have undue barriers to entry through unnecessary prerequisites, the real estate minor becomes more feasible for students with primary majors outside of the College of Business.

Recommendations for educators

Increasing diversity of student enrollment in real estate course work requires the buy-in from many constituencies, including faculty and administrators at the department, college, and university level. You also need to gain the buy-in from individual faculty members who teach the courses you want to put into the real estate program. This is relevant to a program director, irrespective of whether they are leading an undergraduate certificate, concentration, minor or major. This is especially pertinent if a program director or coordinator is relying on professors who do not necessarily view themselves as real estate faculty, but teach in a related field – urban planning, sociology, public policy, law, civil engineering, or architecture, to name a few – to buy into one or more of their classes being part of a real estate curriculum.

Exhibit 13.1 Requirements for Real Estate Minor at the University of Tulsa

*University of Tulsa Undergraduate Real Estate Minor Requirements**

Required Courses (9 hours)

- BL 4013 Real Property OR BUS 4103 Real Estate Market Analysis
- FIN 3053 Principles of Real Estate**
- FIN 4133 Real Estate Finance

Elective Courses (3 hours)

Choose one of the following:

- ECON 4163 Policy Analysis
- FIN 3023 Financial Institutions and Markets
- BUS 4103 Real Estate Market Analysis
- FIN 4513 Finance Internship***
- GEOL 4083 Introduction to Geographic Information Systems
- SOC 3083 Urban Sociology
- Special Topics courses in FIN, ACCT, MGT, MKTG, EMGT, QM, or BUS may be chosen as appropriate****

Notes: *Enrollment in the minor is open to students of any major, but students outside of the Collins College of Business (CCB) may have to take additional prerequisite courses to complete this minor. Students within the CCB will satisfy prerequisites for all required courses and some electives by completing Business Core courses.
**Students with prior knowledge or experience in real estate may test out of Real Estate Principles. Such students would then choose 6 credit hours from the elective courses to complete the minor.
***Internship must be in real estate and approved by an advisor.
****Offerings will vary from year to year. Only special topics courses in real estate topic areas will count toward the minor. This information would be conveyed to students in the posted class description before registration.

Some of the barriers to opening the real estate curriculum to a wider audience are more inherent in universities with a larger number of colleges, higher enrollments, and more constraints on scaling up or down classes, perhaps due to classroom availability, slack in enrollment, scheduling constraints or misalignment of incentives for enrolling students outside of their department or core program. However, smaller private universities are ideal candidates for building interdisciplinary connections across a real estate curriculum; given a smaller number of total faculty, the need to collaborate and coordinate is already baked into the ecosystem of the university. For example, larger universities may have student numbers to be able to fill an introductory real estate course in a finance department as well as an architecture school, which would not be feasible at smaller school. Developing relationships outside of your home discipline can be easier as a member of a smaller faculty. In addition, the closer physical proximity on campus and shared social connections found in a smaller university community can help overcome some of the obstacles to collaboration that may arise in universities with larger faculties that may have fewer natural opportunities for professional interaction and collaborations.

Even though interdisciplinary collaboration may be more straightforward at a smaller institution, opportunities to create curricular connections exist at institutions of all sizes. Key recommendations to program directors interested in increasing real estate's reach and influence across campus include:

- Do a deep dive into your university's course catalog to develop ideas for how to utilize existing courses to build or revitalize your curriculum without requiring significant new resources.
- Do an analysis of the degree programs offered by your university. Identify majors across your institution that have required courses that you have identified as potential electives for your program as well as majors that have significant slack or large number of general elective hours in their programs of study as these students can be a good target for enrollment in your core real estate classes.
- Develop a robust slate of engaging extracurricular opportunities – networking and mentoring events, guest speakers, site tours, and student club activities that students across campus can access, irrespective of their major. Be sure to market that programming widely to attract new potential students to your program early in their course of study.
- Invest time in developing relationships with faculty and staff outside of your home department or college. These relationships will be key in understanding enrollment constraints or opportunities at your institution, while providing the additional advantage of helping develop natural advocates for your program across campus.

As resources at universities are often allotted by enrollments and alumni engagement or donations, educators in the real estate space should carefully consider how to expand their reach at the undergraduate level beyond the traditional audience of finance or economics majors. These efforts can pay dividends beyond simply increasing the number of potential enrollees in your real estate classes. Students who decide on a real estate career path will be engaging with a diverse set of professionals in the course of their jobs; by creating a similarly diverse learning atmosphere in a collegiate setting when students in real estate classrooms include students studying science, engineering, arts, social sciences, as well as business fields, students can better prepare to engage with a wide variety of stakeholders in their future professional lives.

Notes

1 Although some colleges and programs are collaborative in cross-listing courses, college specific prerequisites, limited space in programs of study for electives – especially those that lead to professional licensure such as architecture or engineering – for electives, and availability of classroom seats and faculty resources to allow students from other colleges to enroll in coursework outside of their home college.

2 Introductory finance courses often contain many prerequisites for business students, often including accounting, economics, and statistics coursework; in order to not overly burden non-business students from enrolling in the minor, these prerequisites can be waived on a case-by-case basis.

Chapter 14

Interdisciplinary education

Real estate sustainability as an example

Annette Kämpf-Dern

Introduction

Sustainability challenges and future skills in the built environment

Buildings and urban areas are central to global sustainability efforts due to their high CO_2 emissions, role in social interactions, intense capital requirements, and growing regulatory demands. The real estate sector thus faces the urgent task of developing innovative solutions for energy efficiency, climate protection, social inclusion, economic efficiency, and responsible governance. At the same time, digitalization and new technologies, along with shifting societal expectations, are fundamentally changing the qualifications required of professionals and leaders in this field (Wilkinson et al., 2015).

Objective and chapter question

The question of how higher education can prepare students to effectively and responsibly address the complex sustainability challenges of the built environment is thus gaining importance, with the following question being addressed in this chapter:

How can a higher education course be designed to foster the development of future skills for advancing sustainability in the built environment?

Using the interdisciplinary "Renewable Energies" course at Frankfurt University of Applied Sciences as a case study, the goal is to derive practice-oriented sustainability design principles for university teaching in real estate and the built environment.

DOI: 10.1201/9781032656458-14

Approach and structure

This chapter addresses the main question in four steps:

1. **Competence models:** Key international frameworks (OECD, 2019; World Economic Forum, 2020; UNESCO, 2020, and ISO-26000, 2010) are reviewed and linked to sustainability education.
2. **Teaching approaches:** Effective teaching strategies from multiple disciplines, including architecture, design, and medicine are explored regarding built environment education.
3. **Case study analysis:** The "Renewable Energies" course is presented and evaluated to demonstrate how future skills and sustainability competencies can be practically fostered within an application-oriented, interdisciplinary course.
4. **Deriving course design recommendations:** Based on the case study analysis, transferable course design principles and actionable steps for developing competence-oriented courses in sustainable real estate education are derived, including recommendations for curriculum and teaching approaches, quality assurance and assessment, as well as transfer, practical relevance, and employability.

Readers will gain targeted insights into how higher education courses can be structured to build relevant future skills for sustainable real estate practice, with concrete examples and strategies for effective, applied course design.

Learning outcomes for sustainability in the built environment

Sustainable transformation in the built environment requires competencies that bridge economic, technical, and social expertise, interdisciplinary collaboration, and ethical practice (Ehlers, 2020; Annan-Diab & Molinari, 2017).

In the international context, "learning objectives" describe which competencies in the areas of knowledge, skills, and attitudes (KSA) shall be achieved. Exhibits 14.1–14.3 summarize the most essential learning outcomes, grouped by KSAs, and explain their relevance.

The diversity of required competencies highlights the need for teamwork, leadership, and interdisciplinary approaches. Educational formats that intentionally foster both technical and non-technical competencies are pivotal for preparing future professionals for the complex challenges of sustainable real estate and the built environment.

Exhibit 14.1 Key knowledge areas for sustainability in the built environment

Knowledge area	*Justification*	*Source(s)*
Building physics, renewable energy systems, architectural/ urban design	Design choices impact energy efficiency, user well-being, and environmental outcomes.	Christensen & Worzala, 2010; Ehlers, 2020; Wilkinson et al., 2015
Life cycle environmental impacts (LCA, carbon footprint, and circular economy)	Critical for minimizing long-term ecological harm and resource use.	ISO-14040, 2006; Olubunmi et al., 2016; Schmidt et al., 2020
Economic and financial frameworks (cost-benefit analysis, funding models, and tax incentives)	Ensures projects are economically viable and leverage policy-driven opportunities.	PricewaterhouseCoopers [PWC], 2024 ; Tu et al., 2009
Legal and regulatory frameworks (building codes, ISO 26000, and EU Taxonomy)	Compliance and innovation depend on understanding evolving policy landscapes.	ISO-26000, 2010; Wilkinson et al., 2015
Social equity, user needs, accessibility, and stakeholder dynamics	User-centered design and inclusive processes enhance acceptance and long-term success.	Built4People, 2023; Annan-Diab & Molinari, 2017

Exhibit 14.2 Key skills areas for sustainability in the built environment

Skills area	*Justification*	*Source(s)*
Systems thinking and interdisciplinary integration	Enables holistic solutions that balance technical, economic, and social priorities.	Galuppo & Worzala, 2004; Mathews & Jones, 2008)
Problem-solving and critical analysis	Essential for diagnosing challenges and developing context-sensitive innovations.	Christensen & Worzala, 2010
Collaborative teamwork across disciplines	Reduces siloed thinking and improves project outcomes through diverse perspectives.	C-SanD Project, 2002
Oral and written communication	Essential for communicating complex decisions to stakeholders and being effective.	Tu et al., 2009
Digital tools for modeling and simulation	Supports data-driven decision-making.	Verde et al., 2024

Exhibit 14.3 Key attitudes areas for sustainability in the built environment

Attitudes area	*Justification*	*Source(s)*
Ethical judgment and reflective practice	Prevents greenwashing and ensures decisions align with long-term sustainability goals.	Christensen & Worzala, 2010; ISO-26000, 2010
Adaptability and resilience	Prepares professionals to respond to regulatory shifts, market changes, and climate risks.	Wilkinson et al., 2015
Leadership and advocacy for sustainable practices	Drives organizational and societal change beyond individual projects.	Tu et al., 2009

Teaching approaches and formats for sustainability competence development

Developing the competencies required for sustainability in the built environment calls for innovative, student-centered teaching strategies. Exhibit 14.4 summarizes the most effective teaching approaches and learning formats, with a focus on those most relevant for real estate and the built environment.

These approaches are most effective when combined, allowing students to experience sustainability challenges from multiple perspectives and through various modes of engagement (Wilkinson et al., 2015).

The following section demonstrates how these teaching principles are systematically embedded in an institutional framework at Frankfurt University of Applied Sciences (FUAS).

Institutional framework: Overarching goals and competence orientation

The Interdisciplinary Studium Generale (ISG) is a widely adopted framework at German universities, designed to foster cross-disciplinary learning and generalist education in a country where study programs are very specialized, already on the Bachelor's level. The ISG framework provides the institutional context for a broad range of elective courses that are open to students from all faculties – including those courses focused on sustainability in the built environment. Its primary aim is to equip students with general future-oriented, transferable competencies, such as:

Exhibit 14.4 Teaching approaches and learning formats

Teaching approach / learning format	*Core features*	*Rationale*	*Source(s)*
PBL	Real-world, interdisciplinary projects	Promotes systems thinking, collaboration, and practical problem-solving.	Kolmos & Graaf, 2021
Studio pedagogy	Iterative, hands-on, collaborative; common in architecture and design	Fosters creativity and integration of feedback.	Christensen & Worzala, 2010
Case study analysis	Context-rich, real or simulated scenarios	Encourages critical thinking, application of theory, and ethical reflection.	Galuppo & Worzala, 2004
Interdisciplinary teamwork	Diverse backgrounds	Addresses complex, real-world sustainability challenges and mirrors professional practice.	Annan-Diab & Molinari, 2017
PBL	Tackling open-ended, complex problems	Builds research, analytical, and communication skills.	Savery, 2006
Reflective practice and peer feedback	Structured reflection and peer review	Enhances self-awareness and ethical judgment.	Schön, 1983
Oral and written communication training	Focused training in presenting, reporting, and evidence-based argumentation	Essential for professional and academic success.	Galuppo & Worzala, 2004
Digital tools and simulation	Data-driven analysis, scenario planning, and visualization of sustainability impacts	Provides transparency in complex scenarios and enables better, evidence-based decisions.	Verde et al., 2024
Stakeholder engagement	Involving practitioners and community	Bridges theory and practice.	Boyer & Mitgang, 1996

- **Ambiguity competence:** Recognizing, understanding, and managing complexity and contradictions.
- **Ethical competence:** Identifying and analyzing ethical issues.
- **Communication competence:** Effective, empathetic communication across contexts.
- **Cooperation competence:** Teamwork in diverse, hybrid, and online settings.
- **Reflective competence**: Critical analysis of one's own and others' behaviors, values, and thought systems, adopting multiple viewpoints.
- **Systems competence:** Understanding and leveraging systemic relationships and dependencies, leveraging synergies.

These skills are embedded in all ISG courses, and assessed through project work and presentations, closely aligning with international models of a more generalist education, particularly at liberal arts schools.

Indicative examples in the field of sustainability are the following courses (FUAS, 2025):

- **International Workplace Management Summer School:** Combines online and in-person sessions, excursions/real-world site visits, project and international team work, and practitioner input to address sustainable workplace design and management, and applied project management, and to foster intercultural collaboration.
    - ***Design aspects:*** integration of external expertise and global perspectives in project-based learning (PBL).
- **Simulation of sustainability decision-making:** Students develop and play scenario-based board games to explore negotiation and trade-off management of sustainability goals, fostering systems thinking under uncertainty and cooperation.
    - ***Design aspects:*** experiential, gamified learning for ambiguity competence and decision-making skills.
- **Ecological sustainability:** Teams analyze ecological challenges such as reducing plastic use. Emphasizes the use of life cycle assessment (LCA) and digital tools in interdisciplinary group projects.
    - ***Design aspects:*** method integration and iterative feedback for evidence-based environmental analysis.

These examples show how competence orientation can be operationalized through course-specific learning designs.

Building on this institutional foundation, the next section outlines key course design recommendations and best practices for sustainability courses in the built environment.

Course design for sustainability in the built environment

Designing effective courses for sustainability in real estate education means translating broad future skills and interdisciplinary principles into concrete learning experiences that address the unique challenges of sustainability in the built environment. This section outlines key course design recommendations, typical challenges, and best practices for course development, drawing on current literature and some sustainability course examples experienced and developed by myself.

Key course design recommendations for sustainability in real estate education

To achieve overarching as well as specific learning objectives for sustainability in real estate education, the recommendations listed and explained in Exhibit 14.5 can give guidance.

Exhibit 14.5 Design recommendations for successful sustainability courses

Course design recommendation	*Explanation*	*Source(s)*
Integrate interdisciplinary perspectives	Combine technical, economic, legal, and social viewpoints to reflect the complexity of real-world sustainability challenges.	Wilkinson et al., 2015
Foster systems thinking and ambiguity competence	Use PBL, scenario analysis, and simulation tools from the built environment to help students navigate uncertainty, trade-offs, and interconnected systems that directly relate to this context. Apply principles of sustainable development.	Ehlers, 2020; Savery, 2006;
Emphasize project-based and experiential learning	Engage students in authentic sustainability projects, case studies, or fieldwork that require application of knowledge and skills to these specific issues.	Kolmos & Graaf, 2021; Boyer & Mitgang, 1996

Exhibit 14.5 (Continued)

Course design recommendation	*Explanation*	*Source(s)*
Support reflective and ethical practice	Incorporate structured reflection, peer feedback, and explicit discussion of ethical dilemmas in sustainability decision-making.	ISO-26000, 2010
Develop communication and collaboration skills	Require group work, presentations, and stakeholder engagement activities to build both oral and written communication competence crossing different stakeholder groups.	ISG module guidelines

Exhibit 14.6 Typical challenges and strategies for course design

Challenges	*Strategies*	*Source(s)*
Balancing breadth and depth	Sustainability is inherently broad; courses must focus on selected core competencies and provide depth in application, rather than attempting to cover all possible topics.	Tu et al., 2009
Ensuring relevance and real-world connection	Collaboration with external partners like architects, energy consultants, owners, users, financers, etc., site visits, and use of current case studies ensures contextual relevance.	ISG module pool; Own Experience
Managing interdisciplinary teams	Clear role assignments, structured team processes, and facilitation by instructors are essential for effective collaboration	C-SanD Project, 2002; SESYNC, 2023
Assessment of complex competencies	Use of portfolio assessments – e.g. project reports, presentations, self- and peer evaluations – allows, different from traditional exams, for holistic evaluation of knowledge, skills, and abilities.	Galuppo & Worzala, 2004

Typical challenges and solutions

Course designers face several recurring challenges in implementing competence-oriented sustainability courses. Exhibit 14.6 details effective strategies to cope with these challenges:

Case study: "Renewable Energies" course

To illustrate how competence goals, learning formats, and design principles can be translated and implemented into educational practice, this section presents the "Renewable Energies" course as an exemplary blueprint for sustainability course design.

Course objectives, structure, and assignment

"Renewable Energies" is an interdisciplinary, project-based ISG-course, which is designed to address the multifaceted challenges of sustainability in the built environment. The focus is on energy transition and retrofitting in the multi-family housing sector. It includes students from all faculties with accordingly very diverse backgrounds.

Learning objectives

The course enables students to analyze design, technical, legal, fiscal, economic, and user-centered aspects of energy retrofits in multi-family buildings, to develop and compare alternative solutions, and to present their findings to expert panels.

The course setup ensures that students not only acquire domain-specific expertise but also develop skills necessary to navigate the complexities of sustainability in the built environment.

Structure

The course runs for 12–14 weeks (3 hours/week, 150 hours total workload) and is open to 40 students from all bachelor's programs, taught by three instructors from at least two faculties.

Assignment: Energy retrofit of a multi-family building

Teams analyze a real multi-family building, develop and compare alternative energy retrofit scenarios, and integrate technical, funding, tax, legal, economics, and user perspectives into a simulation model and scientific report. Results are presented and defended before a panel of experts, and documented in a written report.

The course structure and assignment ensure that students experience the full cycle of a complex sustainability project, requiring both deep subject knowledge and advanced professional skills.

Content and methods

The course is structured around four core areas – technical, economic, legal, and social dimensions of sustainable building projects. Students work in interdisciplinary teams and address these areas using a blend of research, group discussion, expert input, and ongoing feedback.

- **Technical:** Students analyze building structures and energy systems, applying scenario modeling to assess sustainability options.
- **Economic:** They evaluate costs, funding opportunities, and financial feasibility for different solutions.
- **Legal:** Relevant regulations and standards are reviewed to assess the practical and legal viability of proposed measures.
- **Social:** User needs, stakeholder perspectives, and broader societal impacts are considered through participatory and reflective methods.

All results are synthesized in a joint project report, simulation model, and presentation, mirroring the complexity and interconnectedness of real-world sustainability challenges. Regular feedback from instructors and peers ensures scientific rigor and professional relevance throughout the process.

This integrated approach enables students to develop both subject expertise and the ability to communicate complex findings to diverse audiences – key skills for future professionals in sustainable real estate and the built environment.

Weekly course flow and organization

The course is structured as a digital, project-based seminar with parallel, interdisciplinary teamwork reflecting real-world complexity and challenges.

Key course features:

- Interdisciplinary teams (6–8 students) select individual focus areas based on interests and project needs.
- Each team appoints a leader responsible for project coordination, timelines, and quality assurance.
- All meetings, presentations, and document sharing occurs online via collaborative platforms.
- Every team member can participate in weekly sessions, ensuring transparency and mutual learning.

- The iterative, parallel work structure requires continuous integration and coordination.
- Each week includes structured peer reviews and expert consultations to ensure the integration and coherence of results.

For the course structure and typical challenges, see Exhibit 14.7.

Exhibit 14.7 Typical phases, activities and tips, and phase-related challenges for "Renewable Energies" course

Phase	*Week(s)*	*Activities and tips*	*Typical challenges*
Kick-off	1	Team formation, role assignment, introduction to project building, and clarification of objectives.	Students don't know each other, uneven skills, unclear roles and responsibilities.
Research	2–4	Parallel data collection on technical, economic, public funding, legal, and user aspects.	Students have strongly varying experience with systematic research and acquiring knowledge in self-study manner.
Analysis and scenario development	5–7	Parallel analysis on technical, economic, public funding, legal, user, and identifying different scenarios.	Data gaps, different speed of individual group members' progress, dependencies and delay lead to communication and coordination challenges.
Integration of individual results	8–9	Synthesis of partial results into joint model and report; mutual scenario development and testing.	Integration of partly siloed work, dependencies become obvious and daunting, need for adaptation.
Draft report	10	Integration of individuals' writings into joint group report.	Differing skills of working with word templates, structuring, and formatting.
Presentation prep	11	Finalization of findings, rehearsal, and coaching.	Missing information, time restriction and time management, and anxiety to present.
Presentation to experts	12	Group defense, Q&A with experts.	Uncoordinated presentation and unexpected questions.
Finalization of report	13–14	Incorporate expert feedback, revise report, and submit final version.	Last-minute issues, coordination, and integration.

In addition to the typical challenges detailed in Exhibit 14.7, some additional tips for teaching this kind of project include:

- Don't assume students will self-organize; assign topics to students in the first week (based on students' preferences).
- Encourage student teams to assign a project manager early and to schedule weekly meetings within their teams.
- Schedule regular meetings between teachers and students; do NOT leave integration to the last week.
- Provide iterative feedback.

Pedagogy

Sustainability and real-life issues define the course structure and form the pedagogy as presented in Exhibit 14.8:

Exhibit 14.8 Pedagogical rationale

Pedagogy	*Rationale*
Iterative, parallel development	Unlike linear courses, this course's structure requires all subtopics to progress in parallel, reflecting the interconnectedness of sustainability projects. This means that delays or gaps in one area can impact the entire team, making coordination, communication, and mutual support critical success factors.
Leadership and project management	Appointing team leaders and explicitly assigning project management roles provides a practical context for developing leadership skills. These students are encouraged to reflect on their experience in the project report, fostering meta-cognitive insights into teamwork and coordination.
Digital collaboration and transparency	The fully online format, including use of collaborative platforms (e.g., SharePoint), not only prepares students for the realities of remote professional work but also ensures that all contributions are visible, traceable, and open to peer review.
Learning from diversity	The interdisciplinary assignment and cross-faculty composition of teams bring together a wide range of academic cultures, knowledge bases, and working styles. This diversity, while sometimes challenging, is a key driver of creativity, problem-solving, and real-world competence development.
Continuous feedback and quality assurance	Weekly expert input, peer feedback, and iterative document development ensure that scientific standards, evidence-based argumentation, and professional communication are consistently reinforced.

In sum, this organizational logic ensures that both the subject-specific and transversal learning objectives are not only addressed in theory but systematically operationalized in practice. Students thus experience the authentic challenges and rewards of collaborative sustainability project work, preparing them for the realities of professional practice in the built environment.

Presentation to experts: Process, assessment, and competence development

A central course element is the final presentation (20% of course grade), where student teams defend their results before a panel of professors, practitioners, and stakeholders. This serves as both summative assessment and a key learning experience.

Process:

- Structured, evidence-based group presentation (each member covers its subtopic in a five-minute presentation).
- Audience includes faculty, industry experts, and user representatives.
- Q&A session probes rationale, evidence, and feasibility.

Assessment criteria:

- **Clarity and structure:** Logical organization, clear argumentation, and effective use of visual aids (25% of presentation grade).
- **Evidence and scientific rigor:** Use of data, references, and evidence-based reasoning (25%).
- **Teamwork and coordination:** Smooth transitions between speakers, consistency of messaging, and demonstration of collaborative preparation (20%).
- **Professional communication:** Ability to explain complex issues to a mixed audience, respond to questions, and defend decisions (15%).
- **Reflection and responsiveness:** Willingness to address critical feedback, acknowledge limitations, and suggest improvements (15%).

Competence development:

- Strengthens oral communication and public speaking.
- Fosters confidence and professional presence in real-world settings.
- Reinforces the importance of teamwork, as each member must both master their own subtopic and understand the overall project to respond to panel questions.

- Safeguards academic integrity, as the live defense ensures that students can articulate and justify the content of their written reports, reducing the risk of plagiarism or over-reliance on external assistance.

Teaching tips:

- Provide students with:
  - A sample presentation template.
  - A clear rubric to structure their arguments.
  - Typical questions from practitioners.

The project report: Structure, assessment, and competence development

The project report (80% of course grade) is the primary vehicle for scientific competence development. It mirrors professional standards in real estate and sustainability, requiring synthesis of technical, economic, legal, user-centered, and project management analyses.

A typical structure for the joint "Renewable Energies" report could be as follows:

- Executive summary
- Project context and building description
- Technical analysis
- Social and user-centered dimensions
- Funding analysis
- Legal and regulatory analysis
- Tax analysis
- Economic analysis
- Scenario development and integration
- Project management and leadership reflection
- Recommendations and conclusion
- References and appendices

Process:

- Developed iteratively, with an initial draft submitted for feedback from the instructors before the final presentation.
- Final version incorporates feedback from both instructors and the expert panel.

Assessment criteria (for each section/team member individually):

- Structure and clarity (25%).
- Scientific quality and rigor, including use of references (30%).
- Quality of individual analyses (10%).
- Own ideas / innovativeness (10%).
- Professional writing (including formatting) (10%).
- Teamwork and project management, integration of others' results in own work (15%).

Competence development:

- Scientific writing, analytical and integrative thinking, project management, and reflective practice

Teaching tip: Use a standardized report template that includes exemplary sections and formatting recommendations for a students' scientific report.

In summary, the "Renewable Energies" course demonstrates how the integration of interdisciplinary content, PBL , and iterative assessment can operationalize future skills for sustainability in the built environment. The following section synthesizes key results, lessons learned, and actionable recommendations for designing similar courses.

Results, lessons learned, and actionable recommendations

Key insights and lessons from "Renewable Energies" implementation

Key lessons from the "Renewable Energies" course include the effectiveness of interdisciplinary, project management, digital collaboration, and iterative feedback (see Exhibit 14.9).

Recommendations for effective real estate sustainability course design

Based on the key course design criteria, combined with the lessons learned from the "Renewable Energies" course, Exhibits 14.10–14.12 synthesize actionable recommendations for effective real estate sustainability course design, regarding (1) curriculum and instructional design, (2) quality assurance and assessment, and (3) transfer, practical relevance, and employability, respectively.

Exhibit 14.9 Challenges and solutions/outcomes in the "Renewable Energies" course

Challenges	*Solutions/ Outcomes*	*Source(s)*
Topical integration	Merging diverse subtopic analyses into a cohesive final report and simulation model required strong coordination and communication. Teams that invested in early integration and regular synthesis meetings were more successful in delivering coherent results.	Baumber, 2024
Interdisciplinary integration to drive innovation	Interdisciplinary teams yielded more creative and robust solutions by integrating diverse knowledge and perspectives.	Podgórska & Zdonek, 2023; Pratt-Adams et al., 2025; Baumber, 2024
Structured project management	Clear role allocation, regular meetings, and the appointment of team leaders were essential for managing complexity, aligning individual strengths with project needs, and ensuring timely progress.	Podgórska & Zdonek, 2023
Digital collaboration and transparency	The fully digital format, with shared platforms and open documentation, not only prepared students for remote professional work but also fostered transparency and mutual accountability. Transparent processes helped mitigate the challenges of asynchronous work and diverse working styles.	Meyer, 2024;
Iterative feedback and reflective practice	Continuous feedback from instructors, experts, and peers improved both the scientific quality of reports and the effectiveness of presentations. Reflections on team dynamics, project management, and process coordination improved students' self-regulated learning and adaptability.	Pratt-Adams et al., 2025; Brundiers et al., 2010

Exhibit 14.10 Instructional recommendations for sustainability courses in the built environment

Instructional Design	*Practical Implementation / Example*
Use project-based/ problem-based assignments	Use authentic projects (e.g., energy retrofit of real buildings) as central course tasks. Use PBL, case studies, and simulations (e.g. solar gains, or economic scenario analysis) to foster student engagement and ownership.
Foster true interdisciplinarity related to BE sustainability	Intentionally compose teams from diverse academic backgrounds and explicitly value the integration of different perspectives. Ensure technical, economic, legal, and social/user aspects are addressed in every project phase. Provide orientation sessions on disciplinary languages and methods to facilitate mutual understanding. Assign clear tasks and responsibilities.
Prioritize project management and leadership training	Assign or encourage the emergence of team leaders and provide guidance on project management tools and best practices. Include structured self-reflection on leadership roles and project coordination strategies / project management as a formal part of assessment. Require milestone meetings to align interdisciplinary results early in the process.
Leverage digital tools for collaboration	Use shared digital workspaces to ensure transparency, version control, and easy access to resources. Offer technical support and training for these tools.
Scaffold skill development	Provide templates, rubrics, and structured milestones to guide students progressively through complex tasks. Encourage early and regular synthesis meetings to align findings and resolve inconsistencies.
Embed iterative feedback and reflection	Schedule interim deadlines for draft submissions and presentations, with structured feedback from instructors and peers. Encourage both group and individual reflection on learning processes, challenges, and solutions. Require reflective assignments or journals.
Align with professional practice	Involve industry partners, simulate professional workflows (e.g., expert juries, project reports, real data).

Exhibit 14.11 Assessment and quality assurance recommendations

Quality assurance and assessment	*Practical implementation / Example*
Provide transparent assessment criteria	Provide detailed rubrics for reports and presentations at the start of the course.
Assess both content and process	Evaluate not only the technical and scientific quality of outputs but also the effectiveness of teamwork, communication, and project management. Make these professional skills explicit in grading rubrics.
Combine formative and summative assessment	Use both ongoing feedback (formative) and final evaluations (summative) for all deliverables.
Integrate peer and expert feedback	Integrate peer- and self-assessment as mandatory components, evaluating both individual contributions and group dynamics. Integrate external expert input at key milestones (e.g., draft and final presentation).
Foster authenticity and academic integrity	Require students to justify and defend their work orally to ensure understanding and reduce plagiarism risk.
Engage real-world jury/panel	Use live defense/presentation before a mixed panel (faculty, practitioners, stakeholders) for final assessment.
Continuously improve course quality	Collect student/instructor feedback after each course iteration and adapt design accordingly.

Transferability and limitations of "Renewable Energies" course design

While the "Renewable Energies" course offers a robust model for interdisciplinary, competence-oriented sustainability real estate education, several factors influence how easily such a course can be adapted by other instructors and institutions worldwide. These include the following:

- **Institutional support and flexibility:** Success depends on institutional frameworks that allow for interdisciplinary courses, flexible scheduling, and digital infrastructure.
- **Team composition and group size:** The optimal balance of disciplinary diversity and manageable group size may vary by context and topic (Meyer, 2024).
- **Instructor expertise and commitment:** Effective facilitation requires a team of instructors with both diverse subject-matter expertise and skills

Exhibit 14.12 Transfer, practical relevance, and employability recommendations

Transfer, practical relevance and employability	*Practical implementation / Example*
Use real-world challenges and data	Select assignments based on current industry challenges and use actual building/project data, current funding programs, and authentic legal scenarios.
Collaborate with practitioners	Involve external experts in teaching, mentoring, and assessment; invite guest speakers from industry and public sector.
Focus on employability skills	Explicitly teach and assess transversal skills (e.g., leadership, communication, systems thinking, and digital literacy) as learning outcomes and assessment criteria.
Adapt to local context	Allow course design to be adapted to different institutional, cultural, or market contexts. Provide guidance for customization.
Support networking and career development	Facilitate student contact with potential employers through project presentations, site visits, and alumni events.
Let students reflect on their professional roles	Encourage students to connect acquired skills with potential career paths through guided reflection exercises.
Foster sustainability mindset and ethical awareness	Encourage critical reflection on professional responsibility, societal impact, and ethical dilemmas in real estate practice.

in managing interdisciplinary, digitally mediated teamwork (Podgórska & Zdonek, 2023).

- **Assessment and recognition of professional skills:** Institutions should formally recognize and reward the development of key professional skills – such as project management, leadership, teamwork, and reflective practice – alongside technical knowledge (Pratt-Adams et al., 2025; Brundiers et al., 2010).

In summary, this case study of "Renewable Energies" illustrates that with intentional design and ongoing support, interdisciplinary, PBL can deliver substantial benefits for sustainability education. However, successful adaptation in other contexts depends on institutional support for quality assurance, practical orientation, and explicit recognition of employability outcomes. Continuous adjustment to local conditions and ongoing improvement are essential for lasting impact.

Conclusion

The "Renewable Energies" course demonstrates that interdisciplinary, PBL can effectively build both subject-specific and professional competencies for sustainability in the built environment. By integrating diverse perspectives and engaging students in real-world projects, the course fosters systems thinking, project management, problem-solving, leadership, communication, and reflective practice. Digital collaboration and structured feedback further enhance learning outcomes and employability.

Limitations and outlook

Transferability to other contexts may be influenced by institutional frameworks, number of involved faculty in one course and faculty expertise, student diversity, and resource availability. The course's success depends on motivated participants and supportive infrastructure. Nonetheless, the course's design principles are adaptable to a variety of institutional and disciplinary contexts.

Looking ahead: interdisciplinary education for sustainable real estate

Interdisciplinary education in sustainable real estate must remain dynamic and responsive. By integrating new digital tools, fostering collaboration with industry and international partners, and adapting to evolving professional demands, such courses can continue to prepare students for the challenges and opportunities of a rapidly changing built environment.

References

Annan-Diab, F., & Molinari, C. (2017). Interdisciplinarity: Practical approach to advancing education for sustainability and for the sustainable development goals. *International Journal of Management Education*, *15*(2), 73–83. https://doi.org/10.1016/j.ijme.2017.03.006

Baumber, A. (2024). Interdisciplinary perspectives on sustainability in higher education. *Frontiers in Sustainability*, *5*, 1416498. https://doi.org/10.3389/frsus.2024.1416498

Boyer, E. L., & Mitgang, L. D. (1996). *Building Community: A New Future for Architecture Education and Practice*. Carnegie Foundation.

Brundiers, K., Wiek, A., Redman, C. L., Fadeeva, Z., & Mochizuki, Y. (2010). Real-world learning opportunities in sustainability: from classroom into the real world. *International Journal of Sustainability in Higher Education*, *11*(4), 308–324. https://doi.org/10.1108/14676371011077540

Built4People. (2023). *Built4People Strategic Research and Innovation Agenda*. www.built4people.eu/

Christensen, P. H., & Worzala, E. (2010). Teaching sustainability: Applying studio pedagogy to develop an alternative post-hurricane housing solution using surplus shipping containers. *Journal of Sustainable Real Estate*, *2*(1), 335–360. https://doi.org/10.1080/10835547.2010.12091797

C-SanD Project. (2002). *Creating, Sustaining and Disseminating Knowledge for Sustainable Construction: Tools, Methods and Architectures*. Loughborogh University, London School of Economics, and Salford University. www.itcon.org/papers/2006_4.content.07629.pdf

Ehlers, U.-D. (2020). *Future Skills–The Future of Learning and Higher Education*. Springer. https://ulf-ehlers.de/future-skills-2/

Frankfurt University of Applied Science (FUAS). (2025). *Course Pool of the ISG Interdisciplinary Studium Generale, Course Descriptions*. Frankfurt University of Applied Sciences. www.frankfurt-university.de/de/studium/interdisziplinares-studium-generale/interdisziplinares-studium-generale-modulpool-sommersemester-2025/

Galuppo, L., & Worzala, E. (2004). A study into the important elements of a master's degree in real estate. *Journal of Real Estate Practice and Education*, 7(1), 25–42. https://doi.org/10.1080/10835547.2004.12091600

ISO-14040. (2006). *Environmental Management Life Cycle Assessment Principles and Framework*. www.iso.org/standard/37456.html

ISO-26000. (2010). *Guidance on Social Responsibility*. www.iso.org/iso-26000-social-responsibility.html

Kolmos, A., & de Graaf, E. (Eds.). (2021). Problem-based and project-based learning in engineering education. In *The Cambridge Handbook of Engineering Education Research* (pp. 141–160). https://doi.org/10.1017/CBO9781139013451.012

Mathews, L. G., & Jones, A. (2008). Using systems thinking to improve interdisciplinary learning outcomes: Reflections on a pilot study in land economics. *Issues in Integrative Studies*, *26*, 73–104. http://static.clexchange.org/ftp/documents/Research/RS2010-01UsingSTtoImprove.pdf

Meyer, M. (2024). Understanding the impact of intercultural project-based learning on students, staff and higher education institutions. *Education and New Developments 2024 Conference Proceedings*. https://end-educationconference.org/wp-content/uploads/2024/07/2024O2OP045.pdf

OECD. (2019). *Learning Compass 2030: Conceptual Learning Framework*. www.oecd.org/content/dam/oecd/en/about/projects/edu/education-2040/concept-notes/OECD_Learning_Compass_2030_concept_note.pdf

Olubunmi, O. A., Xia, P. B., & Skitmore, M. (2016). Green building incentives: A review. *Renewable and Sustainable Energy Reviews*, *59*, 1611–1621. https://doi.org/10.1016/j.rser.2016.01.028

Podgórska, M., & Zdonek, I. (2023). Interdisciplinary collaboration in higher education towards sustainable development. *Sustainable Development*, *32*(4), 3270–3286. https://doi.org/10.1002/sd.2765

Pratt-Adams, S., Warnes, M., & Brown, E. (Eds.). (2025). *Introducing Interdisciplinary Modules in Higher Education: Enhancing Sustainability and Student Employability*. Routledge. www.routledge.com/Introducing-Interdisciplinary-Modules-in-Higher-Education-Enhancing-Sustainability-and-Student-Employability/Pratt-Adams-Warnes-Brown/p/book/9781032755694

Pricewaterhouse Coopers (Ed.). (2024). *Tax & Cash Incentives for Sustainable Real Estate*. www.pwc.com/gx/en/industries/financial-services/assets/sustainable-tax-and-cash-incentives-for-real-estate-brochure.pdf

Savery, J. R. (2006). Overview of problem-based learning: definitions and distinctions. *Interdisciplinary Journal of Problem-Based Learning*, *1*(1), 9–20. https://doi.org/10.7771/1541-5015.1002

Schmidt, M., Crawford, R. H., & Warren-Myers, G. (2020). Integrating life-cycle GHG emissions into a building's economic assessment. *Buildings & Cities*, *1*(1), 361–378. doi.org/10.5334/bc.36

Schön, D. A. (1983). *The Reflective Practitioner: How Professionals Think in Action*. Basic Books.

SESYNC. (2023). *Best Practices for Interdisciplinary Team Research: Shaping the Team's Social Environment*. www.sesync.org/resources/best-practices-interdisciplinary-team-research-shaping-teams-social-environment

Tu, C., Weinstein, M., Worzala, E., & Lukens, L. (2009). Elements of successful graduate real estate programs: Perceptions of the stakeholders. *Journal of Real Estate Practice and Education*, *12*(2), 105–121. https://doi.org/10.1080/10835547.2009.12091660

UNESCO. (2020). *Education for Sustainable Development: A Roadmap*. https://doi.org/10.54675/YFRE1448

Verde, S., Dell'Acqua, F., & Losasso, M. (2024). Environmental data, modeling and digital simulation for the evaluation of climate adaptation and mitigation strategies in the urban environment. *Sustainability*, *16*(5), 2179. https://doi.org/10.3390/su16052179

Wilkinson, S. J., Sayce, S. L., & Christensen, P. H. (2015). *Developing Property Sustainably*. Routledge. www.routledge.com/Developing-Property-Sustainably/Wilkinson-Sayce-Christensen/p/book/9780415835671

World Economic Forum (Ed.). (2020). *Closing the Skills Gap: Key Insights and Success Metrics*. https://www3.weforum.org/docs/WEF_GSC_NES_White_Paper_2020.pdf

Chapter 15

Graduate tracer studies

Using alumni input to update real estate programs and build relationships

Samuel Azasu, Moses Kusiluka, and Sekhoho Ntene

Introduction

Real estate education research has so far answered two questions:

- What skills and competencies should real estate graduates possess on graduation?
- How should real estate degrees and courses be designed to deliver on these skills and competencies?

The first question appears to be the one that has attracted the most attention (Weinstein & Worzala, 2008; Tu, et al., 2009; Poon et al., 2011; Poon, 2012; Poon & Bronlow, 2014; Amidu et al., 2018). These papers highlighted the technical, personal, and interpersonal skills real estate graduates are expected to possess on graduation from the perspective of alumni, employers, and even human resource managers. The findings of these studies reveal a reality of real estate education – it is an investment whose returns appears to be measured almost exclusively in terms of employability skills. The second question has been answered in terms of how stakeholder inputs should be integrated at the program level (Azasu & Gibler, 2016) or within specific courses across the curriculum (Butler et al., 1998; Gibler, 2001; Azasu & Berggren, 2015).

A third question, yet to be answered, is how well have real estate programs done, in delivering on these skills and competencies? This question is particularly much more pertinent to graduate real estate programs not only because real estate markets are very dynamic and heterogeneous but also because, with the exception of the US, parts of Europe and Australia, many stand-alone real estate programs are still relatively new and their nature, objectives and contents vary significantly from country to country depending on, among others, the level of market maturity and historical underpinnings. For instance, whereas in the USA and Germany and some Asian countries real estate programs have their foundation in the field of

DOI: 10.1201/9781032656458-15

finance and business studies, in the UK and many Commonwealth countries they have evolved from land economy and surveying foundations. In some countries, real estate education has even been treated as an integral part of engineering or construction/architecture/planning programs. Roulac (2002) notes that traditional real estate education is biased towards and reflects a narrow, even restricted interpretation of the dimensions and domain of the discipline, often reflecting a limited, culturally narrow, even parochial view of the world. However, over the years, growing interaction among researchers, universities, and professional and regional societies especially those under the umbrella of the International Real Estate Society (IRES – http://iresnet.net/) has allowed for cross-fertilization, which has helped in achieving some level of convergence of the components of real estate programs around the world. It is against this backdrop, that the imperativeness of tracer studies for graduate real estate programs cannot be overemphasized.

Overall, there is limited literature to show whether graduate real estate programs are regularly reviewed to ensure that they are demand driven. One of the relatively recent comprehensive studies was done by Worzala et al. (2013) who compared pre-recession and recession era graduates in the US to examine post-graduation employment outcomes and experience. The question, usually addressed using tracer studies, has largely been overlooked within the real estate academy. Graduate tracer studies have become an essential tool in understanding the outcomes and impact of higher education on students' careers and the labor market (Schomburg, 2003; Badiru & Wahome, 2016; Kraak, 2015). These studies track the trajectories of graduates, shedding light on their employment status, career progression, and the relevance of their education to their chosen professions. This chapter aims to explore the significance of graduate tracer studies in the context of real estate education institutions and their alumni. It emphasizes the benefits, challenges, and how real estate departments could use it to sustain alumni involvement with their universities.

The importance of graduate tracer studies

Higher education is widely recognized as a key factor in shaping individuals' career trajectories and enhancing their employability. The real estate sector is no exception, and the academy has written extensively on the match between degree content, graduate attributes, and employer requirements since 1979 (Rabianski & Black, 1999; Callanan & McCarthy, 2003; Galuppo & Worzala, 2004; Gibler, et al., 2002; Poon et al., 2011; Saginor et al., 2014).

In addition, the academy has also discussed the alternative curriculum models that could deliver on the graduate attributes in these multi-stakeholder studies. Azasu and Gibler (2016) discussed how to use the Conceive, Design, Implement, and Operate (CDIO) model, a curriculum design model originally developed for engineering, to create degree programs that ensure the requisite skills and competencies identified in any stakeholder studies can be integrated, taught, and assessed cumulatively. The model results in the so-called CDIO syllabus, an adapted version of which is shown in Exhibit 15.1.

Within the programs, other studies have compared traditional lecture-based approaches to teaching and learning to experiential learning (McGrath et al., 2020; Hopkins, 2021). Butler et al. (1998) as well as Gibler (2001) also discussed the integration of teamwork and writing skills across the real estate curriculum.

The basic assumption behind this is that real estate departments have subscribed to the belief that college degrees increase the chances of employment and earnings potential (Abel & Deitz, 2019). This belief is backed

Exhibit 15.1 Adaptation of the CDIO syllabus

The CDIO syllabus as a framework for organizing the structure of a real estate degree

Level

1 Technical knowledge and reasoning
- 1.1 Knowledge of underlying disciplines
- 1.2 Core real estate fundamental knowledge

2 Personal and professional skills and attributes
- 2.1 Reasoning and problem solving in real estate contexts
- 2.2 Research and knowledge discovery
- 2.3 Systems thinking
- 2.4 Personal skills and attitudes
- 2.5 Professional skills and attitudes

3 Interpersonal skills: Teamwork and communication
- 3.1 Teamwork (problem solving and collaboration in professional and non-professional settings)
- 3.2 Communications (oral and written in real estate and general contexts)

4 Conceiving, designing, implementing and operating systems in the enterprise and societal context
- 4.1 External and societal context (including civic engagement)
- 4.2 Enterprise and business context
- 4.3 Conceiving real estate business systems
- 4.4 Designing real estate business solutions
- 4.5 Implementing real estate business solutions
- 4.6 Operating a real estate business unit

Source: Azasu & Gibler (2016).

by the substantial wage premium that college graduates enjoy at least in the US (Abel & Deitz, 2014) and by and large in many other parts of the world. However, to the best of our knowledge, no studies have systematically traced real estate graduates from any program over time to verify if these and other benefits associated with college degrees are realized.

Tracer studies are research projects that involve tracking and examining a sample of graduates at different points in their post-graduation lives to assess the impact of their education and training (Schomburg, 2014 & 2016; Brits & Steyn, 2019). Schiefelbein & Farrell (2014) defines tracer studies as research involving a graduate cohort sample at a given time and then located and re-examined at periodic intervals throughout their career. They are also known as graduate destination surveys/studies and alumni research. They are focused on graduate employment destinations and are carried out only after the students have left the university. They are thus different from exit studies and other similar evaluation only surveys in the sense that tracer studies are meant to take a longitudinal view of graduate trajectories in the world of work (Munro & Senekal, 2019). These studies thus analyze a homogeneous group of graduates, who finished their degrees at the same time, retrospectively by means of standardized surveys (Rubal Maseda, 2017). It is done after graduation (normally between 6 months and 3 years).

According to Simister (2017), tracer studies work best when the change from an intervention (like a degree program or a short training program) is intended to be long-term and significant. This is because the extent to which these programs achieve intended outcomes in terms of skills, competence, and career progression of beneficiaries may not be fully ascertained until sufficient time has elapsed after completion. Consequently, these studies are used by higher education institutions to track their graduates (Munro & Senekal, 2019), evaluate their employability (Brits & Steyn, 2019) and career paths (Mouton et al., 2022), assess the relevance of their studies to current jobs (horizontal matching), and the match of position on the job to the qualification obtained (vertical matching), using both objective and subjective data (Rubal Maseda, 2017; Smith & White, 2016).

Tracer studies thus provide important indicators of degree quality and can help identify their effectiveness, their graduates' weaknesses in the workplace, and help programs achieve clarity on the skills and knowledge needed for career success. For example, a study conducted in Poland found that participation in the Erasmus program, which promotes international student mobility, had a positive influence on the subsequent employability and career progression of participants (Bryla, 2015). In this sense, they can be used by institutions to evaluate the success of their career services and support programs in helping graduates secure employment.

The results of graduate destination surveys can also be used by real estate departments to demonstrate their value and impact to stakeholders, such as government agencies, employers, accreditation organizations, like the Royal Institute of Chartered Surveyors (RICS), and prospective students. The accountability provided by the surveys thus encourages institutions to continuously improve their educational offerings and ensure that graduates are well-prepared for the job market. In the UK and Australia, university funding is contingent on graduate employment and employability outcomes, through programs such as the Teaching Excellence Framework in the UK and the Job Ready Package in Australia (Jackson & Dean, 2023).

Tracer studies can help build relationships with alumni by providing an opportunity for institutions to engage with graduates and maintain ongoing contact with them. By inviting graduates to participate in the surveys, institutions can demonstrate their interest in the career outcomes and experiences of their alumni, fostering a sense of connection and engagement.

The surveys can serve as a platform for institutions to gather feedback and insights from alumni, enabling them to understand their experiences and perspectives. The data collected from the surveys can be used to identify success stories and showcase the achievements of alumni, which can further strengthen the relationship between the institution and its graduates. The survey findings can also be used to inform the development of alumni engagement strategies and initiatives, tailored to the specific needs and interests of the alumni community. Overall, graduate destination surveys provide a means for institutions to maintain a connection with their alumni, demonstrate their ongoing interest in their welfare, and foster a sense of community and belonging.

Tracer studies are not without their skeptics. Haigh and Clifford (2011) argue that a university degree must go beyond discipline specific training to general skills to live responsible, productive, and creative lives in a world characterized by rapid and dramatic changes. Good degree programs also prepare graduates for democratic participation, active citizenship, and personal development (Kezar, 2004; Lambert, 2014). As a result, the goal of real estate programs must be broader than just work-readiness with a consequent wider coverage of tracer studies. This appears to be the weakness of many graduate tracer studies. The implication is that the following sections which describe the structure and components of tracer studies must also include goals such as capacity for lifelong learning, democratic participation, and the capacity for ongoing personal development.

Key components of a successful tracer study

Defining objectives and scope

A primary purpose of any tracer study is graduate success after leaving university. In other words, a fundamental question that a graduate tracer study must answer is how successful students have been in transitioning to work. Simister (2017) proposes defining the specific questions that need to be answered in the study, for example, which real estate sub-sectors employ our graduates the most after university? How did our degree programs prepare our graduates for real estate careers? How quick was the transition to work? Which skills from the degree program have been most useful at work? Which professional activities are the graduates engaged in and do these activities enhance career goals such as professional certification? Teichler (2007) also proposes issues such as the time and efforts expended to find jobs, as well as job search methods. In addition, the survey should include typical measures for successful employment such as salary, fringe benefits, full-time employment, job security, social respectability of the job, or career prospects. Care must also be taken to ensure we know who has left the real estate sector altogether. These questions and topics should guide the design of the survey instruments.

This should be followed by identifying the study subjects, for example, graduates who completed their studies in a particular year. Rubai Maseda (2017) recommends between six months to three years after graduation. However, a suggested alternative is a minimum of five years after graduation to measure medium-term effects (Cohen, 2004). It is therefore important for programs to keep good alumni records from the start to enable tracing when it is time to trace them (Munro & Senekal, 2019). One practical way is to allow graduates to keep their university alumni e-mail addresses. This is even more important when a program caters to international students who would be harder to trace when they leave.

Next is to decide how often the data should be collected. When the data is collected too often, it could be difficult to detect changes. If the intervals are too long, the impact of important changes could be missed. In addition, if the data is collected too soon after graduation, the benefits of a real estate degree on job market outcomes may not be noticeable as research shows these effects are sometimes delayed due to lack of significant work experience (Purcell et al., 2006, cited in Coates & Edwards, 2009; Schomburg, 2003). Between one to two years after graduation, many of them would be finishing graduate programs and could be surveyed. Questions about the transition process can also be asked retrospectively. Three to five years after graduation, many of them would become almost established professionals, with a significant number still able to recall their transition to work. Graduates who have been away for more than five years can be harder to trace and not practical to survey. For students with graduate degrees, it would still make sense to survey them within three years for traceability reasons.

Graduate experiences may also vary according to the phase of the real estate cycle in which they graduate. Students graduating into a robust part of the real estate cycle will have a different experience than student graduating into a recession. The time of graduation must therefore guide how eventual data on graduate experience and career success is interpreted. This phase is followed by deciding what data to collect and how.

The typical approach is to use surveys, although surveys may be used in conjunction with interviews and focus group discussions. Coates and Edwards (2009) framing of the results of the 2008 Australian Graduate Pathways Survey provide a point of departure for such surveys:

- Learning and development outcomes.
- Quality of degree.
- Relevance of degree for work and study.
- Participation in further study.
- Participation in employment.
- Industries and occupations of students.
- Graduate salaries.

The components may vary from the above, depending on the specific survey, but common elements include:

- Demographic information, such as gender, age, and educational background to analyze the outcomes and experiences of different groups of graduates.
- Questions about
  - the pathways taken by graduates, including further education (in the same or different discipline), entrepreneurship, or other career transitions. These questions allow us to determine those who transitioned into the real estate industry, the academy and those who have moved into other industries.
  - employment outcomes of graduates, such as their employment status, job titles, and industries they are working in. This allows more specific information in addition to what is available from (a) above.
  - the skills and competencies acquired during the educational program and their relevance to the graduates' current employment. This allows us to assess the relevance of program objectives.

- graduates' perceptions of the value and impact of their education on their career development. While related to (b) above, this offers the graduates an opportunity to reflect on their learning and validate the information from (b).
- the total compensation of graduates, providing insights into their earning potential and financial outcomes. Compensation information allows an assessment of the competitiveness of the degrees.
- satisfaction levels of graduates with their employment and career outcomes. This complements information on (e) above.
- graduates' experiences with career services and support provided by the institution. This enables the institution to evaluate its ability to help graduates transition into the job market.

- Demographic information, such as gender, age, and educational background to analyze the outcomes and experiences of different groups of graduates.
- The pathways taken by graduates, including further education (in the same or different discipline), entrepreneurship, or other career transitions. These questions allow us to determine those who transitioned into the real estate industry, the academy and those who have moved into other industries.
- Employment outcomes of graduates, such as their employment status, job titles, and industries they are working in.
- The skills and competencies acquired during the educational program and their relevance to the graduates' current employment. This allows us to assess the relevance of program objectives.
- Graduates' perceptions of the value and impact of their education on their career development. While related to employment outcomes, this offers the graduates an opportunity to reflect on their learning.
- The total compensation of graduates, providing insights into their earning potential and financial outcomes. Compensation information allows an assessment of the competitiveness of the degrees.
- Satisfaction levels of graduates with their employment and career outcomes. This complements information on their compensation.
- Graduates' experiences with career services and support provided by the institution. This enables the institution to evaluate its ability to help graduates transition into the job market.

In addition, many countries have higher education regulations that specify the skills and competencies bachelor's, and master's degree holders are required to possess on graduation. That can be used to frame some of the competence specifications in a survey like this. For RICS accredited programs, the competence specifications for the Assessment of Professional

Competence pathways may also serve as a frame of reference. This means that the level of interest in the results of this type of survey may span different stakeholders, requiring the survey to be crafted to ensure it simultaneously meets the needs of multiple stakeholders.

Several options exist for survey administration: online/postal questionnaires, interviews, focus group discussions. Online surveys are inexpensive, with a shorter response time than mail surveys (Cobanoglu et al., 2001), with higher response rates. Where respondents are geographically dispersed as in the case of international graduates, a web-based survey would be the most appropriate method of data collection. Interviews and focused group discussions could capture nuances that elude the nature of survey questions. However, they are costly in time and cost and for geographically dispersed graduates, this might not be practical as, despite the high cost, they would not be generalizable. Focus groups or interviews can be used to gather qualitative data and in-depth insights into graduates' experiences and perceptions, as a validating mechanism rather than as a primary method of data collection.

The appropriate data collection methods for graduate destination surveys can vary depending on the target population and the resources available. Longitudinal surveys, conducted over multiple time points, can provide valuable insights into the career trajectories and long-term outcomes of graduates. Data linkage with administrative records, such as tax records or employment databases, can provide objective and reliable information on graduates' employment outcomes. It is important to consider the privacy and confidentiality of respondents when selecting data collection methods and ensure compliance with ethical guidelines and data protection regulations.

To avoid having to develop questionnaires from scratch, it would be helpful to use sample questionnaires from previous studies. One important source document is by Schomburg (2003). However, these questionnaires need to be adapted for real estate-specific skills and competencies (Shah et al., 2004). See Appendix A for a copy of a sample survey.

Sampling frame

The first hurdle is to create a database of standardized graduate contact details. This task gets complicated by dated or incomplete information on their whereabouts. Perhaps the availability and trendiness of social media networks like LinkedIn may offer some help as it is quite common for most people to have at least a LinkedIn social media account. Universities that allow graduates to keep their alumni addresses may also have an easier time tracing their graduates. This step is therefore crucial to the success of the project.

In some cases, the data will need to be constructed from multiple sources, for example, the school/department from which they graduated as well as scholarship offices (du Toit et al., 2014). This data will need to be disaggregated by descriptors such as nationality (local/international), race, gender, degree type (for universities that offer multiple degrees in real estate, for example). For each graduate, a recent contact mobile number and/or email address would be important. Local students could also be traceable by post using their civil registration numbers in countries like Sweden. Extracting a sample from the population is appropriate where the population is large and impractical to survey. However, real estate class sizes tend to be relatively small compared to the typical general business degree. As a result, programs should try to survey the entire cohort of students if they can be traced.

Survey administration

The first step in this phase of the process is to pre-test the instruments even if sample questions from previous instruments have been used (Schomburg, 2003). A potential problem is the risk of non-response (see du Toit [2016] for a discussion of the tradeoffs between web-based surveys and telephone surveys). As indicated earlier, online surveys are commonly used as they are cost-effective, efficient, and allow for easy data collection and analysis.

Postal surveys can be used for reaching graduates who may not have regular access to the internet or prefer a physical questionnaire. Telephone surveys can be effective for reaching graduates who may not respond to online or postal surveys, although they may be more time-consuming and costly. Mixed-mode surveys, which combine multiple data collection methods (e.g., online and telephone), can be used to maximize response rates and reach a broader range of graduates. As a result of the tradeoffs discussed by du Toit (2016), it may make sense to use both web-based surveys and text-based surveys. If the response categories are minimal and interviewers are trained and monitored, telephone surveys may be used for those who may not have responded to the above two surveys.

Using the survey

The next step in the process is data analysis to ascertain whether a relationship exists between requirements and processes of teaching and learning as well as the results of studies and professional success (Schomburg, 2003). Jackson and Bridgstock describe employability as "a multi-dimensional, lifelong, and life-wide phenomenon that is malleable and driven by the individual yet encouraged and facilitated by Higher Education" (2020, p. 724). As a result, one of the basic pieces of information that can be extracted from such studies is the employment/unemployment/underemployment rates of graduates (Mott et al., 2006). This should be followed by teasing out the reasons for the observed employment/unemployment/underemployment rates.

As mentioned earlier, some of this could be due to the phase in the real estate cycle they joined the workforce. For female graduates, it may be important to check which proportion leave the workforce for family reasons as part of the proportion that leave the profession altogether (Mott et al., 2006). It would be equally insightful to see those whose jobs require graduate level skills and those whose jobs require less, which would constitute some form of under employment. All of them should also explain if they had any difficulties finding employment (Shah et al., 2004). For the underemployed, it would be important to probe the reasons for underemployment, especially if there is a possible skills mismatch between the requirements of available jobs and their own skills and competencies on graduation.

Beyond aggregate employment/unemployment/underemployment rates, the professional pathways they have chosen would be important especially for RICS-accredited programs to see if students successfully stay on those pathways or if they leave for other pathways. An interesting issue would also be to seek insights into the point in time when the students made the decision to pursue a particular professional qualification route (Silverton et al., 2003). Respondents can also be disaggregated by socio-economic characteristics such as race, gender, nationality (for international programs), and other relevant socioeconomic characteristics.

Another aspect of post-graduation career development is the number of graduates that have undertaken further studies (Master's/PhD) or obtained professional certification. One of the reasons for accrediting real estate programs is to enable the recognition of the accredited qualifications in partial fulfillment of the requirements for professional certification. Many of these certifications require a minimum of three years of post-graduation work experience. It would thus be natural to expect that if a degree provides the relevant employability skills, graduates should make a swift transition to professional status in three years or more. The number of graduates with professional certification as appraisers, property/asset managers or corporate real estate managers should therefore be a desirable metric of success of a real estate program. This perhaps justifies tracing graduates after three or more years.

Earlier in this chapter, the authors argued against reducing the value of a degree to its ability to provide jobs. Society expects university graduates to play a role greater than just being workers for the state and private businesses. They are expected to be able to effectively function in society (Hess et al., 2021). The idea of embedding civics and social responsibility within technical/business content is credited to Dewey (1916, cited in Hess et al., 2021). The adapted version of the CDIO model alluded to earlier leads to an integrated real estate curriculum that includes technical real estate competence, integrated with personal, interpersonal and professional skills in an enterprise and societal context. The latter could be broadly defined to include civic mindedness, and it is important that real estate degrees address this aspect of graduate preparation and test for it using a tracer study. Hess et al. (2021) used the 30-item Civic-Minded Graduate Scale or CMG Scale, designed to measure a set of citizenship outcomes that embody the qualities of a "civic-minded graduate," a university graduate who is willing and able to work with others to achieve the common good (Steinberg et al., 2011, cited in Hess et al., 2021). Some items on this instrument can be adapted or incorporated to address this aspect of graduate readiness to be a citizen and the extent to which the degree provides skills in civic mindedness.

The next important set of insights from a tracer study relates to the reward structure of graduates. Azasu (2012) argued that the portfolio of pay, benefits, learning and development programs, as well as career progression constitute one side of a social exchange that a real estate company offers employees in exchange for their decision to join, stay with and offer discretionary effort to the company. The quality of the degree program should, all things being equal, contribute to this. A tracer study should therefore measure salaries, benefits, learning and development programs as well as opportunities for career progression.

Moreover, an explicit question must give opportunities for a self-report on the extent to which graduates believe their education has contributed to their career success or lack of it. In particular, the study can ask questions on the employability benefits of programs such as extra/intra-curricula internships, class projects using real world cases, the assistance of university career services (including preparatory programs).

A final set of insights concerns graduates' views of the skills and competencies taught and assessed in their respective degrees, in relation to their current careers. In addition, their views on the desired proficiency level of these skills and competencies is even more important for reasons to be discussed below. Moreover, new skills and competencies not currently taught could be gleaned from the responses, for example, in the current environment, few programs may emphasize ESG (environmental, social, and governance) and AI. Tracer studies allow us to identify these important new skills.

These insights will enable program heads and real estate departments to refine the graduate specifications that form the basis of program design. The difference between tracer studies and other general stakeholder studies found in the literature is that tracer studies are program specific and limited to the alumni of the programs in question. Whereas at the initial stages of the program, surveys seek the input of a broad base of stakeholders, tracer studies are focused on alumni. Their role in improving program relevance completes the loop from planning, implementation to post-implementation evaluation.

Conclusion

A disproportionate amount of real estate education research has focused on stakeholder inputs as a mechanism of ensuring real estate degrees are responsive to stakeholder needs. A slightly smaller number of studies have also addressed how to design real estate programs and courses to reflect these inputs. However, graduate employability outcomes and the transition to work as well as the relevance of these degrees have not attracted equal attention in the real estate academy. Tracer studies or graduate destination surveys offer an opportunity to address this gap.

This chapter describes the opportunities offered by tracer studies or graduate destination surveys. Unlike regular stakeholder studies, these studies are program specific although clusters of universities can organize them for graduates from specific programs to measure graduate success, seek feedback for program improvement and maintain a relationship with graduates. We also described its components and offer guidelines on how to design and implement it. We also show how to categorize and use the inputs.

However, design and implementation are not without its challenges, some which have been discussed above. Tracing graduates who are likely to be geographically dispersed means once programs are up and running, the university must plan how to stay in touch with them. This is even more complicated with female graduates who might drop out of the workforce altogether for family reasons, or with international students who move abroad. Timing also complicates the quality of insights one might be able to gather. Joining the labor force when the real estate cycle is on the rise would lead to different career outcomes than joining during a downturn. Longitudinal studies allow tracing the same cohort of graduates over time which could provide more robust evidence for the objectives already discussed. The merits of that must be compared with cross-sectional studies of different cohorts who graduate as the program presumably undergoes continuous improvement using evidence such as external review and accreditation processes.

The authors hope future real estate education researchers will conduct several graduate destination surveys (cross-sectional and longitudinal) to offer insights on how well real estate degrees have been performing, which changes have impacted the industry and graduate careers, and what changes programs need to implement to ensure that real estate programs continue to produce employable graduates and citizens.

Note

1 A version of this instrument was prepared for graduates from undergraduate and postgraduate programs at the University of the Witwatersrand in Johannesburg. A redesigned and relaunched version of these programs were launched in 2013. This survey traced graduates from older versions of the programs and the new versions that produced graduates from the end of 2014 at the postgraduate level. The first cohort of undergraduates completed at the end of 2016.

References

Abel, J. R., & Deitz, R. (2014). Do the benefits of college still outweigh the costs? *Current Issues in Economics and Finance*, *20*(3), 1–9. www.newyorkfed.org/medialibrary/media/research/current_issues/ci20-3.pdf

Abel, J. R., & Deitz, R. (2019). *Despite rising costs, college is still a good investment.* Federal Reserve Bank of New York. Retrieved December 27, 2023 from https://libertystreeteconomics.newyorkfed.org/2019/06/despite-rising-costs-college-is-still-a-good-investment/

Amidu, A., Ogbesoyen, O., & Agboola, A. O. (2018). Exploring gaps between real estate curriculum and industry needs: A mapping exercise. *Pacific Rim Property Research Journal, 24*(3), 265–283. https://doi.org/10.1080/14445921.2018.1552472

Azasu, S. (2012), A survey of reward management practices in the Swedish real estate sector. *Property Management*, *30*(5), 449–464. https://doi.org/10.1108/02637471211273419

Azasu, S., & Berggren, B. (2015). Using constructive alignment to improve student research and writing skills: a case study of a master's program in real estate management. *International Journal of Learning and Change*, *8*(1), 83–100. https://doi.org/10.1504/IJLC.2015.069076

Azasu, S., & Gibler, K.M. (2016). The CDIO model for real estate curriculum development, *Journal of Real Estate Literature*, *24*(2), 287–308. https://doi.org/10.1080/10835547.2016.12090429

Badiru, E. O., & Wahome, M. (2016). Conducting Graduate Tracer Studies for Quality Assurance in East African Universities: A Focus on Graduate Students Voices on Quality Culture. *Journal of Education and Practice*, *7*(6), 174–181. https://eric.ed.gov/?id=EJ1092473

Brits, H. J., & Steyn, C. (2019). Conducting a graduate tracer study at a University of Technology: A quest to enhance the learning experience. In *Proceedings of the 9th Balkan Region Conference on Engineering and Business Education and 12th International Conference on Engineering and Business Education* (pp. 10–18). Lucian Blaga University of Sibiu. www.researchgate.net/publication/341644973_Conducting_a_Graduate_Tracer_Study_at_a_University_of_Technology_a_Quest_to_Enhance_the_Learning_Experience

Bryła, P. (2015). The impact of international student mobility on subsequent employment and professional career: A large-scale survey among Polish former Erasmus students. *Procedia-Social and Behavioral Sciences*, *176*, 633–641. https://doi.org/10.1016/j.sbspro.2015.01.521

Butler, J., Guntermann, K., & Wolverton, M. (1998). Integrating the real estate curriculum. *Journal of Real Estate Practice and Education*, *1*(1), 51–66. https://doi.org/10.1080/10835547.1998.12091554

Callanan, J., & McCarthy, I. (2003). Property education in New Zealand: Industry requirements and student perceptions. *Journal of Real Estate Practice and Education*, *6*(1), 23–32. https://doi.org/10.1080/10835547.2003.12091590

Coates, H., & Edwards, D. (2009). *The 2008 graduate pathways survey: graduates education and employment outcomes five years after completion of a bachelor degree at an Australian university*. Australian Council for Educational Research. https://research.acer.edu.au/higher_education/12

Cobanoglu, C., Warde, B., & Moreo, P. J. (2001). A comparison of mail, fax, and web-based survey methods. *International Journal of Market Research*, *43*(4), 441–52. https://doi.org/10.1177/147078530104300401

Cohen, R.N. (2004). Introducing Tracer Studies guidelines for implementing Tracer Studies in early childhood programmes. The Hague: Bernard van Leer Foundation. https://issuu.com/bernardvanleerfoundation/docs/introducing_tracer_studies_guidelines_for_implemen

du Toit, J. (2016). Can we augment web responses with telephonic responses to a graduate destination survey? *Assessment & Evaluation in Higher Education*, *41*(4), 560–574. https://doi.org/10.1080/02602938.2015.1033613

du Toit, J., Kraak, A., Favish, J., & Fletcher, L. (2014). From study to work: Methodological challenges of a graduate destination survey in the Western Cape, South Africa. *Assessment & Evaluation in Higher Education, 39*(7), 853–864. https://doi.org/10.1080/02602938.2013.875118

Galuppo, L. A., & Worzala, E. (2004). A study into the important elements of a master's degree in real estate. *Journal of Real Estate Practice and Education*, *7*(1), 25–42. https://doi.org/10.1080/10835547.2004.12091600

Gibler, K. (2001). Applying writing across the curriculum to a real estate investment course. *Journal of Real Estate Practice and Education*, *4*(1), 41–53. https://doi.org/10.1080/10835547.2001.12091573

Gibler, K. M., Black, R. T., & Moon, K. P. (2002). Time, place, space, technology and corporate real estate strategy. *Journal of Real Estate Literature*, *24*(3), 235–262. https://doi.org/10.1080/10835547.2002.12091095

Haigh, M., & Clifford, V. A. (2011). Integral vision: A multi-perspective approach to the recognition of graduate attributes. *Higher Education Research and Development*, *30*(5), 573–584. https://doi.org/10.1080/07294360.2011.598448
Hess, J. L, Lin A., Fore G. A., Hahn T., & Sorge B. (2021). Testing the civic-minded graduate scale in science and engineering. *International Journal of Engineering Education*, *37*(1), 44–64. https://par.nsf.gov/servlets/purl/10480920
Hopkins, E. A. (2021). Leveraging experiential education techniques in the real estate curriculum. *Journal of Real Estate Practice and Education*, *23*(1), 1–9. https://doi.org/10.1080/15214842.2020.1757356
Jackson, D., & Bridgstock, R. (2021). What actually works to enhance graduate employability? The relative value of curricular, co-curricular, and extra-curricular learning and paid work. *Higher Education*, *81*, 723–739. https://doi.org/10.1007/s10734-020-00570-x
Jackson, D., & Dean, B.A. (2023) Employability-related activities beyond the curriculum: how participation and impact vary across diverse student cohorts. *Higher Education*, *86*, 1151–1172. https://doi.org/10.1007/s10734-022-00966-x
Kezar, A. (2004). Obtaining integrity? Reviewing and examining the charter between higher education and society. *The Review of Higher Education*, *27*(4), 429–459. https://dx.doi.org/10.1353/rhe.2004.0013.
Kraak, A. (2015). The value of graduate destination survey data in understanding graduate unemployment: A focus on the universities of technology. *South African Journal of Labour Relations*, *39*(1), 94–113. https://hdl.handle.net/10520/EJC170746
Lambert, M. T. (2014). *Privatization and the Public Good.* Harvard University Education Press. https://doi.org/10.1080/00091383.2015.1031589
Maseda, M. R. (2017) Tracer studies: Evaluating the impact of training programmes. *Skills Anticipation Background Note. European Training Foundation.* www.etf.europa.eu/sites/default/files/m/CEDE612F00BFF6B3C12581A600278816_Tracer%20studies.pdf
McGrath, K., Wang, B., Jackson, B., Kämpf-Dern, A., Malone, K., Funk, D., & Geurts, T. G. (2020). The future of real estate education: A multi-faceted perspective. *Journal of Real Estate Practice and Education*, *22*(1), 40–55. https://doi.org/10.1080/15214842.2020.1757354
Mott, D. A., Doucette, W. R., Gaither, C. A., Kreling, D. H., Pedersen, C. A., & Schommer, J. C. (2006). Pharmacist participation in the workforce: 1990, 2000, and 2004. *Journal of the American Pharmacists Association*, *46*(3), 322–330. https://doi.org/10.1331/154434506777069589
Mouton, J., van Lill, M., Prozesky, H., Bailey, T., Duncan, M., Boshoff, N., Albertyn, C., & Treptow, R. (2022). *A national tracer study of doctoral graduates in South Africa: Report to the Department of Science and Innovation.* Department of Science and Innovation. www.researchgate.net/profile/Tracy-Bailey-2/publication/355757530_A_national_tracer_study_of_doctoral_graduates_in_South_Africa/links/62ef6fcd0b37cc344778ec3c/A-national-tracer-study-of-doctoral-graduates-in-South-Africa.pdf

Munro, N., & Senekal, J. (2019). Lessons learnt from two decades of graduate tracer research: Recommendations for the South African context. *South African Journal of Higher Education*, *33*(2), 230–248. http://dx.doi.org/10.20853/33-2-2628

Poon, J. (2012). Real estate graduates' employability skills: The perspective of human resource managers of surveying firms. *Property Management*, *30*(5), 416–434. https://doi.org/10.1108/02637471211273392

Poon, J., & Brownlow, M. (2014). Competency expectations for property professionals in Australia. *Journal of Property Investment & Finance*, *32*(3), 256–281. https://doi.org/10.1108/JPIF-12-2013-0068

Poon, J., Hoxley, M., & Fuchs, W. (2011). Real estate education: An investigation of multiple stakeholders. *Property Management*, *29*(5), 468–487. https://doi.org/10.1108/02637471111178146

Purcell, K., Elias, P. and N. Wilton (2006) Looking Through the Glass Ceiling: a detailed investigation of the factors that contribute to gendered career inequalities. Liverpool: European Social Fund Higher Education Report/ Coventry: Warwick Institute for Employment Research.

Rabianski, J. S., & Black, R. T. (1999). An international perspective on the importance of real estate concepts and topics. *Journal of Real Estate Practice and Education*, 2(1), 13–32. https://doi.org/10.1080/10835547.1999.12091559

Roulac, S. E. (2002). Requisite knowledge for effective property investment in the global context. In K-W. Schulte (Ed.), *Real Estate Education Throughout the World: Past, Present and Future* (pp. 3–19). Springer.

Saginor, J., Weinstein, M., & Worzala, E. Graduate real estate education: A survey of programs after the great recession. *Journal of Real Estate Practice and Education*, *17*(2), 87–109. https://doi.org/10.1080/10835547.2014.12091738

Schiefelbein, E., & Farrell, J. P. (2014). *Tracer studies*. In G. Psacharopoulos (Ed.), *Economics of education: Research and studies* (pp. 382–385). Elsevier.

Schomburg, H. (2003). *Handbook for Graduate Tracer Studies*. Centre for Research on Higher Education and Work, University of Kassel. https://qtafi.de/images/handbooks/schomburg_2003_handbook_graduate_tracer_studies.pdf

Schomburg, H. (2014). Key Methodological Issues of Tracer Studies–Challenges for a Guide on Tracer Studies. In *Proceedings from Presentation at the Validation Seminar on Methodological Guides for Skills Anticipation and Matching. Cedefop-ILO-ETF Expert Seminar (Prague, 6-7 March 2014). National Training Fund*. http://en.nvf.cz/assets/docs/9639e63aa98c7a8c450f61961c29f4fc/422-0/shomburg-tracer.pdf

Schomburg, H. (2016). Carrying out tracer studies: guide to anticipating and matching skills and jobs: volume 6. www.cedefop.europa.eu/en/publications-and-resources/publications/2218

Shah, A., Pell, K., & Brooke, P. (2004). Beyond first destinations: Graduate employability survey. *Active Learning in Higher Education*, *5*(1), 9–26. https://doi.org/10.1177/1469787404040457

Silverthorne, J., Price, G., Hanning, L., Scanlan, J., & Cantrill, J. (2003). Factors that influence the career choices of pharmacy undergraduates. *Pharmacy Education*, *3*(3), 161–167. https://doi.org/10.1080/1560221031000l623124

Simister, N. (2017). *Tracer studies*. INTRAC. www.intrac.org/app/uploads/2017/01/Tracer-studies.pdf

Smith, E., & White, P. (2016). A "great way to get on"? The early career destinations of science, technology, engineering and mathematics graduates. *Research Papers in Education*, *32*(2), 231–253. https://doi.org/10.1080/02671522.2016.1167236

Teichler, U. (2007). Background and aims of the analysis of African graduates' employment and work. In:Mugabushaka, A-M. et al. (eds.). *Higher education and work in Africa: a comparative empirical study inselected countries*. Kassel: International Centre for Higher Education Research. Werkstattberichte, No 69.

Tu, C., Weinstein, M., Worzala, E., & Lukens, L. (2009). Elements of successful graduate real estate programs: perceptions of the stakeholders. *Journal of Real Estate Practice and Education*, 12(2), 105–121. https://doi.org/10.1080/10835547.2009.12091660

Weinstein, M., & Worzala, M. (2008) "Graduate real estate programs: an analysis of the past and present and trends for the future." *Journal of Real Estate Literature* 16 (3), 385–414. https://doi.org/10.1080/10835547.2008.12090237

Worzala, E., Tu, C., Benedict, R., & Matthews, A. (2013). A graduate real estate program survey: Careers and compensation. *Journal of Real Estate Practice and Education*, *16*(1), 29–40. https://doi.org/10.1080/10835547.2013.12091714

Appendix A

Tracer studies for real estate degrees: Sample survey instrument[1]

There are six (6) sections in this questionnaire. All respondents answer Sections A, B, and F, Section C only those currently employed, Section D by those currently unemployed, and Section E by those currently self-employed.

Section A: Personal information

Q1. Which program did you graduate from?

a. MSc Building (Property Development and Management)
b. BSc Property Studies
c. PG Dip (Property Development and Management)

Q2. To what age range do you belong?

a. Less than 25
b. 25–35
c. 36–45
d. More than 45

Q3. Are you male/female?

a. Male
b. Female

Q4. To which racial category do you belong?

a. African/black
b. Colored (Mixed race)
c. Indian/Asian
d. White

Q5. What is your disability status?

a. I am disabled.
b. I am without a disability.

Q6. In which province do you currently live?

a. Eastern Cape
b. Free State
c. Gauteng
d. KwaZulu Natal
e. Limpopo
f. Mpumalanga
g. Northern Cape
h. Northwest
i. Western Cape

Q7. What was your highest qualification BEFORE you enrolled to study at Wits?

a. Master's degree
b. Matric (High School)
c. Bachelor
d. National Diploma
e. Other (please specify)

Q8. What qualification did you receive at Wits University?

a. MSc Building (Property Development and Management)
b. BSc Property Studies
c. PG Dip (Property Development and Management)

Q9. When did you enroll in the program?

a. Before 2012
b. 2012
c. 2013
d. 2014
e. 2015
f. 2016

Q10. When did you graduate from the program?

a. 2013
b. 2014
c. 2015
d. 2016
e. 2017
f. 2018
g. 2019

Section B

Q11. How did you hear about the program?

a. Word of mouth
b. Material on the internet
c. Brochure
d. Other (please specify)
e. Marketing event

Q12. What were your reasons for choosing to do the program?

a. To improve my chances of getting employed in the property sector.
b. To improve career prospects/Promotion.
c. To be able to move to a different location.
d. To improve my skill set.
e. To gain a formal qualification.
f. I needed a challenge.
g. To access further training.
h. To take advantage of a scholarship/bursary.
i. Other (please explain)

Q13. Have you undertaken any other training/qualification after completing your Wits qualification?

a. Yes (please specify which)
b. No

Q14. What was your employment status at the time you enrolled in this programme?

a. Employed
b. I just came out of high school
c. Self-employed
d. Unemployed

Q15. What is your current employment status?

a. Employed
b. Self-employed
c. Unemployed

Section C: Currently employed

Q16. Which one of the following best describes your main professional activity?

a. Property management
b. Consulting
c. Corporate real estate services
d. Property finance/banking
e. Engineering
f. Architecture
g. Facilities management
h. Property development
i. Town planning
j. Asset management
k. Project management
l. Other (please specify)

Q17. How would you classify your employer?

a. National/Provincial/Local Government
b. Private sector
c. State Owned Enterprise (SOE)/ Parastatal
d. NGO
e. Other (Please specify)

Q18. How long have you been working for your current employer?

a. Less than 6 months
b. 6–12 months
c. 13–24 months
d. 25–36 months
e. Over 5 years

Q19. How many employees are there at your place of work?

a. 1–10
b. 11–49
c. 50–149
d. Over 150
e. Not sure

Q20. Which of the following job-related benefits did you enjoy after the degree?

a. Pension/retirement fund
b. Paid vacation leave
c. Paid sick leave
d. Paid maternity/paternity leave
e. UIF contributions
f. Medical aid
g. Permanent Employment contract
h. Income tax deductions

Q21. How many hours do you work per week?

a. More than 40
b. Less than 40

Q22. Did you ever work during your studies?

a. Yes
b. No

Q23. Which of the following job-related benefits did you enjoy before the degree

a. Pension/retirement fund
b. Paid vacation leave
c. Paid sick leave
d. Paid maternity/paternity leave
e. UIF contributions
f. Medical aid
g. Employment contract
h. Income tax deductions

Q24. What was your job level before the degree/diploma?

a. Senior management
b. Middle management
c. Supervisory level
d. Non-management level
e. Did not work before the degree/diploma

Q25. If your current employer is not the one you had at the time of your studies, why did you leave?

a. Sought after improved salary.
b. Sought after improved working conditions.
c. I needed to change my environment.
d. I wanted a new challenge.
e. Retrenched.
f. I found employment in my area of specialization.
g. Took advantage of an opportunity to use the skills acquired in training.
h. Other (please explain).

Q26. What was your job level after the degree?

a. Senior management
b. Middle management
c. Supervisory level
d. Non-management

Q27. What was your monthly salary range (in Rands) before the degree?

a. less than 10,000
b. 10,001–20,000
c. 20,001–30,000
d. 30,001–40,000
e. 40,001–50,000
f. 50,001–60,000
g. More than 60,000

Q28. How would you characterize your salary expectations after the degree?

a. My expectations have been met.
b. My expectations have not been met.
c. My expectations have been exceeded.

Q29. What do you intend to do in the next few months?

a. Look for another job.
b. Consider self-employment/own business.
c. Enroll for further education or training.
d. Stay in the current job.

Q30. What is your current salary range (in Rands)?

a. Less than 10,000
b. 10,001–20,000
c. 20,001–30,000
d. 30,001–40,000
e. 40,001–50,000
f. 50,001–60,000
g. More than 60,000

Q31. Under-employment refers to workers who are highly skilled but working in low-paying jobs, workers who are highly skilled but working in low-skilled jobs, and part-time workers who would prefer to be full-time. Based on this definition, do you consider yourself under-employed?

a. Yes
b. No

Q32. What is the nature of your under-employment?
a. Under-employment by skill
b. Under-employment by time
c. Both
d. Not applicable

Section D: Currently unemployed

Q33. How long have you been unemployed?

a. Less than 6 months
b. 6–12 months
c. 13–24 months
d. 25–36 months
e. Over 3 years

Q34. What are your sources of income or support for survival?

a. Child support grant
b. Foster care grant
c. Pension in the family
d. Cash/food/clothing from family or friends
e. Disability grant

f. Occasional entrepreneurial activity (specify)
g. Temporary work (roughly indicate how much you earned)
h. Volunteered with pay (roughly indicate how much you earned)

Q35. How long have you been looking for work?

a. Less than 6 months
b. 6–12 months
c. 13–24 months
d. 25–36 months
e. Over 3 years
f. Not looking for work

Q36. If you cannot find the type of work you are looking for, would you settle for other work?

a. Yes, any work
b. Yes, only if I get a high salary
c. No
d. Yes, other, (specify)

Q37. How are you looking for employment?

a. Social media sites
b. Looking up adverts
c. Door to door job hunting
d. Through recruitment agencies
e. Other (please specify)

Q38. Could you speculate as to why you are finding it difficult to find work?

a. I feel discouraged about my prospects of finding a job.
b. There are limited positions available.
c. I did not like working for certain companies.
d. Employers do not recognize my qualification.
e. I do not have relevant work experience.
f. There are limited employment opportunities in my area.
g. I am taking care of children/family members.
h. I don't have any transport money to go to interviews.
i. I am expecting a baby
j. Other (please specify)

Q39. To what extent do you think the following factors influence unemployment among other graduates:

	Agree	*Neutral*	*Disagree*
Lack of information about the job.			
Lack of job searching skills.			
No professional networks.			
Lack of formal working experience.			
Mismatch between skills attained and those that are required by employers.			
Reputation of university.			
Age (too young or too old).			
Race.			
The high cost of searching for employment.			
Geographical area one lives in.			
Lack of self-confidence.			
No contacts in the desired companies.			

Q40. What are your thoughts/ideas/suggestions for improving employment opportunities of the unemployed graduates from property studies at Wits?

Section E: The self-employed respondents

Q41. Are you self-employed in real estate?

a. Yes
b. No

Q42. Do you have any employees?

a. Yes
b. No

Q43. If you're still in real estate, in which sub-sector is your business?

a. Property management
b. Consulting
c. Corporate real estate services
d. Property finance/banking
e. Engineering
f. Architecture
g. Facilities management
h. Property development
i. Town planning
j. Asset management
k. Project management
l. Other (please specify)

Q44. In which province do you currently work?

a. Eastern Cape
b. Free State
c. Gauteng
d. KwaZulu Natal
e. Limpopo
f. Mpumalanga
g. Northern Cape
h. Northwest
i. Western Cape

Q45. Why are you self-employed?

a. No suitable work available
b. Want to make more money
c. Enjoy independence
d. Flexible schedule
e. Can work from home
f. Family business
g. Other, please specify

Q46. How long have you been self-employed?

a. Less than 6 months
b. 6–12 months
c. 13–24 months
d. 25–36 months
e. Over 3 years

Q47. What is your current monthly salary range (in Rands)?

a. less than 10,000
b. 10,001–20,000
c. 20,001–30,000
d. 30,001–40,000
e. 40,001–50,000
f. 50,001–60,000
g. More than 60,000

Q48. Did the program help you in any way to start your own business or have you always been self-employed

a. Yes
b. No (please explain)

Q49. How important is your current job to your career goals?

a. Extremely important
b. Very important
c. Moderately important
d. Slightly important
e. Not at all important

Q50. How useful is the degree you obtained in your current job?

a. Extremely useful
b. Very useful
c. Moderately useful
d. Slightly useful
e. Not at all useful

Q51. How satisfied are you with your current job?

a. Extremely satisfied
b. Somewhat satisfied
c. Neither satisfied nor dissatisfied
d. Somewhat dissatisfied
e. Extremely dissatisfied

Q52. How would you rate your socio-economic status before the degree?

a. I had enough for most necessities but few luxuries.
b. I had enough for food and clothes but was short of many other necessities.
c. I had money for extra things such as going away on holidays and luxury goods.

Q53. How would you rate your socio-economic status after the degree?
  a. I have enough for most necessities but few luxuries.
  b. I have money for extra things such as going away on holidays and luxury goods.
  c. I have enough for food and clothes but was short of many other necessities.

Section F: All graduates

Q54. Please rate the attributes of the program you graduated from? (Select as appropriate.)

	Strength	*Weakness*	*Neither*
Range of courses offered			
Number of optional courses relative to compulsory modules			
Student workload			
Teaching quality			
Interdisciplinary learning			
Teaching and learning facilities			
Research capacity			
Labor market relevance			
Industry linkages			
International real estate markets			

Q55. The following statements relate to your opinions on the effectiveness of the education you have received. Please rank them from strongly agree to strongly disagree. Where this is not applicable, please indicate it.

	Agree	*Neutral*	*Disagree*
The course adequately prepared me for the work I currently do.			
My current employer is satisfied with my level of knowledge and skills.			

(Continued)

	Agree	*Neutral*	*Disagree*
I find myself very effective in my current job.			
My employer values the skills I acquired.			
I am more productive and can do more than I did before attending the course.			
I deliver high-quality work to my employer.			
My working conditions have improved after my studies.			
I can easily change jobs within my area of specialization.			

Q56. How adequately did the degree give you the following skills and competencies? (Select as appropriate.)

	Adequate	*Neutral*	*Inadequate*
Building science and construction technology			
Environmental impact assessment			
Real estate market analysis			
Real estate finance and investments			
Real estate valuation			
Property and asset management			
Real estate development			
Corporate real estate management			
Facilities management			
Statistical/econometric analysis and tools			
Reasoning and problem solving in real estate business situations			
Research, knowledge discovery, and report writing			
Systems thinking			

(Continued)

	Adequate	*Neutral*	*Inadequate*
Collaborative problem solving and team building			
Real estate business report writing (valuation, due diligence, market analysis, etc.)			
Presentation skills			
Awareness of how the real estate sector impacts society			
Understanding of political decisions on the real estate sector			
Participation in local and national elections			
Creating new business ventures			
Implementing real estate business solutions			
Self-awareness, stress management, problem-solving			
Empowerment and delegation, managing and leading change, managing teams			
Difficult conversations, managing office politics, managing conflict, and motivating my team			
Running a real estate business or a unit within a business			
Technologies, tools, and software (ARGUS, EXCEL modeling, etc.)			

Q57. If you were to start your degree all over, what would be the desired degree of proficiency of the following skills and competencies?

	Fundamental awareness	*Novice (limited experience)*	*Intermediate (practical application)*	*Advanced (Applied theory)*	*Expert (recognized authority)*
Generic fundamentals (mathematics, statistics, business law, planning)					
Corporate finance					
Financial accounting					
Building science and construction technology					
Environmental impact assessment					
Real estate market analysis					
Real estate finance and investments					
Real estate valuation					
Property and asset management					
Real estate development					

(Continued)

	Fundamental awareness	*Novice (limited experience)*	*Intermediate (practical application)*	*Advanced (Applied theory)*	*Expert (recognized authority)*
Corporate real estate management					
Facilities management					
Statistical/econometric analysis and tools					
Reasoning and problem-solving in real estate business situations					
Research, knowledge discovery, and report writing					
Systems thinking					
Collaborative problem solving and team building					
Real estate business report writing (valuation, due diligence, market analysis, etc.)					
Presentation skills					
Awareness of how the real estate sector impacts society					

Understanding of political decisions on the real estate sector
Participation in local and national elections
Creating new business ventures
Implementing real estate business solutions
Self-awareness, stress management, problem-solving
Empowerment and delegation, managing and leading change, managing teams
Difficult conversations, managing office politics, managing conflict, and motivating my team
Running a real estate business or a unit within a business
Technologies, tools, and software (ARGUS, EXCEL modeling, AI, etc.)

Chapter 16

Strategy, structure, positioning of college/school of property with a world-class real estate program as the centerpiece

Stephen E. Roulac

Now that we can do anything, what will we do?

This question, provocatively posed by Bruce Mau introducing his *Massive Change* (Mau, 2004), frames how we might think about real estate education's future. My answer is a big tent vision that:

- Transforms university leadership perceptions of real estate programs from marginalized, even disrespected, to prioritizing and championing.
- Emphasizes 'different thing' more so than 'different way' and a 'more, better faster' strategy (Hamel & Prahalad, 1994).
- Models start-ups' flair and ways including innovation, possibility, substantial capital commitment, and a spend now attitude to create value in compressed time horizon.
- Champions creative science while honoring relevant textbook science (Kuhn, 1972).
- Initiates meaningful momentum to enhance social stature, respect for, and influence of real estate in academic and every realm.

My big idea is that a world-class real estate program should be positioned within and as the centerpiece of a College or School of Property (C/SP), along with numerous allied disciplines concerned with places, buildings, and environments, whose Dean reports to the Provost. This vision markedly departs from conventional real estate education, emphasizing professor hires and classroom engagement rather than:

- Prioritizing strategy to achieve scale.
- Structuring programs for the greatest positive stakeholder impacts.
- Positioning real estate education within a broader university context.
- Employing a strategic management perspective, this chapter bridges the Graaskamp Neanderthal frame (Graaskamp, 1972) to post-Neanderthal worlds shaped by proliferating innovations.

DOI: 10.1201/9781032656458-16

Addressing the 'what will we do?' question in the context of improving real estate education, this chapter advances a vision whose implementation follows from strategy. The conclusion of a comprehensive study of corporate business performance by eminent business historian Chandler (1962) found that the most successful companies first determined strategy, next the structure to implement that strategy then, only after clearly, cogently defining and articulating strategy and structure, staffing/hiring decisions. But this 'strategy first, then structure before hiring sequence' is not practiced in university real estate programs. Senior hires, especially those in higher education, too often are pursued independent of strategy; this problematic tactical efficacy is reflected in the book titled: *Searching for a Corporate Savior: The Irrational Quest for Charismatic CEOs* (Khurana, 2002).

When agriculture dominated economic activity, early economics textbooks were largely concerned with land economy issues. Industrialization stimulated innovations and business growth, along with significant managerial advances. These business advances proceeded more pervasively, significantly, and faster than did real estate management and education (Roulac, 2001). *Fortune* magazine reported the industrial revolution forgot real estate with the consequence that real estate missed benefiting from resulting innovation cascades triggering progress: new concepts, patterns, and processes (Roulac, 2019).

While real estate enterprises are rapidly embracing technology, real estate is still far behind other sectors. Despite being by far the largest category of economic activity, real estate is much less concentrated than other sectors, whose companies' business scales tend to dwarf real estate companies. Scale-disadvantaged real estate companies cannot make substantial technology investments, relative to many companies not engaged in real estate. Real estate's scale disadvantages are exacerbated by the accelerating knowledge and decision-making advances – predictive analytics, big data, machine learning, and AI, that have been fueled recently by massive technology investments. These innovations indirectly challenge established real estate practices concerning the relationship of activities to specific purpose physical spaces. As a case in point, three leading technology companies, Alphabet, Amazon, and Microsoft, are reportedly spending $250 billion on AI infrastructure in 2025 (CB Insights, 2025).

Thinking strategically, the most salient is that real estate has significantly lagged behind other economic sectors in managerial theory and practice, generally, and technology adoption, specifically (Roulac, 2019). Company counts at Y Combinator, the leading technology start-up incubator, expanded in approximately 60% in nine of ten categories, yet real estate company counts declined 43% (Tunguz, 2025). The 'smart home' sector of product/service offerings enhancing the performance and experience of houses includes features by numerous start-up companies yet the sector is currently dominated by leading tech players' products and services, Amazon's Alexa, Google's Nest, and Apple's 'Face-ID Door Lock and Smart Display', not real estate companies (Ni & Flanders, 2025). Companies based in technology, consider Airbnb, Compass, and Zillow, have had more profound impacts on real estate than have the real estate companies seeking to apply technology.

Shrinking numbers of real estate professors and universities' lack of strong programmatic presence and strategy excellence commitments, relative to business, economics, and STEM disciplines, mean that in an era of enterprise consolidation and rapid technological advances, real estate's already severely compromised technology competitiveness position inevitably becomes even more exacerbated. In some ways real estate, and most especially in universities, is closer to the ethos, logos, and pathos of Neanderthals than to 21st-century technocrats.

Holistically and comprehensively considered, real estate represents approximately half of economic activity, greater in expanding and emerging economies, and similar proportions of wealth (Roulac, 2001). Yet, no other sector of society and economy is so disproportionately underrepresented in universities' curriculums as real estate, relative to its scale, significance, and importance. Various academic disciplines of far less significance command considerably more faculty positions and resources than do the real estate programs.

Notwithstanding real estate's critically important role in society, culture, and commerce, university real estate programs are of modest scale, generally lacking recognition, prominence, influence, and respect. Most featured programs list only a few faculty and staff (Miller & Weinstein, 2006), which numbers collectively approximate comparable economics faculty and staff counts at a major university. University real estate programs' diminished, marginalized stature sharply contrasts with the prominent and profound roles of physical real estate found on campus, such as offices, classrooms, dormitories, dining halls, and recreation facilities that are designed specifically to attract future students. They help make the processes of learning and social experiences that are the essence of universities' missions.

This disconnect between real estate's overall prominence on many campuses and university real estate educational program's insignificance is most ironic it has been shown that more than 40% of college graduates take economics courses but fewer than 1% take real estate courses

(Roulac, 2015). While the significant role of real estate resources in education is visually evident and intuitively obvious, real estate programs' virtually invisible presence mirrors the 'hidden in plain sight' perception paradox central to Edgar Alan Poe's classic short story, "The Purloined Letter" (Poe, 1844).

The interactions of powerful change forces are disrupting, even destroying established industries, whose persistent, seemingly ever-growing demand for space has long been integral to real estate enterprises. To this point, the retail sector, long a major user of real estate, "faces unprecedented transformation driven by tariff restructuring affecting global supply chains, AI implementation across all business functions, and evolving consumer behaviors that reject mediocrity" (The Robin Report, 2025). Expansion of global warehouse space automation from $28 billion in 2025, to a projected $50 billion in 2029, and $91 billion in 2033 is indicative of accelerating technology impacts on property (Sparsh, 2025).

Real estate program development needs to model tech start-ups best practices

Absent the emergence of major world-class real estate programs at leading universities, real estate's education future shall be characterized by continuing marginalization, lack of respect, and research of limited impact. Real estate programs need to model the best practices of tech start-ups seeking to accelerate growth to a substantial scale accompanied by recognized competence/knowledge to produce a leading product - in this case, a world-class real estate program.

The viable path forward for universities' real estate programs is to embrace what is outlined in this chapter, prioritizing strategy, scale, a tech innovation business model, big tent philosophy, leadership commitment, right organizational positioning and autonomy, financial commitment, and entrepreneurial leadership. Especially important, the world-class real estate program must achieve and operate from a position of scale, for large-scale magnifies reach, success prospects, and impacts. LinkedIn cofounder Reid Hoffman posits that 'changing the world' doing what has not been done before, disrupting old models and building new ones, achieving extraordinary change and perpetuating rapid growth are manifestations of reaching scale (Hoffman, 2021).

If real estate is far behind in technology innovation and adoption, as it is, and other sectors are growing more rapidly than real estate, as they are, then inevitably the real estate tech gap shall increase. Every day that real estate education continues what has been, leads to further marginalization, limited influence, and diminishing respect. Real estate education to varying degrees has been innocent of and removed from technology. Integral to a world-class real estate program is closely embracing technology, not merely applications but, more specifically, the technology start-up business model.

The best way for real estate to address its lagging managerial status and tech shortfalls is to be very close to tech, which can enable real estate embracing the extraordinary *change mindset* that characterizes tech. As Henry Ford observed, "If you always do what you've always done, you'll always get what you've always got!" The tech start-up model is the only viable path for real estate education to achieve necessary extraordinary changes in a compressed time horizon.

The essence of new venture start-up success involves a somehow, some way, against all odds mindset. That is, they are pulling off the 'alchemy magic trick' to travel in a compressed timeframe and moving from an idea with minimal resources and lacking the benefits of scale and established competence to a distant destination of market dominance. Pulling off the alchemy magic trick is the means for realizing the extraordinary transformation from the incipient new start-up into the established enterprise, characterized by significant scale and established competence.

Change, scale, and speed mindsets are critical to enterprise viability, competitiveness, and success in the second quarter of the 21st century. Venture capital firm NFX proclaims that start-up ventures must move 10× faster, asserting that in an AI-centric world, "If you're not making speed your edge, you don't have one" (Currier, 2025). The relevance and sustainability of any higher education real estate program that fails to recognize and integrate into its strategy the implications of change, scale, and speed, is increasingly disadvantaged and compromised.

Manifesting the benefits that may be realized by scale is motivation and reward for pulling off the alchemy magic trick illustrated in Exhibit 16.1. Achieving this incredible magic trick with limited resources requires major doses of pluck and luck, crazy and tenacity, advocates and evangelists converting adopters into believers, enabled by alchemy.

As seen in Exhibit 16.1, the incipient new start-up begins its existence in the lower left corner, with minimal scale and competence, and proceeds upward to the right on the alchemy magic trick path to become, in a compressed timeframe, an established enterprise characterized by both large scale, with the economy/learning/power associated with substantial scale and high competence, and the excellence/expertise/experience associated with substantial competence.

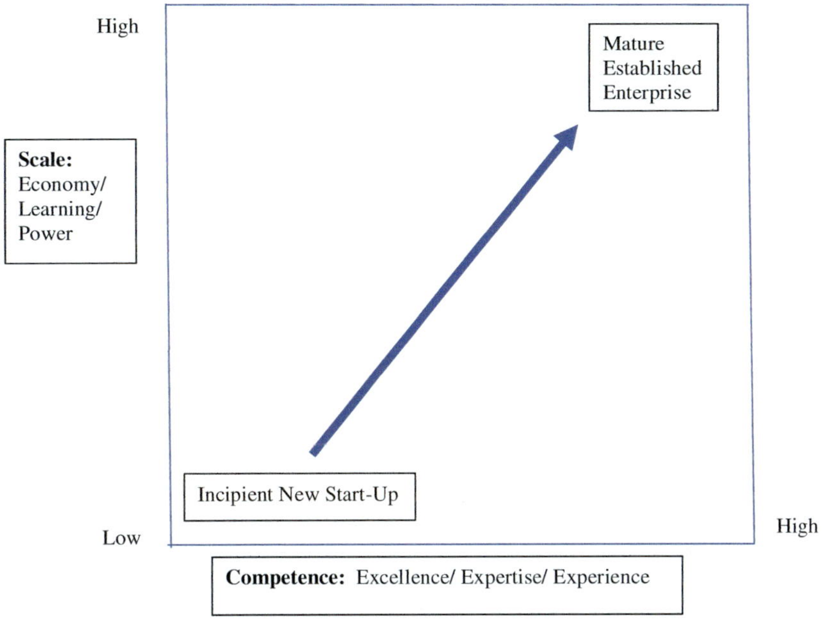

Exhibit 16.1 Alchemy magic trick: Scale and competence.

Below are just a few ways that scale attributes enhance competitive positioning:

- **Economy:** Reduced unit costs may be realized from delivering greater quantities of products and services.
- **Learning:** Larger-sized enterprises may aggregate and apply more knowledge than may be feasible in smaller-scale enterprises.
- **Power:** Bigger organizations may hire more specialized, sophisticated experts and advisors, which absolutely are more expensive but considerably less expensive on a per unit basis, and most especially in terms of value creation net of costs.
- **Excellence:** Larger-scale enterprise, most especially in knowledge work, can consistently deliver a level of excellence that may not be feasible at smaller scale.
- **Expertise:** Greater scale may facilitate higher levels, deeper, and more diverse expertise than is attainable at smaller scale.
- **Experience:** More scale is accompanied by more discovering, learning, accomplishment in compressed time periods than would apply at lesser scale.

The alchemy magic trick path is concurrently mystical and mysterious, ephemeral and fraught, and unknown and unknowable by conventional thinking. Alchemy magic trick transformation is only achievable via what Thomas Kuhn labels 'creative science', which involves extending, challenging, and replacing the received wisdom embedded in 'textbook science' (Kuhn, 1972).

Campus interview lesson: Easy path favored over the strategic path

What follows is the true recounting of a campus interview with an ambitious Dean of a mid-ranked university, known more as the hometown of an iconic rock'n'roll star and place where a beloved political leader was assassinated.

Driving to dinner, the Dean advises the candidate, "Keep in mind that not only is our business school named after the gentleman we're meeting with tonight, but he is one of the University's largest financial backers. This meeting is especially important to him as his name is on the endowed chair and he made his money in real estate. I picked you for your stellar academic record and your extraordinary professional accomplishments. Be sure to communicate your thinking concerning rigor and relevance between research, education, and practice."

Driving back to campus after dinner, the Dean exclaimed: "What an amazing dinner! In all my years, I have never seen anyone impress the most important donor the way you did."

Next morning, in his office, the Dean stated, "Since this Chair Professorship focus is on sustainable real estate, tell me the courses we should offer and how you would teach them."

"We shouldn't offer any courses in sustainable real estate, except perhaps an advanced seminar – primarily for PhD students – concerning how global change forces are impacting the sustainability agenda," the candidate replied.

Hardly masking incredulity, the Dean challenged: "What do you mean?"

"Sustainability considerations should be integral to every course offered. Courses with 'sustainability' in the title would appeal only to a narrow market segment, send wrong signals, and likely discourage the interest of the vast majority. We should embrace a 'big tent' real estate philosophy."

"What is a 'big tent' real estate philosophy?" the Dean inquired.

"The 'big tent' concept means reaching and serving a large, diverse customer base. Think Apple, Google, Microsoft. 'Big tent' real estate philosophy welcomes every student to the introductory principles course, creates close collaborating relationships with related departments by offering courses appealing to students not aspiring to real estate careers, and offers a portfolio of real estate minors," explained the candidate. "A literature major aspiring to write novels would be a more captivating storyteller by understanding and being immersed in issues of place, property, and real estate. Courses exploring the significance of houses and places in Jane Austin's and other writers' work would have wide appeal. There should be close ties to allied disciplines including architecture, planning, construction management, geography, hospitality, urban affairs, urban studies, etc."

Evidencing impatience, the Dean forcefully asked, "What package will it take to motivate you to come here?"

Responding, the candidate replied, "Following our earlier meeting, I invested substantial thought in developing the strategy to create a world-leading real estate program. Let's discuss the strategy, required investment and rewards, and how within several years the program can be substantially cash positive."

"Just tell me the number!" the Dean insisted.

The candidate provided two numbers: the investment and what he expected to earn for taking the university to global prominence for its outstanding real estate program generating millions of dollars annually. The Dean expressed no interest in the thinking behind the investment number, the strategy.

The meeting soon concluded, for the Dean was sufficiently perceptive to recognize that the candidate would not consider an offer not connected to the strategy necessary to be successful. Not unlike many corporate boards, the Dean somehow presumed crafting a quality real estate program through a charismatic hire was all you needed to do. Rather than undertaking and committing to the intellectual heavy lifting involved in crafting strategy, marshalling financial resources, and negotiating requisite institutional buy-in and leadership commitment to pursuing the daunting path that is the precondition to greatness (Khurana, 2002).

Quick fix, easier charismatic star power hires are prioritized over the deliberate, harder work of taking a strategic approach that will lead to organizational and structural priorities for the university. The most consequential decisions are disconnected from strategy, not explicitly but implicitly, for most universities have no strategy for real estate excellence. They simply focus on raising money, recruiting professors, and attracting students. Sadly, this story and its variants are all too prevalent. The moral: universities and their administrations often say one thing but do another. They often take the easy road rather than the strategic path that necessarily involves time, treasure, and talent.

Scale imperative is most effectively realized by creating a college/school of property (C/SP)

Real estate needs multiple strong programs at numerous institutions, but before that can happen, there must be the extraordinary program, serving as model, motivator, and real estate education game-changer, that can raise the bar of excellence. The most efficacious way to jumpstart filling the chasm between today's reality and what is needed is to design and establish that extraordinary real estate program, unlike any now existing, that can readily achieve market leadership and provide inspiration and a model for others to adopt at their institutions.

By its very presence and disciplinary scope, a C/SP embodies the essence of the big tent real estate philosophy. The logical path for launching C/SP is by combining many existing departments related to and allied with real estate together. The entity would be staffed by outstanding teachers, researchers, and administrators, approaching 100 or more, engaged and present both physically and virtually in classrooms, research, community interactions, and symposiums. The conceptual C/SP organization chart is provided in Exhibit 16.2.

The idea here is that the real estate program should be closely associated and affiliated with allied property disciplines. Highlighted below are some of the reasons why the allied property disciplines could benefit by being more closely connected to real estate:

- Combining multiple related fields into C/SP can achieve meaningful economies in teaching, research, and administrative support as well as more efficient use of physical facilities.
- Combined and coordinated operations should motivate more students to take C/SP courses, attract larger class enrollments, and provide superior learning from coordinated, integrated programming.
- Multiple perspectives promote connection and in today's world of polarization, in viewpoints, balkanization of orientations, and silo thinking, broader perspectives are especially important.
- C/SP multidisciplinary character is conducive to expansive, inclusive, and integrated thinking. Because real estate involvements encompass a multitude of sectors, processes, linkages, and decisions, effective comprehension of, interaction with, and most especially direct engagement in real estate requires a knowledge foundation that is both inclusive and congruent with these realities (Roulac, 1996).

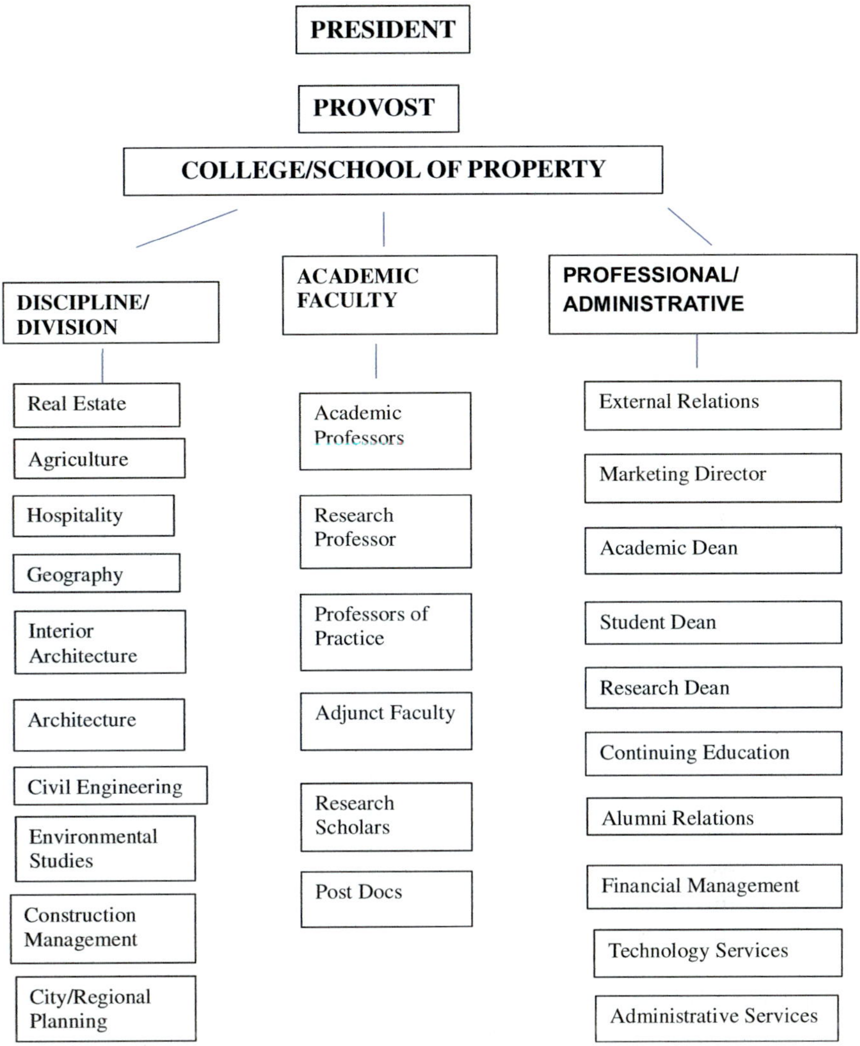

Exhibit 16.2 Conceptual depiction of positioning in an organization structure of college/school of property.

Some of the rationales for proposing the C/SP education model include:

- Career strategy is more important than training for jobs that are dramatically changing and, in some cases, may no longer exist (Category Pirates, 2025).

- In a dynamic world with declining institutional support plus expectations of self-reliance and reinvention, individuals must take more responsibility and initiative to be competitive and rewarded (Category Pirates, 2025).
- With major change forces transforming enterprises and institutions, community memberships and networks are ever more important.
- Rethinking real estate education offers an opportunity to establish lifelong value by creating a learning community with continuing engagement replacing the traditional transactional orientation for real estate decision-making.

Though beyond the scope of this writing, certain fundamentals shall distinguish and differentiate C/SP:

- Curriculum prioritizing what students need to know based on needs of the industry rather than the liberal arts model (Roulac, 1996, Roulac, 2015).
- Some courses/material will be mandatory, especially for masters and PhD students. This could be taught in a 'need to know' principles/foundations course (Roulac, 2015).
- Obligatory dual major, one discipline outside the C/SP, consistent with Peter Drucker's insistence on 'mastering more than one discipline' (Cohen, 2008).

Effectively orchestrated, C/SP learning shall facilitate and promote interaction/cross fertilization/integration of disciplines. It is the intent of the C/SP curriculum (available from the author) to replace the existing learning model used in many real estate programs and the affiliated disciplines where courses are offered in an isolated, siloed setting. Real estate is distinguished from the other disciplines as it precipitates and facilitates the other C/SP disciplines' contracting and practice. Real estate entrepreneurs, investment managers, and developers ultimately control the decisions that determine a project's destiny and the business performance of companies engaged in the allied property fields. Real estate decision-makers initiate projects, seek and secure capital, represent and negotiate terms of space use: the critical actions that trigger the need and demand for the work of allied disciplines.

How-to principles for technology start-ups applied to the C/SP launch

If the right path is chosen and the right steps are implemented in the right way, C/SP can achieve results that are the equivalent to a flywheel effect in which purposeful, focused, sustained intentionality are manifested through market-responsive strategy whose implementation can achieve sustained accomplishment, building on, extending, and magnifying success. Benefits and positive outcomes of the world-class real estate program, effectively envisioned, strategized, and implemented, are reflected in Exhibit 16.3.

Implementing the big idea to create a powerful College/School of Property, with a world-class real estate program as the centerpiece, is a daunting, difficult, and demanding task. Implementation of this big idea involves blending:

- Vision and ambition.
- Evangelism and enthusiasm.
- Persuasion and seduction.
- Invention and innovation.
- Communications and presentations.
- Recruiting and coalition building.
- Talent and time.
- Connections and networking.
- Endorsements and treasury.

Ultimately, two essential pre-conditions must be realized:

- Strong enthusiastic support and commitment by the university president and the most influential trustees.
- A substantial venture investor willing to commit at least $25 million.

If you can secure one of these two, most probably the second critical backer can be recruited.

The appeal to the university leadership are the benefits that C/SP promises:

- Transformational learning outcomes.
- Positively impacting society's most pressing problems and challenges.
- Brand building.
- Thought leadership and research distinction recognition.
- Enhancing professionals' effectiveness.
- Talent recruiting.
- Financial outcomes, specifically strong operating margins and endowment gains.
- Innovating novel educational practice.
- Implementing innovative research/learning/practice partnerships.

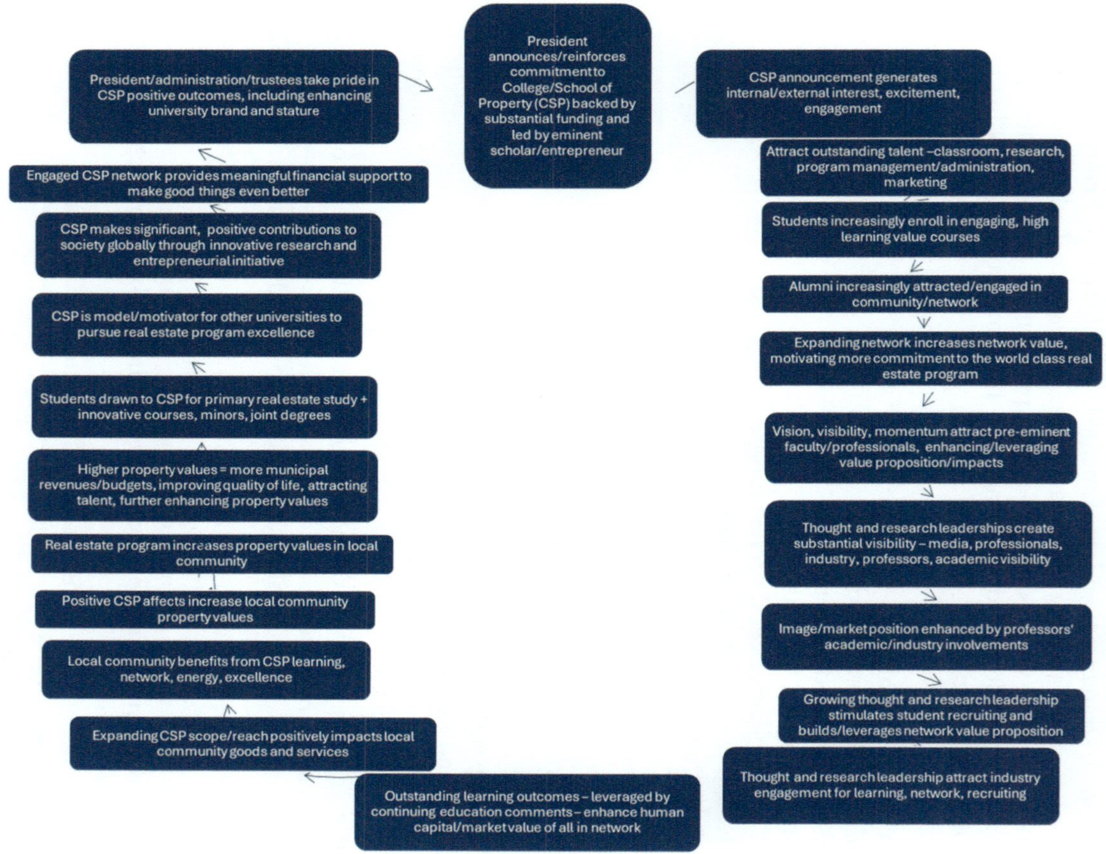

Exhibit 16.3 The virtuous circle of a world-class real estate program.

The C/SP idea and its implementation are differentiated from other real estate programs by the magnitude of the financial resources needed to fund the idea and how those resources shall be spent. Integral to making the C/SP idea a success is to employ a venture capital investing mindset which allows the program to spend (not endow) 100% of the venture money to fund, design, engineer, and scale. Were C/SP to adopt conventional university capital program practices – raising endowed funds and only allocating the interest income to fund the programs – the C/SP launch cost would increase by $100 million or more. Equally adverse from a strategic perspective, going the traditional way can severely compromise the sense of urgency and high-performance expectations that characterize the 'change the world' venture, in addition, it would likely diminish the creative energy so necessary for transformational change. Using a passive finance strategy does not typically fund innovation and transformation but rather it often simply endorses the status quo.

While some extraordinary enterprises are built by individuals with great connections, the best credentials, established track records, and deep financial resources, most extraordinary enterprises are built organically. That is, they are built with ingenuity and enthusiasm, conviction and persistence, relentless hard work, and a do-whatever-it-takes commitment. Most of the extraordinary enterprises are not incubated by insider, establishment-connected, intrapreneurs working at the company but created by ambitious, hard-working entrepreneurs who have no Plan B.

The remainder of this chapter is focused on providing some 'how to' guidance for real estate educators with a passion for teaching and who are focused on making a difference in the world to consider when trying to implement the big tent real estate philosophy of creating a College/School of Property with a world-class real estate program as the centerpiece.

- **Lead with strategy and Jettison bureaucracy:** The C/SP business model challenges traditional thinking and conventional practices, employing differentiated creative science thinking to create value and delight stakeholders through doing different things, not merely doing them in different ways (Hamel & Prahalad, 1996).
- **Position C/SP for success:** This can be done by establishing a dedicated college or school that collects pertinent property disciplines together in a single enterprise. Establishing C/SP changes the conversation about the importance of real estate in higher education, by assuring appropriate positioning within a university's organizational structure. Positioning decisions are a derivative from an explicit strategy informed by and congruent with the priorities, objectives, resources, and commitments, as discussed earlier in this chapter.

- **Report to the top:** The C/SP should report directly to the provost or most senior academic officer and the Board of Trustee Chair, if possible.
- **Establish C/SP organizational autonomy:** The C/SP should have an independent board and guidance that is provided by multiple advisory boards. The governing board chair and its members should not be university employees. The C/SP Dean shall report and be accountable to the C/SP Board. This is mandatory. If the real estate unit reports to the business school Dean, as the current situation in the majority of real estate programs, there is the very real risk of the program's resources being re-directed to the Dean's personal priorities, faculty hijacking those resources for their favored projects, or companies seeking to morph program priorities to promote their particular objectives.
- **Recruit entrepreneurial leadership, and prioritize attracting, incentivizing and rewarding best talent:** Because the strategy for C/SP and the world-class real estate program is inherently challenging, if not overtly disruptive, to existing thinking and practices, extraordinary talent is necessary to successfully implement the C/SP vision. Creating the C/SP and achieving its objectives mirrors the mindset growth pace of a successful Silicon Valley start-up. It requires leadership style and skills, talents and ambition, and track record of prior success that mirror what leading venture capitalists look for in selecting entrepreneurs to back their investments. Concurrently, C/SP must attract a team of highly talented, highly motivated, very ambitious professionals, mirroring the capabilities of individuals who build extraordinary companies. This can be done by offering exciting work, extraordinary colleagues, highly motivated students, a change-the-world mission, and financial participation in value creation for the faculty and staff.
- **Market, market, market:** To succeed, C/SP must model marketing excellence which includes paying attention to content, media, and visibility via ubiquitous omni-channel/multi-modal/multi-market/multi-place presence. High visibility in multiple media is a precondition to achieving substantial scale.
- **Design and deliver a 10× value proposition:** This would include the investors (university), talent (faculty and staff), and most importantly customers (students). This is essential when the very relevance and legitimacy of the college/university value proposition is questioned.
- **Embrace innovation and creative science:** This can be done through a tech-connected, venture-funded, change-the-world commitment and managerial style. Providing leadership that impacts, influences, and changes the disciplines that enable the physical platforms, stages, and structures of culture, society and economy, along with tracking

and being closely aligned to technology and new venture development is fundamental, integral to, and critical for property leaders.

- **Welcome a big tent philosophy of real estate:** The C/SP leaders need to holistically, inclusively, comprehensively integrate and champion the combination, connections, and collaborations of all the disciplines involving and concerned with places, environments, properties, and their stakeholders' interests. The program needs to involve all types of students. Too many real estate programs have a narrow, limiting, small-scale orientation – and lack the informed, worldwide breadth, gargantuan global scale, and phenomenal majesty of what real estate really is.
- **Scale to realize extraordinary impacts and value creation:** This can be done by combining leadership autonomy, high-powered advisors and savvy independent board, top talent, speed-to-market customer satisfaction obsession, and continuing innovation.
- **Backing by influential board members:** This is essential. It is critical to the C/SP to have a strong university commitment which is only really evidenced by the full support of the university president as well as the most influential board members. Preferably these board members also have the personal capacity and/or influence to readily persuade organizational buy-in and arrange funding for the entire C/SP budget. Board leadership commitment is imperative to realize the C/SP vision.
- **Secure substantial financial commitment:** Implementing a 'go to market' path requires substantial initial financial investment. My best estimate is at least a $25 million investment of venture-oriented capital that can be spent immediately would be needed to get the school up and running. Central to the venture financing strategy is raising capital to invest in developmental initiatives that create extraordinary value in the future. The value creation justifies subsequent resource commitments in pursuit of meaningful additional rewards including positive student impacts, brand building, leadership recognition, and talent recruiting. Not to mention, financial outcomes which could come in the form of strong operating margins (profit center for the university) and endowment gains over time.
- **Spend to fund the Alchemy magic trick and expect strong financial performance:** By accelerating the launch and market penetration to realize value creation in a compressed timeframe, the C/SP can recruit extraordinary leadership, professors, and professionals to pursue the vision, implement the program, and realize the outcomes articulated earlier in Exhibit 16.3. The priority is to astutely, aggressively deploy the venture capital funds – $6M/ $5M/$4M/$3M/$2M in each of the first five years – to create great value. Do not passively park the money in the

bank and expect the interest to fund a great, game-changing real estate education initiative. Presuming the right combination of commitment, strategy, talent, and performance realization, it is not unreasonable for the C/SP venture within several years to reach breakeven and within five years it could generate meaningful seven figure margin contributions along with the intangible benefits of recognition as a top real estate program.

- **Pursue thought leadership, research distinction, and market recognition:** The C/SP needs to have faculty with the reputation for thought leadership and research distinction. Their research needs to be connected to and leveraged by a content strategy that couples pervasive dissemination of perspectives with insightful commentary on issues of the day informed by research findings and implications. Together with producing significant research characterized by relevance and rigor, the messaging needs to emphasize connecting-the-dots implications of that research to the most pressing issues of the day. For example, things like housing and homelessness, immigration policy and workforce needs, balancing indigenous place culture and change forces, spatial patterns, and shifting special purpose property dynamics are all relevant and important topics to be studied. The research from faculty and staff in the C/SP produces and enhances the priority to make-a-difference concerning society's most important challenges and priorities.
- **Pioneer a C/SP continuous learning model that prioritizes advancing and disseminating knowledge:** Design courses, certificates, and degrees so they are not one-and-done recognition, but the initiation of an ongoing learning journey in which knowledge is continually updated and re-certified as technology systems are continually updated. Like the tech world, the C/SP should adopt software protocols of sequential updates. That is, promote learning engagement and human capital/market value enhancement rather than the 'four and no more' college degree premise. Technology that was cutting-edge years ago is not only of diminished relevance today but also, in many instances becomes inoperable at some point. In this regard, the C/SP can expand and institutionalize what Harvard Business School class reunions feature: classroom presentations of the latest thinking, research implications, and practices in core disciplines. Harvard effectively offers their returning graduates the means to update and make contemporary the knowledge represented by their MBA degrees.
- **Connect network and promote community:** In the 21st century, networks are virtual tribes, with valuable benefits of membership and powerful social brand connotations. These network attributes are made even more valuable in times of rapid knowledge creation, massive

change, decline of established institutional structures, coupled with diminishing face-to-face personal interactions. The C/SP needs to focus on creating and maintaining the network of alumni.

- **Cultivate a sense of place:** The themes, purposes, and implications of place are integral to every C/SP decision. The history, traditions, and legacy of a location inform and provide a point of reference for contemporary experiences of that place and its buildings. As digital phenomena exert an ever-greater influence over society, culture, and daily life, the importance of the physical environments in which these activities occur is not diminished. It is very important that C/SP curriculum and programming not only be congruent with the growing desire for physical environments that embody a distinct sense of place but it also needs to integrate the significance of a sense of place into curriculum design and learning environments. Specifically, the C/SP must be housed in distinctive world class spaces, facilities, and structures that attract students to want to be on C/SP campuses because these spatial environments are comparable to the very best in the world.
- **Reconcile physical and virtual places, and engage in multiple physical and virtual communities:** The choices we make about where to be – whether in physical or virtual spaces – shape and impact property, decision-making, usage, and economics. The emergence and growing influence of virtual places, especially with recent advances in AI, present extraordinary challenges to how we exist, function, and interact in physical environments. Meanwhile, stress on physical places is increasing. While the ability to choose one's place offers opportunities for a fresh start, safety, or sanctuary to those seeking a new environment, the consequences of unprecedented, large-scale migrations are becoming increasingly apparent. These massive migrations mirror Hardin's concept of *The Tragedy of the Commons (1968)*, where one farmer's decision to graze his cow on shared land encourages others to do the same, ultimately leading to the destruction of the commons. In some regions, such as England, significant migration has so profoundly changed the population's composition that groups once considered minorities are becoming the majority, while those with deep, multigenerational roots, previously the majority, are now becoming minorities. This dynamic is evident throughout the university, local community, major metros, and specialty markets, and extends to research, industry, associations and beyond. Conceptually, this perspective moves beyond an internal view of the C/SP network, to encompass all interactions that connect with the diverse interests of C/SP and its stakeholders. Think of it this way: by interacting with and contributing to the broader society, C/SP gains valuable insights and intelligence: blending

learning and practice, job searching and corporate recruiting, and the roles of continuing students and thoughtful practitioners. Thus, by way of example, rather than companies occasionally visiting campuses and/or randomly for recruiting and select events or courses, C/SP expands the scope and reach of its community and company interactions as well as shared learning experiences beyond the campus. In this regard, C/SP promotes its community participating in external events, such as meetings of the American Real Estate Society and sister's International Real Estate Society meetings.

- **Integrate global awareness and local engagement:** More and more issues and processes of global origins/influences/consequences – military conflicts, drug trafficking, climate, supply chain fragility, competing values, political bifurcation, travel and migration, labor and talent access and opportunity, capital flows, competing interpretations of rights – are played out in the context of and impact on local communities. Ultimately, actions that follow from grand visions, large aspirations, and expansionary strategies are implemented in and have consequences experienced at the local level. This global–local duality is increasingly pertinent, for all real estate decisions so the C/SP curriculum should raise awareness of these issues.
- **Leverage capital attraction and build endowments:** The university with a world-class real estate program has more successful and more loyal alumni that are ready to get involved and get back. They are committed due to the program prominence, scale, and valued-added learning. A compelling case can be made that a university's most important academic initiative, for the purpose of supporting, sustaining, expanding, and enhancing the university's financial resources, should be to have a strong real estate program. By doing so, the university significantly increases its chances of attracting substantial financial support, far beyond what might be achieved without a world-class real estate program anchoring C/SP.

Conclusion

The best future of real estate education is not incremental reform, but radical reimagination. This chapter has made the case that building a world-class real estate program requires more than charismatic hires, more than minor tweaks to curricula, and most certainly more than adherence to outdated institutional structures. What is needed is a bold, comprehensive, and holistic transformation, a strategy-first approach rooted in innovation, scale, speed, and an unwavering commitment to societal impact, enabled by financial strategy mirroring start-up finance backed by venture capital. Integral to this financial strategy is to raise substantial funding that is purposely spent in the near term to create extraordinary value now, rather than the traditional practice of parking donor money being passively parked in a bank.

Establishing a C/SP, with real estate at its core, offers a powerful new model, one that integrates allied disciplines, challenges conventional silos, and operates with entrepreneurial urgency. The C/SP is not merely a structural innovation, but a cultural one, embedding technology, creative science, and a big tent philosophy into every facet of its mission. By addressing the profound disconnect between real estate's dominant role in economic and social life and its marginal presence in the academy, C/SP can profoundly and most positively impact society and its institutions, economies, and peoples.

To realize this vision demands visionary entrepreneurial leadership, institutional courage, significant investment, and the commitment to pursue the path less taken. But the reward is not just academic distinction. It is the creation of a transformative force, one capable of shaping cities, economies, and lives. If universities can commit to this bold path, real estate education will not only catch up to the 21st century, it shall define the intersection between virtual and tangible places. In so doing, real estate education may provide leadership to positively affirmatively address the most pressing issues of today – and tomorrow.

References

CB Insights. (2025, May). Battle of the cloud titans: How Amazon, Microsoft, and Alphabet are preparing for an AI future. Accessed on July 10, 2025. www.cbinsights.com/research/report/battle-cloud-titans-alphabet-amazon-microsoft/

Category Pirates. (2025, May). If not now, when? Accessed on July 10, 2025. www.categorypirates.com/newsletter

Chandler, A.D. (1962). *Strategy and Structure: Chapters in the History of the American Industrial Enterprise*. MIT Press.

Cohen, W.A. (2008). *A Class with Drucker: The Lost Lessons of the World's Greatest Management Teacher*. AMACOM.

Currier, J. (2025). Mindset shift to move 10 X faster. *NFX Newsletter*. Accessed on July 10, 2025. www.nfx.com/post/speed-and-ai

Graaskamp, J.A. (1972). A rational approach to feasibility analysis. *The Appraisal Journal*, 40(4), 513–521.

Hamel, G., & Prahalad, C. K. (1994). *Competing for the future*. Boston, MA: Harvard Business School Press.

Hamel, G., & Prahalad, C. K. (1996). *Competing for the Future* (Revised ed.). Harvard Business Review Press.

Hardin, G. (1968). The tragedy of the commons. *Science, 162*(3859), 1243–1248. https://doi.org/10.1126/science.162.3859.1243

Hoffman, R., Cohen J., & Triff, D. (2021). *Masters of Scale: Surprising Truths from the World's Most Successful Entrepreneurs*. Crown Currency.

Khurana, R. (2002). *Searching for a Corporate Savior: The Irrational Quest for Charismatic CEOs*. Princeton University Press.

Kuhn, T. (1972). *The Structure of Scientific Revolutions*. University of Chicago Press.

Mau, B., Leonard, J., & The Institute Without Boundaries (2004). *Massive Change*. Phaidon Press.

Miller, N., & Weinstein, M. (2006). *Commercial Real Estate Career Education and Resource Guide*. The Hoyt Institute of Real Estate.

Ni, D., & Flanders, S. (2025). Apple's redesign, trouble with coding LLM's, DTC started realities. *TLDR Newsletter*. Accessed on 7 October 2025. https://tldr.tech/tech/2025-05-27

Poe, E. A. (1844). *The purloined letter*. In *The works of Edgar Allan Poe* (Vol. 1). New York, NY: Wiley and Putnam.

Roulac, S. (1996). The strategic real estate framework: Processes, linkages, decisions. *Journal of Real Estate Research*, 12(2), 323–346. www.researchgate.net/publication/5141923_The_Strategic_Real_Estate_Framework_Processes_Linkages_Decisions#fullTextFileContent

Roulac, S. E. (2001). *Stephen Roulac on Place and Property Strategy*. Property Press.

Roulac, S. E. (2015). *What Do Students Need to Know about Property? What do Textbooks Actually Teach about Property?*. No. eres2015-349. European Real Estate Society (ERES).

Roulac, S. (2019). The industrial revolution remembers. *Journal of Property Investment & Finance*, 37(4), 380–397. https://doi.org/10.1108/JPIF-02-2019-0023

Sparsh, I. S. (2025). The floors, no wires, just robots!". *Rustic Flute*. https://RusticFlute.com/the-floors-no-wires-just-robots

The Robin Report (2025). Retail needs reset. *The Robin Report*. Accessed July 10, 2025. https://therobinreport.com/how-to-bridge-the-retail-tectonic-shift/?utm_source=TRR&utm_medium=daily+email&utm_term=07+12+2025&utm_campaign=Retail+Needs+Reset

Tunguz, T. (2025). Patterns across 5 years of YC investing. Accessed on July 10, 2025. https://tomtunguz.com/yc-trends-last-five-years/

Chapter 17

The model is not the market

Teaching responsible AI in real estate

Rebecca L. Johnson

Introduction

AI-driven technologies are transforming how real estate markets operate. AI, including subfields like machine learning (ML), deep learning (DL), and generative AI (GAI), is rapidly reshaping the real estate industry (Arumugam et al., 2024; Seagraves, 2023; Starr et al., 2020). These technologies are already being applied across a range of tasks: gaining a competitive edge, automating time-consuming processes, or simply keeping up with industry trends. While these advances offer clear efficiencies, they also raise important ethical, legal, and societal questions. Given these challenges, a thorough understanding of responsible AI (RAI) should now be integral to any university real estate curriculum. Some types of tasks that AI is applied to in real estate include:

- Property valuations.
- Market analysis and predictive analytics, such as pricing trends.
- Property management, including tenant applications and price setting.
- Investment advice.
- Lead generation.
- Smart buildings, including energy efficiency and security systems.
- Regulatory compliance.
- Real estate marketing, including writing listings and enhancing photos.

RAI is a rapidly growing field that addresses the ethical, legal, and social risks involved in deploying AI systems. Unlike fields such as healthcare, finance, or criminal justice, which have received broad scrutiny, real estate has been comparatively slow to engage with the deeper implications of AI. Most literature in this space focuses on practical and technical benefits, such as increased automation or efficiency, with relatively little attention given to the ethical frameworks required for responsible deployment.

DOI: 10.1201/9781032656458-17

Recent research in real estate AI has rightly flagged issues such as data quality, algorithmic transparency, and risk/compliance. However, these alone do not capture the full spectrum of safety and ethical challenges that arise when AI technologies intersect with housing, investment, and urban development. As a result, real estate professionals, including educators and practitioners, often find themselves navigating fragmented research, with limited guidance for ethical implementation. Fortunately, many of the insights and frameworks developed in broader RAI literature are highly transferable to real estate contexts.

The conceptual tools provided here and drawn from the fields of AI ethics and safety, can empower real estate educators and students alike. As the field matures, a well-rounded approach to RAI will support fairer markets, reduce harm, and improve trust and transparency across the real estate ecosystem.

Foundational concepts in RAI

Teaching AI in real estate requires grounding students in core RAI principles. Concepts like data quality, transparency, accountability, risk, compliance, trustworthiness, and human-centred design are especially critical in real estate, where large volumes of personal and financial data shape high-stakes decisions.

Data

The old adage "Garbage In, Garbage Out" (GIGO) still holds, but it is not the whole story. Modern real estate datasets – often unstructured or incomplete – can skew automated valuation models (AVMs) and bias tenant screening. Ethical concerns extend beyond quality to data provenance and use. Who owns the data? Does it respect privacy or reflect real-world diversity? If crowdsourced data is biased or poorly labelled, models may reinforce inequities. For example, if property images are judged by underpaid crowd-workers with limited context, entire neighbourhoods may be mischaracterised.

Transparency and explainability

Transparency means making AI decisions understandable. In real estate, black-box systems, whether due to complexity or commercial secrecy, make it hard to explain how outcomes like rental prices or credit risks are determined. This erodes trust and allows unfair outcomes to go unchecked. Advances in Explainable AI (XAI) help, but educators should emphasise the importance of interpretable tools, especially when decisions affect people's homes, finances, and futures.

Accountability

When AI harms people, who is responsible? In real estate, the chain includes developers, users, landlords, and regulators. The US Department of Justice recently sued rent-pricing firm RealPage for enabling coordinated pricing via AI, showing how law, ethics, and technology intersect. The case illustrates the urgent need for accountability mechanisms built into both technology and institutional oversight.

Risk and compliance

AI-related risk in real estate includes data breaches, privacy violations, poor business decisions, and legal noncompliance. Effective governance means regular audits, bias testing, and adapting to fast-evolving regulations like the EU AI Act or Australia's AI Ethics Framework. "Ethics washing" (superficial checklists without real oversight) is a growing concern. Educators must equip students not just with current laws but with adaptable RAI thinking skills to navigate this shifting landscape.

Trustworthiness

Trustworthiness in AI-driven real estate tools depends on consistent reliability, transparency, and fairness which are qualities that foster confidence among buyers, sellers, and industry professionals. The EU framework for trustworthy AI (European Commission, 2019) defines three pillars:

- Is it lawful and compliant with applicable laws?
- Is it ethical? Does it align with the ethics and values of the people using and impacted by the AI?
- Is it robust both from a technical and social perspective?

Many governments and major tech firms cite trust as a core AI principle. In 2023, the Biden administration issued an executive order promoting "safe and trustworthy AI" (The White House, 2023), later revoked by President Trump (Shepardson, 2025). Trust in AI platforms and decision-making directly impacts diffusion and adoption of these technologies (Afroogh et al., 2024). A 2022 Oxford study noted property industry reluctance to adopt these tools, citing concerns about accuracy and fairness (Xiong et al., 2022). As such any deployment of AI into the real estate sector should take this factor into consideration and address mitigation issues head-on.

Human-centred

Human-centred AI ensures that tools support, not displace, human judgment. In real estate, this means systems that prioritise user experience, respect community impact, and prevent harm. A tenant screening model might be efficient, but if it reinforces historic discrimination, it fails the human test. Real estate educators should encourage students to think beyond efficiency towards equity and user well-being.

Beyond RAI basics

Building on the above foundational RAI topics, this section delves into more advanced concepts: model design, sociotechnical mapping, and market design. From automated valuations to risk scoring, well-crafted models can drive better property decisions, while poorly designed ones risk amplifying biases and misunderstandings. While the basics remain vital, real estate practitioners and educators increasingly confront complex challenges, such as reconciling multiple stakeholders' interests, managing wide-ranging financial risks, and maintaining fairness in rapidly shifting market conditions.

Model design

A model is an abstraction of the real world; a simplified framework designed to represent a more complex system or phenomenon. By stripping away unnecessary details, a model allows us to focus on specific aspects or dynamics of a system, making it easier to understand, analyse, and predict behaviour in a controlled manner. Models are created through human decisions about what data and parameters to include and exclude, as well as which cause-and-effect relationships to emphasise or ignore. Model designers also decide what tangible, measurable datapoints will serve as proxies for more abstract concepts.

What is critical to remember is that models are not neutral: they are human-guided abstractions and representations of the real world shaped by decisions about data, framing, and emphasis (see Exhibit 17.1). While we often think of models as being driven by mathematics and algorithms, they also reflect the assumptions and perspectives of their creators.

Exhibit 17.1 is a visual depicting the globe on the left with an arrow pointing right labelled "abstraction" to a box with a model designer and

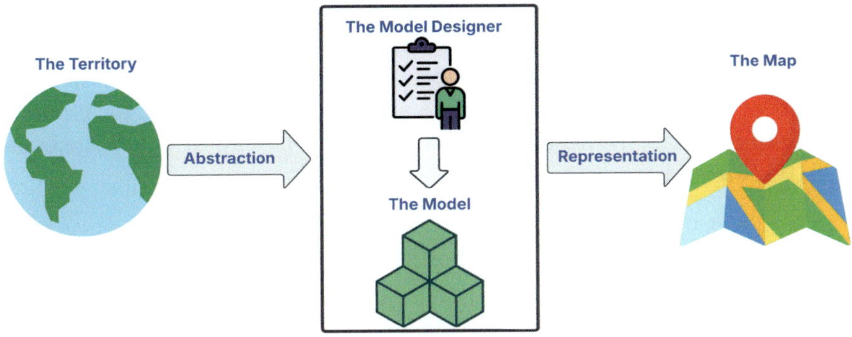

Exhibit 17.1 Examples and categories of GenAI application to real estate.

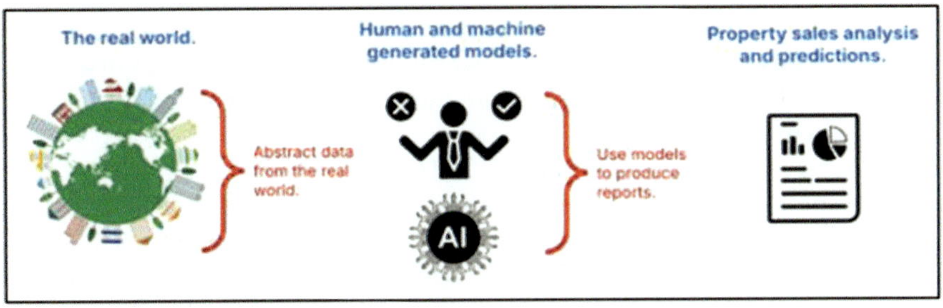

Exhibit 17.2 Human and AI decisions sit between the real world and analysis outputs.

the model. Another arrow points on the other side of the box labelled "representation" points to an abstraction of a map.

Models are everywhere in daily life – from GPS directions to credit scores. In real estate, models underpin automated valuation tools, rent-pricing algorithms, and lender risk assessments. Recognising that these systems are built upon specific data, assumptions, and priorities enables professionals to treat algorithmic outputs critically, rather than as infallible. Whether selecting features for a home-pricing model or deciding which risk variables to include in a tenant-screening tool, thoughtful model design (see Exhibit 17.2) fosters fairer, more reliable outcomes.

Exhibit 17.2 includes three illustrations to demonstrate how humans and AI sit between the real world and analysis outputs: The first image on the left is the abstract data from the real world. The second image in the middle is of a person above an image representing AI and human interfaces, and it states "human and machine generated models," representing how humans use models to produce reports. The final illustration on the right is a report labelled "property sales analysis and predictions."

For further examples of how model representations are not the same as the object being modelled, as well as a suggested class activity, please view the Supplementary Material, Section A: Model Design at routledge.com/9781032625041.

When we remove humans from the center of AI

Placing blind trust in mathematical models risks decentring the very humans such models aim to serve. Many examples show how mathematical and AI models, when applied to complex social systems, can unintentionally cause harm by excluding certain groups or perspectives from their design (O'Neil, 2016).

While these models can offer powerful tools for understanding and prediction, their simplifications can lead to significant oversights, especially when applied to human contexts. A well-known example from outside the real estate sector is the risk recidivism model called Correctional Offender Management Profiling for Alternative Sanctions (COMPAS). A widely cited investigation by ProPublica in 2016 revealed how COMPAS, a tool used by some courts in the United States, was systematically biased against Black defendants. The problem came from the model design.

For an overview of the canonical COMPAS case study and bias in risk recidivism models, of how such bias in model design can perpetuate toxic biases in our social systems, please view the Supplementary Materials, Section B: When We Remove Humans from the Centre of AI at routledge.com/9781032625041.

How AI models work

At its core, AI uses statistical techniques to find patterns in numerical data. The process begins by abstracting a part of the real world, like property features or past sales, and converting it into numbers. AI models then "learn" from these datasets by finding patterns in the numerical representations of the world to make predictions or classifications on new data.

In this text, we use "AI" to refer primarily to neural networks, which is a type of model inspired by the human brain, such as those that drive GAI. These networks contain layers of interconnected nodes ("neurons") that transform input data through weighted calculations and non-linear functions. During training, the model adjusts these weights based on feedback until it can produce accurate outputs. Both the training data and the model's structure (e.g., number of layers, activation functions) shape how well a neural network performs. For example, if an AVM is trained on biased property data, or if the architecture is poorly tuned, the model may return skewed valuations.

The so-called "black box" problem arises because the number of internal calculations makes it difficult for humans to trace how decisions are made, especially when models use thousands of weights and variables. As the diagram illustrates, the process starts with real inputs like location or building size and outputs predictions like property value. Both the data and the way a network is architected shape how effectively, and fairly, a neural network will perform.

For more information on how AI models work, please view the Supplementary Materials: Section C: How AI Models Work at routledge.com/9781032625041.

Importantly, AI models are not autonomous actors. They are human-designed, trained on human-selected data, and applied in human-chosen contexts. This means accountability always remains with us. The emerging field of Explainable AI (XAI) is developing ways to make some model decisions more transparent by exposing intermediate reasoning or simplified outputs.

Real estate already uses AI extensively. For instance, a model might analyse housing demand, interest rates, and economic signals to forecast price trends. These tools offer speed and automation, but only work well if the underlying models are thoughtfully built. The key message: AI models are not neutral or infallible. Their fairness and accuracy depend entirely on design choices, training data, and human oversight.

Sociotechnical mapping

Sociotechnical systems in real estate

AI-real estate is not just about data and algorithms, it's about how those tools interact with people, institutions, market norms, and regulations. Just as a map simplifies complex terrain, real estate models abstract the property market, inevitably leaving out nuance. Removing all bias from these systems is impossible, especially when models are built on historical data shaped by uneven development, policy, and access. Sociotechnical mapping helps us unpack how AI tools in real estate, like valuation engines or tenant screening systems, are influenced by and influence the broader ecosystem, including agents, buyers, lenders, and government bodies.

When we speak of AI applications to real estate or Proptech, we are in reality creating models to describe the world of real estate that use AI-powered technologies to apply statistical methods to make predictions or decisions based on the model and data we provide to the machine. Our decisions about what data to include in these processes directly impact the results that AI models produce and thus, the outputs of that model. For example, in the case of an AI-generated property valuation report, someone decides which data is relevant and which will be included or excluded. Then, an AI is employed to glean deeper insights.

As Alfred Korzybski (1933) famously put it, "The map is not the territory." Every output is a simplified version of reality, built from numerous design choices. Overfitting a model with too many parameters can make it unwieldy; conversely, under-specification can obscure key insights. Navigating this balance is central to responsible model use.

For a case study on how bias in a real estate algorithm can impact outcomes, as well as four additional examples of built-in bias and two supporting in-class activities, please view the Supplementary Materials, Section D: Sociotechnical Mapping. The materials supporting this section are presented along with examples supporting the following section due to the scaffolding and interwoven aspects of these sections at routledge.com/9781032625041.

Bias is inevitable

To truly grasp the ethical risks of applying AI technologies to the real estate industry, it is important to understand why it is impossible to remove all bias. Often, you hear in business literature that some organisation or AI model has been built to "remove" all bias: this is a nonsensical statement that indicates a fundamental lack of understanding of both AI technologies and model building. Some students are only taught about the risks of AI at a superficial level, such as "poor data going in leads to poor data coming out." Whilst GIGO is an important part of the story, it is not the entire picture. Trying to eliminate bias from a model is like attempting to remove the perspective from a photograph – the angle always shapes what's seen and what's left out.

Claiming that you can completely remove bias from an AI model is like saying you can design a house that's completely free of any architectural style or regional influence. Every house inevitably reflects design choices influenced by the builder's taste, local traditions, and practical considerations. Another example can be found in human resources: every hiring decision is influenced by bias, even when recruiters use structured interviews and scoring systems. The criteria they prioritise, such as experience over potential, cultural fit over diversity, or technical skills over soft skills, reflect implicit values that shape who will be hired.

The word bias is often used as short-hand for toxic-bias. Certain biases in AI models, particularly those that reinforce discrimination or harm, raise ethical concerns. Toxic bias in AI is a real and significant problem that many scholars and researchers have studied for several years. However, bias in a model doesn't necessarily imply negative or harmful perspectives; it refers to the inescapable vantage point or weighting that emerges from the data, the algorithms, and the goals chosen by those building or deploying the model. Early Generative AI models (GenAI) often exhibited obvious toxic bias (Abid et al., 2021; Floridi & Chiriatti, 2020; Johnson et al., 2022); and, whilst most tech companies have put in notable effort to mitigate these biases, they have often been addressed with "band-aid" type fixes such as system prompts and content warnings rather than removing the toxic proclivities from the underlying model.

Bias in AI is not merely a technical problem but a contextual one. Rather than aiming to eliminate bias, RAI focuses on understanding and mitigating it within context. Think of it as understanding the system rather than trying to fix the system. AI ethicists focus on recognising and acknowledging bias, assessing its potential harmful impacts within the specific context where a model will be used, and then determining whether, and how, that bias should be mitigated. This approach ensures that the model remains both effective and equitable, aligning its outcomes with the needs and values of the communities it serves.

For a case study on how bias in a real estate algorithm can impact outcomes, as well as four additional examples of built-in bias and two supporting in-class activities, please view the Supplementary Materials, Section D: Sociotechnical Mapping. The materials supporting this section are presented along with examples supporting the previous section due to the scaffolding and interwoven aspects of these sections at routledge.com/9781032625041.

Visualising sociotechnical relationships with STS maps

A sociotechnical system (STS) is a model that involves humans (people and societies) and technology (machines and software) and seeks to map the relationships between these two key aspects, as well as other influencing factors (Emery & Trist, 1973; Trist, 1981). An STS may include relationships between humans, technology, and complex infrastructures that the system operates within (see Exhibit 17.3).

Exhibit 17.3. This is a picture of a large box with a dashed line down the middle, making two sides. Each side includes two boxes, each connected by two-sided arrows to each of the other three boxes. The two boxes on the left in green represent the social subsystem and are labelled

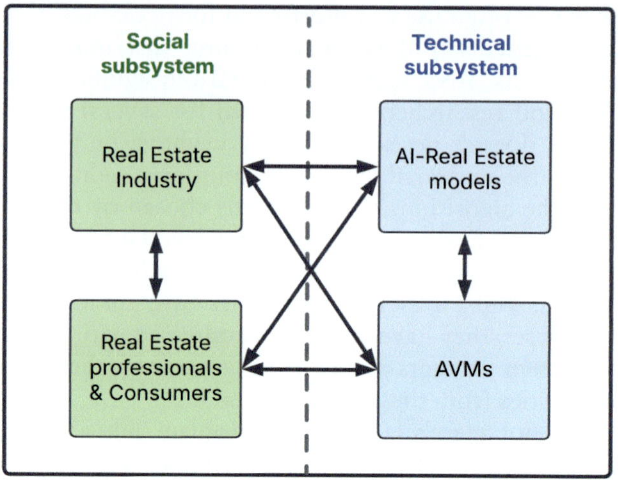

Exhibit 17.3 Solution generated by ChatGPT.

"Real Estate Industry" and Real Estate Professionals and Consumers" top to bottom. The two boxes on the right in blue represent the technical subsystem and are labelled "AI Real Estate Models" on the top and "AVMs" on the bottom.

Sociotechnical mapping in RAI illuminates how AI models, organisations, social structures, individuals, and industry norms interconnect and influence one another. Rather than existing in isolation, AI models operate within specific social and institutional contexts, shaped by human decisions, cultural norms, and regulatory frameworks. Understanding these interdependencies between social and technical subsystems, and identifying where data enters the system, who has authority over model decisions, and how end-users interpret outputs practitioners can pinpoint potential biases, power imbalances, and ethical risks – such as biased datasets or unchecked automation.

Exhibit 17.4 is a diagram illustrating an STS map and its feedback loops. Representing "Human-Centred" at the top-centre is an illustration of a group of people labeled "human oversight and diverse stakeholder engagement". Representing "Regulation & Audits" at the bottom-centre is an image an audit document labeled "Regulatory audits and explainability frameworks ensure each stage meets ethical benchmarks". Both of these have arrows pointing to two images in the middle left. The top left image represents Data Collection and is labelled "Diverse and accurate data. Ethically collected and independently audited. Transparent metadata is essential". The lower left image represents Model Design and is

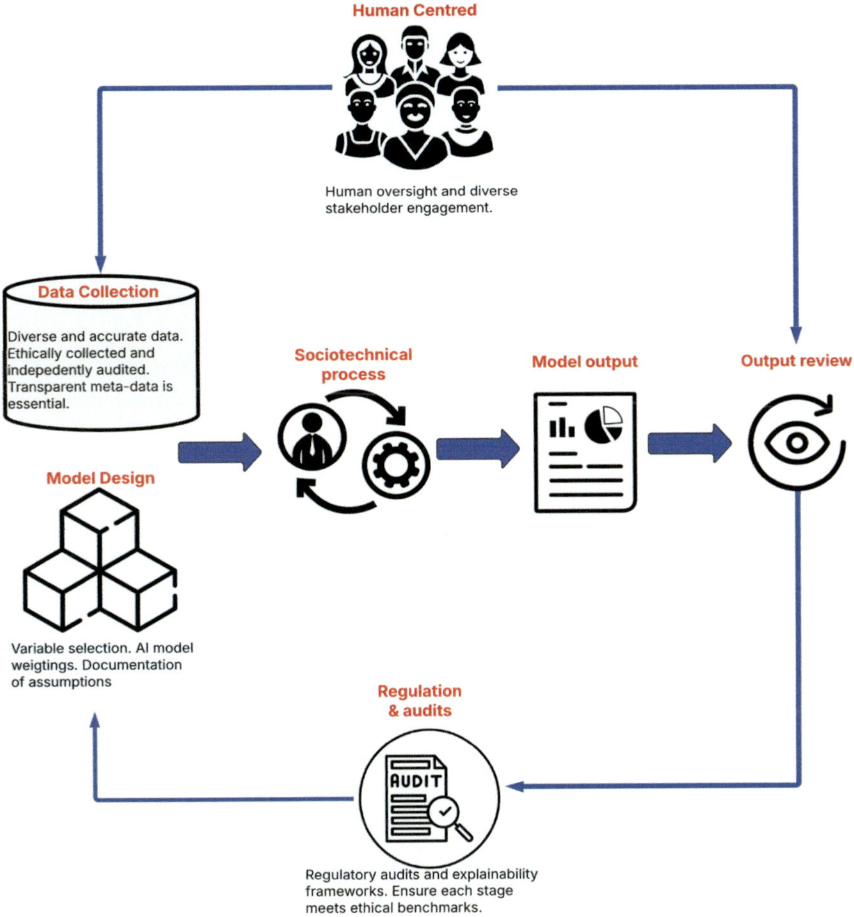

Exhibit 17.4 Prompt instructing ChatGPT to use direct YP formula.

labelled "Variable selection. AI model weightings. Document of assumptions". Across the centre of the image are a series of three arrows, interspersed with an image following each arrow. The first arrow points to an image representing Sociotechnical Processes, depicted by two circles, one with a human and one with a mechanical cog at their centre, connected by two arrows demonstrating that each influences the other. After the second arrow is an image representing Model Output, depicted by an image of a report with data visualisations on it. The final arrow points to an image representing Output Review and is depicted by an image of an eye with a circular arrow around it. Finally, there is an arrow from the top-centre image "Human Centred" to Output Review, and an arrow from Output Review to the bottom-centre image "Regulation & Audits".

This holistic perspective encourages interdisciplinary collaboration (e.g., between data scientists, urban planners, and community advocates) and ensures that each node in the system is accountable for its role. Moreover, mapping the feedback loops between AI-generated valuations and real-world market behaviour helps highlight moments where human oversight or policy interventions might be critical to prevent runaway effects. In essence, STS mapping offers a roadmap for embedding ethical, transparent, and context-sensitive practices throughout the AI lifecycle.

Understanding that AI-driven real estate systems do not function in isolation, and that they are embedded within complex STSs that involve people, institutions, and industry practices is critical to ethical decision-making. Each decision made, whether by a human or an AI system, is shaped by prior knowledge, contextual influences, and institutional constraints.

Exhibit 17.5 has three boxes, each within another, depicting layers of the STS system. The outer box is labelled "Complex Environment: The Human World" at the top, and includes "human social structures, normative beliefs, ideologies, politics, socioeconomic forces, history, media influences, education, existing inequalities, and laws". The middle-layer

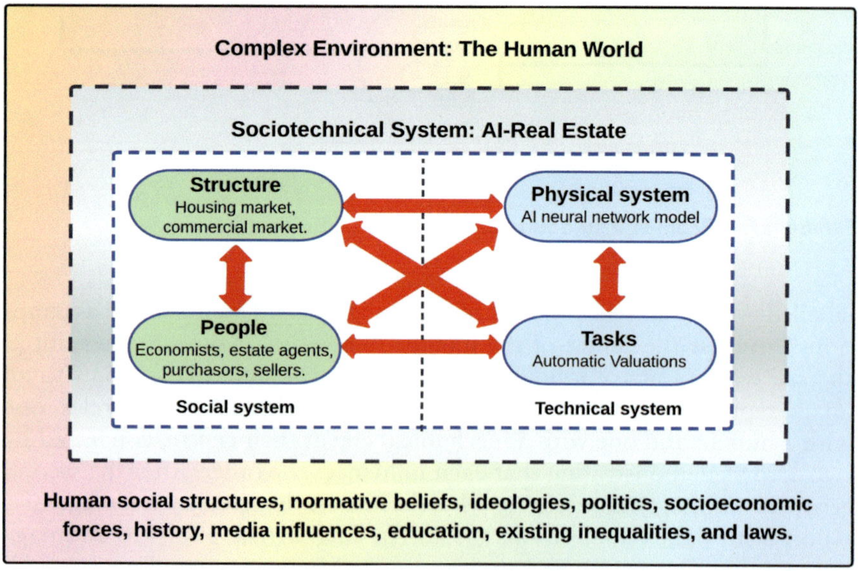

Exhibit 17.5 Solution by ChatGPT using YP formula.

box is labelled "Sociotechnical System: AI-Real Estate", as a title for the inner box, which depicts a four-part diagram. The diagram is split into two sides by a dashed line. On the left are two green ovals representing the social system, with "Structure" on the top and "People" on the bottom. Structure is labelled as "housing market, commercial market", while People is labelled "Economists, estate agents, purchasers, sellers". On the right are two blue ovals representing the technical system, with "Physical System" on the top and "Tasks on the bottom. Physical system is labelled "AI neural network model" and Tasks is labelled "automatic valuations". Two-sided arrows connect each of the four boxes to the other three boxes.

For more information on how to represent an STS, please view the Supplementary Materials, Section D: Sociotechnical Mapping, Example 3: Economic Models affect interest rates, and Supplementary Exhibits 5 and 6 at routledge.com/9781032625041.

Feedback loops in AI systems

A key feature of STS is its non-linearity, moving beyond simplistic cause and effect. These are sometimes called cybernetic processes and include feedback loops, which help identify when relationships or actions impact one another. These concepts are often applied to better understand how AI might ethically and responsibly align with our expectations (Selbst et al., 2019). For example, data inputs into an AI model are themselves products of human decisions – decisions about what to measure, how to measure it, and what to exclude. AI models then process these inputs, generate insights, and present outputs that influence human decisions, which in turn affect the next cycle of data collection and modelling.

STS mapping helps us identify these feedback loops. Exhibit 17.4 shows how both humans and the outputs of an AI model impact the model design and the data collection. By identifying where data enters the system, who has authority over model decisions, and how end-users interpret outputs, stakeholders can pinpoint potential vulnerabilities, such as biased datasets or unchecked automation.

STS mapping encourages interdisciplinary collaboration (e.g., between data scientists, estate agents, regulatory bodies, urban planners, and community advocates) and ensures that each node in the system is identified for its accountability. The technique also helps highlight where human oversight or policy interventions might be critical to prevent runaway effects. In essence, STS mapping offers a roadmap for embedding ethical, transparent, and context-sensitive practices in AI real estate.

For an example of how to map an AI Real Estate report, please view the Supplementary Materials Section D: Sociotechnical Mapping section, Example 4: Mapping AI Real Estate Reports at routledge.com/9781032625041.

AI-powered models don't merely reflect patterns in real estate markets; they also play a role in shaping them. For instance, in AI-powered Purchasing Recommendations, algorithmic preferences can reinforce specific property trends, influencing which areas receive investment and visibility. Over time, such loops can evolve beyond individual market behaviours to affect systemic structures, impacting property values in whole areas, urban planning, and even social mobility.

For a suggested classroom activity on mapping AI-driven real estate platforms, please view Supplementary Materials, Section D: Sociotechnical Mapping, Activity 2: Mapping AI-Purchasing Recommendations at routledge.com/9781032625041.

Market design

Models don't just describe reality; they help shape it. This recursive dynamic, where models influence the systems they model, is known as co-construction. Economic theory offers a clear example, as it has long grappled with how its models can alter market behaviour.

Economists are often seen as neutral observers, but many scholars now argue that economic models are performative, they reshape the very systems they analyse (D. MacKenzie et al., 2020). For example, a central bank's interest rate change based on a model can shift investor behaviour and market outcomes.

> Economics often seems abstract. ... yet it also articulates with, influences, is deployed in, and restructures concrete economies in all their messy materiality and their complex sociality.
>
> (MacKenzie et al., 2020: 2)

Even academic norms shape which models gain traction. As MacKenzie (2006) notes, financial theorists are incentivised to create models that are solvable, publishable, and intellectually novel criteria that can distort what is modelled and how.

> The most influential models ... yielded as their solutions relatively simple equations. However, a good model also could not be "obvious" and thus at risk of being seen by theorists' peers as trivial.
>
> (MacKenzie, 2006)

These internal pressures affect external decisions, such as monetary policy, where models directly inform choices around interest rates and inflation.

For a case study on how economic models can impact interest rates and property prices, please view the Supplementary Materials, Section E: Market Design, Case Study 1: Economic Models Impact Interest Rates and Property Prices at routledge.com/9781032625041.

Market design by governments

"Market design" refers to the deliberate structuring of systems to guide participant behaviour – what some scholars call "smart markets" (Frankel et al., 2019; Kahlen et al., 2024). Governments often engage in this form of structured intervention. For example, in March 2020, the US government used US treasury auctions to smooth out price swings (Rilinger, 2023). Due to the impact on society of this method of market manipulation, market design has been seen by some scholars as a form of social engineering (Rilinger, 2023). Governments are not the only ones who engage in market shaping: individuals and investment groups can also manipulate or nudge markets using similar mechanisms.

For more case studies on this topic, please view the Supplementary Materials, Section E: Market Design, Case Study 2: Singapore GLS; Case Study 3: Market Design by Individuals; and Case Study 4: Market Design by Investment Groups at routledge.com/9781032625041.

These examples reveal that the line between modelling and market-making is far thinner than it first appears. Real estate is not a neutral terrain onto which we apply tools – it is an evolving STS shaped by values, incentives, and design choices, both human and machine. As AI systems increasingly influence how property is priced, sold, financed, and developed, small shifts in model assumptions, or deliberate manipulation, can have wide-reaching consequences. Without robust oversight and a deep understanding of how models interact with social and economic contexts, we risk undermining public trust and amplifying existing inequities. For real estate educators, the challenge is not only to teach how these models work, but to equip students with the critical tools to question who designs them, whose interests they serve, and how they shape the markets we live in.

Real-world implications

AI-driven models in real estate have far-reaching consequences beyond mere efficiency gains in property valuation. The very act of model building, deciding which data to include, the weighting of features, and the abstraction level, plays a critical role in shaping market outcomes. In

Australia, for example, research on mass valuation using big data has demonstrated that even state-of-the-art AVMs can produce skewed estimates if the input data or model assumptions embed historical biases. These biases not only affect property prices and investor confidence but also influence broader urban development trends, potentially reinforcing patterns of disinvestment or overvaluation in certain neighbourhoods. The sociotechnical feedback loops inherent in AVM systems illustrate how human decisions in model design interact with machine outputs to drive real-world market dynamics, ultimately impacting sustainability and social diversity.

In the realm of investment advice, AI-powered platforms in Australia, such as those used for mass valuation by CoreLogic, Pricefinder, and Pointdata (The Australian Property Institute, 2022), can inadvertently create self-reinforcing cycles. If an AVM consistently overvalues properties in high-demand areas, it may draw investor attention to those regions, inflating prices further and exacerbating regional inequality. These feedback loops contribute to speculative bubbles while leaving other areas undercapitalised. The ethical implications extend beyond pricing, impacting mortgage eligibility and even housing insurance access (Cheung, 2023; Yiu & Cheung, 2024).

The issue of toxic-bias plays a significant role when AI is used for residential tenant selection. The residential rental crisis is impacting many people of lower incomes across many countries in 2025. Increasingly, landlords and agencies are turning to AI to sift through applications and make decisions on renters, often with unfair outcomes.

For a relevant case study, please view the Supplementary Materials, Section F: Real-world Implications, Case Study 1: Senior Denied Housing Based on Someone Else's Crime at routledge.com/9781032625041.

Regulatory bodies are beginning to respond to these challenges. In Australia, there is growing momentum among policymakers to establish stronger oversight of AI-driven valuation models. Concerns about transparency, data quality, and algorithmic fairness have led to calls for mandatory algorithmic audits, explainability standards, and improved data governance. These steps are crucial to ensure that AI supports equitable outcomes in lending, leasing, and land-use planning.

For a relevant case study, please view the Supplementary Materials, Section F: Real-world Implications, Case Study 2: Core Logic at routledge.com/9781032625041.

The provided examples highlight how AI is not just a tool, but an active agent in shaping markets, communities, and access to housing. When left unchecked, it can reinforce existing inequalities and create barriers to economic mobility.

For activities to bring these case studies together, please view the Supplementary Materials, Section F: Real World Implications, Activity 1: Compare Concept Tables; and Activity 2: Map and Evaluate AI-driven Real Estate Models at routledge.com/9781032625041.

Mitigating challenges

Mitigating the ethical challenges inherent in AI-driven real estate models starts with rigorous data governance and careful model design. Ensuring that training datasets are diverse, accurate, and free from historical prejudices is paramount. This involves implementing regular audits of data sources, pre-processing steps to identify and correct imbalances, and incorporating techniques such as explainable AI (XAI) to illuminate the model's decision-making processes.

- **Model developers:** Are responsible for shaping the overall model architecture. They can reduce systemic biases by sourcing diverse datasets and documenting design decisions, including the parameters included or excluded, the abstraction boundaries drawn, and the provenance of all data used.
- **Model technicians:** Play a critical role in implementing and maintaining model transparency. This includes logging variable selections, detailing how features are weighted, and articulating the assumptions embedded within the algorithmic logic.
- **Regulatory bodies and oversight professionals:** Must ensure that models used in real estate comply with legal and ethical standards. This includes mandating documentation, requiring algorithmic audits, and supporting explainability measures that make models understandable to end users and affected parties.

As we have discussed in detail, creating concept tables and STS maps is an excellent start to mitigating some of the RAI challenges in AI real estate. There are additional RAI techniques that real estate can draw from, such as model cards, diverse stakeholder engagement, accountability practices, mechanisms for recourse, and sustainability integration that together help build a more trustworthy ecosystem.

Model cards

One practical tool for communicating how an AI model operates is the model card (Mitchell et al., 2019). Originally introduced in general AI contexts, model cards are equally relevant to real estate, especially when building on earlier concept tables. A model card functions as a kind of "meta-tag" for AI systems, outlining critical aspects of a model's purpose, data, performance, and limitations. When published alongside AI-real estate tools, they can enhance transparency and support responsible use. Key components of a model card might include:

- **Purpose and scope:** Outline the model's intended purpose: Is it designed to estimate property values, screen potential tenants, recommend investment strategies, or something else? By clarifying these objectives, stakeholders can more easily evaluate whether the model is being used in contexts that align, or conflict, with its original design.
- **Dataset provenance and known biases:** Where did the training data come from? Was it compiled from property sales, demographic records, or user applications? Highlighting known gaps or imbalances – for example, underrepresented neighbourhoods – helps stakeholders assess how the model may behave in different contexts.
- **AI-model choice:** There are many AI models available for use. Document which model was used and why that model was selected.
- **Performance metrics and validation:** In real estate, metrics might include the mean absolute error (MAE) of property valuations, the correlation with actual market sale prices, or false-positive rates in tenant screening. The model card should describe how these metrics were validated – what timeframe was used, which geographic regions were sampled, and whether external validation data was employed.
- **Intended usage context:** Specify which usage scenarios are appropriate (e.g., short-term market trend analysis, preliminary mortgage risk assessment). Also, state the model limitations, such as not capturing rapid neighbourhood gentrification or relying on outdated historical data.

These are only a few suggestions for factors that could be included in model cards. A working model card is likely to have many more aspects. It is important that model cards don't become a tool for "ethics washing", and care must be made to ensure this risk mitigation strategy is incorporated with other factors.

Model cards are not a silver bullet. Nor are they, as Google (2025) notes, "one-size-fits-all" solutions. They may need to be embedded within broader transparency frameworks. Students and future professionals should be encouraged to create and critique model cards as part of their AI literacy. Real estate students should be encouraged to develop their own model cards after examining a range of examples (Crisan et al., 2022).

Diverse stakeholder engagement

RAI development depends on engaging a wide range of stakeholders throughout the model lifecycle. This includes domain experts, community representatives, regulators, and those most impacted by real estate decisions. These voices help ensure that models reflect lived realities, align with ethical values, and remain accountable to public interest. Establishing **formal feedback loops**, where model outputs are regularly tested against real-world outcomes, enables iterative improvement and correction. In high-stakes contexts such as tenant screening or housing investment, regulatory frameworks and independent audits are essential for ensuring fairness, preventing harm, and maintaining public trust.

Accountability

Accountability in AI-driven real estate applications requires clear delineation of responsibilities across every stage of the model lifecycle, from data collection and curation to deployment and monitoring. Developers of the models should maintain detailed records of their decisions, including which variables are selected and how they are weighted, so that the rationale behind any valuation outcome is transparent and traceable. Making these decisions legible, especially to regulators, end-users, and affected communities, is foundational to building trust and ensuring AI systems in real estate remain open to scrutiny.

Mechanisms for recourse

When AI systems cause harm, such as delivering inaccurate valuations or unfairly screening out tenants, there must be clear paths for **investigation, explanation**, and **redress**. This includes both technical review and human oversight.

Real estate regulators and professional bodies can reinforce this by requiring:

- Publicly documented scoring criteria.
- Transparent error correction processes.
- Appeal mechanisms for disputing algorithmic decisions.

By making recourse possible, the system signals that accountability doesn't end with automation. Such measures not only build trust among stakeholders but also underscore that, even in automated processes, ultimate responsibility and accountability lie with human actors who design, deploy, and oversee the technology.

Sustainability

Sustainability in AI-real estate goes beyond efficiency. It involves aligning economic, environmental, and social priorities to support resilient communities and long-term urban planning. Well-designed models can forecast infrastructure needs, environmental risks, and demographic shifts, helping to guide policy and investment towards inclusive, eco-conscious outcomes. For example, models that integrate environmental indicators can help identify areas where green building initiatives will have the most impact. Embedding sustainability principles into model design ensures that AI does more than reflect short-term trends, it helps shape future-ready cities that serve all.

Summary of mitigation strategies

In short, humans must remain at the centre of AI real estate ecosystems. Models may abstract, calculate, and optimise; but, it is human decisions, values, and oversight that determine whether these technologies serve the public good or exacerbate existing inequities. Humans are ultimately accountable, and it is humans who will be positively or negatively impacted.

These mitigation strategies, ranging from rigorous data governance to stakeholder engagement, are not only theoretical tools, but practical frameworks that students can apply in real-world contexts. Educators may wish to encourage students to apply these principles by designing their own more ethical AI models.

For an activity to help cement these ideas, please view the Supplementary Materials, Section G: Mitigating Challenges, Activity 1: Design a More Ethical AI Real Estate Model at routledge.com/9781032625041.

Conclusion

AI is reshaping the real estate industry, but without critical oversight, its adoption risks reinforcing inequality, eroding trust, and compromising decision-making. For educators, this chapter offers more than a conceptual overview; it provides practical tools to help students think critically about how models are built, used, and interpreted in real estate contexts.

By integrating activities such as concept tables, STS mapping, and ethical model redesign, educators can move beyond theoretical RAI principles and into the specifics of how AI shapes property valuation, investment, and tenant screening. These exercises not only deepen technical understanding, but also cultivate judgment, fairness, and accountability, skills essential for tomorrow's real estate professionals.

In equipping students to ask who designs these models, whose interests they serve, and how they shape the markets we live in, real estate educators play a vital role in ensuring AI enhances, not undermines, the integrity, sustainability, and inclusiveness of the profession.

For a suggested final assessment for the AI & Ethics module in your subject, please view the Supplementary Materials, Section H: Conclusion, Activity 1: Reflection at routledge.com/9781032625041.

References

Abid, A., Farooqi, M., & Zou, J. (2021, January 18). *Persistent Anti-Muslim Bias in Large Language Models*. https://doi.org/10.48550/arXiv.2101.05783

Afroogh, S., Akbari, A., Malone, E., Kargar, M., & Alambeigi, H. (2024). Trust in AI: Progress, challenges, and future directions. *Nature: Humanities and Social Sciences Communications*, 11(1), 1–30. https://doi.org/10.1057/s41599-024-04044-8

Arumugam, T., Arun, R., Anitha, R., Swerna, P. L., Aruna, R., & Kadiresan, V. (2024). Advancing and methodizing artificial intelligence (AI) and socially responsible efforts in real estate marketing. In S. Singh, S. Rajest, S. Hadoussa, A. Obaid, & R. Regin (Eds.), *Data-Driven Intelligent Business Sustainability* (pp. 48–59). IGI Global Scientific Publishing. https://doi.org/10.4018/979-8-3693-0049-7.ch004

Cheung, K. S. (2023). Real Estate Insights – Unleashing the potential of ChatGPT in property valuation reports: The "Red Book" compliance chain-of-thought (CoT) prompt engineering. *Journal of Property Investment & Finance*, 42(2), 200–206. https://doi.org/10.1108/JPIF-06-2023-0053

Crisan, A., Drouhard, M., Vig, J., & Rajani, N. (2022). Interactive model cards: A human-centered approach to model documentation. *Proceedings of the 2022 ACM Conference on Fairness, Accountability, and Transparency*, 427–439. https://doi.org/10.1145/3531146.3533108

Emery, E., & Trist, E. (1973). *A Social Ecology: Contextual Appreciation of the Future in the Present*. Springer.

European Commission. (2019). Ethics guidelines for trustworthy AI. *Independent High-Level Expert Group on Artificial Intelligence, European Commission. Ethics Guidelines for AI.*

Floridi, L., & Chiriatti, M. (2020). GPT-3: Its nature, scope, limits, and consequences. *Minds and Machines*, 30, 681–694.

Frankel, C., Ossandón, J., & Pallesen, T. (2019). The organization of markets for collective concerns and their failures. *Economy and Society*, 48(2), 153–174.

Google. (2025, March). *Google Model Cards*. https://modelcards.withgoogle.com/about

Johnson, R. L., Pistilli, G., Menédez-González, N., Duran, L. D. D., Panai, E., Kalpokiene, J., & Bertulfo, D. J. (2022). The Ghost in the Machine has an American accent: Value conflict in GPT-3 (No. arXiv:2203.07785). arXiv, Cornell University. https://doi.org/10.48550/arXiv.2203.07785

Kahlen, M., Schroer, K., Ketter, W., & Gupta, A. (2024). Smart markets for real-time allocation of multiproduct resources: The case of shared electric vehicles. *Information Systems Research*, 35(2), 871–889.

Korsybski, A. (1933) Science and sanity. *An introduction to Non-Aristotelian Systems*. New York: Science Press Printing.

MacKenzie, D. A. (2006). *An Engine, Not a Camera: How Financial Models Shape Markets. MIT Press Scholarship Online. An Engine*, Not a Camera: How Financial Models Shape Markets | MIT Press Scholarship Online | Oxford Academic.

MacKenzie, D., Muniesa, F., & Siu, L. (2020). *Do Economists Make Markets?: On the Performativity of Economics*. Princeton University Press. https://doi.org/10.1515/9780691214665

Mitchell, M., Wu, S., Zaldivar, A., Barnes, P., Vasserman, L., Hutchinson, B., Spitzer, E., Raji, I. D., & Gebru, T. (2019). Model cards for model reporting. In *Proceedings of the conference on fairness, accountability, and transparency* (pp. 220–229). https://doi.org/10.1145/3287560.3287596

O'Neil, C. (2016). *Weapons of Math Destruction: How Big Data Increases Inequality and Threatens Democracy*. Crown Publishing.

Rilinger, G. (2023). Conceptual limits of performativity: Assessing the feasibility of market design blueprints. *Socio-Economic Review*, 21(2), 885–908. https://doi.org/10.1093/ser/mwac017

Seagraves, P. (2023). Real Estate Insights: Is the AI revolution a real estate boon or bane? *Journal of Property Investment & Finance*, 42(2), 190–199. https://doi.org/10.1108/JPIF-05-2023-0045

Selbst, A. D., Boyd, D., Friedler, S. A., Venkatasubramanian, S., & Vertesi, J. (2019). Fairness and abstraction in sociotechnical systems. In *Proceedings of the conference on fairness, accountability, and transparency* (pp. 59–68). https://doi.org/10.1145/3287560.3287598

Shepardson, D. (2025, January 22). *Trump revokes Biden executive order on addressing AI risks. Reuters*. www.reuters.com/technology/artificial-intelligence/trump-revokes-biden-executive-order-addressing-ai-risks-2025-01-21/

Starr, C. W., Saginor, J., & Worzala, E. (2020). The rise of PropTech: Emerging industrial technologies and their impact on real estate. *Journal of Property Investment & Finance*, 39(2), 157–169. https://doi.org/10.1108/JPIF-08-2020-0090

The Australian Property Institute. (2022). *Big visual data analysis using artificial intelligence for mass valuation of residential properties in Australia*. Australian Property Research and Education Fund. www.api.org.au/apref/

The White House. (2023, October 30). *President Biden Issues Executive Order on Safe, Secure, and Trustworthy Artificial Intelligence*. The White House. https://bidenwhitehouse.archives.gov/briefing-room/statements-releases/2023/10/30/fact-sheet-president-biden-issues-executive-order-on-safe-secure-and-trustworthy-artificial-intelligence/

Trist, E. L. (1981). *The evolution of socio-technical systems* (Vol. 2). Ontario Quality of Working Life Centre Toronto.

Xiong, Q., Graham, L., & Baum, A. (2022). The Future of Automated Real Estate Valuations (SSRN Scholarly Paper No. 4927480). Saïd Business School at Oxford University. https://papers.ssrn.com/abstract=4927480

Yiu, E., & Cheung, W. (2024, October 10). Use of AI in property valuation is on the rise – but we need greater transparency and trust. *The Conversation*. http://theconversation.com/use-of-ai-in-property-valuation-is-on-the-rise-but-we-need-greater-transparency-and-trust-240880

Chapter 18

Generative AI in real estate pedagogy

Gavin Boyce, Olayiwola Oladiran, Tunbosun Oyedokun, and Andrew Stanton

Introduction

The real estate industry is experiencing significant "disruption" with the advancement of innovation and digital transformation. As part of this industry-wide digital transformation, generative AI (GenAI) tools are now being introduced to various areas of real estate practice and services. For instance, JLL GPT was unveiled in 2023 as the first GPT model for commercial real estate (Pereira, 2023), ushering in an era of GenAI models in the real estate industry. JLL GPT is a purpose-built GenAI technology that will be used by JLL's 103,000+ workforce around the world to provide CRE insights to clients in a whole new way. Bibit is another GenAI that can create property listings with compelling descriptions in multiple languages, conduct market research, draft reports, and script property tours for virtual or in-person presentations. The emergence of these and other GenAI platforms suggests that the real estate industry is beginning to embrace GenAI. According to a recent report by McKinsey & Company, this technology is expected to have a significant impact across all industry sectors, including professional services (Chui et al., 2023).

Real estate education is also rapidly evolving in line with the broader education transformation. Digital technology has played a cardinal role in the educational transformation in recent years leading to changes in teaching, learning support and skills development (Tondeur et al., 2013). For instance, digital tools and techniques such as digital storytelling (Puvlou, 2020) and digital quizzes (Wilkinson et al 2020, Mao et al., 2022) are becoming regular features in teaching delivery. Teacher education and training institutions are, therefore, engaging in various initiatives to reshape their curriculum to prepare educators for the effective integration of technology into their teaching practices (Tondeur et al 2017; Pavlou, 2020; Rafi, 2019).

As part of the advancement of technology-enhanced pedagogy, GenAI became prominent following the launch of OpenAI's ChatGPT platform in

DOI: 10.1201/9781032656458-18

November 2022. This has since led to global conversations and discussions about the role and impact of GenAI in education. Reconciling divergent and often opposing views regarding the benefits and challenges of GenAI in education is therefore valuable. This chapter examines education-related issues associated with GenAI, focusing on real estate pedagogy. It overviews GenAI and highlights its use within the real estate industry. It also provides a critical analysis of the issues surrounding the use of this technology in real estate pedagogy. This chapter offers real estate educators' insight into the various channels through which GenAI can enhance teaching, learning support, and skills development in real estate. Additionally, it highlights some strategies that can be used to mitigate unethical GenAI use in education.

What is GenAI?

GenAI is a technology that is used for generating text, images, sound, or virtual environments in response to a prompt. The outputs will make sense to a human observer, mainly due to the immense amount of data that has been used to train the models that generate them. If asked to generate a script, then the model's response will resemble a script, if asked for an essay plan the response will look like an essay plan and if asked for a CV, the output will be aligned to a CV. The capabilities of this technology bring with it several benefits including addressing the "blank page" problem. When faced with starting a new project or task, it is a simple matter to generate something that might look roughly appropriate whether it be a starting page to a new detective novel or the opening stanza to an epic poem on modern-day train travel, for example. Once started, the user can amend/adjust/add/delete as appropriate until there is a finished product.

Too often we ask: "what is Gen AI good at?" rather than "what is Gen AI good for?" – this sleight of hand can lead to confusion. The first question is understandable given our propensity to take the intentional stance (Dennett, 1971) to explain the behaviors of others; however, it can also be unhelpful as it distracts from the important question. GenAI tools are "stochastic parrots" (Bender et al., 2021) not intelligent agents. Commentators often stray into questions of whether GenAI is actually "intelligent" rather than considering it as a tool that exists and can be used for purposes defined by the user. A high-level understanding of Large Language Models (LLMs) and how they represent the statistical relationships of words to one another in various contexts will certainly help the criticality with which they are used.[1] However, explanations of GenAI in terms of LLMs, transformers, or deep neural networks are themselves of less value for decision-makers and educators. It is therefore important to focus more on what these tools are useful for and how they may be abused.

Stokel-Walker and Van Noorden (2023) reported that users of GenAI have stated that this technology has made them more productive and efficient. They, however, note that there are several "widespread concerns" associated with the technology ranging from the propensity to return falsehoods to worries about people passing off AI-generated text as their own. Another potential effect is the Too Long: Didnt Read (TLDR) society. TLDR refers to a societal trend where people have shorter attention spans or limited patience for lengthy texts or information. In this context, individuals prefer quick and concise summaries rather than engaging with lengthy content. In the context of this phenomenon, Forrin et al. (2021) suggest that students may be more likely to engage with more bite-sized segments of information compared to longer chunks of texts; this can further lead to unintentional mind-wandering while students are reading academic passages with relatively longer sentences. Furthermore, when faced with getting up to speed on an unfamiliar topic, it is all too easy to ask for a brief synopsis from a GenAI tool. One might not think this is much different than relying on Wikipedia. In reality, it is highly likely that the tool has "ingested" Wikipedia. However, the largest of these tools have been trained on many other sources as well and without knowing what data has been used to train the model one cannot be sure of the veracity of the output. Additionally, bias in the training of LLMs is an oft-repeated criticism of GenAI tools.

Ultimately GenAI tools will be used if they are useful regardless of whether users understand the fundamentals and mechanism or not. Like Google search, it is poised to continue to transform our work practices, learning, and several other areas of society.

GenAI and the real estate industry

Proptech is the buzzword that is being used to describe the recent digital transformation in the real estate sector and AI has played a significant role in this transformation. AI has been particularly highlighted as one of the three digital technologies that will drive further innovation within the sector (Oladiran and Dickins 2024). GenAI is also gradually permeating the industry. According to Fitzpatrick et al. (2023), GenAI is maturing in the real estate industry, and it is now being used to perform tasks such as identifying opportunities for investors, building and interior design, as well as marketing and customer services. According to Chui et al. (2023), GenAI is projected to generate \$110 billion to \$180 billion in value for the real estate industry.

Exhibit 18.1 lists areas GenAI can be applied in real estate practice and service delivery. These examples are categorised based on the four Cs

Exhibit 18.1 Examples and categories of GenAI application to real estate

Task/impact	*Description*	*"Cs" category*
Advanced analytics and modeling	Real estate professionals and practitioners with little or no experience in advanced analytics and coding can use genAI tools to generate, interpret, and translate code.	Coding solutions
Documentation	Information can be pooled from a large volume of documents such as lease agreements providing a summary and response to specific questions or issues.	Concision
Design	Enhancing the design and drawing of architectural and structural plans based on underlying design principles and concepts. This can be optimised to create desired outcomes in space. It can also introduce IoT sensors and computer vision algorithms that collect data points on space use.	Creation
Interaction	Can be used for a wide range of real estate interactions such as tenants' request management, lease terms negotiation, maintenance management, and other forms of client support. Copilots (GenAI-powered bots) are important tools that support this function.	Concision Customer engagement
Investment decision	Improving precision and timeliness in investment decisions. It enables various forms of analysis of structured and unstructured data, providing valuable insight into location, assets, and markets more broadly.	Concision

(Continued)

Exhibit 18.1 (Continued)

Task/impact	*Description*	*"Cs" category*
Visualisation	Prospective tenants/buyers/ investors can visualise the exact layout and outlook of properties and spaces. This can enhance conversion rates and opportunities for revenue maximisation.	Creation Customer engagement

highlighted by Fitzpatrick et al. (2023). The first C is customer engagement supported by tools such as conversational chatbots that answer questions and remove doubt from customer decisions; the second C is creation taking the form of tools that generate new creative content, including text and images; the third C is concision which entails the synthesis of unstructured data, interpreting conversations, and querying large data sources; and the fourth C is coding solutions including interpreting, translating, and generating code.

The potential benefits of Gen AI to the real estate industry are enormous and according to D'Angelo et al., this automation of creativity and imagination (2023) could become more widespread sooner rather than later. Jones Lang LaSalle (2024) further reveals that AI and GenAI are among the top three technologies expected to have the biggest impact on real estate with near and long-term impacts ranging from the emergence of new markets and asset types to innovations in investment and revenue models. For these reasons, real estate educators must understand this technology and how it can be introduced to students, so they are prepared to use it in their jobs as well as how it can be used to facilitate teaching and learning support for faculty teaching real estate.

GenAI in real estate education: Prospects and challenges

Due to the scope of real estate practice and services, education in this area often covers a broad spectrum of subjects such as economics, management, planning, finance and building services. Furthermore, various real estate programmes and courses have different philosophies, objectives, priorities, and learning outcomes (Oladiran & Nanda, 2021). Regardless, the rapid utilization of GenAI over the last couple of years has created commonalities in both opportunities and concerns associated with its use.

The launch of ChatGPT in November 2022 has particularly made the technology a recurrent conversation in education. While the response of many higher education institutions and educators could be described as averse, there is emerging evidence that points to changing perceptions and the growing adoption of GenAI for learning and teaching purposes. The *New Principles on the Use of AI in Education*, published on July 4, 2023, by The Russell Group universities (Russell Group 2023),[2] suggests GenAI can be beneficial for learning. Rather than viewing it as a risky tool, they advocate for its responsible application by both educators and students to harness its potential opportunities.

As a support tool, GenAI can perform a wide array of tasks related to learning and teaching. Broadly speaking, these tasks encompass learning design, lesson preparation, teaching delivery, assessment, and feedback. Taking lesson preparation as an example, educators utilise GenAI as a tool to create educational resources, leveraging the technology to generate teaching content, including handouts, worksheets, images, model answers, multimedia, and quizzes. Real estate is practical. Teaching the subject often requires the use of real-life data and case studies which have been found helpful for keeping students engaged and interested in the learning. Using GenAI, the process of curating data and case studies for workshops is expedited, as AI tools can quickly gather, analyse, and organise relevant information from a variety of sources. This enables educators to focus more on delivering interactive lessons rather than spending excessive time searching for and compiling data. Data scrapping is an example of how AI can be used to download web-based data in a structure that can be used for quantitative data analysis (see Oladiran et al., 2023).

The use of GenAI for assessment is growing but remains largely experimental and limited to "assessment for learning". This is also known as formative assessment which refers to a range of evaluative activities used by educators to monitor student learning and provide ongoing feedback during the learning process. Educators provide suitable prompts that students can use to generate questions with GenAI, and subsequently solve and cross-check with solutions produced by GenAI tools. When done properly, this approach offers a quicker way for students to receive feedback on their learning, whether in class or during self-study (see Exhibits 18.2–18.7 for examples of how prompts can be used to generate problems and solutions and Oyedokun (2025) for a demonstration.

GenAI can also be used to support students in developing their critical thinking. One way this is achieved is by setting activities for students to critically evaluate the materials produced by GenAI and assess, for instance, their reliability, accuracy, and consistency. In fact, through this practice, educators themselves acquire further knowledge and skills

Create and solve a simple example problem to illustrate the use of the discounting formula in estimating the present value of future payments. Make this example suitable for students in MSc Real Estate. Use £ as the currency. All calculations and final answers should be presented to two decimal places.

Example Problem – 5-Year Rental Income

A property investment is expected to generate **£10,000 per year for 5 years**. The appropriate discount rate is **6% per annum**.

Question:
What is the present value (PV) of this 5-year series of future rental payments?

Formula

For multiple future payments (an **ordinary annuity**), the PV is calculated as:

$$PV = \sum_{t=1}^{n} \frac{CF_t}{(1+r)^t}$$

where:

- CF_t = Cash flow in year t (£10,000 each year)
- r = Discount rate (0.06)
- n = Number of periods (5 years)

Exhibit 18.2 Prompt and a question generated by ChatGPT.

essential in guiding students on the ethical and responsible application of GenAI technologies. For instance, using the illustrations in Exhibits 18.6 and 18.7, students can be provided with an MS Excel present value model that requires them to input the annuity, discount rate, and duration. They can use this model to confirm whether the answer generated by GenAI is correct. If an incorrect result is produced, another prompt can be issued to recalculate. This process provides a learning opportunity for students to understand the limitations of the technology. Exhibit 18.8 shows further examples of how GenAI can be applied in RE education.

There is growing evidence of the adoption of GenAI among students since the introduction of ChatGPT. Students are using GenAI largely because the technology offers an easier and quicker way to complete

Step-by-Step Calculation

Year 1:

$$PV_1 = \frac{10,000}{(1.06)^1} = \frac{10,000}{1.06} = 9433.96$$

Year 2:

$$PV_2 = \frac{10,000}{(1.06)^2} = \frac{10,000}{1.1236} = 8900.92$$

Year 3:

$$PV_3 = \frac{10,000}{(1.06)^3} = \frac{10,000}{1.1910} = 8396.36$$

Year 4:

$$PV_4 = \frac{10,000}{(1.06)^4} = \frac{10,000}{1.2625} = 7918.64$$

Year 5:

$$PV_5 = \frac{10,000}{(1.06)^5} = \frac{10,000}{1.3382} = 7466.50$$

Total Present Value

$$PV_{\text{total}} = PV_1 + PV_2 + PV_3 + PV_4 + PV_5$$

$$PV_{\text{total}} = 9433.96 + 8900.92 + 8396.36 + 7918.64 + 7466.50$$

$$PV_{\text{total}} = 42,116.38$$

Exhibit 18.3 Solution generated by ChatGPT.

assignments. However, this comes with unwanted consequences that are a major concern in the higher education sector. For instance, anecdotal evidence suggests that the use of GenAI is increasingly becoming a tool for "contract writing", where students may over-rely on it for their assignments. While students traditionally engaged human services for writing help, they are now turning to GenAI tools. This shift not only raises concerns about plagiarism but also constitutes a serious issue of academic

Use the Year's Purchase (YP) formula for this calculation.

Perfect! The **Year's Purchase (YP) method** is a simplified way in real estate to estimate the present value of a series of future cash flows, assuming a **fixed annual payment** and a **constant discount rate**.

Year's Purchase (YP) Formula

$$PV = CF \times YP$$

where:

- CF = Annual cash flow (£10,000)
- YP = Years Purchase factor

For a **finite number of years (n)** at a discount rate r, the Years Purchase (YP) is:

$$YP = \frac{1 - (1 + r)^{-n}}{r}$$

where:

- r = Discount rate (decimal)
- n = Number of years

Exhibit 18.4 Prompt instructing ChatGPT to use direct YP formula.

misconduct related to authorship (Michel-Villarreal et al., 2023). Culpable students are penalised, but a sorer challenge is the additional workload it creates for lecturers to identify AI-generated works and report any misconduct found. Turnitin has attempted to integrate AI into its studio, but this has been met with considerable unease across the sector, due to concerns about the rate of false positives (i.e., content which is not AI-generated but which is wrongly suspected to be as such).

Preiksaitis and Rose (2023) highlight some other challenges with the use of GenAI in an academic setting:

- Overdependence on the use of the technology might hinder critical thinking and creativity.
- Inequities in access among educators and learners might further widen the digital divide and attainment gaps.

Step 2: Substitute values into the formula

$$PV = 10,000 \times \sum_{t=1}^{5} \frac{1}{(1+0.06)^t}$$

This shows **exactly how the formula is used**: you replace CF, r, and n with the known numbers and then sum the discounted fractions for each year.

Step 3: Use a calculator or software to sum the series

$$\sum_{t=1}^{5} \frac{1}{(1+0.06)^t} = 4.2123669$$

$$PV = 10,000 \times 4.2123669 = 42,123.6690$$

Exhibit 18.5 Solution by ChatGPT using the YP formula.

Generate another sample question that involves using the discounting formula, but do not solve it.

Sure! Here's a clear, MSc Real Estate–style sample question:

Sample Question

A real estate investor is considering purchasing a small retail property. The property is expected to generate **annual rental income of £15,000** for the next **7 years**. The investor requires a **discount rate of 5% per annum** to reflect the risk and opportunity cost of capital.

Exhibit 18.6 Prompt instructing ChatGPT to generate another question.

- Since GenAI technologies depend on the information and data available to them, they may contribute to propagating biases and inaccurate information.
- Difficulty in adhering to data protection and privacy regulations, such as General Data Protection Regulation (GDPR), for the processing of sensitive information.

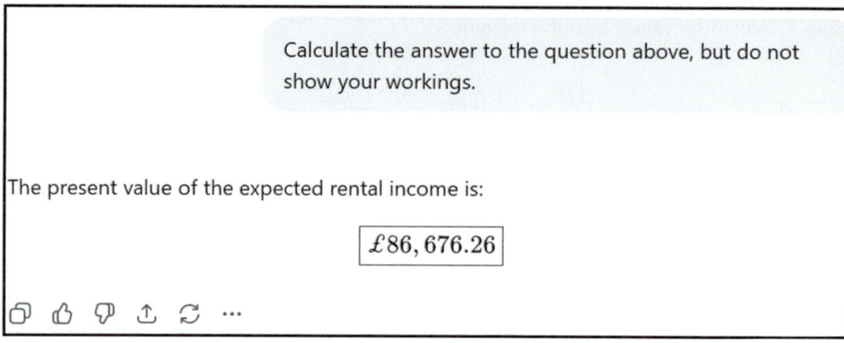

Exhibit 18.7 Prompting ChatGPT to solve problems without showing workings.

Exhibit 18.8 Examples of GenAI Application in RE Education Source

GenAI Application	*Relevant Courses/Module*
Creating site-specific building plans and development designs to teach development appraisal.	Real Estate Valuation & Appraisal and Real Estate Development
Developing simulations and case studies to practice decision-making on investment, negotiation, conflict resolution, client management, etc.	Real Estate Finance & Investment, Strategic Real Estate Management, and Professional Practice & Ethics
AI-powered real estate market analytics to compare real estate submarkets.	Real Estate Markets, Real Estate/ Urban Economics, and Feasibility & Viability Appraisal
Using GenAI as chatbots to provide instant responses to queries on various topics. e.g., definition of terms and application of theories.	All modules
Creating property listings for training purposes.	Real Estate Agency/Marketing
Generating diverse and challenging automated exam questions, quizzes or tests that assess different levels of understanding and skill sets.	All modules
Developing immersive 3D models of properties that students use to explore various property types, neighbourhoods, and renovations virtually.	Real Estate Valuation & Appraisal, Real Estate Market, Real Estate Development, Urban Economics and PropTech
Supervising and supporting students in dissertation writing and researching, e.g., generating prompts/ideas; project outline/structure; searching for literature sources; proofreading; etc.	Research Methods and Dissertation

Regardless of the concerns that the majority of educators share about students' use of GenAI, we know that many academics are already welcoming it into their practice, particularly as workload pressures get more intense.

It is likely that soon, higher educational institutions offering real estate programs will be compelled, either through competition or as part of accreditation requirements, to include topics relating to AI use in their curricula to support students in developing essential skills and competencies in property professional practice. Modules and programs may therefore be revised to incorporate GenAI-related content. While caution must be exercised in using the technology, real estate educators and institutions should be prepared to support students in developing relevant skills to leverage the numerous opportunities that the technology offers that have already been detailed earlier in this chapter.

Some strategies can be used to mitigate the abuse and unethical use of AI by real estate students. First, students should be sensitised about the pitfalls of using these tools and more importantly, the consequences of abuse. Second, unassessed and non-summative feedback can be used to provide the students with an opportunity to test their knowledge without consequences on their overall scores. Online quiz platforms such as Kahoot would be useful for this purpose. Some of these tools provide educators with insight on the questions that the students performed best/worst and this can be used to identify potentially problematic topics and content that the teacher can provide support for. Third, the ethical use of GenAI can be promoted if students are encouraged to acknowledge and cite its use.

Conclusion

In conclusion, the use of GenAI technology in various aspects of real estate education has created a plethora of opportunities and complexities. Real estate educators can use GenAI to enhance the speed of lesson preparation, curriculum design, assessment, and student support. However, ethical concerns such as plagiarism bias, and overdependence on GenAI can mask some of these benefits and create negative sentiments towards the technology. Thus, while the tool holds immense potential to positively transform real estate education (including teaching, learning support, and learners' experience) for good, it is important that careful consideration is given to its use and proactive measures are put in place to mitigate its abuse.

With digital technology transforming real estate with resounding calls for a general real estate curriculum refresh to meet the demands of a digital tech-enabled real estate future, integrating GenAI-related content into real estate programs becomes increasingly imperative. By equipping both educators and students with the necessary skills, knowledge, and criticality to harness the capabilities of GenAI, real estate education will be well-positioned to groom the next generation of professionals poised to lead the digital transformation in the real estate sector and the built environment industry.

Notes

1 See Feuerriegel et al. (2024) for an overview of a detailed overview of GenAI and its mechanism.
2 The Russell Group represents 24 leading UK universities.

References

Bender, E. M., Gebru, T., McMillan-Major, A., & Shmitchell, S. (2021, March). On the dangers of stochastic parrots: Can language models be too big? In Proceedings of the 2021 ACM Conference on Fairness, Accountability, and Transparency (pp. 610–623). https://doi.org/10.1145/3442188.3445922

Chui, M., Hazan, E., Roberts, R., Singla, A., Smaje, K., Sukharevsky, A., Yee, L., & Zeemel, R. (2023). *The economic potential of generative AI: The next productivity frontier.* McKinsey Digital. www.mckinsey.com/capabilities/mckinsey-digital/our-insights/the-economic-potential-of-generative-ai-the-next-productivity-frontier#/. Accessed on 18 August 2024 at 14:07 am.

D'Angelo, J., Coy, T., & Bhargava, P. (2023). *RE-generative AI: How technology can transform commercial real estate.* Deloitte Centre for Financial Services. https://www2.deloitte.com/us/en/insights/industry/financial-services/generative-ai-in-real-estate-benefits.html. Accessed on 15 April 2024 at 12:28 pm.

Dennett, D. C. (1971). Intentional systems. *The Journal of Philosophy*, *68*(4), 87–106.

Feuerriegel, S., Hartmann, J., Janiesch, C., & Zschech, P. (2024). Generative AI. *Business & Information Systems Engineering*, *66*(1), 111–126.

Fitzpatrick M., Gujral, V., Kapoor, A., & Workomir, A. (2023, December). Generative AI can change real estate, but the industry must change to reap the benefits. *McKinsey Quarterly*. www.mckinsey.com/industries/real-estate/our-insights/generative-ai-can-change-real-estate-but-the-industry-must-change-to-reap-the-benefits. Accessed on 15 April 2024 at 10:19 am.

Forrin, N. D., Mills, C., D'Mello, S. K., Risko, E. F., Smilek, D., & Seli, P. (2021). TL; DR: Longer sections of text increase rates of unintentional mind-wandering. *The Journal of Experimental Education*, *89*(2), 278–290.

Jones Lang LaSelle (2024). Artificial intelligence: Real estate revolution or evolution. *JLL Trends and Insights Research*. www.jll.co.uk/en/trends-and-insights/research/artificial-intelligence-and-its-implications-for-real-estate Accessed on 15 April 2024 at 12:35.

Mao, K., Dong, Q., Wang, Y., & Honga, D. (2022). An exploratory approach to intelligent quiz question recommendation. *Procedia Computer Science*, *207*, 4065–4074.

Michel-Villarreal, R., Vilalta-Perdomo, E., Salinas-Navarro, D. E., Thierry-Aguilera, R., & Gerardou, F. S. (2023). Challenges and opportunities of generative AI for higher education as explained by ChatGPT. *Education Sciences*, *13*(9), 856.

Oladiran, O., & Dickins, L. (2024). *PropTech and real estate innovations: A guide to digital technologies and solutions in the built environment* (1st ed.). Routledge. https://doi.org/10.1201/9781003262725

Oladiran, O., & Nanda, A. (2021). *PropTech Education Integration Framework (PEIF),* www.researchgate.net/publication/356420161_PropTech_Education_Integration_Framework_PEIF_integrating_innovation_and_digital_technology_in_real_estate_higher_education

Oladiran, O., Sunmoni, A., Ajayi, S., Guo, J., & Abbas, M. (2023). What property attributes are important to UK university students in their online accommodation search? *Journal of European Real Estate Research*, *16*(1), 130–151. https://doi.org/10.1108/JERER-03-2021-0019

Oyedokun, T. (2025 May 20). *ChatGPT for independent learning* [Video]. YouTube. https://youtu.be/aWF4WVbtbA0?si=YlGTBzZptrLEjrDX

Pavlou, V. (2020). Art technology integration: digital storytelling as a transformative pedagogy in primary education. *International Journal of Art & Design Education*, *39*(1), 195–210.

Pereira, D. (2023). JLL unveils first GPT model for commercial real estate. *JLL News* Release August 01, 2023. www.jll.co.uk/en/newsroom/jll-unveils-first-gpt-model-for-commercial-real-estate Accessed on 15 April 2024 at 13:40.

Preiksaitis, C., & Rose, C. (2023). Opportunities, challenges, and future directions of generative artificial intelligence in medical education: scoping review. *JMIR Medical Education*, *9*(1), e48785. https://doi.org/10.2196/48785

Rafi, M., JianMing, Z., & Ahmad, K. (2019). Technology integration for students' information and digital literacy education in academic libraries. *Information Discovery and Delivery*, *47*(4), 203–217.

Russell Group (2023). New principles on use of AI in education. *Russell Group*. https://russellgroup.ac.uk/news/new-principles-on-use-of-ai-in-education/ Accessed on 15 April 2024 at 12:55 am.

Stokel-Walker, C., & Van Noorden, R. (2023). What ChatGPT and generative AI mean for science. *Nature*, *614*, 204–216. https://doi.org/10.1038/d41586-023-00340-6

Tondeur, J., Roblin, N., van Braak, J., Fisser, P., & Voogt, J. (2013). Technological pedagogical content knowledge in teacher education: in search of a new curriculum. *Educational Studies, 39*(2), 239–243. https://doi.org/10.1080/03055698.2012.713548

Tondeur, J., Roblin, N., van Braak, J., Voogt, J & Prestridge, S. (2017). Preparing beginning teachers for technology integration in education: Ready for take-off? *Technology, Pedagogy and Education*, *26*(2), 157–177. https://doi.org/10.1080/1475939X.2016.1193556

Wilkinson, K., Dafoulas, G., Garelick, H., & Huyck, C. (2020). Are quiz-games an effective revision tool in anatomical sciences for higher education and what do students think of them? *British Journal of Educational Technology*, *51*(3), 761–777.

Chapter 19

Integrating generative AI into urban planning education for real estate students

A semiotic perspective

Luis Lozano-Paredes

Introduction

The intersection of urbanism and real estate education represents a pivotal opportunity for equipping future professionals with tools to navigate the complexities of modern development. This chapter explores how urbanism offers a foundational understanding of regulatory frameworks, societal structures, and environmental considerations, which are indispensable for designing projects that balance economic feasibility with social responsibility. The chapter further investigates the transformative potential of generative AI (GenAI) and large language models (LLMs), systems trained on vast text datasets to understand and generate human-like language, in enhancing real estate education. By enabling students to merge rigorous technical analysis with interpretive, context-sensitive approaches, these tools help foster a more integrated understanding of real estate's cultural, social, and environmental dimensions. Through the lens of urban semiotics, design methodologies, and practical applications, this chapter underscores the importance of embedding AI-driven insights into a holistic framework that aligns professional goals with societal needs.

Urban planning and real estate education

Urban planning and urbanism are a cornerstone of real estate education, providing critical insights into the regulatory frameworks, societal structures, and environmental considerations that shape land use (Phibbs & Gurran, 2021; Yigitcanlar & Teriman, 2015). For students pursuing careers in property development, understanding urban planning is essential, not only for navigating complex legal and regulatory systems but also for anticipating community responses and designing projects that balance financial feasibility with social and environmental responsibility. Core concepts such as zoning regulations, infrastructure planning, environmental sustainability, and community engagement are integral to understanding

DOI: 10.1201/9781032656458-19

how property development contributes to broader societal objectives, particularly in addressing challenges like housing affordability in cities such as Sydney, Australia.

This comprehensive understanding is vital in preparing students to engage with the multi-dimensional demands of socially responsible development. By integrating the capabilities of GenAI and LLMs into the curriculum, educators can enhance students' ability to draw connections across disciplines, themes, and contexts. LLMs offer a dual advantage: they support rigorous technical analysis while facilitating more interpretive explorations of urban planning's social and cultural dimensions. This enriched learning experience equips future real estate professionals to complement their necessary and valuable profit-driven goals with a nuanced appreciation of their work's environmental, social, and cultural impacts.

Urban semiotics: Decoding the language (model) of cities

Cities are far more than physical spaces defined by buildings and infrastructure; they are dynamic cultural landscapes, layered with symbols, narratives, and shared meanings (Gottdiener & Lagopoulos, 1986; Nas, 2011). Urban semiotics – the study of signs and symbols within the urban environment – provides an analytical lens for understanding how cities communicate their identity, history, and communal values. Features such as architectural styles, public spaces, and neighborhood layouts function as expressions of cultural and social identity, offering a narrative that reflects the aspirations and character of the communities they serve. For real estate students, developing the ability to interpret these urban "languages" is critical for creating developments that align with local cultural contexts and resonate socially.

The integration of LLMs into this analytical framework offers transformative possibilities. LLMs can support students in uncovering the narratives embedded in urban spaces, enabling more profound engagement with the cultural and symbolic dimensions of their real estate projects. By incorporating these semiotic insights into their design and planning processes, students are better prepared to produce developments that reflect and uphold local cultural values. This perspective fosters a functional, marketable, socially, and culturally meaningful approach to real estate.

The role of LLMs in real estate education

LLMs, leveraging extensive datasets to provide human-like comprehension and language generation, have emerged as powerful educational tools (Zhai et al., 2021). Their application in real estate education extends beyond technical problem-solving to include, as addressed above, the interpretation of complex urban narratives and stakeholder perspectives.

In one transdisciplinary exercise and subject at the University of Technology Sydney, Australia, students specializing in property economics (real estate) collaborated with peers from diverse disciplines, including law, health sciences, cybersecurity, interior architecture, communications, engineering, and environmental science to reimagine how industry-relevant technologies and practices could address pressing societal issues. By employing LLMs, they were able to generate fresh insights by simulating stakeholder dialogues, simulating scenarios, contextualizing and exploring the broader implications of technologies standard in their work environment, geographic information systems (GIS), drones, and building information modeling (BIM) (Batty, 2018; Bender et al., 2021).

This process encouraged students to think critically about their disciplines, exploring both technical possibilities and societal implications. For instance, rather than focusing solely on the efficiency gains offered by GIS or BIM, students used LLMs to examine how these technologies could enhance community engagement, environmental stewardship, or housing equity. Through this critical engagement, real estate students began to see their profession as a vehicle for addressing societal challenges, not merely a commercial enterprise but a field with the potential to contribute meaningfully to sustainability, equity, and cultural preservation.

Design thinking, computational thinking, and AI in problem-solving

Here, the intersection of design thinking and computational thinking provides a valuable framework for reimagining real estate education. Design thinking is particularly suited to addressing "wicked problems" – complex, ill-defined challenges that require user-centered and context-sensitive solutions. By contrast, computational thinking emphasizes abstraction and structured problem-solving, offering tools for developing specific, replicable solutions to well-defined problems (Kelly et al., 2021).

GenAI sits at the nexus of these approaches, enabling students to bridge the gap between creative exploration and analytical rigor (David et al., 2023). For example, LLMs can guide students through the iterative and exploratory phases of design thinking, helping them develop innovative and contextually relevant solutions. At the same time, these tools can assist in applying computational thinking by supporting the abstraction and optimization of solutions. In real estate education, this dual capability enables students to address challenges such as urban redevelopment or sustainable housing design with both imaginative and practical approaches.

Educators can cultivate a more integrated understanding of real estate's role in society by positioning AI as a mediator between design thinking and computational thinking. This interdisciplinary and transdisciplinary approach encourages students to view real estate not merely as a technical or economic domain but as one deeply interconnected with societal, cultural, and environmental priorities. By equipping students with this holistic perspective, real estate education can prepare them to address the specific challenges of their profession and the broader issues facing urban development.

Practical applications of LLMs in real estate education

Overview of the transdisciplinary project

As previously introduced, this chapter builds from a transdisciplinary project conducted at the University of Technology Sydney during 2023–2024. The project involved up to 160 undergraduate students, including students from property economics (real estate) and other subjects across the University in an elective subject. Students worked in mixed-discipline teams of four to five members over a semester to reimagine how industry technologies could address urban challenges.

The project utilized Microsoft Copilot as the primary LLM tool, with students developing prompt engineering skills through the structured approach outlined in this chapter. Students progressed through four phases: technology exploration, stakeholder analysis, scenario development, and solution design. Weekly workshops included AI literacy training, critical evaluation exercises, and reflection sessions where students compared AI-generated content with their disciplinary knowledge.

Simulating stakeholder dialogues

Real estate development involves negotiations and collaborations with various stakeholders, including city planners, community representatives, investors, and regulatory agencies. LLMs can simulate dialogues between these parties, giving students a controlled environment to practice effective communication. For example, students in the transdisciplinary project previously mentioned used LLMs to simulate community meetings where residents shared their concerns about proposed developments. Through these exercises, students not only learned to respond to diverse stakeholder concerns but also gained an appreciation of the sociopolitical dynamics that can shape real estate projects and the tools they use to engage with them.

While artificially generated, these simulations offered students insights into the nuances of stakeholder communication. They were encouraged to practice empathy, consider opposing viewpoints, and develop well-rounded responses. In the future, real estate students may use LLMs to explore how differing priorities among stakeholders can affect development projects and how thoughtful dialogue can lead to more inclusive and responsive urban spaces.

Generating scenario-based analyses

LLMs are highly effective in generating and analyzing scenarios based on specific variables, helping students consider potential outcomes in a structured manner. In the transdisciplinary project, real estate students used LLMs together with their peers from other disciplines to craft three key scenarios for their reimagined technologies and practices – optimistic, pessimistic, and realistic. For instance, one student exploring GIS technology in the context of disaster management envisioned an optimistic scenario where GIS enabled emergency response teams to prepare and act more efficiently, enhancing overall community safety. A contrasting pessimistic scenario highlighted potential privacy concerns and misuse risks, showing how inadequacies in regulatory frameworks could lead to unintended consequences.

The realistic scenario represented a balanced perspective where students envisioned GIS effectively used for disaster management with appropriate safeguards. In this scenario, students projected how proper regulatory frameworks, data privacy protocols, and community involvement could harness GIS capabilities while mitigating potential risks.

Regarding the LLM implementation, as previously addressed, students primarily used Microsoft Copilot (Using GPT-4) for these exercises, with institutional access provided through the university. Before beginning the project, two dedicated workshops were conducted on prompt engineering and design.

Many students initially struggled with vague prompts that produced generic outputs, so we implemented a structured approach where they would:

- Draft initial prompts collaboratively.
- Review and refine prompts in small groups.
- Compare outputs from different prompt variations.
- Iterate based on the specificity and usefulness of results.

For example, an effective prompt template taught after first student iterations was: "Generate a realistic scenario for how GIS technology might be implemented in disaster management in Sydney over the next 5 years. Consider technological limitations, regulatory requirements, community acceptance, and privacy concerns. Include perspectives from emergency services, local government, and residents."

This systematic approach helped students develop critical AI literacy skills alongside their subject knowledge, enabling them to direct the LLMs toward meaningful scenario exploration rather than accepting superficial responses.

Through these scenario-building exercises, students could assess various approaches' societal, economic, and environmental impacts. These exercises provided a space where students could reflect on how regulatory, financial, and ethical factors might influence urban planning decisions, giving them an appreciation of the complexity and interconnectedness inherent in real estate and urban development.

To guide this critical thinking process, students were provided with a structured analytical framework and specific prompting techniques. Students worked through a three-step evaluation process.

First, students used "consequence mapping" when crafting their prompts. For example, instead of simply asking "What are the impacts of using drones in urban planning?", students learned to create prompts like: "Analyze the potential second and third-order consequences of widespread drone adoption in urban planning across environmental, privacy, equity, and regulatory dimensions."

Secondly, students employed a "stakeholder lens matrix" to examine each scenario through five different perspectives (government, residents, developers, environmental advocates, and future generations). For each stakeholder group, students prompted the LLM to identify potential benefits and concerns, then critically evaluated these outputs by comparing them with course materials and their disciplinary knowledge.

Finally, "critical comparison sessions" were facilitated where student teams exchanged their LLM-generated analyses and identified gaps, biases, or oversimplifications. Students were specifically instructed to note where the LLM:

- Presented technological solutions without addressing implementation challenges.
- Overlooked local contextual factors specific to Australian urban environments.
- Failed to consider equity implications for different demographic groups.
- Made assumptions about regulatory frameworks that didn't align with current practices.

This guided approach helped students move beyond accepting AI outputs at face value, instead developing the ability to use LLMs to expand their thinking while maintaining critical awareness of the tools' limitations (Ruiz-Rojas et al., 2024). Students documented their analytical process, including how they modified or challenged AI-generated content, as part of their assessment deliverables.

Providing contextual information

To navigate their roles effectively, real estate professionals need a firm grasp of the cultural, historical, and economic contexts that shape the communities in which they work. LLMs can also provide comprehensive background information on urban areas, including historical developments, cultural landmarks, policy frameworks, and socio-economic data. During the transdisciplinary project, students accessed GenAI-driven insights to enrich their understanding. For example, a student reimagining drones for community wellbeing could envision how drones could be used for property monitoring, detecting environmental hazards, and identifying land suitable for affordable housing.

By providing students with such rich contextual information, LLMs support a more holistic approach to real estate development. This enables students to think beyond market trends and property values, aligning their projects with market demands and urban planning objectives that consider their work areas' cultural and socio-economic intricacies.

Enhancing hermeneutic approaches with LLMs

A hermeneutic approach, focused on interpreting texts and symbols to uncover deeper meanings, is highly relevant to both urban planning and real estate. In their transdisciplinary project, students employed LLMs to analyze planning documents, policy statements, and historical texts, helping them identify underlying narratives and themes that shape urban development. This approach allowed students to evaluate GenAI-generated proposals critically, distinguishing where AI-generated insights offered value and where they required modification to fit local contexts.

The experience of combining LLM insights with their interpretations gave students a more nuanced understanding of the regulatory environment, societal trends, and cultural factors influencing urban landscapes. It taught them to use GenAI not as a conclusive authority but as a tool to enhance their analysis, encouraging them to integrate their insights and adapt suggestions thoughtfully.

Developing this critical AI literacy required a structured pedagogical approach that balanced freedom of exploration with guided critical thinking. The following section outlines how these reflective skills were fostered.

Practical implementation process

- **Guided demonstration sessions:** Instructor-led demonstrations analyzing documents both manually and with LLM assistance were developed, explicitly highlighting where AI excelled (synthesizing lengthy documents) and where it fell short (understanding local planning nuances in Sydney, for example). Students observed how to evaluate AI outputs against authoritative sources critically.
- **Comparative analysis exercises:** Students received two analyses of the same document – one human-written expert analysis and one LLM-generated. They worked in groups to identify differences, discuss the strengths/weaknesses of each approach, and create an improved version that leveraged both.
- **Scaffolded assignment structure:** Rather than simply allowing or forbidding AI use, three-part assignment structure was designed:
  - **Part 1:** Initial AI-generated analysis (students submit their prompts and unedited AI response).
  - **Part 2:** Critical evaluation (students identify limitations, biases, or gaps in the AI analysis).
  - **Part 3:** Enhanced final product (students integrate their expertise with AI insights).
- **Reflective documentation:** Students maintained "AI interaction logs" documenting their prompts, their conversation with the language model, the valuable insights gained, and where they needed to override or significantly modify AI suggestions based on their disciplinary knowledge. These logs were required as part of the submission of the assignment as an appendix.

This approach addresses the tension many educators feel around AI use in assignments. Rather than trying to detect or prevent AI use (which becomes increasingly complex), the critical evaluation of AI outputs became central to the assessment itself. This transformed AI from a potential academic integrity concern into a pedagogical opportunity.

Key benefits of this approach include:

- **Transparency:** By requiring submission of both AI-generated content and student enhancements, the assessment process becomes transparent.

- **Skill development:** Students develop crucial skills in prompt engineering and design, critical evaluation, and appropriate integration of AI tools.
- **Authentic assessment:** The ability to critically enhance AI outputs better reflects real-world professional skills than attempting to work without these increasingly common tools.
- **Adaptability:** This framework can be applied across disciplines by adjusting the evaluation criteria to reflect domain-specific considerations.

The most successful students demonstrated their expertise not by avoiding AI, but by showing sophisticated judgment about when and how to enhance, modify, or override AI suggestions based on their disciplinary knowledge – precisely the skills they'll need in AI-augmented professional environments.

Challenges and considerations

Within the abovementioned exploration, a significant concern in using AI for education is the potential for bias in AI-generated content (Mehrabi et al., 2021). Since LLMs are trained on historical datasets, they may inadvertently reinforce biases related to race, gender, socio-economic status, and other societal factors. In the transdisciplinary experience, students were encouraged to critically evaluate GenAI outputs and identify potential biases that could reinforce systemic inequalities. This exercise underscored the importance of critical thinking and the need for students to approach AI outputs with scrutiny and responsibility rather than accepting them uncritically.

For example, when analyzing GenAI-generated recommendations for urban development (for those students focusing on that aspect in one of the workshops in class), they often identified systematic biases in how LLMs approached affordable housing locations. The AI responses typically favor development in already disadvantaged neighborhoods while overlooking opportunities in more affluent areas, despite no instructions about economic stratification in the prompts. This pattern appeared to reflect and reinforce existing housing segregation rather than promoting more equitable distribution. By identifying this tendency, participants were able to develop more balanced prompts that explicitly required consideration of social equity across diverse neighborhood types. This discovery highlighted how AI systems can inadvertently perpetuate systemic biases in urban planning when not subjected to critical evaluation.

The use of AI in real estate education also raises important ethical considerations. Although LLMs can provide valuable insights, they should not replace human judgment, especially in fields with significant impacts on communities. Real estate and property development students and professionals must carefully consider the ethical implications of their projects, such as the potential for gentrification, displacement, and environmental harm. Throughout the transdisciplinary exercise, for example, students discussed these implications in their scenario analyses, weighing GenAI insights against ethical considerations related to data privacy, environmental sustainability, and social equity.

Technical limitations and data privacy

Despite their advanced capabilities, LLMs have limitations, such as the inability to access up-to-date data or account for nuanced, local specifics crucial to real estate development. Additionally, using AI tools entails significant data privacy and security considerations, especially when dealing with sensitive or proprietary information. In the transdisciplinary project, students were encouraged to recognize these limitations and learn best practices for responsible AI use, fostering an understanding of AI's potential and constraints in real estate and urban planning (see Appendix A for more information on suggested best practices).

Integrating student experiences into real estate education

The students, focused initially only on their degree in property economics, emerged from this experience with a broader understanding of real estate's potential to impact communities positively. By collaborating with peers from diverse fields, they learned to approach technology from multiple perspectives, developing an ethical awareness that will guide them as they step into their professional roles. This educational experience models how GenAI can deepen interdisciplinary learning in real estate, preparing students to be reflective, responsible, and innovative professionals (Zawacki-Richter et al., 2019). An implementation guide for educators is presented below to direct future applications of LLM in education.

Implementation guide for educators

For educators interested in implementing similar LLM-enhanced learning experiences, the following step-by-step approach is recommended:

- **Tool selection and access:** Choose an accessible LLM (e.g., ChatGPT, Claude, etc.) and determine how students will access it. Options include:

  - Institution-sponsored accounts.
  - Student personal accounts with reimbursement.
  - Computer lab sessions with provided access.

- **Prompt development framework:** Create structured prompts that:
  - Begin with clear role assignments and "persona" patterns (e.g., "Act as a community planner").
  - Include specific context relevant to course content.
  - Request multiple perspectives or scenarios.
  - Example: "Act as an urban planner. Given the following zoning regulations [insert local regulations as an upload file into the language model], generate three approaches to increasing affordable housing while maintaining neighborhood character."

- **Critical evaluation scaffolding:** Develop worksheets that guide students to:
  - Identify potential biases in AI responses.
  - Compare AI suggestions with course materials.
  - Annotate AI outputs with their insights.
  - Sample question: "Identify one assumption in the AI response that might not apply to our local context. Explain why."

- **Assessment design:** Create assessments that evaluate:
  - Quality of student prompts (clarity, specificity).
  - Critical enhancement of AI outputs.
  - Integration of disciplinary knowledge with AI insights.
  - Example criteria: "Student has substantively enhanced AI-generated content with discipline-specific considerations not present in the original output."

Integration timeline: Start with small, structured exercises before progressing to more complex applications:

Weeks 1–2: Basic AI literacy and prompt engineering
Weeks 3–4: Guided stakeholder simulations with reflection
Weeks 5–8: Scenario development with critical evaluation
Weeks 9–12: Independent application to course projects

Conclusion

The exploration of urban planning and real estate education presented in this chapter underscores the growing significance of integrating technological innovation with socially responsible development practices. By employing tools like LLMs, educators and students can reimagine traditional real estate and property development education approaches, addressing technical and financial considerations and their work's broader societal, cultural, and environmental impacts. This dual focus equips students with the ability to approach real estate development as a transformative field capable of fostering sustainability, equity, and cultural and heritage preservation.

At the heart of this shift is the interplay between design thinking and computational thinking, mediated by AI, which enables students to develop creative yet structured solutions to the complex challenges of urban development. Through scenario-based exercises, stakeholder simulations, and critical engagement with AI-generated insights, students are encouraged to think beyond profit margins, reflecting on their projects' ethical and societal implications.

This chapter concludes by emphasizing the need for real estate education to prepare students for the multi-dimensional realities of urban development. By fostering interdisciplinary and transdisciplinary learning experiences, incorporating technological tools thoughtfully, and promoting critical reflection, educators can shape a new generation of professionals ready to address the immediate challenges of their field and the broader issues of sustainability and societal wellbeing.

References

Batty, M. (2018). Artificial intelligence and smart cities. *Environment and Planning B: Urban Analytics and City Science*, *45*(1), 3–6.

Bender, E. M., Gebru, T., McMillan-Major, A., & Shmitchell, S. (2021). On the dangers of stochastic parrots: Can language models be too big? In M. C. Elish, W. Isaac, & R. Zemel (Eds Chairs.), *Proceedings of the 2021 ACM Conference on Fairness, Accountability, and Transparency* (pp. 610–623). Association for Computing Machinery. https://doi.org/10.1145/3442188.3445922

David, Y., Krebs, A., & Rosenbaum, A. (2023). The use of generative AI tools in design thinking academic makeathon. *CERN IdeaSquare Journal of Experimental Innovation*, *7*(3), 43–49.

Gottdiener, M., & Lagopoulos, A. P. (Eds.). (1986). *The city and the sign: An introduction to urban semiotics*. Columbia University Press.

Kelly, N., & Gero, J. S. (2021). Design thinking and computational thinking: A dual process model for addressing design problems. *Design Science*, *7*, e8.

Mehrabi, N., Morstatter, F., Saxena, N., Lerman, K., & Galstyan, A. (2021). A survey on bias and fairness in machine learning. *ACM Computing Surveys*, *54*(6), 1–35.

Nas, P. J. (2011). *Cities full of symbols: A theory of urban space and culture*. Leiden University Press.

Phibbs, P., & Gurran, N. (2021). The role and significance of planning in the determination of house prices in Australia: Recent policy debates. *Environment and Planning A: Economy and Space*, *53*(3), 457–479.

Ruiz-Rojas, L. I., Salvador-Ullauri, L., & Acosta-Vargas, P. (2024). Collaborative working and critical thinking: Adoption of generative artificial intelligence tools in higher education. *Sustainability*, *16*(13), 5367.

Yigitcanlar, T., & Teriman, S. (2015). Rethinking sustainable urban development: Towards an integrated planning and development process. *International Journal of Environmental Science and Technology*, *12*(1), 341–352.

Zawacki-Richter, O., Marín, V. I., Bond, M., & Gouverneur, F. (2019). Systematic review of research on artificial intelligence applications in higher education – where are the educators? *International Journal of Educational Technology in Higher Education*, *16*(39), 1–27. https://doi.org/10.1186/s41239-019-0171-0

Zhai, X., Chu, X., Chai, C. S., Jong, M. S. Y., Istenic, A., Spector, J. M., Liu, J.-B., Yuan, J., & Li, Y. (2021). A review of artificial intelligence (AI) in education from 2010 to 2020. *Complexity*, *2021*, 1–18.

Appendix A

Best practices for responsible AI use in real estate education

Data and privacy considerations

- **Data sensitivity:** Avoid inputting sensitive property data, personal information, or proprietary market analyses into public LLM platforms.
- **Institutional accounts:** Use institution-provided AI accounts with appropriate data protection agreements rather than personal accounts when possible.
- **De-identification:** Remove or modify identifying information before submitting real case studies or project data to LLMs.
- **Compliance awareness:** Maintain awareness of relevant privacy regulations when using LLMs for real estate data analysis.

Mitigating bias and ensuring accuracy

- **Cross-verification:** Always verify AI-generated market data, regulatory information, or demographic statistics against authoritative sources.
- **Local context specification:** Explicitly include local regulatory frameworks, market conditions, and cultural contexts in prompts to improve relevance.
- **Multiple perspectives:** Request diverse stakeholder perspectives to counteract potential biases in AI-generated analyses.
- **Temporal awareness:** Recognize that LLMs have knowledge cutoffs and may not reflect current market conditions or recent regulatory changes.

Academic and professional integrity

- **Transparent attribution:** Document which aspects of work were AI-assisted and how the outputs were critically evaluated.
- **Value addition:** Focus on how disciplinary expertise enhances, contextualizes, or corrects AI outputs rather than simply accepting them.
- **Prompt documentation:** Maintain records of prompts used to generate content for later reference and refinement.
- **Process emphasis:** Assess learning based on the quality of critical thinking and enhancement of AI outputs rather than just the final product.

Effective prompting for property economics and real estate contexts

- **Specificity:** Include relevant market sectors, geographic locations, and regulatory jurisdictions in prompts.
- **Constraint recognition:** Acknowledge financial, regulatory, environmental, and social constraints in scenario prompts.
- **Stakeholder identification:** Explicitly name relevant stakeholders for comprehensive analysis (e.g., "Consider perspectives of developers, local residents, planning authorities, and environmental agencies").
- **Time horizons:** Specify relevant timeframes for market analyses or development projections.

Ethical considerations

- **Impact assessment:** Routinely consider how AI tools might affect different community groups, particularly vulnerable populations.
- **Algorithmic awareness:** Maintain awareness of how algorithmic processes may reproduce existing inequalities in housing and development.
- **Critical distance:** Cultivate the ability to question AI-generated assumptions about property markets and development "best practices."
- **Value alignment:** Ensure that AI use aligns with professional values of social responsibility, environmental sustainability, and ethical practice.

Index

For Product Safety Concerns and Information please contact our EU representative GPSR@taylorandfrancis.com Taylor & Francis Verlag GmbH, Kaufingerstraße 24, 80331 München, Germany